A Critical History of English Literature

VOLUME II

DAVID DAICHES

A Critical History of English Literature

IN FOUR VOLUMES

VOLUME II

LONDON · SECKER & WARBURG

First published in England 1960 by
Martin Secker & Warburg Limited
14 Carlisle Street, London W.1

Reprinted 1960, 1961, 1963, 1968

SBN (Hard covers) 436 12110 7
(Paperback) 436 12106 9

Made and printed in Great Britain by
Morrison and Gibb Limited, London and Edinburgh

Contents

VOLUME I

VOLUME II

VOLUME III

VOLUME IV

A Critical History of English Literature

VOLUME II

CHAPTER NINE

Shakespeare

William shakespeare (1564–1616) doubtless saw himself as merely another professional man of the theater who moved almost casually from play acting to play writing. And indeed he was very much a man of his time, a man of the Elizabethan theater, who learned to exploit brilliantly the stagecraft, the acting, and the public taste of his day. It happens very rarely in the history of literature that a craftsman who has acquired perfect control of his medium and a masterly ease in handling the techniques and conventions of his day is also a universal genius of the highest order, combining with his technical proficiency a unique ability to render experience in poetic language and an uncanny intuitive understanding of human psychology. Man of the theater, poet, and expert in the human passions, Shakespeare has appealed equally to those who admire the art with which he renders a story in terms of the acted drama or the insight with which he presents states of mind and complexities of attitude or the unsurpassed brilliance he shows in giving conviction and a new dimension to the utterances of his characters through the poetic speech he puts in their mouths. It is a remarkable combination of qualities. Shakespeare has been praised for his "knowledge of the human heart," for his superb poetry, for his esthetic cunning in his disposition of the action, for his theatrical skill, and for his ability to create living worlds of people while himself remaining (as James Joyce's Stephen Dedalus said of the artist) "like the God of creation, within or behind or beyond or above his handiwork, invisible, refined out of existence, indifferent, paring his fingernails." Yet this was no poetic genius descending on the theater from above, but a working dramatist who found himself in catering for the public theater of his day. Unquestionably the greatest poetic dramatist of Europe, he was also Marlowe's successor, the heir to a tradition of playwriting which we saw developing in the preceding chapter. His contemporaries saw him as one dramatist among others

—a good one, and a popular one, but no transcendent genius who left all others far behind—and to the end of his active life he showed no reluctance to collaborate with other playwrights.

It was the eighteenth century—contrary to the popular view that this was a period of grudging admiration of Shakespeare as too wayward a genius to be of the very highest order—which first recognized Shakespeare's pre-eminence, and ever since Rowe's edition of 1709, editors, scholars, critics, biographers, and later bibliographers, psychologists, and many other varieties of inquirers have been building up a body of knowledge and of ideas about the plays (little enough about Shakespeare the man, whose biography has many blank passages) which cannot possibly be even summarized in a short history of literature. Shakespeare's apparent indifference to the publication of his plays, his preoccupation with their performance rather than their production as books, meant that no authoritative "works" supervised by the author ever passed through the press. Texts of sixteen of the plays were printed individually in quarto editions in Shakespeare's lifetime, sometimes from the author's "foul papers," with inevitable errors. Some were corrupt and pirated editions, so that we have "bad" as well as "good" quartos, and the best were casual enough publications in which the author had no hand. For eighteen of Shakespeare's plays we have only texts published after his death (sometimes apparently from his own heavily corrected original drafts), notably in the First Folio, the first collected edition, edited by Heminge and Condell in 1623; for four we have only the Folio text and that of a corrupt quarto; for others we have both quarto and First Folio texts, sometimes more than one of the former, with variations among them which raise the question: Which represents what Shakespeare wrote? Into such problems the general literary historian cannot enter, nor can he pause to discuss the evidence on which scholars have come to arrange Shakespeare's plays in some sort of chronological order. Reference to a given play in a work of known date and reference in a play to an event of known date can help to determine the date of composition, and of course the publication of a quarto edition of a play gives a date before which it must have been written. Having constructed a skeleton chronology of the plays in this way, we can note shifts in style and technique and, very cautiously, draw some conclusions about the way in which Shakespeare's art developed which can then be applied to deciding the approximate date of other plays. Generations of scholars have worked on this problem; the literary historian can only accept such of their conclusions as seem most convincing, while relying for Shakespeare's text on the findings of those textual editors whose work seems soundest (though, except in the "bad quartos," the textual errors of even the worst printed plays are not serious enough to effect any major distortion). As for Shakespeare's relations with his company, and the fortunes of the companies of which he was such an important member (from 1594, the Lord Chamberlain's men, who became the King's men after 1603), that belongs to the history of the English theater rather than to English literary history, and can be only mentioned here as representing the conditions under which Shakespeare's genius operated.

Shakespeare's earliest identifiable plays, his prentice work, show him interested in a variety of Elizabethan dramatic traditions. The three *Henry VI* plays (ca. 1590–92) show him developing the chronicle play on English history which was already a popular variety of drama by the time he came on the scene. *Titus Andronicus* (ca. 1593) shows him—if it *is* by Shakespeare—exploiting the popular taste for blood-and-thunder Senecan drama as Kyd had done. *The Comedy of Errors* (ca. 1590) takes its plot from the *Menaechmi* of Plautus and exploits the comic possibilities of two pairs of indistinguishable twins, complicating the intrigue by some of the devices standard in Roman comedy and untying the various knots with reasonable skill at the conclusion. *Richard III* (ca. 1592–93) shows Shakespeare following Marlowe's footsteps and building a tragedy around a central villain. *The Taming of the Shrew* (with a problematical relationship to a play entitled *The Taming of A Shrew*, first printed in 1594, which *may* be a "bad quarto" of Shakespeare's play) shows him combining a certain amount of knock-about humor with a romantic love element in a kind of play which has been called "low romantic comedy," to distinguish it from the "high romantic comedy" of such plays as *Twelfth Night*. Of these early plays, only *The Comedy of Errors*, with its Roman affinities, was not written for the public theater. The others show a beginning dramatist trying his hand successively at the different kinds of play that were already popular on the public stage. Robert Greene's attack on Shakespeare, in a pamphlet written on his deathbed, as "an upstart crow beautified with our feathers" seems to indicate that here was a player who had the effrontery to try writing plays as well as acting them—the reference is apparently to the second and third parts of *Henry VI*. As a player, Shakespeare was in an excellent position to judge public taste.

Into the complicated problems of the relation between these early plays and other plays, which in some cases can be regarded as either sources or corrupt versions of Shakespeare's, we cannot here enter, except to note that recent scholarship restores to Shakespeare much that earlier scholars had taken away from him. But a working dramatist interested in providing actable plays for his company would have had no compunction in revising or rewriting other people's plays; such activity was regarded as perfectly ethical, and there is no doubt that Shakespeare used other people's material when he found it serviceable or when he had to get something together in a hurry. This is truer of the beginning of his career than of Shakespeare in his maturity; once his own genius found itself it took complete control and so reworked any alien material that it emerges as thoroughly and uniquely Shakespearean. The view that Shakespeare only wrote bits and pieces of his own plays is as completely false as the equally exploded view of him as the illiterate rustic from Stratford. Further, it represents a complete misunderstanding of the nature of a work of literary art. Shakespeare in almost every instance derived his plots from somebody else's work, but that is no more to his discredit than the Greek dramatists' use of popular myths is to theirs. It is by the shaping of the material and its bodying forth in language that a crude tale can be made into a profound work of art. A study of Shakespeare's sources, in Italian *novelle* or English chronicles or in other plays, only emphasizes the remarkable power of his "shaping spirit of imagination."

If Shakespeare had written nothing more than the early plays enumerated above, he would still be an interesting dramatist, and *Richard III* in particular would receive respectful attention as a remarkable dramatic presentation of the rise and fall of a villain-hero who succeeds by wit and cunning, by Machiavellian policies (as the Elizabethans understood them) and Renaissance *virtù,* and at the same time as a contribution to the Elizabethan conception of English history emerging from the horrors of the Wars of the Roses and the climactic evil of Richard III's reign to the glories of Tudor peace and unity. Modern interest in Tudor historians has led to an emphasis, perhaps an overemphasis, on Shakespeare's concern to present English history, in his history plays, as an ordered sequence of events beginning with the deposition of Richard II, the last medieval king in the true original succession. The sequence proceeds through "the unquiet time of Henry IV" (as the chronicler Hall calls it) to the temporary glories of Henry V's military achievements in France before nemesis strikes the Lancastrians in the latter part of Henry VI's reign; civil war shatters the peace and unity of England until the reign of Richard III finally unites all that is decent in the country against this monstrous tyrant, with the result that Henry Tudor wins at the battle of Bosworth in 1485, unites the "two noble houses," and, representing both the ancient Celtic line and the English line, begins a new and glorious epoch in history. It is true that the Tudor historians—Polydore Vergil, Edward Hall, Raphael Holinshed, among others—built up something like this picture between them (in Hall it is especially clear); it is true also that the Elizabethans regarded history as a "mirror for magistrates," and saw lessons in the deposition of Richard II, the military virtues of Henry V, the Wars of the Roses, and the accession of the Tudors which they felt could be usefully applied to contemporary politics. It is true, too, that there is some evidence that in his gallery of English kings Shakespeare was seeking to indicate, directly or indirectly, his view of the ideal king, and that Henry V's education as Prince Hal, his acquaintance with all strata of life and his final refusal of the opposite extremes of riot (Falstaff) and vainglory (Percy) to choose justice and true kingship, as presented in the *Henry IV* plays, show a morality play element which cannot be ignored. And it is convenient to arrange Shakespeare's history plays (with *King John* standing somewhat outside the group) into two groups of four, with the three parts of *Henry VI* and *Richard III* in one group, and *Richard II*, the two parts of *Henry IV* and *Henry V* in the other; the first group giving the second part of the epic story—civil war and tyranny followed by Tudor regeneration—and the second giving the original causes of it all with Henry V's stay of execution of nemesis by his personal virtue as the good king. But to look at the plays this way is to miss much—if not most—of what makes them interesting as plays, and to impose on the subtlety and complexity of Shakespeare's art a schoolroom patterning which sacrifices several levels of meaning to pedagogic convenience. Richard III is not merely an evil monster who by representing the culmination of tyranny and horror forces England to find herself in rebellion against him. He is, in his way, a hero as well as a villain; his psychology is far from simple; the stylized rhetoric in which he and other characters often express themselves is a way of exploring paradoxes of character as well as presenting simplified historical truths. As Dr. Johnson said of Shakespeare, "his story requires Romans or kings, but he thinks only on men." The character and behavior of Shakespeare's kings illuminate aspects of the human situation as well as displaying the Tudor view of history, and it is the former function that is the more important.

Shakespeare at no period in his career wrote only one variety of play, so that any attempt to discuss his works chronologically cannot treat the plays in kindred groups, nor, conversely, can a discussion of the plays by types keep to a chronological line. One gets a clearer picture of his achievement by sacrificing, in some degree, chronology to a more logical grouping. *The Two Gentlemen of Verona* (ca. 1594) is the first of a series of romantic comedies which includes *Love's Labour's Lost* (1594)—though with some qualifications—and *A Mid-*

summer Night's Dream (ca. 1596), *The Merchant of Venice* (1596–97), *Much Ado about Nothing* (ca. 1598–99), *As You Like It* (1599–1600), and *Twelfth Night* (1599–1600). The *Two Gentlemen* is clearly experimental: Shakespeare cannot yet handle with assurance the different elements (deriving from Lyly and Greene as well as from the Spanish pastoral romance *Diana Enamorada* by Jorge de Montemajor and from Italian comedy) which he blends with such extraordinary skill in *Twelfth Night. Heroine* disguised as a boy; a story of love and intrigue with a low comedy subplot; talkative clowns; neat pairing of characters; intermittent verbal fireworks; male friendship versus heterosexual love—these are some of the elements in the play which we meet again in later plays, more effectively handled. The *Two Gentlemen* has a sprightly stiffness which shows a gift for comedy, however slightly developed, but it lacks the stylized brilliance of *Love's Labour's Lost,* which is immature in a different way—it is an admirable example of a relatively immature kind of art rather than an imperfect example of something more ambitious.

Love's Labour's Lost was first published in a quarto volume in 1598, described on the title page as "a pleasant conceited comedy . . . presented before her Highness this last Christmas. Newly corrected and augmented by W. Shakespeare." It is a stylized and courtly play, of which the 1598 text apparently represents a corrected version to replace a lost "bad" quarto; it was probably originally written and later augmented for specific private performances. The play shows that Shakespeare was aiming not only at popular successes in the public theater but also at something more sophisticated, appealing to the witty and the educated. How Shakespeare acquired his intimate knowledge of Elizabethan courtly wit and his friendship with members of the nobility we may only surmise: we know that his *Venus and Adonis* (1593) and *Rape of Lucrece* (1594) were dedicated to the Earl of Southampton, the first respectfully, the second in language suggesting deep personal affection, and there is other evidence of his having made friends in the highest social circles. He was familiar by this time with both popular humor, courtly wit, and current intellectual fashions, and he could imitate or satirize any of these. *Love's Labour's Lost,* with its action resembling one of the entertainments offered to Queen Elizabeth by noblemen whom she visited on her "progresses," its many topical allusions, its delicate satire of romantic idealism on the one hand and pedantic affectation on the other, its echoing notes of love and melancholy, of royal grace, male vanity, and rustic reality, its combination of wit combats, formal speeches, and singing lyricism, its balance and precision and ballet-like movement, is clearly designed for a highly educated taste. The plot is rudimentary—indeed, the play can hardly be said to have a plot at all. Ferdinand, king of Navarre, and his three lords, Biron (or Berowne), Longaville, and Dumain, resolve together to spend three years in study and contemplation, turning the court into "a little Academe, Still and contemplative in living art." In that period they will see no woman, and eat and sleep sparingly. The arrival of a diplomatic mission from France, consisting of the Princess and her three ladies, Rosaline, Maria, and Katherine, destroys their resolution. The four men fall in love with the four ladies, who tease them with witty mockeries. Finally, news of the death of the Princess' father, the King of France, puts an end to this mocking sport. The ladies explain that they had received the gentlemen's protestations of love as "pleasant jest and courtesy, as bombast and as lining to the time," but now that they realize that they are meant in sober earnest, they propose to put these conceited and exuberant young men on trial for a year, after which they will reconsider their refusal.

The pairs of lovers, particularly the self-opinionated Biron and the witty Rosaline, are the first of a Shakespearean line of which better known representatives are Beatrice and Benedick in *Much Ado about Nothing*. But wit combats between the suitor and his beloved are far from constituting the main texture of *Love's Labour's Lost*. The minor characters—the pompous and fantastical Armado and his page Moth; the curate Sir Nathaniel, "a foolish mild man, an honest man, look you, and soon dashed"; Holofernes, the pedantic schoolmaster; Dull, the stupid constable; Costard, the clownish rustic—not only develop in their dialogue a constant stream of ironic criticism of contemporary manners and fashions by means of parody, but also act out within the play a countermovement to the formal motions of the principal characters. The minor characters put on, for the entertainment of the principal characters, the Masque of the Nine Worthies, with Armado as Hector, Costard as Pompey, Sir Nathaniel as Alexander, Moth as Hercules, and Holofernes as Judas Maccabeus. The actors are mercilessly mocked by their noble audience, but somehow Shakespeare contrives that the noble mockers lose, and the ignoble mocked gain, dignity in the end. Armado, boastful and grandiloquent though he is, and ludicrous though his rhymed speech as Hector sounds and is meant to sound, remains patient and courteous under the cruelest mocking. "The sweet war-man is dead and rotten; sweet chucks, beat not the bones of the buried; when he breathed, he was a man. But I will forward with my device. Sweet royalty, bestow on me the sense of hearing." And when he is mockingly asked to strip for combat, he excuses himself with the unexpected and quietly genuine remark: "The naked truth of it is, I have no shirt. I go woolward for penance." Similarly, when Holofernes is mocked off the stage by the noble lords, his retreating cry, "This is not generous, not gentle, not humble," contains both dignity and truth. The battle of the sexes ceases before the battle of the social classes, and the nobility join in mocking the pretensions and inadequacies of their inferiors. But the mockers are themselves mocked by Shakespeare. And the players—after an interruption when the messenger brings news of the death of the King of France and the main action is then concluded—return to conclude their pageant with a simple presentation of the Winter and Spring, singing two charming and simple songs ("When daisies pied" and "When icicles hang by the wall"), each representing one of these two seasons. On that simple lyrical note the play ends.

Love's Labour's Lost owes something to Lyly, something to the Italian *Commedia dell' Arte* with its conventional character types and improvised plots, something to the shows and pageants so frequent in Elizabethan courtly and country-house life. But it is far more than a combination of derivative elements. Its extravagant verbal play, set exercises in wit, and many topical allusions have helped to make it relatively unpopular among general readers, particularly in the nineteenth century. But more recent criticism and dramatic production have helped to show the kind of stylization which is the play's medium, so that it is now produced—most successfully—with something of the formality of a Mozart opera and the grace of movement of ballet. It was never the most popular of Shakespeare's plays, and nobody would claim for it the profundity and brilliance of the work of Shakespeare's maturity. But it was (except perhaps for *Richard III*) Shakespeare's first important and successful original play. It is significant that he began by writing for the popular taste of the public theater and achieved his first technical success (as it might be called) in writing for private performance: his greatest work was to combine both kinds of appeal and profit from both kinds of experience.

But it was the public theater which claimed Shakespeare's chief attention throughout his career. Only three of his plays—*Love's Labour's Lost, A Midsummer Night's Dream,* and *The Tempest*—were written originally for private performance.[1] *A Midsummer Night's Dream* was first written to be performed as part of a wedding festivity before being adapted for the public theater (or perhaps vice versa): it lacks the somewhat self-conscious wit of *Love's Labour's*

[1] Whether *Troilus and Cressida* was originally written for a private performance is still a matter of conjecture, and scholars have argued for and against the view.

Lost and shows Shakespeare moving toward an ideal of "romantic comedy" in which the fortunes of love and the humors of character are skillfully blended. The play is lyrical in tone and masquelike in movement. It lacks the graver undertones that are audible in Shakespeare's later comedies: it is a dream, a jest, a presentation of the comic irresponsibility of young love whose variations are lightheartedly attributed to the mischief-making (half deliberate, half accidental) of Puck. There are several strands, the marriage of Theseus and Hippolyta providing the background or the enclosing brackets which contain the play. In the foreground are the two pairs of lovers, the women constant, the men changing their affections as the magic herb "love in idleness" bids them. In the background is the fairy world, centering on Oberon and Titania and their quarrel, which involves (though they do not know it) the human lovers. Puck moves between the human and the fairy world, and it is interesting that the only human being in the play who comes into direct contact with that world is not any member of Theseus' court or one of the lovers, but Bottom the weaver. The incongruity of bringing the grossest element in the human world into contact with the gossamer world of fairy is exploited by Shakespeare with delicate brilliance. Bottom and his companions, thoroughly English figures for all their classical setting (just as the fairy element comes from English folklore, even though Titania's name is from Ovid and Oberon's from the medieval romance *Huon of Bordeaux*), show Shakespeare bringing a new dimension into English dramatic humor. Bottom is far from being the conventional clown of the sixteenth-century stage, though he doubtless derives from him: he is an affectionately mocking study of a kind of character who flourishes in every society, given precise and convincing localization and individualization. The way in which the love plot, the fairy plot, and the activities of Bottom and his fellows are brought together by means of the Theseus-Hippolyta background shows Shakespeare at ease in his dramatic technique in a new way. The "tedious brief scene of young Pyramus and his love Thisby" is at the same time a hilariously funny parody of the cruder kinds of drama still popular in Shakespeare's day, a vehicle for further developing Bottom's character, and a means of establishing the relation of the different social groups to each other. Theseus himself is a paternal figure, the benevolent ruler who governs with justice and humanity:

> I will hear that play:
> For never anything can be amiss,
> When simpleness and duty tender it.

But the vagaries of love are beyond even his beneficent control. The concluding benediction on the newly married couple for whose wedding the play was written is sung by the fairies; and the last word of all is Puck's. Thoroughly successful, thoroughly charming, delicate, happy, lyrical, *A Midsummer Night's Dream* shows Shakespeare the easy master of a new kind of comedy.

The Merchant of Venice (1596–97), *Much Ado about Nothing* (1598–99), *As You Like It* (1599–1600), and *Twelfth Night* (1600–01) show Shakespeare developing his variety of romantic comedy with increasing technical brilliance and new ways of counterpointing poetry humor. Though these plays have common features—the lively and witty heroines, the carefully placed moments of poetic hush, the delicate and happy treatment of love, the undertones of melancholy or prevented disaster, the element of fairy tale or folklore—each has its distinctive atmosphere and unique pattern. In *The Merchant of Venice* Shakespeare sets himself the almost impossible task of combining the fairy tale plot of the caskets, in which Bassanio figures as the lucky adventurer who wins the girl by a sort of predestinate good fortune, with a story of male friendship in true Renaissance vein (Bassanio and Antonio) and, more significantly, with the story of Shylock and the pound of flesh, a theme of larger dimensions and greater dramatic possibilities than the other strands in the play. For the story of the pound of flesh and the incident of the rings, Shakespeare drew (as he so often did) on an Italian short story or *novella;* in creating Shylock he was probably thinking of Marlowe's *Jew of Malta* as well as contemporary prejudice and the unhappy case of Roderigo Lopez, the Queen's Portuguese-Jewish physician. But he treats everything in his own way, and the result is an original and remarkable play on which Shakespeare's genius carried him beyond the limits of this kind of drama. In the casket plot and the Bassanio-Portia relationship, as well as the character and behavior of Shylock's daughter Jessica, we are in the realm of fairy tale, where characters act in a simple symbolic way and the moral and psychological implications of their behavior are not investigated. In a fully realized moral world, Bassanio would appear as a selfish adventurer and Jessica as a cruel and heartless daughter. But in the enchanted air of Belmont (and though much of the action takes place in Venice, it is Belmont that provides the golden fairy tale atmosphere) we see human beings only in a simple symbolic relationship, with good luck implying worthiness, movement from the Jewish to the Christian orbit seen always as good, and young love justifying all. Shakespeare, however, seeks to combine this world not only with a world of pure comedy, which can go with it perfectly safely, but with a world of moral and psychological realism. The result is—or perhaps this is the cause, not the effect, for it is likely that Shylock grew in his hands beyond his intention—that the character of Shylock is not simply that of a stylized villain, the alien devil who is bad because he does not accept the religion and the social standards of his environment, but a figure of power and dignity whose speeches and behavior, for all his conventional villainy, almost redeem him into tragedy. Even when we make allowances for the Elizabethan state of mind on these matters, and even though we realize that Shylock must not be played as a sympathetic and tragic figure, it is impossible not to feel that the fully realized moral world to which Shylock belongs challenges and even in a sense destroys the simple enchantment of Belmont. For a non-Christian girl to leave her ancestral faith and her family to join her Christian lover is wholly admirable according to the tradition of medieval romance and popular thought; but Shakespeare brings in a new dimension when he shows us Shylock's anguish, and indeed the whole fierce reality of Shylock's character produces a new level of probability in the play on which Bassanio and Jessica and even Portia have a much less real existence. The gap between the fairy tale and the real world shows in the play. Shakespeare tries to cover it up by sheer poetry. The simple beauty of Portia's speech when she gives herself to Bassanio mediates somewhat between the two worlds and brings her nearer the real one, while the famous scene between Lorenzo and Jessica at the beginning of Act V dissolves all disparities in music and moonlight. Portia's and Nerissa's tricks with the rings, childish though the whole incident is, help to mitigate in retrospect the realities of the great court scene, where Portia's speech on mercy rings out with (to modern ears) ironic overtones challenging the Christian attitude to Shylock as well as Shylock's attitude to his victim. *The Merchant of Venice* is a complex play whose different elements do not really belong to the same world. It is held together by moments of poetry as well as by Shakespeare's theatrical skill—for it is good theater throughout. Considered as a dramatic poem rather than as a play to be acted, it can, however, be seen to possess a unity in the pattern of imagery that suggests further meanings: the world of Antonio and Bassanio becomes almost a mirror-image of Shylock's world which in turn is a distorted but recognizable version—and so a deep criticism—of the Christian society about him.

In Shakespeare's next three "romantic comedies"—*Much Ado about Nothing, As You Like It,* and *Twelfth Night*—this form of Elizabethan drama reaches its golden perfection. Like *The Merchant of Venice, Much Ado* combines two plots, one of which has tragic overtones. In the wit combats between Beatrice and Benedick, Shakespeare brings to a more richly human level, and anchors more profoundly in human experience, a dramatic device with which he had earlier sported in a more distinctly formal manner. In the Claudio-Hero story, where the bridegroom is deluded by the wicked Don John into believing in his innocent bride's criminal wantonness and so denounces her at the altar, Shakespeare (taking his plot, as so often, from an Italian *novella*) provides a context in which the merry world of witty attitudinizing is shaken into a deeper reality. There is not here, as in *The Merchant of Venice*, a gap between a world of romantic magic and one of grim reality: the plots not only interlock neatly but also reinforce each other emotionally. Beatrice and Benedick, man-hater and misogynist tricked by friends into believing that each loves the other, discover their real mutual love in the shadow of Hero's tragedy, and the modulation of tone here between the tragic and the romantic is achieved with remarkable art. But Shakespeare keeps the tragic overtones muted by contriving that the forces of evil are already in the process of being discovered and exposed even before the terrible accusation against Hero at the altar, and we know that it is a matter of time before justice is done and Hero is vindicated. The elimination of potential tragedy by the exposure of evil—not too rapidly, but quickly enough to prevent irreparable harm being done—is achieved by the introduction of a third strand into the play, the comic-realistic strand represented by Dogberry and Verges, the officers of the watch who accidentally stumble across the villains and proceed, in their slow-witted and comically clumsy manner, to examine them. This third strand is pure English in inspiration, deriving from Shakespeare's own experience and observation of native character, and it is the first fully developed example of his genius in handling this kind of comedy. Don John's henchmen, and so the truth about Don John's villainy, are safe in the hands of these bumbling public servants from a relatively early point in the play; that the ultimate exposure should be delayed until potential tragedy has sealed the love of Beatrice and Benedick, and that at the same time this delay should be achieved by richly comic means, constitute a striking example of Shakespeare's mastery both of dramatic structure and of modulation of tone.

Of *As You Like It* (whose plot derives from Thomas Lodge's prose pastoral romance, *Rosalynde*) and *Twelfth Night* (the basic idea of whose plot derives ultimately from Greek comedy, via Plautus and sixteenth-century Italian comedy) there is little left to be said by the literary historian. The most popular of Shakespeare's comedies, they represent the ripest fruits of his imagination in its happy golden phase, the perfection of romantic comedy in English. Of the two, *As You Like It* is the lighter in tone, its moral pattern simpler, its happy solution of problems of love and politics in the carefree atmosphere of the greenwood achieved with careless ease. Rosalind, disguised as a boy in the greenwood, teasing her lover in the happy confidence that she is loved by him without having yet to declare her own love, is perhaps the most attractive of all Shakespeare's pert and resourceful young heroines. The exiled duke, "fleeting the time carelessly as they did in the golden world" in the forest of Arden, which is a deliberate mixture of a conventional romantic forest (the Arden of the original story was the Ardennes in France) and the Arden of his native Warwickshire; the melancholy Jacques, commenting on affairs with exhibitionist melancholy, Shakespeare's amused portrait of the traveling intellectual returned to sneer at everything at home; Touchstone, the clown, a new type of character for Shakespeare, and the first of a series which culminates in the Fool of *King Lear;* Touchstone and Audrey representing love between the sexes in its simplest physical aspect, contrasted with the romantic love between Rosalind and Orlando as well as with the exaggerated pastoral passion of Silvius for the scornful Phebe; these and other characters circle round Rosalind, who, once she has arrived in Arden, remains the center of the play. The dialogue is as much in prose as in poetry: the former is a far cry from Lodge's euphuistic prose, though it is in some degree based on it; it is light and sparkling and has the speed of talk as well as the form of art. The poetry has a lyrical clarity with overtones of gravity, shifting in tempo in accordance with the mood and character of the speaker. And the songs—"Under the greenwood tree," "Blow, blow, thou winter wind," "It was a lover and his lass" —echo through the play with a grave sweetness. The concluding wedding masque is perhaps more to the Elizabethans' taste than to ours, and the perfunctory solution of all remaining difficulties at the end not wholly acceptable even in terms of the level of probability set up by the play. It can be argued, too, that a note almost of mawkishness, of schoolgirl romanticism, occasionally comes to the surface, but this is a minority view and it represents a criticism of the theme rather than of the treatment. As a lyrical comedy of romantic love in a simple moral context whose basic pattern derives from folklore or at least from popular imagination working on a literary tradition, *As You Like It* stands supreme.

Twelfth Night, or What you Will (the first title indicates when it was first performed and the second, Shakespeare's cheerful carelessness about titles), uses similar elements to those found in *As You Like It,* but in different proportion, and with a somewhat more adult tone. The texture is richer, the overtones subtler. The comic elements enrich and comment on the romantic elements, and the romantic attitude itself is gently mocked at the same time it is glorified. The result is a play which presents an attitude to life through the combination of romantic and comic elements into a unity essentially lyrical in nature. Shipwreck, disguises and misunderstandings, romantic love, friendship, boisterous mirth, wit, trickery, self-deception, and above all and throughout all *music*—the songs, the references to music in the verse, the instrumental music off stage—music with a faintly melancholy tone underlying the whole play: these themes and devices Shakespeare welds together in what is perhaps the most perfect of all his comedies. If the light playing on *As You Like It* is that of the morning sun, the sun in *Twelfth Night* is now mellower and later, afternoon sunshine with a hint of sunset in its quality. From its opening, with the sad-sweet, self-indulgent music of the Duke's speech, "If music be the food of love, play on," to the Clown's concluding song, "When that I was a little tiny boy, With hey, ho, the wind and the rain," with its sense of wistful futility, the play moves through different phases of the romantic-comic combination to create a world in which passion, adventure, melancholy, and folly coexist and help to define each other. The comic scenes are rich in appreciative sense of human absurdity. There is no finer fool in literature than Sir Andrew Aguecheek, and the dialogue between him and Sir Toby Belch is splendid in its cheerful folly. It is significant, too, that it is against the background of this comic dialogue that Feste the clown sings what is perhaps the most haunting of all Shakespeare's songs, "O mistress mine, where are you roaming?" with its philosophy of comedy present in the second stanza:

> What is love? 'Tis not hereafter.
> Present mirth hath present laughter. . . .

The gulled Malvolio, "sick of self-love," is presented for our comic disapproval; the love-sick duke is loved by his own page, a girl in disguise, whose love for her master redeems him from sentimentalist into true lover; Viola, the shipwrecked, the resourceful, the disguised, steers her course as best she can, and in the process keeps the plot moving, until the happy ending can be worked out; the lady Olivia, like the Duke, is turned by events from self-indulgent emotion into a truer emotional life. And always we have the feeling that the comedy is balanced on a razor-edge: this world of afternoon sunlight is ringed round with traps and dangers, and eventually the dark will come anyway. Danger, misadventure, self-delusion, self-indulgence, misunderstanding, and the constant rise and fall of the human passions and appetites, all work out here to a happy ending, except for the mocked Malvolio. It is appropriate that they should; it is this kind of world and this kind of play; but in the distance we hear the sadder notes underlying the romantic—

> What is love? 'Tis not hereafter.
> Present mirth hath present laughter;
>   What's to come is still unsure.
> In delay there lies no plenty;
> Then come kiss me, sweet and twenty,
>   Youth's a stuff will not endure.

The golden moment passed, and Shakespeare was not to write this kind of play again.

Parallel with his development of romantic comedy, Shakespeare was maturing his handling of the history play. The three Henry VI plays, with which he opened his career, are of interest to those concerned with Shakespeare's attitude to English history as well as to those numerous scholars who have been attracted by the bibliographical and other problems which they raise. Uneven and sometimes crude both in dramatic movement and verse technique, they have their "Shakespearean" moments and show Shakespeare seeking a way from the episodic chronicle play to a more dramatic and more fully integrated handling of historical material. In *Richard III* he solves the problem of form by concentrating on the central character, a Marlovian villain redeemed from mechanical badness by his wit and energy; Richard projects his own character by the thoughtful rhetoric of his speech and the Machiavellian virtuosity of his actions, and the element of heroism which he acquires in his final defeat is kept from raising any moral difficulties by the passionate picture of the victorious Richmond, founder of England's Tudor dynasty, as the savior of his country. *Richard II* (1595–96) is a more complex and interesting play, deliberately ritualistic—even sacramental—in tone to suggest the Elizabethan view of the Middle Ages. The deposition of the last of England's medieval kings—for Shakespeare clearly thought of Henry IV as "modern," belonging to Shakespeare's own world, and his succession the result of personal ambition rather than divine right—had long acquired an aura of mystery and pathos in the minds of those who looked back to it, and Shakespeare deliberately set out to render that aura dramatically, providing both adequate psychological explanation and impressive poetic expression. Richard himself, petulant, childish, emotionally self-indulgent, incapable of asserting his authority over factious nobles but brooding and poetizing over his royal status once he is on the point of losing it, is the most complex character that Shakespeare had so far created, and the way he manipulates the audience's sympathy (first against, then in favor of Richard) shows remarkable dramatic cunning. Richard was the Lord's anointed, the last English king to rule in virtue of his direct and undisputed descent from William the Conqueror. His deposition was in a sense sacrilege, and after his death his supporters built up a picture of him as saint and martyr. The other side, the Lancastrians, who supported the claims of Henry IV and his successors, saw Richard as a weak and foolish king who voluntarily abdicated because he recognized his own unfitness to carry out his royal duties. Shakespeare combines both pictures with complete dramatic consistency. And in the ritual note which pervades the play he pictures a phase of English civilization very different from the breezy background of power politics we see in the *Henry IV* plays. The deposition scene is a careful inversion of the coronation ritual, and Bolingbroke's impatience with Richard's histrionics is also the modern man's impatience with the stylized forms of medieval life. The self-indulgent lyricism of many of Richard's own speeches reflects the predominantly lyrical interest that seems to have been a feature of Shakespeare's dramatic art in this phase of his development (we see it also in *Romeo and Juliet,* written at about the same time), but it also helps to build Richard's character and to differentiate it from that of his more realistic and practical supplanter.

Henry IV Part I and Part II (1597–98) show Shakespeare combining the political with the comic in a new and striking manner. The central theme is the education of Prince Hal, Henry IV's son and later Henry V, and this is worked out with many echoes of the older moralities. But the figure who represents Riot is so much more than a character in a morality play that the whole tone and character of the two plays are altered by his presence. Falstaff is no conventional Vice, but a comic figure of immense proportions who embodies in his speech and action an amoral gusto in living at the same time as he stands for a way of life which the prince must repudiate before he can be king. Shakespeare uses the Percy rebellion in Part I in order to put Falstaff in some degree in his proper moral place: the colossus of the Boar's Head tavern, so richly amusing in his comic vitality in his habitual environment, becomes less satisfactory as a human being when he is found using his authority as an officer to line his own pockets and impair the strength of the king's forces or, on the battlefield against determined rebels, faking a heroic action for himself. The way for the final and inevitable rejection of Falstaff by his former boon companion now become king is prepared throughout the latter section of Part I and the earlier section of Part II. Much ink has been spilt on the rejection of Falstaff: the simple fact is that he is (and is meant to be) engaging but not admirable, that he belongs to the amoral world of the Boar's Head, not to the moral world of the dedicated Christian ruler. He enters the latter world only to be ejected from it, and though we are properly sorry for him we must realize that the amoral becomes the immoral in this new context, and must be removed from it.

This is to consider the two Henry IV plays as a single dramatic unit, and there are convincing arguments for and against this view. It is perhaps simplest to take the common-sense position that Shakespeare wrote the first part as a play complete in itself, but when he continued it in the second he adjusted his continuation to a comprehensive and consistent view of the meaning of the whole action of both parts. In Part I the three levels of the action—the high political, surrounding Henry IV; the low comic, surrounding Falstaff; and the plausible, even attractive, but politically immoral world of Hotspur and his fellow rebels—each has its appropriate language and its place in the total politico-moral pattern. Hotspur's heroic egotism and Falstaff's unheroic egotism are both contrasted with the attitude of heroic unselfishness which is the implied ideal attitude for the ruler. In Part II, the country justices, Shallow and Silence, represent yet another level, and in a sense a deeper one: they represent the England which remains unchanged throughout all the political struggles of ambitious men to achieve control of the state, the world of inefficient innocence, unconsciously comic (unlike Falstaff, who is consciously so), foolish and pretentious, yet impressively and averagely human. The juxtaposition of different moral and social levels in both parts helps to give the play its richness and brilliance. Statesmen, rebels, roisterers; the King and his sons and advisers; Falstaff with Peto and Bardolph and Mistress Quickly and Doll Tearsheet; Percy and his friends; Shallow and Silence—each group has its place in the unfolding action (or series of actions), each reveals something about England, about the relation between moral character and human behavior, about the nature of man. The Henry IV plays can be seen as part of the general pattern of Shakespeare's picture of English history from Richard II to the Tudor; but they are, much more significantly, entertaining, stimulating, and esthetically satisfying plays whose subject, like the subject of all great drama, is human nature. And Falstaff remains, greater even than the plays which contain him, the richest comic creation in English literature.

Henry V (1598–99) concludes the historical series. It is narrower in scope and interest than the Henry IV plays, concentrating, according to tradition, on Henry as ideal warrior and man of action with a conventional piety and a gift for military rhetoric that impressed Shakespeare's contemporaries more than they impress us. The witty and aloof prince of the Henry IV plays has become a copybook model for a conquering prince, a much narrower concept than that of the Renaissance gentleman. Henry V has none of the tortured idealism of Brutus or the intellectual and moral complexity of Hamlet; his kind of success comes to simpler and in some respects less attractive characters. A brisk, well-constructed, happily varied play, *Henry V* is good theater and contains some admirable rhetorical verse. But it is the narrowest and occasionally the stuffiest of all of Shakespeare's maturer plays, and one for which the modern reader or audience has to make a special effort to align his sensibility with that of the Elizabethans.

King John (ca. 1596–97) stands somewhat apart from Shakespeare's other history plays, where he deals with the cycle of English history from the deposition of Richard II to the founding of the Tudor dynasty by Henry VII in 1485. Its relation to an older play, entitled *The Troublesome Reign of King John*, published in two parts in 1591, remains problematical: there is clearly some connection, and perhaps the *Troublesome Reign* is a "bad quarto" of an earlier version of Shakespeare's play as we have it. The older play covers the whole of King John's reign, portraying him as a champion of English ecclesiastical independence against intolerable papal claims to supremacy; its tone is strongly anti-Catholic. In Shakespeare's *King John* the anti-Catholic tone has been significantly moderated and John himself (though not the simple villain of later historians) is far from a hero. The character of the Bastard Faulconbridge; the dramatic conflicts between Queen Eleanor, King John's mother, and Constance, mother of Arthur, John's nephew; Pandulph, the Papal legate, succeeding by his cunning rhetorical argument in persuading King Philip of France to turn against John with whom he has recently sworn amity; the pathetic scene between Hubert and young Prince Arthur—these are some of the elements in the play which show Shakespeare bursting the bounds of the older chronicle form, not to concentrate on the psychological and moral problems of an individual character, as he did in *Richard III* and *Richard II*, but to give free rein to a curiosity and an exuberance which make the play lively and fascinating in spite of its structural deficiencies. The political interest which emerges so strongly in the Henry IV plays is visible here—the concern with the ethics of rebellion and the unity of England and the character of the good ruler—but the play's true appeal lies elsewhere: in the Bastard's vividly presented quality of the forthright Englishman, in the vitality and variety of the whole. Altogether, *King John* is a most interesting and promising transitional play, which occupies an important though lonely place in the Shakespeare canon.

In the years when he was experimenting with different kinds of history plays and perfecting his romantic comedy Shakespeare was also thinking about tragedy. *Richard III* was tragedy of a kind, but Shakespeare was soon dissatisfied with this kind of play and never wrote another like it. About the same time that he wrote *Richard II* (1595–96) he also produced *Romeo and Juliet,* a play of star-crossed lovers based on an Italian story which had already been handled in English (via the French) both in prose and in verse. Shakespeare's immediate source was the verse rendering, Arthur Brooke's poem *The Tragical History of Romeus and Juliet,* though he produces a quite different effect by speeding up the action and by giving the characters new life and motivation. It is, however, as Shakespeare tells it, a tragedy of circumstances rather than of character, brilliantly rendered in passionate lyrical-dramatic terms. Romeo and Juliet themselves are the quintessence of young love; the speed and ardor of their mutual adoration are symbolic of the recklessly dedicated love that is the mark of first real passion (how different from the maturer and more sophisticated love of Antony and Cleopatra!), which banishes alike sentimentality and false modesty to burn brightly and honestly until fate brings all to an untimely close. We first see Romeo as the conventional, sentimental lover of Rosaline, sighing histrionically, though not forgetting to ask, "Where shall we dine?" His first sight of Juliet, daughter of the Capulets with whom his own family of Montague is engaged in deadly feud, banishes all that nonsense and makes a man of him. When his lively and mocking friend Mercutio sees Romeo again for the first time since he and Juliet have declared their mutual love, he is struck by his liveliness and wit: "Why, is not this better now than groaning for love? Now art thou sociable; now art thou Romeo. . . ." Throughout the play Shakespeare, by a variety of devices, sets the love of Romeo and Juliet against other views of love: to Capulet, it is a matter of a suitable family alliance; to the Nurse, a matter of physical, sexual satisfaction; to Paris, Capulet's chosen husband for his daughter, a matter of good breeding and decorum.

The norm of the play's expression is both lyrical and declamatory. When Romeo, disguised, first meets Juliet in the home of his family enemy, they share the speaking of a sonnet together, and with its last line comes their first kiss. Juliet's surging speech as she impatiently awaits her bridegroom's arrival for the one night fate is to allow them to spend together is a formal epithalamium as well as an expression of physical passion so honest and frank that it shocked Victorian editors (Shakespeare makes no attempt to conceal the physical element in ideal romantic love). And the lovers' reluctant recognition of the dawn which brings to an end their first and last night of love is in the form of a traditional "aubade" or dawn poem. At the same time, each character has his own idiom which rings true to his personality. And the characters themselves are clearly conceived and brilliantly presented. The Nurse, that well-meaning but gross figure whose failure to understand that love is more than mere sex finally leaves Juliet to face her fate alone, is one of Shakespeare's great comic creations; Mercutio, the witty, mocking gallant, is the ideal Renaissance bachelor, and almost steals the show before his death—resulting from his getting mixed up in the Montague-Capulet feud—takes him out of the way and at the same time helps to precipitate the tragedy. Capulet, Friar Lawrence, Tybalt, Benvolio, and the others play their parts as less fully realized but clearly presented and deftly handled characters whose speech and actions are always both appropriate to themselves and helpful to the working out of the play. The picture of the two ideal young lovers discovering their love only to be trapped by circumstance into premature death is not profound tragedy; it has no meaning other than to present the glory of true love and the fatuity and futility of those hatreds and conventions that destroy it. But it is sheer bad luck rather than either the fatal feud or Capulet's sudden impulse to marry off his daughter to Paris immediately that finally brings on the tragedy. Life is not indicted; true love remains a glory, and the lovers die without disillusionment. Ophelia and Desdemona, who die bewildered, ignorant of the cause of their own destruction and of their hero's cruelty, are part of a sadder world and products of a profounder imagination.

During the next few years Shakespeare produced histories and comedies, and when he turns to tragedy again, in *Julius Caesar* (1599–1600), he is seeking a profounder way of finding individual human tragedy in history than he did in either *Richard III* or *Richard II*. The source of the play, as of all Shakespeare's Roman plays, is Sir Thomas North's *Lives of the Noble Grecians and Romans*, translated from the Greek of Plutarch via the French of Jacques Amyot. In Plutarch's lives of Caesar, Brutus, and Mark Antony, Shakespeare read history through biography and went on to show dramatically some of the paradoxical ways in which private character influences and is influenced by public affairs. In a sense, the theme of the play is the relation between private and public virtue: they are not identical, as Brutus thought, and the humanitarian idealist does not necessarily make the best politician or even the best patriot. In *Richard II* Shakespeare showed how qualities which, in a private person, though far from admirable might yet have a certain charm, were fatal in a ruler. In *Julius Caesar* he probes much more subtly into this problem, and shows the liberal idealist bringing about the very opposite result to that which he intended. Brutus, like Hamlet and in some degree like Othello, is destroyed largely by his own virtues. In Brutus, nobility of character implies political innocence; in Hamlet, intelligence and sensitivity produce inability to face the world as it is; in Othello integrity and forthrightness produce credulity and, through credulity, tragic mistrust of the one person whom above all he should have trusted. Each of these characters may well have acted better if he had been a less good man. A more worldly Brutus, a less morally sensitive Hamlet, a tougher and more cunning Othello, would have done less harm in the world. This goes far deeper than simply the relation between private and public virtue. It includes, among other problems, that of the relation between innocence and virtue, or at least between innocence of character and effectiveness of moral action. It is an old problem: Milton was to treat it, in his own way, in *Paradise Lost,* where "our credulous mother, Eve" allowed herself to be fooled by Satan into tasting of the forbidden tree. Eve's real fault was lack of sophistication; she was unsuspicious of what Satan, in his serpent disguise, told her; she was a "sucker" and swallowed his story. But would she have been more virtuous to be suspicious? Is it morally wrong to be a "sucker"—as Eve was with respect to the serpent, as Othello was with respect to Iago, as Brutus was with respect to such political sophisticates as Antony, as Hamlet was—we might almost say—with respect to life?

A man destroyed by his own virtues is a truly tragic theme, and one familiar enough in the modern world where the tragedy of the liberal intellectual is a commonplace. But of course this is not the only theme of *Julius Caesar.* Cassius is the co-hero, and, skilled politician though he is, with little scruple in playing on Brutus' finer feelings, he admires Brutus and cannot help allowing Brutus to achieve moral ascendancy over him, once the murder of Caesar is accomplished. The coarser nature is dominated by the finer—to the destruction of both of them and of the ideal to which they had sacrificed everything. In the quarrel scene it is Cassius who first gives way, and it is under the influence of this moral domination by Brutus that, against his better judgment, Cassius allows Brutus to have his way in his ill-advised plan of seeking immediate battle at Philippi. Nowhere is the Epicurean Cassius more like the stoic Brutus than when he commits suicide because he is ashamed of having lived "so long, /To see my best friend ta'en before my face." And that suicide, rather than military defeat, seals the doom of the republican forces. Cassius is not as unlike Brutus as he thinks. Both are made fools of by Antony—Brutus, of course, especially, for it was Brutus who, against Cassius' advice, insisted on Antony's being given permission to speak. If Cassius is shrewder and more practical than Brutus he is basically an idealist too, an intellectual, whom Caesar had come to suspect because "he thinks too much." If he appears a cunning man of action beside Brutus, he is almost equally a babe in the wood when seen beside Antony, the man without innocence, the man who knows how to unite his personal affections with his political ambitions. (Though it is an unstable equilibrium and, as Shakespeare shows us later in *Antony and Cleopatra,* it cannot be maintained throughout a lifetime.)

Julius Caesar is thus a political tragedy, exploring the relation between private and public virtue, between personal morality and political efficiency, between innocence and action. A well-knit, lean play, with no superfluous fat or subsidiary levels of action (though we must remember that the text we have may represent a shortened acting version), it is one of the most clean-cut and straightforward of Shakespeare's tragedies. The blank verse is fluent and businesslike, rising where necessary to a noble eloquence and falling to a quieter colloquial movement where the action demands it. The moments of quiet in the play—Brutus with Portia, Brutus with his sleepy page, Lucius—are beautifully managed and add that note of controlled pathos which emphasizes the personal tragedy of the public figure. And at the end victorious efficiency pays its tribute to defeated innocence. "This was the noblest Roman of them all." The words are Antony's, referring to Brutus, and they represent his "real" opinion, as they do Cassius'—and Shakespeare's. The failures are, in an important sense, the better men. Henry V is a mechanical figure beside Brutus or Hamlet.

Hamlet (1600–01), the most popular and the most discussed of Shakespeare's tragedies, is both more complex in theme and more subtle in treatment than *Julius Caesar*. The existence of three separate texts—a "bad quarto" (1603), which is apparently a garbled reconstruction, largely from memory, of Shakespeare's play put together by a player who doubled the parts of Marcellus and the Second Player; the "good" quarto of 1604 which represents Shakespeare's full text; and the Folio text of 1623, a cut acting version, with nevertheless some passages not in the 1604 quarto—has deflected a great deal of critical attention to purely textual matters, while the relation of the play to a lost earlier *Hamlet*, probably by Kyd, has also led to much speculation. The story itself is an ancient one, originating in Scandinavia as the tale of Amleth, a prince who pretended madness in order to fool his usurping uncle and regain his throne. Late in the twelfth century it was told—already an old story, that had come down through oral tradition—by the Danish historian Saxo Grammaticus in his Latin *Historia Danica.* In Saxo's version we find important elements which remain in Shakespeare's play and which critics have long argued about. Amleth's madness, in Saxo, is assumed so that his usurping uncle would regard him as a completely mindless lunatic not worth killing: its purpose is sheer self-preservation. The usurping uncle sends agents to try to find out whether Amleth's idiocy is genuine—and one of these agents is a girl, the original of Ophelia, while another, the original of Polonius, hides himself in the straw of Amleth's mother's room to overhear a conversation between mother and son, and is discovered and killed by Amleth. Amleth in the end achieves his revenge, slays his wicked uncle, and becomes king. This story—a tale of revenge from the heroic age—underwent some modifications in later versions, and then, apparently in the late 1580's, a dramatist who is generally taken to have been Kyd dramatized it as a Senecan revenge play in the Elizabethan mode, incorporating some of the devices that had been so successful in *The Spanish Tragedy*. Here for the first time we get the ghost—a Senecan device—crying for revenge, and here, too, the original murder is done secretly by poisoning, not openly as in Saxo, so that the wicked uncle is not publicly known as wicked and the ghost is required to reveal the truth to Hamlet. This makes it unnecessary for Hamlet to feign madness in order to save his life, as he does in Saxo, but Kyd was a great hand at madness and kept this element in the story (indeed, he added to it by making the Ophelia character go mad also) though the motivation for it is now much less clear. He also, true to the Senecan fashion, killed off the hero and the other major characters in the end, and introduced Laertes, the fencing match, and the poisoned rapier and drink. We know something of this lost *Hamlet* largely from a degraded version of it which exists in German, and our knowledge is important, because it enables us to see Shakespeare's play as a reworking of a melodramatic Senecan revenge play into a profound poetic tragedy.

Shakespeare's task was to impose a new, tragic meaning on this traditional story, by his arrangement and presentation of the action, by the kind of life and motivation he gave to the characters, and by the overtones of meaning and suggestion set up by his poetic handling of the characters' language. Though T. S. Eliot has questioned the success with which he transformed the old material into a consistent work of dramatic art, the experience of generations of play-goers and readers is sufficient proof that Shakespeare has given it profound and disturbing new dramatic life. In the character of Hamlet he takes the Brutus type and by giving him increased complexity and sensitivity within the story's traditional atmosphere of ambition, murder, and revenge gives the play a wholly new dimension. This is the tragedy of moral sensitivity in a wicked world, the tragedy of the idealist come suddenly face to face with reality, the tragedy of imagination betraying its owner. Or so the play has been read by many. Hamlet, his innocent world shattered by the marriage of his adored mother to the uncle who has succeeded his hero-worshiped father to the throne which in any case rightly belongs to Hamlet himself, is in a bad enough mental state before the ghost reveals that his "uncle-father" has more than incest (for marriage with a sister-in-law was technically incest), ambition, and drunkenness to answer for: he is also guilty of fratricide. Old-fashioned revenge in the heroic tradition is not going to restore his lost world or bring back to health an imagination increasingly "tainted" by disgust and horror at sex, Court life, and politics. Surrounded by the suspicious Claudius, the bewildered Ophelia, the lost Queen, the worldly busybody Polonius (to whose coolly self-interested support Claudius owed the throne), and the spies and opportunists of the Court, Hamlet can do nothing but brood and indulge his festering imagination. He can confide in nobody—not even fully in Horatio, his one trustworthy friend. His madness is partly real hysteria, partly an attempt to fence off curiosity about his real state of mind and intentions. It serves only to increase suspicion, while his reckless baiting of Claudius, which he seems unable to resist, plays into the usurper's hands. No one can help him. In Ophelia he sees only tainted womanhood—tainted because of his mother's sin; in Horatio, the happy extrovert, "the man who is not passion's slave," whom he can admire but not imitate. Occasionally we get glimpses of the old Hamlet, gentle, accomplished, princely; occasionally, when the event presses and his sudden temper is roused, he can break away into violent action, as in his slaying of Polonius—which again plays right into the King's hands. When he tests the truth of the ghost's story by putting on the play within the play, his baiting of the King and the way he presents the play ("one Lucianus, *nephew* to the king") allow the Court to think that his trouble is thwarted ambition and that he is threatening to get rid of the King and succeed to the throne himself (as the old Amleth did), and determines Claudius to get rid of him immediately. His one clear chance to kill Claudius he will not take, making the excuse that the villain is praying and he would prefer to slay him when he is engaged in some activity which will ensure his immediate descent to Hell; and he goes on to the famous scene in his mother's bedroom where he rubs her face in the dirt in a desperate attempt to make her see and feel how she has shattered his world and betrayed everything that was decent in the Hamlet family. He escapes Claudius' plot by a mixture of luck, courage, and contrivance, and comes back to find Ophelia dead and Laertes incensed against him, meeting his doom at last by Laertes' poisoned rapier, but not before he has finally, in a surge of contemptuous anger, killed Claudius. In the end, all the principal characters are dead—Polonius, Ophelia, the Queen, Claudius, and Hamlet—and Fortinbras, the man of action, the soldier who believes in such crude sentimentalities as military glory, the Henry V type, succeeds to the throne.

Does Shakespeare give proper dramatic shape and conviction to it all? That the play is tremendously effective on the stage there can be no doubt. From the tense, quiet opening, with the sentries apprehensive and jittery, to Fortinbras' final elegy on Hamlet, scene succeeds scene with mounting dramatic interest, moments of tension are adroitly followed by more relaxed interludes, characters create themselves by speech and action with astonishing vividness and humanity, and the struggle between Hamlet and his destiny is played out. Is Hamlet consistent? Are his actions properly motivated? Do his soliloquies sometimes reveal their author's distresses and speculations rather than Hamlet's? Is there not some disproportion between Hamlet's behavior and the situation that calls it forth? We can answer all these questions unfavorably to Shakespeare—Hamlet is not always consistent, the motives for his actions are sometimes in doubt, sometimes in the soliloquies Shakespeare rather than Hamlet seems to be speaking, there is not always a close and easily demonstrable connection between the situation and Hamlet's response to it—but this does not mean that Shakespeare has bungled the problem of giving satisfying dramatic shape to the old story. The element of mystery in Hamlet's motivation helps to enlarge the dimensions of the play. Personality is not a cut-and-dried affair which can be explained by a simple cause-and-effect relationship. If there are elements in the original story that Shakespeare feels obliged to use even though they do not appear to be directly connected with his conception of the action and the characters, it is to his credit as an artist that he uses them to help suggest the mystery of personality rather than as mere mechanical appendages to the action. We may be told that Hamlet's rash killing of Polonius and his contemptuous treatment of the corpse derives from elements in the old story that

Shakespeare felt he had to include, but the important fact is that in Shakespeare's play these things are dramatically compelling and esthetically satisfying to those who know nothing of the sources of the plot. It is a mistake to confuse the dramatically and artistically successful with the psychologically explicable. Hamlet may remain in part a mystery, but that mystery is bound up with the mystery of life. And the play has the dimensions of life together with the formality and completeness of art.

Scholarship can concentrate on Shakespeare's treatment of his sources, on the way in which Elizabethan dramatic conventions helped to determine his treatment of any given point, or on the degree in which a knowledge of the Elizabethan view of the world explains Hamlet's attitude to the ghost or Polonius' behavior at Court. All this knowledge is helpful, but it must not be allowed to obscure the fact that in his handling of an older story, his use of contemporary dramatic conventions, and in his Elizabethan habit of mind Shakespeare operates as a successful dramatist, creates a moral world that challenges and illuminates, builds up a pattern of tragic action that does arouse "pity and fear" to leave us in the end "in calm of mind, all passion spent." That Shakespeare does this so brilliantly in *Hamlet* is partly due to his having discovered by now a method of enabling his principal characters, at selected moments in the play, to render their state of mind to the audience or the reader. The Shakespearean soliloquy, which reaches its maturity in *Hamlet,* is not merely an expansion of the conventional "aside" or a simple speaking aloud of a coherent stream of thought. It is a poetic rendering of a character's complete mental and emotional state at a critical point in his development, drawing on all the resources of imagery and rhythmic movement for its total expression. For this is poetic drama, not "realistic" drama, and the recurrence of related images, the rise and fall of certain rhythms, the sounding of certain overtones of meaning and suggestion, are as important in building up the total significance of the play as the mere sequence of events or paraphrasable content of the speeches.

Containing something of the larger dimensions of life within the limiting formality of art, *Hamlet,* perhaps more than any other of Shakespeare's tragedies, lends itself to a variety of interpretations. Hamlet is both the ideal Renaissance prince and the conventional malcontent, the traditional avenger and the sensitive idealist in a brutal world, and other things besides. And, in lesser degree, the same multiple description can be given of the other characters. The play is not, however, simply a series of portraits; the action is what gives it shape and primary meaning, and it is a mistake to remove the characters from the action and speculate about them as though they are characters in a psychologist's case-book (though the fact that critics have been tempted to do this is surely a tribute to Shakespeare's dramatic skill). Of the many meanings that can be extracted from the action of *Hamlet*, perhaps the most tragic, and the one which fits in best with what appears to be Shakespeare's view of the essential tragedy of human life at this time, is that here is a presentation of the paradox of guilt and justice. Justice demands appropriate action where a crime has been committed, but in fact no action is ever appropriate. The tragedy of *Hamlet*, as in some degree of *Othello*, is that moral outrage demands action when no action can be of any use. In a sense, we can say that the ghost was at fault in appearing to Hamlet in the first place and setting him—for what might be called purely selfish reasons—a task which, even if accomplished, could do no possible good. When Hamlet's whole nature was outraged by his mother's behavior and then by the news of his father's murder, he naturally felt that something must be done. But what? What could be done that would make any difference—any difference at all to the things that really mattered? Would a dagger through Claudius' ribs restore Hamlet's shattered universe? Would it restore his earlier idealized image of his mother or remove the "blister" that had been set on his innocent love? This is a tragedy of moral frustration. What are you going to do about past crimes which have shattered your preconceptions about the nature of life? There is nothing you can ever do about the past, except forget it. And yet, of course, Hamlet could not forget. Revenge is no real help—what sort of action, then, *is* of help? None that is directed toward undoing the past: only purposive action directed toward the future can ever help. And that is at least one explanation of Hamlet's long delay in carrying out the ghost's command: he wanted action that would undo the past, and no action could do that, revenge least of all, for that would only re-enact the past.

The punishment can never fit the crime, for it can never undo it. We may think we may be able to find appropriate action, as Lear thought:

> I will have such revenges on you both
> That all the world shall—I will do such things—
> What they are yet, I know not; but they shall be
> The terrors of the earth;

but in fact we never do, and it is impossible that we ever should. Lear's frustration at feeling a deep moral indignation which can have no "objective correlative" in action is, in part, the cause of his madness, as it is of Hamlet's moods and Othello's self-torture (for in *Othello* there is no action that can take care of the supposed fact of Desdemona's infidelity). Only when he gives up the whole idea of action does Lear recover and achieve redemption. The morally outraged man, the finer and more sensitive he is, will feel all the more need for action, the need to do something about his shocking revelation; and his frustration at finding no adequate action produces tragedy. Even the ghost in *Hamlet* learns at last—perhaps learns sooner than Hamlet himself—the futility of trying to undo the past by physical action. He declines from the armed warrior whom we first see to become on his last appearance a pathetic domestic figure ("enter the ghost in his night gown") only interested in trying to make contact with his morally lost wife and in saving her from Hamlet's morbid rage. This remarkable scene—the only one in which we see the Hamlet family together, father, mother, and son—has a strange kind of pathos, with the Queen unable because of her guilt to see her husband's spirit so that the ghost, after a vain effort to re-establish the family unit, as it were, departs in silence forever. On the other side is the Polonius family, all destroyed, too, through involvement in Hamlet's tragedy—innocent involvement on Ophelia's part, almost innocent on Laertes', and only relatively guilty on the part of Polonius. We last see *them* together fairly early in the play, when Laertes is being seen off by his devoted father and sister—also a touching domestic tableau, with its own meaning in the play. The tragedy of Hamlet concerns more than the wreck of a noble spirit, and the longer Hamlet dwells on the past and searches for a way of undoing it, the more innocent—as well as guilty—people become involved in it. And so interpretation can go on, for the meaning of *Hamlet* echoes on indefinitely.

Othello (1603–04), the second of Shakespeare's great tragedies, is a more closely packed and concentrated play. Exploring again some of the paradoxes of good and evil and the irony of evil being bred out of innocence, Shakespeare here concentrates on a domestic issue and produces the most relentless and the saddest of his tragedies. Iago, the "realist," the man who thinks he knows how to get on in the world, who relishes his power to manipulate people like puppets, is more than a mere device to get the plot started, as some modern critics see him, or than the embodiment of "motiveless malignity" that Coleridge saw; he is both the disgruntled professional soldier and the hard-boiled cynic who feels personally outraged when a simple-minded hero like Othello gets ahead in the world and he, who knows the world so much better, fails to get on. Othello himself, the romantic Moor with his background of "antres vast and deserts idle," can fight for Venice and save her from her enemies but knows that he does not really know these people, and that knowledge makes him Iago's prey. The story of a jealous ensign inventing slanders to make his Moorish captain believe that his devoted white wife has been faithless to him and then helping him to slay her comes from the Italian writer Cinthio's collection of stories, the *Hecatommithi,* and as Cinthio tells it is a crude enough tale, far from promising material for a tragedy. Shakespeare makes it into a tragedy by his arrangement and patterning of the details, by his characterization, by the symbolic use of detail, and by the language in which he makes the characters express themselves. The opening, with the whispering at street corners flaring suddenly into Othello's confrontation with his unrecognized enemies and his noble defense of his marriage before the Senate, is a little play in itself, and one with a happy ending. Othello's simple dignity carries all before it:

> Keep up your bright swords, for the dew will rust them.

And the habit of command:

> Hold your hands,
> Both you of my inclining and the rest.
> Were it my cue to fight, I should have known it
> Without a prompter.

And the superb combination of respect and self-assurance:

> Most potent, grave, and reverend signiors,
> My very noble and approv'd good masters,
> That I have ta'en away this old man's daughter,
> It is most true; true, I have married her:
> The very head and front of my offending
> Hath this extent, no more . . .

It is this self-assurance that Iago sets out to destroy. Iago the puppet-master, who enjoys life most when he can manipulate the lives of others from behind the scenes, sets himself to manipulate this commanding Moor. And because he is a Moor, and noble, and so deeply in love with Desdemona that he can scarcely believe his good fortune, and inexperienced and therefore self-distrustful in domestic matters (especially where Venetians are concerned), Iago succeeds in destroying him. That Iago destroys Desdemona too is (in Shakespeare's play but not in his source) incidental: he has no malice against her; he is out to destroy successful innocence, which to him ought to be a contradiction in terms, and he can only get at that through Desdemona. He wants nothing out of it all except the destruction of Othello: he makes this heroic figure dance to his piping, makes a puppet out of him—and what happens after that, he scarcely thinks about. If he had thought, he would have known that sooner or later the truth would have come to light; but he never looked beyond his immediate aim.

What makes it all possible is Othello's incredulity in the face of his own supreme happiness—a kind of modesty, which makes him vulnerable to Iago's suggestion that he does not in fact enjoy the happiness he has thought was his.

> It gives me wonder great as my content
> To see you here before me. O my soul's joy!
> If after every tempest come such calms,
> May the winds blow till they have waken'd death! . . .
> If it were now to die
> 'Twere now to be most happy for, I fear,
> My soul hath her content so absolute
> That not another comfort like to this
> Succeeds in unknown fate.

Desdemona does not share his sense of insecurity, and replies:

> The heavens forbid
> But that our loves and comforts should increase,
> Even as our days do grow.

She has defied her own father and chosen Othello and takes her happiness as a right. And when Othello, inflamed by Iago's cunning and plausible lies, turns on her, she is hurt and bewildered, but does not lose her faith. She goes to her death not knowing what it is all about, and that is what makes the play almost unbearably painful; only the fact that in spite of everything her faith in Othello and in herself for choosing him remains, prevents her tragedy from being altogether too painful to read or witness—and even so, it only just prevents it.

Othello is not a study in jealousy—for that, as Coleridge pointed out, we must go to Leontes in *The Winter's Tale*. Iago has to work desperately hard to catch Othello in his trap, and even then he is helped by coincidence before he can succeed. It is not jealousy, but anguish that this beautiful and innocent-seeming creature, whom he loved, could be so horribly guilty, that so torments him. All reason and order and beauty are shattered: "chaos is come again." A soldier, a man who was used to meeting a situation with the appropriate action, he here confronted a situation so monstrous, so destructive of reason, that nothing could be done about it. Something had to be done, but nothing could be done. Othello was not a philosopher like Hamlet who could at least mark time by introspection and speculation while pondering the problem of the irrevocability of performed evil. The man of action must do something—but what? "Othello's occupation's gone," his world is shattered, here was the outrage of irreversible evil. Something had to be done—and the only action that seemed at all relevant and proper in the circumstances was to kill Desdemona. He did not kill her in jealous rage. He made no move himself to kill his supposed rival Cassio. He killed Desdemona for the sake of his moral universe, as the only action somehow appropriate to the situation. "It is the cause, it is the cause, my soul." And when the truth is finally known, though it cannot make life tolerable for Othello, it at least restores his moral universe and he can resume his former dignity of bearing before performing the now inevitable act of self-slaughter.

King Lear (1605–06), which Swinburne called "the most elemental and primeval" of Shakespeare's plays, is in sharp contrast to the concentrated domestic tragedy of *Othello*. The main story goes far back into ancient British mythology; Lear himself is originally the old Celtic sea-god, and the folk tale of the king and his three daughters was attached to this character by Geoffrey of Monmouth in the twelfth century. The story as Geoffrey told it was repeated several times in English literature before Shakespeare (by Holinshed and Spenser among others), and there was an older play on the subject which Shakespeare used as one of his sources. With the main story Shakespeare combined the tale of Gloucester and his two sons —the substance of which he found in Sidney's *Arcadia*—to achieve an extraordinary double-plotted tragedy where the main action is echoed and commented on, as it were, by the subplot. And, as though instinctively recognizing the mythological and folklore elements in the original story, Shakespeare fills his play with archetypal images and ideas which combine and reverberate to produce a large cosmic view of man's fate at the same time as the individual tragedies of Lear and his daughters, and Gloucester and his sons, are played out. *King Lear* is thus the largest in conception and implication of all Shakespeare's tragedies; it is poetic drama heightened to a grand symbolic level without losing that uncanny insight into ordinary human psychology that continues to astonish us in Shakespeare. The play is thus a happy hunting ground for those who are interested in discovering the symbolic pattern of imagery in Shakespeare, for in his handling of images of nature, of sex, of astronomy, of order, in the paradoxical counterpointing of symbols of light and dark, of sight and blindness, of knowledge and ignorance, of good and evil, Shakespeare brings his highest poetic and dramatic powers to bear. It is an immense play, immense in power and meaning and in the weight of tragic knowledge which it conveys. Both poetically and dramatically it goes as far as poetic drama can go.

The tragedy in *Lear* is Shakespeare's own: the old play ends happily. Indeed, though Shakespeare got his crude raw material from the old play and from other sources, he has reworked it so completely that his play is in every sense that matters a wholly original work of the imagination. The simple folk characters become fraught with moral and psychological meaning. Lear, the passionate old king who seeks to indulge his vanity by arranging for public protestations of the daughters' love, pretending that this is to determine how much of his kingdom he is to give to each, provokes his youngest and best-loved daughter, whose share he had already decided to be the largest and whose victory in the love protestations he took completely for granted, to a stubborn understatement. She is her father's daughter, and the palpably exaggerated speeches of her sisters, together with the whole idea of assessing love by extravagance of assertion, arouse her pride. Her father's anger, the product of frustrated vanity, produces her banishment and leaves the two evil sisters with the power. In his powerful presentation of this opening situation Shakespeare sets going the themes of true and false vision, of self-knowledge and self-blindness, that are to be handled with so many variations throughout the play. Kent's protests against Lear's act of supreme folly brings only the cry "Out of my sight!" to which Kent replies, "See better, Lear, and let me still remain /The true blank of thine eye." Already Shakespeare has found means of introducing Gloucester and his bastard son Edmund, who is determined to revenge the unjust shame of his bastardy by acting as he was begot, "naturally," as though kindness and justice and the affection that binds families together were unnatural inventions of human "art." But Lear's banishment of his best-loved daughter is unnatural in the opposite sense, just as Goneril and Regan's behavior to their father afterward is unnatural. But what *is* natural, and what are the principles that govern human affairs? Every important character has his own answer to this question, and the action of the play itself provides a larger answer than any individual can arrive at. Lear himself, being king, being used all his life to pomp and circumstance, to the trappings of rank and the automatic protestations of loyalty and devotion to which his position entitles him, has never had the opportunity of seeing things "naturally," of understanding himself or others. Only when Goneril and Regan have combined to strip him of the signs of rank he had reserved for himself in giving away his kingdom, does Lear begin to see the difference between what man needs as a biological organism and what he wants to sustain his human dignity:

> O, reason not the need! Our basest beggars
> Are in the poorest thing superfluous.
> Allow not nature more than nature needs,
> Man's life is cheap as beast's. . . .

(Here is a different "nature" again, life in its simple biological aspect.) Lear achieves self-knowledge through suffering: he learns for the first time in his life to see "naturally" as a man rather than artificially as a king; but the conditions of his education are too hard and he learns at the cost of his reason and, in large measure, of his personality.

Only the Fool realizes from the beginning that, having given way his kingly power, his artificial personality, Lear can no longer count on the artificial relationships which it produced:

> *Lear.* Dost thou call me fool, boy?
> *Fool.* All thy other titles thou hast given away; that thou wast born with.

The Fool is a remarkable transformation of a stock Elizabethan dramatic character into a species of chorus, whose wry commentary on Lear's actions between his "giving all to his daughters" and his succumbing to madness helps to add a new ironic dimension to the play. The king is foolish, the Fool is wise; like Yeats' Crazy Jane, Lear's Fool explores the paradoxes of pretention and reality, but he is also a dramatic character himself, whose destiny is pathetic rather than tragic. In Act I, scene 4, the banished Kent (returned in disguise to serve his ungrateful master), the Fool, and Lear, engage in a conversation that is both realistic (it is in prose, except for the Fool's snatches of song) and stylized, almost, as Granville-Barker points out, ritualistic; Lear, now first beginning to realize faintly the consequences of his folly; the Fool, heartbroken and reckless, flashing bitter home truths at his brooding master; Kent listening and waiting, to see how he can be of service to the doomed old man. When the truth about his daughters' intentions is finally apprehended by Lear, incredulity gives way to epic anger, and anger to a desperate attempt to come to terms with this unthinkable new knowledge; and he finally goes out into the storm to face "nature" at its most uncompromising, to realize elemental facts about life from which he had hitherto been completely shut away, and at last to lose his reason under this rough schooling.

Meanwhile, Shakespeare has gone ahead with the Gloucester story and presented Edmund's plot against his noble but simple-minded brother Edgar, who is driven to flee into the countryside disguised as a mad beggar. Here, as in his other tragedies, Shakespeare raises the question of the relation between innocence and moral effectiveness: it is Edgar's naïve credulity which produces his own plight and his father Gloucester's cruel treatment. Edmund calls Edgar

> a brother noble
> Whose nature is so far from doing harms
> That he suspects none.

It is Eve and the serpent again.

It was a bold stroke of Shakespeare's to bring together Edgar, feigning madness, Lear, now going truly mad, and the Fool, but he succeeds in keeping the different levels of folly distinct, and, more than that, each contributes its own strand of meaning to the complex symbolic statement about life that the play makes. Lear begins by being solely concerned with the injustice he has received at the hands of his two daughters, accepting the storm because it is "natural" and not malicious and seeing in Edgar's plight confirmation of his own fate. A concern for impersonal justice succeeds his earlier immediate concern for revenge, and gradually, as his madness grows, a new kind of moral insight emerges to end in the recognition that there is no division into the just and the unjust: "None does offend, none." This comes near the recognition that we all share in everybody else's guilt, which is one of the underlying themes of *Measure for Measure*. The artifice of rank can produce an apparent division into judge and criminal, but with the "natural" vision of madness this is seen to be a false picture. This is more than the movement from vengeance to compassion for the sinner, which it is often taken to be; the statement that "none does offend" follows a fierce picture of universal lechery and deceit which shows the same kind of bitter disgust with sex that some of Hamlet's speeches show. It is because all are equally guilty that none does offend. The road to true humility runs through these bitter insights.

Gloucester, the moral simpleton who pays a terrible penalty for his simplicity and finds a new dignity in suffering, sees better blind than he had seen when he had his eyesight, just as Lear sees the world more clearly after he has gone mad. But of course it is not as simple as that. The moving scene where Lear, recovered from his madness to find Cordelia bending over him, fully achieves his new character of the humble and ambitionless private man also shows us a Lear who had lost the pride and dignity which, moral pitfalls though they were, gave stature to his personality. Pride is both a good and a bad quality, and Shakespeare was to treat the problem more particularly in *Coriolanus*. But he is much concerned with it in the great tragedies. Lear is not redeemed until he loses his pride, but the redeemed Lear is but the pale shade of a man. Yet when Hamlet regains his pride ("It is I, Hamlet the Dane") he recovers our sympathy. And Cleopatra redeems herself when she acquires pride. Macbeth has ambition and courage, but no pride, and none of Shakespeare's true villains has pride. (Othello has it, but not Iago, and it is perhaps partly true to say that Othello's *pride* is hurt when he thinks he has discovered Desdemona's infidelity.)

Lear is full of such moral ambiguities; it says more about man than any other of Shakespeare's plays. The ambiguity of the moral world is never so effectively illustrated as by the rapid and apparently effortless way in which Shakespeare can turn out fierce disapproval of Lear into profound sympathy for him. In this teeming tragedy, with its cunning alternation of prose and verse, its paradoxical play with reason and madness and innumerable other pairs of apparent contraries, Shakespeare challenges all the categories with which men comfort themselves into a delusion that they know the moral universe they live in. Perhaps the ultimate statement made by tragedy is that the moral universe is more complicated and more self-contradictory than we can allow ourselves to think in our daily lives.

In *Macbeth* (1606) Shakespeare took two different stories from Holinshed's *Chronicles of Scotland* (Donwald's murder of King Duff and the career of Macbeth) and worked this somewhat primitive material into a profound dramatic presentation of the progress of evil within a human personality. The shortest of the tragedies (though the text as we have it may have been cut), it is given power and scope by the poetic expansion of meaning through imagery as well as by the persuasive and moving projection of character. Shakespeare here solves the problem of the hero-villain in a more subtle and impressive fashion than he did in *Richard III*. Macbeth is first presented as a true heroic figure, loyal and brave, in whom the witches' prophecy precipitates a phase of consciousness that had hitherto lain submerged below his acknowledged thought. (It does not matter whether we take the witches as real or symbolic: the psychological meaning is the same.) Lady Macbeth, the most devoted of wives, steels herself to encourage her husband to win a crown whose meaning for both of them is mystical rather than clearly apprehended in terms of power and glory. She speaks of the crown as

> . . . the golden round
> Which fate and metaphysical aid doth seem
> To have thee crown'd withal.

and neither she nor Macbeth ever dwells on any specific advantage it will bring them. The crown is the symbol of the ultimate earthly ambition, of something beyond the grasp of ordinary man, as it was for Tamburlaine

> . . . the ripest fruit of all,
> That perfect bliss and sole felicity,
> The sweet fruition of an earthly crown.

They both shrink from the deed that is to bring them this symbolic reward, and Lady Macbeth, who makes the greater initial effort and seems more unscrupulous at the beginning, collapses most completely in the end. They are both aware of the unnatural quality of their act—indeed, contrasts between the "natural" and the "unnatural" are as frequent in the poetic imagery of *Macbeth* as they are in *Lear,* though somewhat differently used, and when the deed is done they know that they are committed to a way of life that is at war with nature. No sooner is the murder committed than Macbeth feels that he has lost forever the great natural means of refreshment and renewal:

> Methought, I heard a voice cry, "Sleep no more!
> Macbeth does murder Sleep,"—the innocent Sleep;
> Sleep, that knits up the ravell'd sleave of care,
> The death of each day's life, sore labour's bath,
> Balm of hurt minds, great Nature's second course,
> Chief nourisher in life's feast.

And Lady Macbeth professes to believe that the difference between the temporary death of sleep and true death is illusory:

> The sleeping and the dead
> Are but as pictures; 'tis the eye of childhood
> That fears a painted devil.

But appearance and reality are willfully confused at one's peril, as Macbeth's hallucinations and his wife's sleepwalking are later to show.

Macbeth's disillusion begins almost immediately after the commission of the crime. Hallucination begins at once:

> What hands are here? Ha! They pluck out mine eyes,

and hands and eyes—doing, seeing, contradicting and confusing and terrifying each other—persist throughout the imagery of the play. His question that follows at once—

> Will all great Neptune's ocean wash this blood
> Clean from my hand?—

is echoed later by Lady Macbeth's

> What, will these hands ne'er be clean?

in the sleepwalking scene. She faces it out bravely enough at first: "A little water clears us of this deed," but the note is already one of desperate encouragement to her husband rather than of real confidence. And when the knock at the gate comes immediately afterward, Macbeth wishes the deed undone:

> Wake Duncan with thy knocking: I would thou couldst!

It all turns to dust and ashes, with no interval for enjoyment of the crown so dearly won. Lady Macbeth plays the perfect wife, encouraging and cheering her husband, for as long as she can (except for Brutus and Portia, the Macbeths are the most happily married couple in Shakespeare), but as he is driven by the logic of his position to ever more crimes, to become at last the obsessed nihilist, she cannot keep up in body or spirit and takes her own life at last. By this time Shakespeare has modulated Macbeth from haunted villain to a man rendered heroic by sheer lack of hope, a man who faces the total lack of meaning in his life with fatalistic determination. There is a sort of dignity in this, witnessed by the moving expression of the nothingness he finds in life that is provoked by the news of his wife's death. This is a very different kind of tragedy from *Julius Caesar* or *Othello,* where innocence can help to produce evil; the Macbeths are never innocent, but they are ignorant, deluded, self-deceived about what they really want in life and about the meaning of it all. In the end Macbeth is not so much damned as reduced to moral nothingness, in the midst of which he can keep on acting only by an almost superhuman exertion of will power. Thus the villain is a hero in a sense, and though Macbeth is destroyed by the evil he does, he does not let down the human species in his manner of facing that destruction.

Macbeth is no moral monster; he is a sensitive and able man driven by an obsession with an unexamined ambition to do what he knows to be evil and what at first his whole nature shrinks from. Of course he becomes bloodier as he proceeds, for that is the nature of crime, but the real tragedy lies in his discovery of the meaninglessness of his ambition almost as soon as it is achieved and his condemnation to carry on and pay over and over again the price for what he knows is worthless. He is left with nothing at all but physical courage. But this is a drastic oversimplification of the tragic theme. As in *King Lear,* Shakespeare in *Macbeth* creates a whole symphony of meaning by the patterns of recurring images in the play and overtones of suggestion of the nature of good and evil, of problems of choice and responsibility, of the relation of human behavior to the natural order, of appearance and reality, and many other things besides.

Antony and Cleopatra (1607) is the most spacious of Shakespeare's tragedies, and in a sense the most relaxed. In *Hamlet* and *Othello* and *Lear* the tone and the imagery often suggest that the dramatist is putting into dramatic terms some personal obsession or emotional disturbance of his own; in *Macbeth* we are more at a distance and the tragedy does not appear to be one in which the author's personal emotional history is involved. In *Antony and Cleopatra* we feel this to an even greater degree. Shakespeare is clearly at the height of his powers; his confident mastery of dramatic structure is as obvious as his positively negligent control of language. The poetry of the play is abundant and magnificently handled, serving always to increase the area of relevant dramatic meaning. The movement to and fro between Rome and Egypt (with Athens in between), the simple yet cunning way in which the Elizabethan platform stage is exploited to enable the action to flow with uninterrupted movement (an effect spoiled by the modern division of the play into scenes separated by a dropped curtain), the devices Shakespeare uses to suggest that the whole Roman world is involved in Antony's struggle between Roman loyalty and Egyptian magic, the evocative suggestions of the old Antony (whom we saw in *Julius Caesar*) contrasting with the Antony we now see, "the nemesis of the sensual man," as Granville-Barker has put it—these among other features of the play sufficiently demonstrate the author's superb craftsmanship. From the very beginning the contrast between the Roman and the Egyptian view is emphasized: the Roman soldier watched the Egyptian pageantry in Cleopatra's palace:

> Nay, but this dotage of our general's
> O'erflows the measure. . . .

The lovers' passion is dotage to Roman eyes, but Antony is still "*our* general." And a moment later we see the other side. "The triple pillar of the world transformed /Into a strumpet's fool," in the Roman view, is then shown as he appears in his own and the strumpet's eyes.

> *Cleopatra.* If it be love indeed, tell me how much.
> *Antony.* There's beggary in the love that can be reckoned.

But then the summons from Rome comes: Antony learns that his wife Fulvia is dead and war threatens, and he who has said

> Let Rome in Tiber melt and the wide arch
> Of the rang'd empire fall! Here is my space.
> Kingdoms are clay; . . .

is struck by "a Roman thought" and mutters to himself:

> These strong Egyptian fetters I must break
> Or lose myself in dotage.—

echoing Philo's word "dotage" that we heard in the first line of the play. Cleopatra tries all her tricks to keep him in Egypt, but, when she sees he is determined to go, puts on her noblest bearing to become, no longer the shrew or the temperamental lover, his protecting goddess of Victory:

> Upon your sword
> Sit laurel victory, and smooth success
> Be strew'd before your feet!

We hear the lewd chatter of the Egyptian court, with Cleopatra trying to while away the time in her lover's absence, in scenes adroitly interspersed with those which show the wary reconciliation of Octavius Caesar and Antony, sealed by Antony's marriage to Octavia, Caesar's sister. The Roman empire (not yet formally an empire) holds; its enemies are cowed by the reunion of Antony and Octavius, and a cynical truce with the rebels is celebrated by the drunken scene in Pompey's galley, where the three rulers of the Roman world get drunk and the well-meaning Lepidus, the ineffectual third in the triumvirate, has to be carried out. Enobarbus, Antony's hard-boiled follower, suggests a song and dance, and joins the hands of Antony, Octavius, and the ill-fated Sextus Pompeius as, tired and surfeited, they sing "Come, thou monarch of the vine"—a scene which can be compared with that in *Othello* when Iago "fastens a cup of wine" on Cassio and strikes up a forced merriment with the song, "And let me the canakin clink."

But, in spite of Octavia, we know that Antony will go back to Egypt, and Enobarbus knows it too. "You shall find the band that seems to tie their friendship together will be the very strangler of their amity. Octavia is of a holy, cold, and still conversation," he tells Menas as they are chatting after the great reconciliation. And we have already heard Antony, seizing the lame excuse of a soothsayer's prophecy, saying:

> I will to Egypt;
> And though I make this marriage for my peace,
> I' th' East my pleasure lies.

The struggle is not a tragic one. Octavius Caesar is a cold fish and his sister a conscientious Puritan: the sensual man belongs in Alexandria.

Up to this point the interest of the play lies in the rapid alternation of different points of view and different kinds of character, until a full picture of the whole Roman position is built up. Shakespeare was never more brilliantly at ease in the creation of character. The slightest minor figure has his own accent. Lepidus, the poor third member of the triumvirate, hero-worshiping Antony and awed by Caesar; Sextus Pompeius, the would-be rebel who has not the courage of his own ambitions; Enobarbus telling the wide-eyed Agrippa and Maecenas all about the wonders of Egypt, like a modern businessman returned from a trip to France telling the boys back home what Paris night life is really like (and including in his account the great description of Cleopatra when she first met Antony—most appropriately introduced here)—in these and other scenes and characters a shrewd and humorous knowledge of human nature manifests itself in language continually shifting in tone and scope in accordance with the dramatic and poetic needs of the moment.

So Antony returns to Cleopatra and the breach between him and Octavius Caesar is made final. The second movement of the play shows the aging roué and the temperamental sensualist facing the vengeance of the cold and confident Octavius. There is never any doubt as to who will win; the interest here lies in the changes and passions that the varying fortunes of war produce in Cleopatra and in less degree in Antony. Antony, influenced by Cleopatra's foolish exhibitionism, weakly decides to fight by sea instead of on land, and when Cleopatra (against Enobarbus' advice) joins the fleet with her flagship, only to flee when the battle begins and draw Antony after, the stage is set for an explosion of passionate self-contempt on Antony's part which shows at last that he has lost his grip. He gives way to self-pity and sentimental speeches to his servants, and for once Cleopatra has nothing to say. A temporary improvement of his fortunes brings back the old Antony again, but it is a brief Indian summer. In the sea fight that follows, the Egyptian fleet surrenders and Antony believes that Cleopatra has deliberately betrayed him. His impotent rage frightens her into sending him a false message of her suicide, and then at last Antony—his accent moving ever into richer poetry—knows that the end has come; in following Cleopatra to the grave he is reconciling Rome and Egypt, for suicide is the Roman way out. When he dies at last in Cleopatra's arms he boasts that he does

> not basely die,
> Not cowardly put off my helmet to
> My countryman—a Roman by a Roman
> Valiantly vanquish'd.

Cleopatra's lament over him first begins to raise this passion between a middle-aged sensualist and a royal prostitute to a higher level. She realizes that the world for her is destroyed—

> O, wither'd is the garland of the war,
> The soldier's pole is fall'n. Young boys and girls
> Are level now with men. The odds is gone,
> And there is nothing left remarkable
> Beneath the visiting moon—

and at the same time that she is, after all, but a mortal woman with ordinary human passions:

> No more but e'en a woman, and commanded
> By such poor passion as the maid that milks
> And does the meanest chares.

Her problem now is how to come to terms with what remains of life.

Shakespeare does not hurry, however, to elevate Cleopatra to tragic stature. The final movement of the play is Cleopatra against Octavius Caesar: she tries every way of finding out what Caesar (in spite of his polite protestations) means to do with her, and humiliates herself in the process. But at last she learns from Dolabella (whom she has twisted round her finger with a word) that Caesar's intention is to take her to Rome and exhibit her there; then and only then does she find the courage to follow Antony in the Roman way. And this is the measure of Shakespeare's genius, that he spares neither Antony nor Cleopatra anything; he bungles his own death; she, after his death and her great lament, becomes for a while a low trickster apparently only interested in saving what she has left. Only when the game is finally up does she admit that without Antony life is impossible; but in that admission and in the splendid poetic gesture of her final suicide, she is redeemed at last into tragedy. She finds true pride, and dignity, and the quiet humor that sees over the other side of death without panic or self-pity. Yet she does not lose her original character. Her dying speech is as sensual as all her other speeches, and almost her final thought is that she must die before Charmian in case Charmian gets to the next world before she does and kisses Antony first. As everything is hushed into the final pageantry, with the crowned and royally robed queen awaiting death from the asp at her breast, the language becomes ritualistic while losing nothing of its sensuality:

> *Charmian.* O Eastern star!
> *Cleopatra.* Peace, peace!
> Dost thou not see my baby at my breast,
> That sucks the nurse asleep?
> *Charmian.* O, break! O, break!
> *Cleopatra.* As sweet as balm, as soft as air, as
> gentle—O Antony! . . .

The final pageant, the dead queen flanked by her two dead handmaidens, meets Caesar's gaze as he enters, and the play ends with the Romans held by the strange and moving spectacle.

Clearly, this is tragedy of a very special kind, tragedy in a very different sense from that of *Hamlet* or *King Lear*. The theme is not the conflict between love and duty that Dryden made of it in his *All for Love*. True, Shakespeare makes clear that the fate of the civilized world is involved in Antony's decisions, but the conflict between public duty and private passion is not his major interest, nor is he chiefly concerned with the conflict between the Roman and Egyptian ways of life, though this, too, is an element in the play and one of the themes suggested by the pattern of its imagery. Cleopatra is shown as shrewish, hysterical, sadistic, dishonest, and cowardly, as well as beautiful, queenly, and heroic. Antony is selfish and fatuous as well as generous and noble. Are they great lovers or merely great sensualists? They are both experienced in the ways of sexual pleasure and often talk as though that is all that love involves. Yet this is far from being a disillusioned or a cynical play. We are continually fascinated by the richness and variety of character and the way in which history is bound up with psychology. There is little pity or fear in the play, but rather a lively human curiosity throughout. And the poetry keeps enlarging the moment, showing experience as ever livelier and richer. We watch fascinated as Antony, most Roman when most enslaved by Egypt, goes to his self-inflicted death, and then follow Cleopatra's twistings and turnings with ever increasing interest and wonder. We make no new moral judgment on either, because that is decided at the beginning and is never in question: they are both behaving badly, and their sophisticated passion does not excuse them. But there is a wonder in it all, and Cleopatra in her death finds, as it were, the objective correlative of that wonder. The sensual life ends in a blaze of ritual pageantry: it has its own amoral nobility.

Hamlet, Othello, Lear, and *Macbeth* were apparently written between 1600 and 1606, the phase of Shakespeare's career generally known as his great "tragic period." It has been held that the note of personal disillusion, sex nausea, and bitterness which some have seen in these plays, and which came to a climax in the savage misanthropy of *Timon of Athens* (written sometime between 1605 and 1608), not really a tragedy at all but a picture of human ingratitude and hypocrisy turning the world of men into a world of beasts, lacking all order and health, indicates that Shakespeare was going through a desperately disillusioned period in his own life at this time, of which *Timon* marks the climax and which later (after, it has even been suggested, a nervous breakdown) gave way to a new serenity, reflected in the last plays. This is possible, though it is dangerous to correlate too closely literal biography and the life of the imagination. Whatever biographical inferences we may draw, the fact remains that Shakespeare looked on the dark side of life during these years, and the comedies which he wrote during this period (except for *The Merry Wives of Windsor,* an uninspired professional farce written to order, which in any case may be as early as 1597) have a very different atmosphere from those written immediately earlier. *Troilus and Cressida* (ca. 1602), *All's Well that Ends Well* (1602–04), and *Measure for Measure* (1604) have been called "problem plays" or "bitter comedies," because, though not technically tragedies and, in the case of the last two, having a "happy" ending, they have nothing of the golden cheerfulness of the "middle comedies" and show human behavior as (to put it mildly) gross and unedifying. That Shakespeare's state of mind during these years was such that, when asked by his company for a comedy, he could produce only this kind of "bitter comedy," is a view which was once popular, but more recent critics have refused to see these plays as hybrids produced by the working of a tragic imagination on comic material and have adduced many arguments to show that each has its own unity and its own impressive pattern of meaning and that the concept of "problem play" is irrelevant and misleading. It is true that careful and continued reading of each of these plays produces an increasing impression of their literary value, and *Troilus and Cressida* and *Measure for Measure* have both been hailed as masterpieces of the very highest order by modern scholar-critics, instead of as the interesting failures which their predecessors had judged them to be. Nevertheless, the reader (or spectator) who takes these plays together will certainly find something different and puzzling about their tone, and the academic snobbery which denies the validity of this impression to explain away all difficulties in terms of Elizabethan sensibility or Shakespeare's sources runs counter to the critical judgment of three hundred and fifty years. (The preface to the second of the two 1609 quartos of *Troilus and Cressida* suggests that the first audiences found the play puzzling.)

Troilus and Cressida takes two themes—the story of Troilus and Cressida as developed in medieval and subsequent literature and the background theme of the siege of Troy, also familiar in medieval and later writing—and treats them in a spirit of restless disillusion. Much in the background is taken for granted: Troilus is already in love with Cressida when the play opens, and Cressida's coyness is brief and superficial; the whole Troy story and the place in it of the various Greek and Trojan characters is assumed, so that to those who do not know the Troy story as it appeared in medieval and early Renaissance literature the play appears extremely allusive and sometimes even sketchy. The title theme does not dominate the play. At least as much interest is centered on the difference between the Greek and the Trojan attitude (the Greek, represented by Ulysses, being realistic and "modern," the Trojan, represented by Hector and by Troilus himself, being old-fashioned and "romantic"), and on character conflicts such as those between Ajax, Achilles, and Ulysses on the Greek side and Hector, Troilus, and Pandarus on the Trojan. On the Trojan side, Hector admits that it is unjust and unnatural to hold Helen, yet he refuses to surrender her to the Greeks and so end the war because his muddled notions of honor demand that the struggle be carried on. On the Greek side, Ulysses gives his famous speech on order and demonstrates how the Greeks' failure to take Troy up till now results from a lack of proper order and subordination in their behavior. The romantic rhetoric of the Trojan council of war contrasts with the opportunist rhetoric (reminiscent sometimes of *Henry V*) of the Greek. And Thersites, the licensed fool, covers everything with his scabrous comment, reducing all human actions to their lowest animal level. Pride is exposed, chivalry degraded, prudence mocked, and ideal passion rewarded with casual faithlessness. The boorish Ajax scores over Achilles; the wise Ulysses constructs a brilliant plan for bringing the sulky Achilles back into the fight, only to have it proved wholly unnecessary when the death of Patroclus achieves the same end in a moment; Achilles treacherously slays Hector when he finds him resting with his armor doffed; and Troilus, the prudent Ulysses by his side, watches with tortured incredulity while his beloved Cressida, the very night after she has left him, gives herself to Diomede. Shakespeare uses chivalric devices (the personal challenge, and its consequences) to bring the two camps together, so that passionate Trojan and worldly-wise Greek can watch the betrayal side by side—while, from the other side of the stage, the foul-mouthed Thersites observes and comments on both watchers and watched, both Cressida and Diomede on the one hand and Ulysses and Troilus on the other. The play ends with Hector slain and his corpse ignominiously treated, Troilus in a frenzy of revenge against all Greeks, Cressida Diomede's mistress, and the repudiated Pandarus (who has the last word) reduced to a bawdy "trader in the flesh."

Troilus and Cressida may well have been written in the first instance for performance at one of the Inns of Court, which may account for the peculiar kind of sophistication found so often in the play. It may also have been influenced by a new fashion of dramatic satire introduced by Ben Jonson and John Marston. And in the treatment of Cressida, Shakespeare was following the tradition as it had developed after Chaucer, just as his presentation of the Trojan war derives in large part from Lydgate's *Troy Book* and Caxton's *Recuyell of the Histories of Troy.* But the flavor of the play as a whole remains strange. Shakespeare presents an unfinished story—a story much more familiar to his contemporaries than that of Hamlet or Lear—whose end was already known to the Elizabethan audience. They knew what the fate of Troy finally was, and what happened at last to Achilles, Troilus, and Cressida. It is as though Shakespeare has deliberately arrested time, to show the plans and expectations of men in a double perspective, first in the context of the moment and then in the larger context of past, present, and future. And indeed time is much referred to in the play. When Trojans and Greeks meet in chivalric courtesy, Ulysses prophesies the fall of Troy and Hector replies:

> I must not believe you.
> There they stand yet, and modestly I think
> The fall of every Phrygian stone will cost
> A drop of Grecian blood. The end crowns all,
> And that old common arbitrator, Time,
> Will one day end it.

Ulysses replies to this: "So to him we leave it." The disposition of human affairs is left to Time. Meanwhile, men behave as their beliefs or their passions or their apparent self-interest demand. Ulysses' speech to Achilles—

> Time hath, my Lord, a wallet at his back,
> Wherein he puts alms for Oblivion,
> A great-siz'd monster of ingratitudes—

makes the point that a man is judged by his present behavior, not his past reputation:

> O, let not virtue seek
> Remuneration for the thing it was;
> For beauty, wit,
> High birth, vigour of bone, desert in service,
> Love, friendship, charity, are subjects all
> To envious and calumniating Time.

But Ulysses' shrewd opportunism is no safeguard. The future reveals the true meaning of the present in its own fashion; Cressida in Calchas' tent with Diomede is the final gloss on Cressida protesting eternal love to Troilus, and Troilus' speech at the spectacle expresses his anguished recognition of the fact that both present and past are equally true. Time tests all ideals and finds us all out in the end. *Troilus and Cressida* ends without a climax or a resolution: the true end, as Shakespeare's audience well knew, lay in the death of Troilus, the degeneration of Cressida, and the sack of Troy.

All's Well that Ends Well (which may be a reworking of an earlier play) is a "problem play" in a very different sense. In spite of its element of formlessness (which seems deliberate), *Troilus and Cressida* is a mature and interesting play, the product of a powerful imagination and an astringent wit. But *All's Well* is a somewhat mechanical handling of a folk theme which Shakespeare found in the story of Giletta of Narbon as translated in William Painter's *Palace of Pleasure* from Boccaccio's *Decameron.* There are indeed two folk themes: the story of Helena's curing the King and her reward in obtaining a husband of her choice, and the story of the deserted wife winning back her husband by substituting herself, unknown to him, in the bed of his mistress and so fulfilling seemingly impossible conditions. Neither theme is interesting or credible to the modern mind, and our difficulty with the play lies, not, as perhaps in *Troilus* and certainly in *Timon,* in the bitterness of spirit with which Shakespeare handles his material, but in his inability to present it dramatically with sufficient poetic and imaginative force to create a level of probability that can convince us. There are interesting poetic moments and some fine touches in the play, and the character of Parolles (an inglorious Falstaff, with only the shabbiness and the nastiness apparent) has its possibilities, though only superficially exploited; but the main action moves stiffly, and the atmosphere remains that of an early comedy such as *The Two Gentlemen of Verona.* Bertram, the physically courageous but morally weak hero who repudiates the gifted wife who has chosen him, remains a cad until the end, in spite of the machinery of redemption which Shakespeare appears to have prepared for him, while Diana (the lady whom Bertram thinks he is with the night he sleeps with his own wife) and her mother exist simply to speak the words that carry forward the story to its required end. We tend to think that it is the morality of the play that is offensive and "bitter"; but the morality is the folk morality which Shakespeare had successfully embodied in earlier comedies: the failure here is a failure of the imagination. Whatever the reason, the story did not light up for Shakespeare in terms of his art, and it remains a cold and baffling play.

Measure for Measure, the final comedy in this group, is at once the most interesting and the most challenging. The plot, found both as a tragedy and as a prose tale in the work of the Italian writer Cinthio, and thence used by the English George Whetstone, also in both a play and a prose tale, in a version somewhat nearer to Shakespeare's, contains in itself a multiplicity of overtones which in part account for the disturbing nature of the play as Shakespeare wrote it. The basic theme is indeed older than either Whetstone or Cinthio: the story of the judge or ruler who offers to save the girl's lover or husband or brother if she will yield herself to him and who, after the girl has yielded, deliberately breaks his promise, goes back into the mists of folklore. In pre-Shakespearean versions the girl does yield to the ruler, but Shakespeare, by means of a device he had already used in *All's Well*—the secret substitution of one girl for another in the bed of the seducer—keeps his heroine chaste throughout; further, he follows Whetstone (and not Cinthio) in saving the girl's brother and having the ruler only imagine that he has been put to death. There are many themes involved in this apparently simple story. In the first place there is the ironical theme of the judge himself guilty of what he has others punished for. (Claudio, the brother in *Measure for Measure,* is sentenced to death for premarital intercourse with his fiancée.) *Quis custodiet ipsos custodes?* Who shall guard the state's guardians, and what happens when the judge is more guilty than the man he condemns? This is bound up with a theme not unrelated to the deep-seated Oedipus motif—the ruler, in an honest attempt to uncover guilt, reveals that he is himself the guilty one. This is the detective story where the detective, conscientiously following the clues, proves himself to be the criminal. Such a notion has both its comic and its tragic side. The uncovering of the hypocritical judge as the true villain can easily be made the subject of pure comedy, and this, as Dr. Hanns Sachs pointed out, was done in Heinrich von Kleist's comedy *Der zerbrochene Krug* (The Broken Jug), in which a judge is forced by circumstances to conduct a careful cross-examination which proves himself to have been the criminal in the case under investigation. Finally, there is the Christian element in the story, which Shakespeare emphasizes in his title. (Cf. Luke, Chapter vi: "Judge not, and ye shall not be judged; condemn not, and ye shall not be condemned: forgive, and ye shall be forgiven. . . . For with the same measure that ye mete withal it shall be measured to you again.") In *Measure for Measure* everybody is in some degree guilty, and it is only after the much injured heroine has pleaded for mercy for the man who has injured her that it is revealed that the injury was in intention only. All are guilty, and mercy rather than justice saves the day.

Shakespeare further complicated the story by having a disguised duke, the real ruler, watch over all the proceedings unknown to the actors. The Duke, before leaving the country on a temporary absence, gives over his rule to Angelo, hoping that Angelo, a sternly puritanical character, will have the firmness to revive laws which the Duke himself has been too kindhearted to enforce, with resulting increase of sexual immorality among all classes. Angelo begins by sentencing to death young Claudio for intercourse with his fiancée and refusing to listen to any pleas for mercy. Claudio's sister Isabella, passionately chaste and about to enter a nunnery, pleads with Angelo for her brother's life, and Angelo, suddenly smitten with lust for Isabella, agrees to save him if she yield herself to him for one night. She of course refuses, but the Duke disguised as a friar persuades her to agree to a plot whereby Mariana, formerly betrothed to Angelo but later deserted by him when her dowry was not forthcoming, is substituted for Isabella without Angelo's being aware of the substitution. After spending some hours secretly at night with the supposed Isabella, Angelo goes back on his word and orders Claudio to be immediately executed, but the disguised Duke arranges for the head of a man who has died in prison to be brought to Angelo as Claudio's, and Claudio is spared. Finally, in a carefully contrived denouement, Angelo is exposed and, after a plea for his forgiveness made by Isabella while she still thinks Claudio has been executed, forgiven. Behind this main action runs a stream of sordid low life, with bawds, brothels, and much talk of venereal disease.

The play puzzles largely because of the different and sometimes mutually conflicting themes bound up in the story as Shakespeare develops it. The "gulling" of the hypocrite (in the manner of Ben Jonson's comedies) is one way of treating Angelo, but he is at the same time presented as a genuinely puritanical character who suddenly discovers, to his dismay and even horror, that he is as much subject to sensual temptation as ordinary men—he might even be said to be a man who has sublimated his tendencies toward sadistic sensuality in the practice of stern justice, but who, on being faced with a beautiful woman pleading for mercy for a brother condemned to death, regresses into the sensualist and sadist. Similarly, Isabella is both a stern, otherworldly character who fiercely abuses her brother for a momentary lapse in his desire to have death rather than have his sister lose her chastity and who at the same time cheerfully plays the procuress with Mariana, and a symbol of radiant purity who, at the end of the play, embodies its Christian moral of mercy before strict justice. The gulling of the hypocrite, the testing of the puritan, the judge discovered to be the criminal, the discovery that all are guilty and none has the right to judge, and that mercy rather than justice is the proper "measure for measure"—here is, indeed, an intermingling of tragic and comic themes. No wonder that *Measure for Measure* has elements of Jonsonian comedy, Sophoclean irony, and Christian morality. That Shakespeare should have chosen such a theme is doubtless some evidence of his state of mind at the time he wrote it; but it is worth noting that *Measure for Measure* is not a "bitter comedy" simply because he was asked to write a comedy when he was in the middle of a "tragic period," but a serious play between tragedy and comedy whose complications and difficulties arise from the implications of its plot. And there is no point in complaining that no character seems wholly sympathetic, that even virtue is made to appear uncongenial, if one realizes that a basic theme in the play is precisely that none are guiltless and that in judging one another we have no right to condemn but only to forgive. This is in a sense a deeply pessimistic position, but the notion that man's duty is to be merciful to his neighbor because all men are in some degree evil was not original with Shakespeare. *Measure for Measure* is Shakespeare's most comprehensive treatment of the notion of original sin, with which he was much concerned at this stage of his career.

Coriolanus, probably written between *Antony and Cleopatra* and *Cymbeline,* the latter being the first of Shakespeare's final group of plays, stands somewhat alone. It is in a sense a political play, dealing with the fortunes of a hero whose aristocratic pride provoked popular ill-will, but it is not political in the way that *Julius Caesar* is political: in *Julius Caesar* Shakespeare explores the tragic implications of private virtue operating without the requisite political shrewdness in a public context. The tragedy of Coriolanus is not that of Brutus, and the play in which he is the hero has none of the wider implications and overtones of *Julius Caesar*. Coriolanus, egotistical, aristocratic, contemptuous of the people, is opposed by the tribunes for his antipopular attitude and, in spite of his great military services to Rome, is exiled after the tribunes have maneuvered to make him lose his temper and display his "treasonable" attitude to the people. His virtues are immense personal courage and a certain boyish arrogance which is not without charm; his defects of character lie in complete lack of self-knowledge, his total inability to handle people (even soldiers, for though he is a magnificent fighter he has not the qualities of a great military leader), and lack of any kind of imaginative understanding of other people. It is partly this lack of understanding which leads him to treat the people with such contempt, for to him they are not human beings but an aggregate of foul-smelling changeableness.

There is immense irony in Coriolanus' objection to the variability of the people—

> Hang ye! Trust ye?
> With every minute you do change a mind,
> And call him noble that was now your hate—

in the light of his own subsequent behavior. Enraged at his banishment, he joins his country's enemies and leads a Volscian army against Rome. His action here is that of a man with no awareness of his own nature or the basis of his own principles, and when he is finally prevailed upon by his mother to spare Rome (which means ultimately his own death at the hands of the Volscians) it is because he is overcome by an unfamiliar emotion which is all the more powerful because of its unfamiliarity. His revenge on Rome is instinctive and irrational, and it destroys the basis of his own personality, which has hitherto been a fierce pride in his own aristocratic patriotism and an almost religious feeling for his own class. Though his mother, who had brought him up in the military virtues and in disdain of the common people, learns through hard experience another point of view (in her final speech to her son she pleads that he should act not as the warrior but in the more blessed role of peacemaker), Coriolanus does not develop at all. His enraged reversal of his natural role involves him in a much more profound instability of purpose than anything he had charged the common people with, and with the resulting emptying of his personality he can respond to his mother's plea, which temporarily fills the vacuum, as it were, but he cannot advance to any understanding of the superiority of the peacemaker to the warrior or to any redemption through suffering. He meets his death the same boyish, bewildered, instinctive character he is at the beginning, and it is through this immaturity, almost, in a sense, this innocence, that Shakespeare preserves throughout the play sufficient sympathy for him to enable his fall to be seen as tragic at all.

Coriolanus is thus one of the most limited in scope of Shakespeare's mature plays. The design is more rigid, the verse is more compact and workmanlike, the implications are more strictly controlled, than in any of the great tragedies. The design has not the flexibility which allows him in *Hamlet* or *King Lear* to ring in through overtone and suggestion the most far-reaching comments on the human situation, and even in *Macbeth,* the most compact of the great tragedies, the human context is richer. It is not surprising that after this Shakespeare moves on to a different kind of play altogether: *Coriolanus* suggests that he had done what he could with tragedy and was now looking at the dramatic possibilities of the tragic situation with less excitement. From now on he moves not only toward new themes but toward new dramatic conventions.

Shakespeare's final group of plays, the so-called "romances," have certain characteristics in common and seem to reflect a new attitude both to life and to his art. *Pericles, Cymbeline, The Winter's Tale,* and *The Tempest* all deal in one way or another with evil and innocence, guilt and atonement, uncorrupted youth undoing original sin and starting life afresh. Mythology, folklore, and magic find their way into these plays to a greater degree than in any other of Shakespeare's mature work, so that it can hardly be claimed (as some critics have asserted) that they represent a new faith in the essential goodness of man: the remoteness of the setting and the introduction of the magical element indicate a different level of probability from that found in *Hamlet* or *Othello,* a symbolic world where (unlike the real world) innocence can triumph and the gods enable the evil past to be undone. In *Pericles,* Marina and her mother, both assumed to be dead, are found in the end alive and innocent; in *Cymbeline,* Imogen similarly comes alive again; in *The Winter's Tale* the statue of Hermione proves in the end to be the living Hermione, long thought dead; and in *The Tempest,* Alonso and his company are miraculously redeemed from drowning to find repentance and new virtue. The dramaturgy in these plays is relaxed, almost casual, with masque elements and other spectacular devices introduced to emphasize the note of symbol and ritual. Shakespeare has done with probing directly the tragic paradoxes of human nature, and he now reaches out to a larger poetic symbolism through which the moral patterns and possibilities of human life can be presented with the calm beauty of one who is no longer tortured by his own involvement.

Pericles, of uncertain date and probably of composite authorship, is the least satisfactory of these plays. The text we have (a corrupt Quarto: *Pericles* does not appear in the First Folio) seems to consist of several layers, indicating revision, and some parts are very crude. The story, too, deriving from a widely dispersed tale of Greek origin, told by John Gower in his *Confessio Amantis* (and the use of Gower, rather crudely, as chorus, indicates plainly enough that he was the source), is too crowded with incident to be easily rendered dramatically. Antiochus, king of Antioch, has incestuous relations with his own daughter; Pericles, prince of Tyre, discovers this, thereby arousing Antiochus' anger. To avoid the effects of Antiochus' wrath, Pericles flees from his own kingdom of Tyre and after succoring starving Tarsus sets sail again, is shipwrecked, lands at Pentapolis, where he marries Thaisa, the King's daughter, then sets off by sea again for Tyre. But he is again shipwrecked; during the storm Thaisa gives birth to a daughter, Marina, before apparently dying, and her body is committed to the sea in a chest. The chest is washed up at Ephesus, where Cerimon restores the apparently dead Thaisa to life and she becomes a priestess of Diana. Meanwhile Pericles and Marina arrive at Tarsus, where Pericles stays a year before returning to Tyre, leaving Marina in the care of Cleon, governor of Tarsus and his wife Dionyza. But Dionyza grows jealous of Marina, who outshines her own daughter, and plans her murder; before she can be murdered, however, she is carried off by pirates to Mytilene, where she is sold to a brothel, but her angelic innocence converts the customers to virtue and she retains her chastity. Pericles is told by Cleon and Dionyza that his daughter is dead, and he devotes himself to grief. But fate brings his ship to Mytilene where he finds Marina in a moving scene of mutual discovery. Finally, under Diana's guidance, he proceeds to Ephesus, where he finds his wife, long supposed dead.

To get all of this complicated story across requires the use of choruses and dumb shows, employed clumsily enough. But the main theme centers on Marina, lost and found again, subjected to the corrupting influence of the brothel yet preserving always her shining innocence. And the sea, on which Marina was born and into which Thaisa disappears to be cast up later alive, dominates the play, a symbol of purification, of "death by water" which precedes resurrection. T. S. Eliot's poem "Marina" distils the essential meaning:

> What seas what shores what grey rocks and what islands
> What water lapping the bow
> And scent of pine and the woodthrush singing through the fog
> What images return
> O my daughter.

Pericles is a symbolic play, a religious play, dealing with death and resurrection, with ritual purification and the redemptive power of innocence. Uneven and botched up in places as it is, it has its Shakespearean moments of grave beauty; and though by itself—so uncertain is the text and the authorship—it could tell us little about the direction in which the later Shakespeare's imagination was moving, taken with the following three plays it helps to build up a picture of a Shakespeare who has turned away from what (with all the necessary qualifications) might be called the psychological realism of the great tragedies to a new, more symbolic, kind of play in which he could come to terms with the problem of evil in a different manner.

Cymbeline, The Winter's Tale, and *The Tempest* all appear to have been written (in this order) between 1609 and 1612. In *Cymbeline* Shakespeare took a story from the *Decameron* (of a husband, making a wager on his wife's virtue, tricked by his friend into believing that the friend has succeeded in seducing her) and the setting from that part of Holinshed which deals with the ancient British kingdom. He got some details from various parts of Holinshed and other elements in the plot from other sources, including folklore, and wove them all together into a story almost as complicated as *Pericles.* An element of fairy tale runs right through the play. Imogen, the princess who marries against her parents' wishes; Cymbeline's Queen, the wicked stepmother; the potion which brings apparent death but really only sends the drinker into a prolonged swoon; the "Snow White" theme of the apparently dead girl being covered with flowers by her simple companions—these are familiar enough elements in any folk literature. The evil Cloten, son of the wicked stepmother by an earlier husband, is also a folk character, though Shakespeare gives him a fully individualized personality. Imogen herself is pure Shakespeare, idealized yet real, one of those spirited heroines whom he created so happily in his "middle comedies" and who here is subjected to much more grievous trials than anything which befell Rosalind or Viola. For the theme of this play, as of *Pericles,* is innocence triumphant, emerging victorious from the darkest possible circumstances. Her own banished husband turned against her by the vile trick of Iachimo; the wicked Cloten pursuing her; misfortune and evil dogging her footsteps wherever she goes; she yet takes her destiny into her own hands and, having survived the shock of hearing that her husband has ordered her to be murdered and the counter shock of seeing what she thinks is the dead body of her husband, survives to win her husband back in the final scene of explanation and reconciliation.

Evil mounts to an ugly climax in the play before the countermovement sets in, and Shakespeare leaves us in no doubt of its reality. Iachimo, the subtle Italian, is as nasty a case of small-minded pride and perverted ingenuity as one can find in literature, and Cloten is a sadistic boor. Only the Queen, the wicked stepmother, with her stagy asides and her poison potions, remains a purely fairy tale character, and her final suicide is as unreal as the rest of her actions. This is a tragicomedy, a play in which all the terror of tragedy is given full vent before the tide is allowed to turn. Those who maintain that Shakespeare now felt in a kindly mood toward life have surely paid too little attention to Cloten or to the tortured speech Posthumus makes when he thinks his wife has betrayed him, a speech full of the sex nausea we find in *Hamlet* and *Lear*. Tragicomedy was the fashion now, the Blackfriars audiences wanted all the thrills of tragedy with the happy ending of comedy, and they wanted, too, the masque-like devices, the music and pageantry, which Shakespeare, yielding to public taste, now freely gave them. It may be that this is the only explanation one needs for these final romances or tragicomedies: Shakespeare, the professional playwright, was changing his style in response to public demand. Yet one cannot be satisfied with this explanation. The themes of these final plays are too similar and the ritual of forgiveness runs too persistently through them all, for this not to be a reflection in some way of Shakespeare's mind at this time. The point is, however, that it was not an easy forgiveness resulting from a new optimistic belief that vice is always defeated by virtue. Evil in all its horror is imparted directly in these plays. Salvation comes by magic or coincidence, and the ritual of pardon is performed in the serenity of a brave new world in which we cannot literally believe. Even so, in *Cymbeline,* the grosser villains are disposed of first. Cloten has his head cut off by Guilderius with cheerful matter-of-factness and the Queen conveniently ends her own life. Those who are pardoned are those whose acts, in spite of themselves, turn out to have brought forth nothing but good. As in *Measure for Measure,* time has brought good results out of evil intentions, and no one standing on the stage in the remarkable last act of *Cymbeline* has managed to achieve any lasting evil. That is their good luck, or rather the playwright's magical manipulation of events. And so, as Cymbeline says, "Pardon's the word to all."

Cymbeline (like *Pericles,* though to a smaller extent) has its moments of dramatic awkwardness and crudity, which make one wonder whether the text as we have it is Shakespeare's throughout. But *The Winter's Tale* presents no such problem. The source of this play is Robert Greene's prose pastoral romance, *Pandosto, or The Tri-*

umph of Time, and in working the essential features of this story into a play Shakespeare produced the greatest of his tragi-comedies. *The Winter's Tale* is notorious for flouting the "unity of time" as well as of place with supreme confidence. The first three acts take place in Sicily, and form almost a complete play in themselves. Leontes grows causelessly jealous of his wife, Hermione, imagining that she is having an affair with his friend Polixenes, king of Bohemia; Polixenes, warned in time, flees for home, and Hermione is brought to trial and accused of adultery with him. The obsessed Leontes insists on believing her guilt, even when the Oracle of Apollo has declared her innocence, but news of the Queen's death in prison shocks him to his senses, and we leave him a sadder and wiser man. Meanwhile Hermione's infant daughter, born in prison and suspected by Leontes of being Polixenes' bastard, has been ordered by Leontes to be put to death, but Antigonus, on whom the charge is laid, carries the baby off to sea, to leave her on the seacoast of Bohemia before being himself pursued and eaten by a bear. This last piece of action is a simple device to provide a bridge to the next part of the play and at the same time get rid of the inconvenient Antigonus. Apart from this, the first three acts constitute a brilliant tragic play. The sudden growth of causeless jealousy in Leontes is presented with remarkable psychological insight and an assured poetic diction which combines colloquial overtones with an almost casual richness of poetic suggestion. Hermione faces her accuser with tragic dignity. Paulina, her faithful attendant and wife of Antigonus, stands up for her lady before the obsessed Leontes and is the only one who dares tell him home truths to his face. Mamillius, the young son of Hermione and Leontes, is introduced in the best child scene in Shakespeare, before his death is reported as a result of his mother's imprisonment. At the end, Mamillius dead, Hermione dead and her infant daughter on the way to destruction, the consequences of Leontes' wicked jealousy appear to have worked themselves out. He knows better now, but it is too late to do anything about it.

Part of the essential tragedy of *Hamlet* and *Othello* is that one can never undo the past; evil once done is done, and there is no way of restoring the lost world of innocence. But in these last plays Shakespeare finds a way of at least partially undoing evil. It is done by trickery, one might say—Hermione is not really dead, but hidden by Paulina; the infant daughter is saved and brought up as a shepherdess—but it is a symbolic trickery, whose function is to suggest, once again, a ritual of redemption. Act IV takes us to Bohemia sixteen years later, and it is a new world, where even roguery is innocent. The lost princess is now Perdita, a shepherd's supposed daughter, and—true to the logic of fairy tale—she bears in her face and manners the hereditary stamp of her royal birth, so that she attracts Prince Florizel, Polixenes' son, and the two fall in love. Autolycus, the rogue, is the most engaging of all Shakespeare's minor villains (if villain he can be called). Bohemia is fairyland, real enough in its pastoral atmosphere, its sheep-shearing feast and flowered countryside, but fairyland none the less, where time keeps innocence until the opportunity has come for sending it back to do its redeeming work in the real world. The freshness and beauty of the Florizel and Perdita scenes have been noted by everyone who has ever discussed the play: the idyllic pastoral note is sounded here more splendidly and movingly than anywhere else in English literature, yet the psychology—the psychology of young love—is real, and the countryside the real English countryside. When Polixenes breaks in on this idyll to discover Florizel's identity and abuse both Florizel and Perdita for daring to fall in love so out of their degree, his vile temper and cruel threats do not seriously disturb us: fathers are expected to be angry in such circumstances, and Polixenes' anger, though mean-spirited and selfish, has not the tragic overtones of Leontes' jealousy. Besides, Perdita knows that

> The self-same sun that shines upon his court
> Hides not his visage from our cottage, but
> Looks on all alike.

So the couple flee to Sicily, where Leontes receives them kindly until Polixenes arrives in pursuit and reveals his son's disobedience; but the final discovery of Perdita's identity turns all to happiness.

This, significantly, is not the end of the play, and the climax of reconciliation between the young lovers and their parents is not presented, only related in the conversation between several gentlemen. The climax is reserved for the discovery by Leontes that Hermione is still alive. Paulina introduces her as a newly finished statue of the dead queen, but the statue turns out to be the living queen, kept in seclusion all these sixteen years. But is the past really undone? For sixteen years Hermione has deliberately allowed her husband to think her dead, and she returns to life now to greet her daughter. The text gives her no greeting to her husband; her first words are to ask a blessing on her daughter. And there is no return to life for Mamillius. The curse is not fully lifted from the older generation: what Leontes has done he has done, and it cannot after all be undone. The younger generation can do better; they bring new innocence and new hope; and Hermione returns from the grave to give her blessing to them. She says to Perdita

> . . . thou shalt hear that I,
> Knowing by Paulina that the oracle
> Gave hope thou wast in being, have preserv'd
> Myself to see the issue.

She says nothing about being happy to live with Leontes again: all her thought is for her daughter. And the play ends with Leontes trying in his pattering speech to act the part of the leader of this group who have eyes for one another rather than for him.

The Tempest treats the theme of forgiveness and the younger generation most explicitly of all, and at the same time most symbolically. Prospero's island—Shakespeare's imagination had been turned in that direction by news of a shipwrecked crew surviving nine months in the Bermudas—is not subject to the normal laws of human destiny, for Prospero controls all with his magic and he can set the stage for the desired solution. In a sense this compact and familiar story is less Christian than any of Shakespeare's earlier treatments of guilt and justice. *Measure for Measure* leaves us with a final sense of identity with the guilty: all are guilty, and we forgive each other for that reason. But Prospero has no real kinship with the other characters; he stands outside the action and stage-manages it, with Ariel's help. The ritual of forgiveness is conducted by a priest who is not himself in need of pardon. That is perhaps why many readers and spectators of *The Tempest* have found Prospero a pompous bore, with his prosy expositions of earlier events to both Miranda and Ariel and his easy loss of temper with inattention or weakness. Though he may not be, as was once held, Shakespeare himself taking his farewell of the stage, he is certainly in a sense the creator of the other characters in the play, controlling them from above, a godlike figure who renounces his godhead only at the end of the play when, the action satisfactorily concluded, he breaks his magic staff to take his place among common humanity. He is in some respects like the Duke in *Measure for Measure,* for both manipulate the other characters in a godlike way; but the Duke is involved in his world more than Prospero is, and symbolizes that involvement by marrying Isabella at the end.

Miranda is youth and innocence, and her union with Ferdinand has the same symbolic meaning as that of Florizel and Perdita. Trinculo and Stephano represent gross animality, mankind at its lowest, and the spirits that serve them are not like Ariel, but alcoholic spirits which destroy the judgment—and it is the alcohol that attracts Caliban:

That's a brave god, and bears celestial liquor.
I will kneel to him.

Ariel is the wise man's spirit, representing the scientist's control over nature. The other characters represent different degrees of good and evil at the human level—except for Caliban, who remains a somewhat puzzling character. He is the conquered savage who has rejected the education of his master and is punished by slavery for that rejection. "I pitied thee," Prospero tells him,

Took pains to make thee speak, taught thee each hour
One thing or other: when thou didst not, savage,
Know thine own meaning, but wouldst gabble like
A thing most brutish, I endow'd thy purposes
With words that made them known. But thy vile race,
Though thou didst learn, had that in't which good natures
Could not abide to be with; therefore was thou
Deserv'dly confin'd into this rock, who hadst
Deserv'd more than a prison.

And Caliban replies:

You taught me language, and my profit on't
Is, I know how to curse.

Yet the island was Caliban's, "by Sycorax my mother," and Prospero took it from him by force. Prospero, as the superior order of being, would have, on the Elizabethan view, the right to dominate the inferior, so Shakespeare does not seem to be posing an ethical problem here. Caliban, savage son of a witch, the denier of civilization, who refuses to fit into Prospero's scheme of things and is punished for his refusal, is in a strange way both evil and innocent. He is, in his own way, a child of nature; he loves music; he is credulous, and easily fooled by human art. There is perhaps more to be said for him than for the human villains whose treachery to each other constitutes a deeper evil than does Caliban's crude villainy: *corruptio optimi pessima.*

The action takes place throughout on the island, washed by the purifying sea. It is shipwreck which saves Alonso and Antonio from their wickedness; as in *Pericles,* death by water proves to be redemption. It is shipwreck, too, that brings Ferdinand to Miranda, and having done that, brings to her gaze other representatives of the outside world, causing her to exclaim:

O wonder!
How many goodly creatures are there here!
How beauteous mankind is! O brave new world,
That has such people in't!

She is deceived: it is not a brave new world but a shabby old one. Her innocence is ignorance; she takes the motley assortment of schemers and traitors to be angels; and one is left wondering how she will cope with the realities of the everyday world when she has left the island for Italy. One remembers that it was Othello's ignorance of the "civilized" way of life which led him to trust Iago.

So in the end Shakespeare avoids tragedy by shifting his action to a magic island in which all can be controlled by a benevolent will: *The Tempest* is a magical play, full of grave beauty and rich poetry, a play out of this world, a wish-fulfillment play in which virtue has all the power and innocence meets its appropriate destiny. This is the Garden of Eden, with God, as Prospero, personally in charge to prevent the Devil from prevailing; Miranda is a prelapsarian character who, as the play ends, is about to leave the shelter of Paradise to test her virtue in the wicked world. When Eve, "our credulous mother," left Paradise she had already been tempted and had fallen, and she and Adam went out into the world disillusioned and knowledgeable. But credulous Miranda goes out unfallen into the world, whither Shakespeare refuses to follow her. His last gesture is to avert his eyes from the workaday world at the same time as he sends his characters back into it. There they may become figures in other plays—tragedies no less than comedies, since they will now be unprotected by Prospero's magic.

Shakespeare's last word can hardly be Prospero's

> We are such stuff
> As dreams are made on, and our little life
> Is rounded with a sleep,

for if that is all that life is, it is a strange thing to spend one's career interpreting it dramatically. No; life is worth something after all. The characters in *The Tempest* leave the magical island of redemption to go back into civilization with all its imperfections and temptations; and this is a good thing, for man belongs with his kind, and there is a glory even in the tragic paradoxes of the human situation. In the epilogue Prospero asks to be released, by the applause of the audience, from "this bare island," and the adjective is significant. "Let me not," he says

> Since I have my dukedom got
> And pardon'd the deceiver, dwell
> In this bare island by your spell; . . .

The magic world is but a "bare island" after all, compared with the ordinary world of men. Just as, in *Paradise Lost* "all th' Eastern side of Paradise, so late their happy seat" appeared to Adam and Eve as flaming and terrible when they looked back for a moment before going down into the world that was all before them, so Prospero's Eden becomes uninhabitable at the end. Perhaps Shakespeare's last word, like Milton's, was that man cannot live in Paradise.

Shakespeare spent the last seven years or so of his life at Stratford, in New Place, the large house he had bought there in 1597. After an active life as man of the theater, playwright, and man of property, he seems to have retired in some degree from the London theatrical world. His company, the King's men (earlier the Lord Chamberlain's men), had now both the Globe as a "public" theater and the "private" theater of Blackfriars, in both of which Shakespeare's last plays were acted. Beaumont and Fletcher, two promising younger playwrights, were now writing for the company, having already established themselves with their courtly and sentimental plays at the Blackfriars. Shakespeare wrote his last group of magical romances from Stratford; his imagination had moved away from the everyday human scene to dwell in a more symbolic world. Twice, in 1612–13, he gave his younger colleague John Fletcher a hand with a play, the first time with *Henry VIII*, the larger part of which has, on somewhat dubious internal evidence, been attributed to Fletcher, and the second with *The Two Noble Kinsmen,* where Fletcher seems to have worked over Shakespearean scenes and fitted them into the finished play. *Henry VIII* is a lively dramatic rendering of the high points of that King's reign, with some fine dramatic moments and some great spectacles, emphasizing at the end the Tudor succession and the glories of Queen Elizabeth's reign to come. Henry's repudiation of his first wife, Katherine of Aragon and his love for Anne Boleyn; the proud Wolsey at the height of his power provoking his own fall; the trial of Katherine; the rise of Cranmer and Cromwell; the birth of Elizabeth—these are treated in sequence, with little dramatic unity but considerable dramatic verve. Most of the better scenes in the play appear to be Fletcher's, though the character of Queen Katherine—the most sustained success in the play—is probably Shakespeare's own throughout. *The Two Noble Kinsmen* is a dramatization of the story told by Chaucer in his *Knight's Tale;* it was first published in 1634 as the joint work of Fletcher and Shakespeare, and recent scholarship is still busy trying to distinguish the contribution of each. In conception and tone the play is Fletcher's.

In the last few years of his life Shakespeare appears to have written nothing at all. The reasons can only be conjectured. It may be that his imagination had transcended the limits of dramatic expression and he now felt that language was too weak an instrument. Certainly in his later plays he used language with a poetic force and subtlety which indicated that he was prepared to beat more meanings out of verse expression than ordinary logical use of words allows. Especially from *Antony and Cleopatra* on do we find a daring lack of metaphorical consistency in favor of a fiercer and richer kind of meaning:

> The hearts
> That spaniel'd me at heels, to whom I gave
> Their wishes, do discandy, and melt their sweets
> On blossoming Caesar.

Or consider the curious elliptical construction of these lines from *The Winter's Tale:*

> I am question'd by my fears, of what may chance
> Or breed upon our absence; that may blow
> No sneaping winds at home, to make us say
> "This is put forth too truly."

Not that Shakespeare's later poetry is always complex and packed; he achieves some of his greatest effect by a magical simplicity:

> Finish, good lady; the bright day is done,
> And we are for the dark.

We must not forget that Shakespeare was more than a brilliant dramatist and man of the theater: he was also the greatest poet the English language has yet produced, and any adequate account of his achievement would have to include a discussion of his poetry. From the "sugared" style of

> But soft! what light through yonder window breaks?
> It is the east, and Juliet is the sun, . . .

to the bold syntax and packed thought of

> Was this taken
> By any understanding pate but thine?
> For thy conceit is soaking, will draw in
> More than the common blocks: not noted, is't,
> But of the finer natures? by some severals
> Of head-piece extraordinary? lower messes
> Perchance are to this business purblind? say, . . .

Shakespeare's poetic usage covers an enormous range. The later poetry, with its flexible rhythms, startling vocabulary, and syntactical audacity achieves a quality and depth of expression that seem to exhaust the utmost possibilities of language. Scholars, seeking for methods of dating uncertain plays, have discovered that in the later plays there is a large number of "weak" endings (an extra light syllable added to the iambic pentameter line), a trick that Shakespeare may have picked up from Fletcher, with whom it was a regular practice. But, however useful for purposes of dating plays, this extra light syllable is the least part of the flexible richness of Shakespeare's style. It is a style whose packed elliptical treasury of meaning and suggestion achieves blinding clarity on the very threshold of total obscurity. Nothing more was left to be done with language.

Shakespeare began his literary career as a poet, and he never ceased to be fascinated by the poetic possibilities of image, conceit, metaphor, and symbol. The lyrical music of *A Midsummer Night's Dream*, *Richard II*, and *Romeo and Juliet* succeeded the Marlovian rhetoric of *Richard III* and gave way to the richer orchestration of *As You Like It* and *Twelfth Night*, which in turn is deepened and further enriched in the great tragedies, to emerge with its most potent magic in *Antony and Cleopatra*. The movement is from conceit to a more original and exploratory use of language, from metaphor to symbol. At the end, in *The Tempest*, after the brilliant audacities of the immediately preceding plays, he returns to a more formal Elizabethan utterance, which gives us the grave beauty of Prospero's great speech in which he renounces his magic: "Ye elves of hills, brooks, standing lakes and groves, . . ."

Shakespeare's use of prose, for comic, ironic, mad, or simply realistic scenes, and the different uses to which he puts prose in different phases of his career, are also worth attention. Most of all, one must realize what Shakespeare did to the vocabulary at his disposal. He inherited a language that was in the process of expansion by translation and borrowing, a language flexible enough to enable him to cast his own stamp on it, to manipulate it, enlarge it, wrest it to his purpose, with remarkable freedom. Spenser was behind him, and Marlowe and Lyly, and the Elizabethan song writers and Petrarchan sonneteers, and Ovid and Mantuan and Italian poets and short story writers, and translations from the classics and from the Bible. He was conscious, as other writers of his time and later were, of the advantages to be derived from combining and counterpointing the Anglo-Saxon and the Latin elements in English. Above all, as for all truly great poets, language was for him not only expressive but cognitive and exploratory; for him, the nature of reality could be probed by the very fact of rendering it in poetic speech. This great poetic gift was put at the service of an equally great dramatic gift. He had the true objectivity of the artist, the supreme craftsmanship of the man of the theater, a humane curiosity about man and his nature, an extraordinary ability to conceive and create character, and an unrivaled mastery of the English language. That was William Shakespeare: he remains the unchallenged champion in the whole field of English literature.

CHAPTER TEN

Drama from Jonson to the Closing of the Theaters

As for Jonson, . . . I think him the most learned and judicious writer which any theatre ever had. . . . He was deeply conversant in the Ancients, both Greek and Latin, and he borrowed boldly from them. . . . If I would compare him with Shakespeare, I must acknowledge him the more correct poet, but Shakespeare the greater wit. Shakespeare was the Homer, or father of our dramatic poets; Jonson was the Virgil, the pattern of elaborate writing; I admire him, but I love Shakespeare." So wrote Dryden, in his *Essay of Dramatic Poesy* (1668), expressing a view which was not only common to his age but which also corresponds in some degree to what all subsequent critics have felt about the difference between Shakespeare and Ben Jonson. Shakespeare, with a largeness of vision and flexibility of technique, worked with the popular dramatic tradition of his time and produced an English poetic drama which owed nothing to any external doctrine of correctness but which developed, out of the pressure of its own vitality, its own kind of form and unity. Jonson, more learned and deeply concerned with classical precedent, approached his art from a quite different point of view. With him the formula came first, and the classical model was the source of the formula. He knew in advance what the function of comedy was, and what sort of humor was proper to it. He knew the rules of dramatic structure and he understood what propriety was, from the same sources. When he wrote plays based on Roman history, he knew what Roman historians to quote from and what phases of Roman life to refer to. Pedantic, imitative, and supremely self-confident in his learned art, he is the one great example in English of the Renaissance Humanist (in the narrowest sense of that term) turned dramatist and poet.

If he were only that, he would be remembered more as a literary curiosity than as a great literary figure. But he was also a rugged Englishman with a sardonic relish for the varied and colorful London life of his day; he had a boisterous and even a cruel sense of humor which manifested itself in his best comedies with a bizarre brilliance; he showed enormous vigor and impressive originality even when most closely following classical models or applying rules derived from classical theory or practice; and he had in addition a quality which is not often associated with those already mentioned—a delicate artfulness in the handling of word and image in lyrical verse which enabled him to produce such well remembered examples of perfect verbal patterning as "Drink to me only with thine eyes," "Slow, slow fresh fount," and "Queen and huntress, chaste and fair." The contrast between Jonson and Shakespeare is not therefore the simple one between the Renaissance Humanist obsessed by classical rule and precedent and the "natural genius" inventing his own kind of art with the help of a popular tradition. Jonson's sardonic view of human nature owed nothing to classical sources, while his lyrical gift, however much it may have been stimulated by classical epigram and the Greek Anthology, reflected an important facet of his personality. No English writer was more highly idiosyncratic than Jonson, and his picturesque and violent life—which included (after bricklaying and soldiering) the slaying of an actor in a duel and consequent imprisonment and branding, a temporary conversion to Roman Catholicism, a fierce literary quarrel with his fellow dramatists Marston and Dekker, a journey to Scotland on foot, a career as principal purveyor of masques to King James I's court, and a bitter feud with Inigo Jones, the architect and stage designer who had provided the sets for his masques—is sufficient testimony to his individuality and self-confidence. In the latter part of his career he was the leader of an important literary group and indeed something of a literary dictator, the first significant example of that species in English literature. His life, which ran from 1573 until 1637, not only spanned the flowering time of that literary era which we loosely call Elizabethan, but reached well into the reign of Charles I and into a very different cultural atmosphere from that which prevailed at the end of the sixteenth century, when Spenser was working on his *Faerie Queene* and Shakespeare was developing his true powers.

That Jonson was eclipsed as a dramatist by Shakespeare is clear enough to later eyes, but to the critics and playgoers of the seventeenth century it was not so clear. Jonson had a claim on literary men that Shakespeare had not; he bullied them into admiration by the force of his literary claims and the supreme confidence he showed in pressing them. It was a long time before a critical theory developed which was adequate to cope with the richness and subtlety of Shakespeare's plays and the incredible wealth of his genius; but from the beginning Jonson could be proved good by the available critical apparatus. Dryden, in *An Essay of Dramatic Poesy,* provides a model analysis of a play, and the play is Jonson's *Epicœne, or the Silent Woman.* "I will take the pattern of a perfect play from Ben Jonson, who was a careful and learned observer of the dramatic laws." Shakespeare could not be so analyzed; he drew on the images of Nature "not laboriously, but luckily"; "he needed not the spectacles of books to read Nature; he looked inwards, and found her there." Jonson was thus the more respected in the seventeenth century because his plays were more amenable to criticism.

Jonson's first important and successful play was *Every Man in his Humour* (1598),[1] a comedy of intrigue owing much to Roman comedy but highly original in tone and manner. He wanted to present a satiric picture of his own age, to write with cool irony of contemporary human foibles, as he considered Plautus and Terence had done. (But he thought of himself also as an English Juvenal.) He considered himself a realist, and in the Prologue he attacked both the themes and the conventions of contemporary drama and contrasted his own aim. He will not "serve the ill customs of the age" and refuses

> To make a child, now swaddled, to proceed
> Man, and then shoot up, in one beard, and weed,
> Past threescore years: or, with three rusty swords
> And help of some few foot-and-half-foot words,
> Fight over York and Lancaster's long jars,
> And in the tiring house bring wounds to scars.
> He rather prays, you will be pleased to see
> One such today as other plays should be,
> Where neither chorus wafts you o'er the seas,
> Nor creaking throne comes down, the boys to please,
> Nor nimble squib is seen, to make afeard
> The gentlewomen, nor rolled bullet heard
> To say, it thunders, nor tempestuous drum
> Rumbles, to tell you when the storm doth come;
> But deeds and language such as men do use,
> And persons such as comedy would choose
> When she would show an image of the times
> And sport with human follies, not with crimes.

[1] The dates given for Jonson's plays are those of their first performance. None of the plays was published singly in Jonson's lifetime, but he brought out a collected volume in 1616, reprinted with a second volume in 1640. Plays of other dramatists are also dated by their first performance when it is known.

This is the language of a conscious reformer of the stage, who sees himself doing something both artistically better and morally worthier than his contemporaries are producing. He was to be more correct in structure, more contemporary in theme, and more improving in effect. The function of comedy was the reproving of human foibles by holding them up to ridicule, and he adapted the old explanation of human character by the four humors to develop a "comedy of humours," a comedy, that is, in which each character is seen to be dominated, and even obsessed, by one particular quirk. He explained his view in the "induction" to his next comedy, *Every Man Out Of His Humour:*

> Why, humour, as 'tis *ens,* we thus define it
> To be a quality of air or water,
> And in itself holds these two properties,
> Moisture and fluxure; as, for demonstration,
> Pour water on this floor, 'twill wet and run;
> Likewise the air, forced through a horn or trumpet,
> Flows instantly away, and leaves behind
> A kind of dew; and hence we do conclude
> That whatsoe'er hath fluxure and humidity,
> As wanting power to contain itself,
> Is humour. So in every human body
> The choler, melancholy, phlegm and blood,
> By reason that they flow continually
> In some one part, and are not continent,
> Receive the name of Humours. Now thus far
> It may by metaphor apply itself
> Unto the general disposition,
> As when some one peculiar quality
> Doth so possess a man that it doth draw
> All his affects, his spirits and his powers,
> In their confluctions, all to run one way:
> This may be truly said to be a humour.

[*ens:* an existing thing.]

He goes on to say that those who "affect a humour" merely by some trick of costume, and boast of these petty and affected humors, are apes who ought to be scourged:

> . . . I will scourge those apes
> And to these courteous eyes oppose a mirror,
> As large as is the stage whereon we act,
> Where they shall see the time's deformity
> Anatomized in every nerve and sinew
> With constant courage, and contempt of fear.

Jonson's insistence on the humors was at cross purposes with his realistic intention, though he never seems to have realized this. A "humorous" character is bound to be a caricature, never presented as a fully realized human being but only as the fop, the blusterer, the jealous husband, the anxious father, the uncouth country cousin aping city manners, the hypocritical Puritan, or some similar type. Jonson lacked tenderness, and he lacked, too, that ability to enjoy the essential humanity of his immoral characters, as Shakespeare so clearly did with Falstaff. He was never faced with the problem that in some degree has troubled so many of the greatest dramatists and novelists—the problem of preserving a moral pattern while at the same time showing such a thorough awareness of the humanity of his evil characters that (to know all being to forgive all) moral disapproval is almost dissolved in psychological understanding. The comedy of humors inevitably avoids that problem. Comedy becomes satire, character becomes oddity, evil becomes culpable folly. There is humor enough (in the modern sense) in Jonson's comedy; he presents his obsessed characters with wit, liveliness of comic extravagance, and cleverly manipulated absurdity (of which one of the most effective examples is the scene in *The Poetaster* where Crispinus, who represents John Marston, is given an emetic which forces him to vomit up his long Latinate words), and at times comedy in his hands degenerates into farce; it is however splendid farce, which deals not with ridiculous situations merely, but with ridiculous situations as they arise from ridiculous elements in human nature. It is Dickensian in some respects, but when Dickens laughs the overtones are humanitarian. Jonson's laughter is sterner, and underlying it is his own enormous self-confidence, which at times rises to arrogance.

Every Man In His Humour was first set in Italy but the scene was soon changed to London, whose life and manners were always Jonson's real interest. The action of the play is designed to exhibit the fatuities, the follies, the obsessions, the pretentions, and the absurdities of the different characters; the foolish and boastful are "gulled" and exposed; plots and disguises help to forward the intrigue, and the play ends in reconciliation and mirth. Much of the dialogue is in prose, a vigorous and basically colloquial prose which bears the impress of the idiosyncrasy of the speaker. The blank verse, which is largely confined to expository passages and scenes where the tension is fairly relaxed, is firm and workmanlike, with again colloquial overtones. *Every Man Out of His Humour* (1599) concentrates with greater single-mindedness on the illustration of ridiculous "humours." The satiric note is dominant throughout; the characters (who in the folio edition of Jonson's *Works*, 1616, are each described in an introductory note somewhat in the manner of the "character writers" of the period) are given names indicating their particular foible: Carlo Buffone, "a public, scurrilous and profane jester"; Fastidius Brisk, "a neat, spruce, affecting courtier, one that wears clothes well, and in fashion; practiseth by his glass how to salute"; Sordido, "a wretched hob-nailed chuff, whose recreation is reading of almanacs, and felicity, foul weather"; Fungoso, "the son of Sordido, and a student; one that has revelled in his time, and follows the fashion afar off, like a spy"; Sogliardo, "an essential clown, brother to Sordido, yet so enamoured of the name of a gentleman, that he will have it, though he buys it"; and so on. Jonson himself is introduced as Asper, explaining and commenting on the action in conversation with his friends Cordatus and Mitis. The latter two act as a sort of Chorus. The play is more episodic than its predecessor, and incidents are contrived to illustrate the follies and idiosyncracies of the different characters with little regard to the development of the main action, although everything is tied up at the end with considerable ingenuity. Every one is finally shaken out of his absurd humor by suitable punishment or exposure. In spite of the Italian names this, too, is a London play full of the atmosphere of contemporary London.

Cynthia's Revels was first acted in 1600 by the boys of the Queen's Chapel, and it is full of that special kind of virtuosity which Elizabethan child actors could display so brilliantly. A satire on contemporary gallantry using mythological characters does not represent a very happy convention; the plot is overelaborate and confused; masques are introduced, with music and dancing; and altogether one has the impression that Jonson has let his ingenuity run away with him. The play shows many kinds of skill—it includes some cleverly mannered prose, some carefully chiseled blank verse, and the perfectly wrought lyric, "Slow, slow fresh fount"—but they do not contribute to a dramatic unity. (It is worth noting that Jonson, for all his concern with classical rule and precedent, often has less artistic unity in his plays than Shakespeare. The reason is easy to see: Shakespeare developed the unity appropriate to his original art form, while Jonson often imposed an external unity on his material.) It was typical of Jonson that he should have concluded the play with an Epilogue in which he aggressively asserted:

By God, 'tis good, and if you like't, you may.

By this time Jonson was involved in that quarrel with Marston and others which is known as the War of the Theatres, and his play

The Poetaster (1601) was a vindication of his position against his enemies. The scene is set in Augustan Rome. We see Horace (Jonson) moving with dignity in the literary world of Rome, friend of Virgil and of Augustus Caesar though pursued by the envy of fools and knaves. Ovid, Propertius, Tibullus, among others, are introduced, and there is much learned reference to Latin literature. Ovid's famous encounter with a bore which he records in Book 1 of his *Sermones* is turned into an encounter with Crispinus (Marston) in an amusing street scene. The whole play has more life and vigor than one would expect from such exhibitionist use of classical reading, but the satire is very limited in scope and the author's patent self-glorification sometimes irritates. The effortless identification of himself with one of the principal figures in the Golden Age of Latin literature and of his enemies with Roman impostors and poetasters who yapped at the heels of the great Augustans illustrates both the way in which his imagination dwelt in the Rome of his studies and the importance which he attached to literature and its practitioners, symbolized most effectively by Virgil and his contemporaries. In this respect Jonson's attitude to life and letters was that of the true Renaissance classical Humanist.

Fortunately, Jonson turned aside from those literary controversies which so confined his satirical talent, to enrich and develop his own species of satiric comedy. *Volpone, or the Fox* (1605) is the first and the greatest of a series of comedies which show Jonson's characteristic mixture of savagery and humor, of moral feeling and grim relish of the monstrous absurdities of which human nature is capable, disciplined with a new sharpness and given new depth and scope. Taking a hint from the *captatores,* legacy hunters of Rome, described by Petronius and others, Jonson contrived the story of a cunning rich man who feigned a mortal illness so that his wealthy neighbors would court his favor in the hope of being named his heir. Volpone is childless, and thus of obvious interest to the legacy hunters. His servant Mosca cunningly plays on their hopes and fears, promising each that Volpone is on the point of naming him as his heir and urging him to speed the process by a further proof of regard and friendship. Thus each is induced to bring gifts to the supposedly dying Volpone in the expectation of receiving them back together with all of Volpone's property when he dies. But Jonson does more than exploit the irony of this situation. The eager legacy hunters, falling over themselves in their haste to prove their devotion to Volpone, are played with cunningly by Mosca to the point where they become not only willing but anxious to do much more than merely give Volpone gifts. One disinherits his son in order to name

Volpone his heir, thus proving his friendship, while another, normally extravagantly jealous of his pretty wife, is induced to persuade her to give herself to the dying man in the confident hope that this supreme gift will clinch Volpone's choice of him as his heir. In the end everyone is overreached; Mosca overreaches his master, and both finally overreach themselves so that their villainies are exposed and punished. The scene is set in Renaissance Italy, accepted by the English imagination of this time as the proper home of vice, but the satire is general and deeply misanthropic. The working out of the plot is extremely ingenious; the mounting pace of the trickery and the villainy raises a horrified interest which never flags, and the progressive exposure of the depths to which lust for wealth can degrade the human character is made with an obsessive fierceness that shows Jonson at the height of his satiric powers. The tone is set at once by Volpone's opening words as he pays his daily worship to his wealth:

> Good morning to the day; and next, my gold!—
> Open the shrine, that I may see my saint.

The blank verse moves with speed and vigor; less subtle and flexible than the mature Shakespeare's, it does combine strength with a conversational movement. In the extravagance of imagery with which Volpone and Mosca express their ambitions and designs, Jonson not only suggests the obsessive nature of their drive for wealth and power but also, through the infatuated exaggeration of the tone, provides an implicit criticism of this attitude. The characters are deliberately restricted in scope in the interests of the satiric purpose. There are moments when the play moves close to tragedy, and the scene where Celia, Corvino's wife, expresses her horror when she discovers that her husband intends to force her to Volpone's bed shows Jonson moving closer to what one might call Elizabethan romantic tragedy than he ever moved again. It is in this scene that Volpone, now revealed as a cunning old lecher as well as a sadistic miser, sings to his shrinking victim the song, "Come, my Celia, let us prove, /While we can, the sports of love," which has in its context much grimmer overtones than can be imagined when it is read or sung separately.

Volpone was followed by *Epicœne, or The Silent Woman* in 1609, *The Alchemist* in 1610, and *Bartholomew Fair* in 1614. *Epicœne*, though much admired by Dryden and analyzed in his *Essay of Dramatic Poesy* as a perfectly constructed comedy, is the slightest of these mature comedies and is more concerned with the "gulling" of fools and hypocrites than with the satiric exploration of vice. The principal character, Morose, has the "humour" of being unable to stand noise, and lives surrounded by silence; he marries a young girl, supposed to be perpetually silent, in order to disinherit his nephew. But the girl turns out to be an incessant talker and the nephew finally agrees to arrange a divorce in return for a satisfactory financial settlement. In the end it is revealed that the girl is a boy in disguise; the whole thing has been a plot by the nephew to gull his uncle. A bare summary of the plot, however, tells little about the qualities of the play, which is full of odd characters and fantastic humor—a Jonsonian holiday in which the author gives full play to his characteristic blend of learning and realism, of boisterous humor and contrived grotesquerie. The play is in prose throughout, and thus lacks that criticism through obsessive imagery that is found in Jonson's greatest comedies. *The Alchemist* is more in the vein of *Volpone,* though it lacks the latter's misanthropic fierceness. It is a satiric comedy, dealing with a pretended alchemist whose victims include a great variety of characters all of whom are attracted by the hope of easy gold. This situation enables Jonson to display a great variety of human weakness and hypocrisy. As in *Volpone,* a principal theme is the way in which greed can make people gullible. In the absence of his master Lovewit, Face brings Subtle, the quack alchemist, to his master's house and there he proceeds to raise money from the gullible greedy, who include Drugger, a tobacco merchant, Dapper, a lawyer's clerk, the ambitious and sensual Sir Epicure Mammon, and two Puritan Brethren of Amsterdam whose conversation and behavior give Jonson the opportunity to ridicule Puritan hypocrisy and absurdity. Each character has his own characteristic extravagance of language as well as the mental fatuity which makes him a preordained dupe; it is a brilliant portrait gallery. Again like *Volpone,* the plot is cunningly developed and the action moves fast until the unexpected return of Lovewit puts an end to the activities of Face and Subtle. But Lovewit does not represent impartial justice or the moral norm; Face confesses to him and is pardoned, for Lovewit loves a jest, and only the unfortunate Subtle and Doll Common, the third in the trio of tricksters, meet some kind of retribution in the end. Jonson continually varies the system of mirrors, as it were, which he uses to reflect his moral position. In *Volpone,* the principal characters, Volpone and Mosca, batten on the greed of others, exposing to the full their selfishness and avarice; but this battening and this exposure arise from greed, selfishness, and avarice even greater than that of the victims. Similarly, in *The Alchemist,* Face and Subtle are motivated by greed in playing on the greed of others. But here there is no simple poetic justice at the end; Lovewit's return does not destroy Face, for the master cannot resist the situation Face presents him with, and the play ends with Lovewit in possession of the money and goods which the gulled fortune-seekers had deposited with Face. This wry twist in the end provides a further comment on society. But Jonson's true criticism of his characters, here as in most of his mature comedies, lies in the verse he makes them speak; the obsessive extravagance with which they express their ambitions makes clear, by the very fact that it *is* obsessive extravagance, that here is a wide deviation from the true moral and social norm. A well-known example of this is a speech of Sir Epicure Mammon:

> I will have all my beds blown up, not stuft:
> Down is too hard: and then, mine oval room
> Filled with such pictures as Tiberius took
> From Elephantis, and dull Aretine
> But coldly imitated. Then, my glasses
> Cut in more subtle angles, to disperse
> And multiply the figures, as I walk
> Naked between my succubae. My mists
> I'll have of perfume, vapoured 'bout the room,
> To lose ourselves in; and my baths, like pits
> To fall into; from whence we will come forth,
> And roll us dry in gossamer and roses.

Bartholomew Fair is the most expansive of Jonson's mature satiric comedies and the most English in atmosphere. The plot here is less important than the speech and action of the individual characters and the roistering atmosphere of the Fair at which most of the play is set. The humors and follies of the complacent Littlewit and his wife Win; of the Puritan Zeal-of-the-Land Busy anxious (for pecuniary reasons) to marry Win's mother, the widowed Dame Purecraft; of Justice Overdo, who gets himself into trouble by appearing at the Fair in disguise in order to discover what villainies really go on there; of Bartholomew Cokes of Harrow on the Hill, whose fatuous complacency makes him an easy victim of the professional pickpocket Ezekiel Edgeworth and his accomplice Nightingale the ballad seller—these are revealed against the noise and bustle of the Fair, where Ursula the pig-woman, Joan Trash the gingerbread woman, and many others carry on their raucous business. The play is full of life and color, and if the structure is less artful than that of his other mature comedies, this is compensated for by the boisterous high spirits and the zestful rendering of London life that Jonson here gives us. The satirical note is sounded clearly enough, but (unlike *Volpone* and even *The Alchemist*) satire is subordinated to comedy and the main interest of the characters (even Zeal-of-the-Land Busy, who is shown as alternately stupidly fanatical and grossly hypocritical) lies in the rich humor of their folly. Here indeed, Jonson "sports with human follies not with crimes," and the play ends with everyone chastened by experience but not otherwise punished.

Jonson also produced two tragedies on Roman themes, *Sejanus* (1603) and *Catiline* (1611), moved probably by Shakespeare's success with *Julius Caesar*. But his approach was very different from Shakespeare's. Not only did he choose much less well-known incidents from Roman history, but he drew on the original Latin sources—Tacitus, Suetonius, Juvenal, Seneca, and Dion Cassius in the case of *Sejanus*—and introduced numerous details from these works. He even cited in his preface the actual editions of the Latin authors that he had used. Nevertheless, he allowed himself some liberty in shaping the tragic pattern of the action. In *Sejanus,* he did not keep to the classical unity of time, though his preface shows that he had some qualms of conscience about this. There he conceded that he had not observed "the strict laws of time" or employed the classical chorus, but pleaded that he had "discharged the other offices of a tragic writer . . . in truth of argument, dignity of persons, gravity and height of elocution, fulness and frequency of sentence [i.e. moral sayings]." The play does move with dignity and achieves a certain tragic force in the ironic way in which the hero's intriguing ambition and final reversal of fortune are handled. Though the characters are not probed beyond their more obvious qualities which help to motivate the plot, Jonson succeeds in giving dramatic force to his picture of a police state in which the most unscrupulous and egotistical planning cannot yield any permanent power, for everyone is spying on everybody else and the Emperor himself spins his secret web at a distance. The climactic scene where Tiberius' letter about Sejanus is read to the Senate shows Jonson's special kind of dramatic irony at its most successful: the Senate, anxious to follow the Emperor's line, is deliberately baffled by his ambiguous and shifting references to Sejanus, and does not know whether to hail him or denounce him; until, at the end, the meaning is made clear and denunciation follows. *Catiline* is a more "regular" play, complete with ghost and chorus. The story of Catiline's conspiracy is told with conspicuous use of classical sources; the usual vein of savage satire runs through the play, and the attempt to provide motivation for Catiline's action (he becomes indirectly involved with jealous women and one of them worms the story out of one of the conspirators) provides an ironic commentary on the relation between the lower human passions and the shaping of political history, but the characters are not developed nor are their motives explored with any real dramatic subtlety. *Catiline* lacks the ironic vigor of *Sejanus*.

Of Jonson's later comedies—*The Devil is an Ass* (1616), *The Staple of News* (1625), *The New Inn* (1629), *The Magnetic Lady* (1632), and *A Tale of a Tub* (1633)—all that need be said is that they show him playing variations, with differing degrees of success, on his favorite satiric-comic themes; though each has its bright moments, and even some splendid passages, none is of the quality of his best mature comedies and there is little reason to dispute the conventional view that these later works show Jonson in decline. An exception must, however, be made for the unfinished pastoral drama, *The Sad Shepherd, or, A Tale of Robin Hood,* which shows an attractive vein of poetic fancy, combining the pastoral with the realistic.

That Jonson possessed this kind of poetic fancy is made abundantly clear by his masques, of which he wrote a large number throughout his career. The purpose of the masque was entertainment at Court or at a great house. Spectacle and movement were an important part of it, and the arts of the stage designer and the composer were often as important in its production as that of the poet. The origin of the masque is a matter for the anthropologist; it is connected with mumming and with seasonal revels on Twelfth Night, May Day, and similar occasions. From a fairly early period in England we find the custom of masked visitors arriving at a party to dance, present gifts, and mingle with the guests; eventually the masque, in its more stylized Italian form, became a regular part of festivities accompanying coronations, state visits of foreign princes, and royal or noble marriages. These masques drew on classical mythology for their characters and themes, which were treated with deliberate fancifulness. Throughout the reigns of Henry VIII, Elizabeth, James I, and Charles I the court masque flourished. Jonson was a principal purveyor of masques to James I and his queen. His saturnine wit and misanthropic irony disappeared when he turned to the production of these courtly entertainments, in which he showed a very different side of his genius—a delicate fancy, a lyrical grace, and a lively sportiveness. His lines may lack fluidity, but they have the other virtue of a finely chiseled shape. This is perhaps a two-dimensional art, lacking all complexity and that infinite reverberation of meaning which marks the greatest poetry. There is no echoing profundity in such lines as

Beauties, have you seen this toy
Called Love, a little boy
Almost naked, wanton, blind,
Cruel now, and then as kind?
If he be amongst ye, say:
He is Venus' runaway;

or in

Stay, my sweet singer,
The touch of thy finger
A little, and linger
For me, that am bringer
Of bounds to the border,
The rule and recorder
And mouth of your order,
As priest of the game
And prelate of the same.

But they represent excellent workmanship, and they take their place very effectively in the masques of which they are part. In the "antimasque" (which Jonson introduced), with its deliberate change of tone from the masque proper, he could show something of his other side and add many different kinds of contrasting notes, from the comically realistic to the gruesome and the grotesque. Jonson's long career of collaboration with the architect and designer Inigo Jones (which ended with their quarrel in 1630) meant that his masques were produced with particular visual effectiveness.

Finally, one must mention *Eastward Hoe* (1605), a play written jointly by Jonson, Marston, and Chapman, though we cannot be certain about the limits of the contribution of each. This attractive comedy displays qualities which none of its three authors shows in his independent work. The Jonsonian comedy in it has a lightness of touch not typical of Jonson, and Chapman's reflective psychology and Marston's melodramatic bitterness are both subdued to a brighter, gayer mood. The plot is a bourgeois morality, dealing with a city goldsmith's two apprentices, one virtuous and one vicious, and their respective fates, which are balanced by the fates of the goldsmith's two daughters, the younger sweet and modest and the elder foolish and worldly. The bad apprentice lands in jail but is saved from the gallows by timely repentance; the virtuous apprentice ends by marrying his master's younger daughter and eventually, as deputy-alderman, mercifully judging his erring former colleague. The foolish elder daughter is duped by an unscrupulous adventurer and after being humbled by misfortune is reduced to seeking mercy from the sister and father she had previously scorned. The lively realism of the action, the glimpses of middle-class London life and manners, the strong character drawing, the good-natured humor, combine to give *Eastward Hoe* unusual charm. Whether its morality is intended seriously, or, as seems probable, it is really a subtle burlesque of tradesmen's morality, it stands apart from the work of its joint authors as a more genial kind of play than any of them ever managed to produce alone.

Shakespeare and Jonson are the two giants among Elizabethan and early Jacobean playwrights; but there were many others who wrote with success both for the public and the private theater, sometimes individually, sometimes in cooperation, sometimes anonymously. Writing for the theater was the obvious way for a literary man whom destiny had placed on the lower slopes on Fortune's Hill (to use a common Elizabethan figure) to secure public acclaim and economic satisfaction. In some respects the drama in the late sixteenth and early seventeenth centuries can be compared to the novel in the nineteenth and twentieth centuries, and a theatrical success might be compared to a modern best seller. But there are important differences. Though plays were printed, generally in cheap quarto editions, and were often eagerly read by the literate, it was as acted plays that they made their impact and achieved popularity. The audience, though varied in its class composition, was not large enough to make long runs possible, so that there was a continuous demand for new plays. Old plays were rehashed, new plays on themes that had proved popular rushed out, and every possible variation played on the kinds of tragic and comic situation that appealed to the Elizabethan and Jacobean imagination. Dramatists drew for their plots on Italian *novelle,* on classical history and on recent English and European history, on old plays, stories, legends, and on any source that provided or suggested a plot in which injured men sought revenge, ambitious men overreached themselves, characters displayed heroic dignity in holding out for a while against the encroachment of inevitable doom, passion led men—and women—into strange jungles of horror or self-deception or pathos or all three, obsessed or foolish men demonstrated their folly and were duly gulled by their superiors in wit—indeed, anything that provided the opportunity for the dramatic display of emotional and physical violence and a presentation of the absurdities and the wonders of which passionate man is capable. Some dramatists, like George Chapman, infused an ethical and philosophical spirit into their plays; some, like John Marston, became intoxicated by exuberant language and produced some quite extraordinary fustian; some, like

Cyril Tourneur (if he really is the author of the anonymous *Revenger's Tragedy*) played variations—sometimes strangely impressive ones—on the old revenge theme; some, like John Webster and, rather differently, John Ford, explored the individual moment of passion with haunting poetic brilliance. Others explored in comedy conflicts between the social classes—especially between citizens and courtiers—and pointed the way toward that counterpointing of gullible bourgeois respectability and amoral aristocratic sophistication which is the theme of so much Restoration comedy. Others again churned out routine stuff in reasonably competent blank verse, presenting again and again the kinds of situation which had proved themselves most popular. Many plays of the period have not survived. Printed copies of plays were regarded as ephemeral light literature unworthy of the attention of any librarian: the first librarian of the Bodleian Library, Oxford (which was opened in 1602) was instructed by Sir Thomas Bodley to reject plays and similar "baggage books" for fear of scandal. One must remember, too, that in spite of the enormous popularity of the drama during this period, Puritan hostility toward the playhouse increased rather than diminished, and when the Puritans finally gained control of the government they closed the theaters. The closing of the theaters in 1642 brought this greatest of all periods in the history of English drama to an end; but it is arguable that the form of poetic drama developed by the Elizabethans had by this time completely run its course and that, quite apart from the closing of the theaters, there was no further road that way. The next phase of English drama, which appeared after the Restoration, produced a very different kind of dramatic literature.

It is impossible for the historian of English literature to do justice to a dominant literary form such as poetic drama between 1580 and 1640 and the novel in the nineteenth century and after; to do so would mean taking up so much space that there would be no room for anything else. If Shakespeare and Ben Jonson had not existed, the literary historian would devote pages to Chapman and Middleton and Webster and Ford and Beaumont and Fletcher without any disproportion; each of these is more interesting and produced plays of greater intrinsic value than any playwright of the eighteenth century and perhaps even of the nineteenth. But in the light of the peak achievements of their period, they must remain minor figures, paying the penalty of the period's dramatic richness.

George Chapman (ca. 1559–1634) has been generally known, ever since Keats wrote his famous sonnet, as a translator of Homer; but his somber ethical imagination (which is reflected in the way he handles the Homeric heroes) produced five tragedies which show the Elizabethan interest in Stoic philosophy in an original and impressive form. *Bussy d'Ambois* (1604) is a study of an old soldier (like Othello) lost and betrayed in a peacetime world of courtly intrigue: but the traitor is as much his own passion, which takes him completely by surprise in welling up in affection for a married lady of the Court, as the sophisticated characters who resent his blunt martial manner. Chapman's dramatic verse has its own dark and crowded intensity; it is sometimes congested and not always dramatic, but it bears the stamp of a brooding, original mind. Sometimes we feel that Chapman has not properly come to terms with the theater, or adequately reconciled his ideas about man's behavior and destiny with his sense of character in action. His great men try to achieve a Stoic calm; sometimes, like Bussy d'Ambois, they are surprised and betrayed by passion; sometimes, like Clermont d'Ambois in *The Revenge of Bussy d'Ambois* (ca. 1610), he does achieve a Senecan detachment, but the spectacle of a Stoic character philosophizing and debating with himself against a somewhat perfunctory background of traditional revenge-play properties is an odd one (though in *Hamlet,* Shakespeare manages it without oddness), and suggests that Chapman was searching for a kind of intellectual drama which the conventions of the Elizabethan stage denied him. In both these plays, Chapman derived his plot from recent French history. He did this also in *The Conspiracy and Tragedy of Charles, Duke of Byron* (1608), a tragedy in two parts where again a man of potentially heroic stature is destroyed by his own passions, on which his enemies find it easy to play. *Chabot, Admiral of France* (ca. 1613) and *Caesar and Pompey* (printed 1631) explore different aspects of stoical virtue. The loyal and noble Chabot is bayed by his barking enemies, and stands stiffly honest until his innocence establishes itself, but not before his sense of injustice has eaten into his heart, to produce his eventual death. In *Caesar and Pompey* the interest centers on the exemplary Stoic calm of Cato, and the achievement of such calm, after much vacillation, by Pompey.

Chapman's attempt to produce a philosophical drama within the conventions of the Elizabethan theater, while not wholly successful in dramatic terms, produced some of the most interesting and individual plays of the period. His comedies, deriving both from the intrigue of Latin comedy and the "humours" of Ben Jonson, are less individual, but at least one, *All Fools,* in its deftly constructed plot (from Terence) and kindliness of tone, is still capable of affording civilized pleasure.

John Marston (d. 1634) is a very different sort of dramatist. Having begun as a writer of coarse and violent verse satires, which display a certain ingenious pedantry in their lavish vocabulary of abuse, he turned to drama, where he shows the same extravagant language in melodramatic tragedies of love and revenge and cynical comedies which combine bitter exposure of human folly and ambition with wild farce. *Antonio and Mellida* (1599) and *Antonio's Revenge* are, like so many Elizabethan and Jacobean plays, set in Italy, which was now seen as a land of political violence and psychological extravagance, where the claims of rank and power could be set against those of proud poverty in startling patterns of cunning intrigue and twisting passion. The first of these twin plays deals with the intercomplications of private passion and political malice in a plot made up of elements from many different stock Elizabethan dramatic situations; the second, similarly drawing on stock situations, shows stoical characters dedicated to revenge, and so involved in that conflict between self-control and passion which we have seen was of such interest to Chapman. The conflict is resolved in a peculiar kind of philosophical rant which is nevertheless quite unlike Chapman's philosophical speeches. In the midst of the rant and the general extravagance of vocabulary, a strange kind of poetic excitement occasionally breaks through, showing that Marston is more than a writer of melodramatic fustian. *The Malcontent* (printed 1604), the story of a supplanted Duke who returns to his dukedom in disguise and vents his bitterness by cynically assisting his supplanter, comes to an unexpectedly happy ending when the usurping Duke gives the dukedom back to the Malcontent who then contemptuously pardons everybody. As not infrequently happens in Marston's plays, the motivation sometimes becomes obscure, and we are allowed to forget the reasons for the Malcontent's behavior in the virtuosity of his cynicism. The manipulation of passion, as well as the handling of the more purely comic scenes and the minor complications of the plot, show a fundamental uncertainty between diagnosis and rhetoric and between an interest in Jonsonian "humours" and an interest in moral situations. But *The Malcontent* is a remarkable performance, none the less. Of Marston's other comedies, *The Dutch Courtesan* is the most interesting. It is a complex and sordid story of love, lust, and conspiracy, with a subplot concerning the gulling of a stupid and miserly citizen by a sprightly trickster. As in *The Malcontent*, the happy ending of the main plot does violence to its predominant tone.

Marston is the Crispinus of Ben Jonson's *Poetaster*, and Jonson's picture of him vomiting up his strange, invented words has its justification. The animosity between Marston and Jonson is part of a somewhat tedious chapter in Elizabethan stage history known as the War of the Theaters. Dekker was also involved in this quarrel and also both attacked and was attacked by Jonson. Dekker is the Demetrius of *The Poetaster* and he in turn ridiculed Jonson in his play *Satiromastix, or the Untrussing of the Humorous Poet* (1601). Other plays by all these dramatists also contributed to the controversy, in which Marston showed himself the most ill-tempered. But Marston became reconciled to Jonson later, at least temporarily; he collaborated with him, as well as with Chapman, in *Eastward Hoe,* and dedicated *The Malcontent* to him in 1604.

Thomas Heywood (ca. 1570–1641) was a professional man of the theater and miscellaneous writer who produced many more plays than the twenty-three or so that survive as his and had a hand in very many others. He himself claimed to have "had either an entire hand or at least a main finger in two hundred and twenty plays," and there is no reason to suppose that he was not telling the truth. The theater of his day demanded constant new material, and Heywood was professionally equipped to provide it. He wrote on historical and patriotic themes; he glorified the London citizenry and prentices in plays which showed him appealing to urban middle-class feeling; he had a vein of somewhat ribald comedy which he worked into his most serious plays with little or no sense of construction or appropriateness; and, in *A Woman Killed with Kindness* (1603) and *The English Traveller* (ca. 1627), produced two impressive examples of the kind of play that has been called "domestic tragedy," plays, that is to say, that deal with the tragic results of passion or lust in ordinary family situations, in an atmosphere of sentimental morality.

Charles Lamb's well-known description of Heywood as a "prose Shakespeare" has some justification if it means that he dealt with many of the themes that Shakespeare handled without any of Shakespeare's poetic power or dramatic cunning but with fluency and facility and with a keen eye for the pathetic. His language is pedestrian, but it rises to occasional heights in moments of simple emphasis on pity or passion or regret. *A Woman Killed with Kindness* is the story of a happy marriage broken when the wife is seduced by the husband's friend; the husband, on discovering his wife's infidelity, has his moment of rage and horror, but controls himself with an effort and decides to punish his wife only by sending her away to live with her servants in one of his manors. The sinning wife realizes and acknowledges her sin at the moment of discovery, and dies repentant and brokenhearted, having summoned her husband to her bedside, where he assures her of his forgiveness. *The*

English Traveller deals with a similar theme, though the plot has a curious complication: the hero is chastely in love with a woman happily married to an old man; she returns his love, and they agree to marry on the old man's death. Both have an affection for the old man and repudiate any desire to hasten his death. The hero's friend seduces the wife, whose sin is discovered, and she dies almost immediately, repentant and self-reproachful. There is (as so often in Heywood) a completely irrelevant comic subplot, but the main story is developed with skill and considerable power. A certain delicacy of feeling, the author's combination of compassionate heart with inquiring mind, and a quiet but confident moral tone, give these plays their distinctive character. Heywood can be boisterous enough elsewhere, as in his early play celebrating the heroic exploits of four prentices, *The Four Prentices of London*, which Beaumont made fun of in 1608 in his *The Knight of the Burning Pestle*.

Thomas Dekker (ca. 1570–1641) was another versatile professional who turned his hand to a variety of kinds of writing, including prose pamphlets which show a remarkable knowledge of London low life. Again, only a small proportion of his plays survive. Apparently of humble origin and self-educated, he gives in all his work the impression of an untrained talent making the most of itself with whatever material comes to hand. Like so many other dramatists of his day, he collaborated with others whenever he got the opportunity, and it is not always possible to determine the extent of even his existing work. Of the comedies written by Dekker alone, *Old Fortunatus* (1599) and *The Shoemaker's Holiday* show his characteristic combination of a romantic imagination with an eye for realistic detail. *The Shoemaker's Holiday* (1599) retains its popularity as a lively, boisterous comedy of London life, taking its plot from Thomas Deloney's prose story of Simon Eyre, the London shoemaker who rose to become Lord Mayor and virtually the patron saint of prentices. The play brings together urban realism with a happy folk element. Dekker had a genuine poetic talent, a real gift for delineating character and a sentimentally optimistic view of human nature, and the combination produces his characteristic note. *Old Fortunatus*, published in 1600, is a morality play, based on German legend: Old Fortunatus is offered a gift by Fortune; he chooses an unexhaustible purse rather than a wiser gift, and the choice eventually produces his own death and that of his two sons. It is an ill-organized and uneven play; but its impressive opening scene contains some of Dekker's finest dramatic poetry.

Perhaps Dekker's greatest achievement is *The Honest Whore*, a play in two parts in the first of which (1604) Middleton is thought to have had a hand. But the second part, which is the more interesting and original, is all Dekker's own. The first part tells the story of Bellafront, the prostitute who redeems herself and is finally married to her original seducer. The second shows her being pressed to resume her former life both by her debauched and ruined husband and by the very man who had instigated her conversion, but she stands firm, watched over (unknown to herself) by her father, Orlando Friscobaldo, who turns out to be the *deus ex machina* of the play. In spite of a crude and implausible subplot, *The Honest Whore* (Part II, ca. 1605) is a remarkable and original play; indeed both these plays show a new kind of moral imagination closely linked to an almost Dickensian sense of character. Orlando Friscobaldo is one of the few characters in Elizabethan and Jacobean drama outside Shakespeare who, besides playing an integral part in the moral pattern of the play, is also a convincing and memorable character in his own right, remembered after the details of the play are forgotten. Dekker resembles Heywood in his fluency and his feeling for middle-class urban life; but he has both a vein of poetry and a sense of character that Heywood lacks. The "citizen comedy" produced by these and other dramatists of the period is a reminder that, although Puritan opposition to the stage was centered in London, the London citizenry as a whole were eager theater goers and developed a taste for seeing themselves glorified on the stage.

Other dramatists of the period turned to the revenge theme. After the subtilizing and deepening of the revenge play in *Hamlet* there would seem to be little enough left to do in this line, but some of the Jacobean dramatists took it up again and sought further variations. Cyril Tourneur (ca. 1575–1626) in *The Atheist's Tragedy* (ca. 1608) and *The Revenger's Tragedy*, especially in the latter (if this play, published anonymously in 1607, really is by Tourneur), explored the corrupting power of revenge, constructing a kind of tragedy whose chief interest lies in the spectacle of injured innocence turning monstrous in the endeavor to avenge its wrongs. *The Revenger's Tragedy* has echoes from Hamlet, as in the opening scene, with Vendice standing aside to meditate bitterly on a skull while the wicked and lecherous Duke with his equally lecherous wife and son pass across the stage, but the tone is quite un-Shakespearean. The plots, the disguises, the moments of calculated frightfulness, the melodramatic ingenuity of the Duke's murder, illustrate the avenger's mounting hysteria, his insane self-confidence, his utterly obsessive concern with his revenge and with that only, his savoring of the actual moment of revenge by gloatingly revealing himself and his motives to the dying victim—all this produces an atmosphere of contrived horror which, while splendid in its way, is too deliberately artful to enable the reader or spectator to lose himself in the dramatic situation. At the end of the play, Vendice and his brother Hippolito, who started off as injured innocents, have become monstrous connoisseurs of cruelty who have ceased to have any contact with the ordinary world. With the Duke and his son dead, Antonio, who takes over the government, wonders "how the old duke came murdered," and the two brothers admit their responsibility with a lunatic cheerfulness:

> Hippolito: 'Twas all done for the best, my lord.
> Vendice: All for your grace's good. We may be bold to speak it now.
> 'Twas somewhat witty carried, though we say it—
> 'Twas we two murdered him.

And Vendice is astonished when the new duke orders them to execution. His single-minded pursuit of revenge has destroyed his sanity and humanity. *The Atheist's Tragedy* (ca. 1608) is a more general study of corruption of personality through ambition and lust, but it has the same lingering over the contrived grisly episode. The blank verse in both plays combines a conversational quality with a somber power; the movement is conversational but the imagery is often exotic or deliberately shocking. The most effective lines (and we remember Tourneur, as we do Webster, for specific passages rather than for complete plays) are, however, simple and forthright in diction as well as movement, and owe their effectiveness to their terrible simplicity, as in Castiza's speech to her mother when the latter has agreed that Castiza should be the duke's mistress:

> Mother, come from that poisonous woman there.

Simplicity of diction combined with an exotic touch in the imagery is found in many of Vendice's speeches, as in the often quoted:

> And now methinks I could e'en chide myself
> For doating on her beauty, though her death
> Shall be revenged after no common action.
> Does the silkworm expend her yellow labours
> For thee? For thee does she undo herself?
> Are lordships sold to maintain ladyships,
> For the poor benefit of a bewildering minute?
> Why does yon fellow falsify highways,
> And put his life between the judge's lips,
> To refine such a thing—keeps horse and men
> To beat their valours for her?

John Webster (ca. 1580–1625) is a greater poet than Tourneur but he has less control over dramatic structure. Ambition, covetousness, and lust are the motivating factors in the cunningly cruel behavior of his villains, and sometimes we have the impression that motive is really unimportant and the interest of the plays lies in the virtuosity with which cruelty is manifested or the nobility with which even a vicious character confronts his doom when there is no alternative. *The White Devil* (ca. 1610) and *The Duchess of Malfi* (ca. 1614) are far and away his best plays, and they are both episodic in structure, allowing the author to arrest the dramatic movement while he exploits with brilliant poetic effect the terror or grandeur or pathos of the moment. The moral lines are less clearly drawn than in Tourneur. Vittoria Corombona, the heroine of *The White Devil,* is also the villain, or at least one of the villains. She is false to her husband and becomes the mistress of the Duke of Brachiano, who for her sake murders both her husband and his own duchess. She is not, however, fully implicated in the Duke's guilt, while those who bring her to trial and condemn her for her adultery are themselves corrupt and ambitious men. The true villain is Vittoria's brother Flamineo, the Duke's pander, but even he achieves dignity in dying:

> I am i' the way to study a long silence:
> To prate were idle. I remember nothing.
> There's nothing of so infinite vexation
> As a man's own thoughts.

The ramifications of the plot defy summary, and the play resolves itself into memorable scenes: Vittoria's trial, where she dominates the proceedings by her superb dignity; Cornelia's lament over her murdered son (an episode which has nothing to do with the action of the play but which Webster dwells on because it provides him with an opportunity of building up an atmosphere of wild pathos); Flamineo's final duel of wits with his sister, concluding in the death of both and Vittoria's dying cry:

> My soul, like to a ship in a black storm,
> Is driven, I know not whither.

The ambitions and lusts which drive the characters in Webster's plays are beyond ordinary human compass; there is something Faustian about them—they are after they know not what. They kill and betray and contrive for reasons which, though connected with some kind of self-interest, are deliberately left vague. And surrounding all is the corruption of Court life, which helps to breed these ambitions and poisons the virtue in everybody. Vittoria's last words curse the Court:

O, happy they that never saw the court,
Nor ever knew great men but by report.

Thus, traditional satire of Court life, the theme of the Machiavellian man and the cruelties and luxuries of Italy, the revenge theme, and the notion that in moments of ultimate crisis even evil characters can redeem themselves by a stoic dignity—all these threads are woven together by Webster and given color and strength by the morbid splendor of his verse.

The Duchess of Malfi is structurally a much simpler play and its plot can be briefly summarized: the young widowed duchess is forbidden by her brothers to remarry but secretly marries her own steward, and when this is discovered the brothers prepare cunning horrors for her and then have her killed. As usual with Webster, the motivation is obscure. Early in the play it appears that considerations of honor have led the brothers to forbid their sister's remarriage, while, at the end, one of them confesses that he had hoped to inherit her wealth if she remained a widow. But this does not matter. The interest and value of the play lie in the individual episodes. The piling up of horrors for the Duchess by Bosola, the brothers' instrument, trembles occasionally on the brink of the ridiculous, but Webster never allows a scene to fall over the edge. Even the masque of madmen—the imprisoned duchess is surrounded by lunatics released from a madhouse, and one of them howls a dismal dirge—stops short of the ridiculous because Webster keeps our eyes fixed on the stoical duchess who, made to sup her fill of horrors, retains the dignity to say

I am Duchess of Malfi still.

Before her execution every conceivable emblem of death, every kind of morbid horror, is brought to her; in Charles Lamb's words, "she has lived among horrors till she is become 'native and endowed unto that element.' She speaks the dialect of despair, her tongue has a snatch of Tartarus and the souls in bale." At the end she is no longer terrified by the prospect of rough strangulation:

What would it pleasure me to have my throat cut
With diamonds? or to be shot to death with pearls?
I know death hath ten thousand several doors
For men to take their exits; any way, for Heaven sake,
So I were out of your whispering.

When Ferdinand, her brother, sees his sister dead, he has a fit of remorse:

Cover her face; mine eyes dazzle: she died young.

There are more stratagems and horrors before the play comes to an end with the violent death of both brothers and of Bosola.

In the Court atmosphere of ambition, jealousy, deceit, lust, and sadism this strange and terrible tale unfolds itself, with Webster using every opportunity to pull out all the stops and arrest the action in a sense of perverse poetic beauty. Webster's art, like Tourneur's, is decadent, if by decadence we mean the desperate search for effect indulged in by those who work in a literary tradition after it has been fully exploited by a consummate genius. Perhaps after Shakespeare only this kind of brilliant sensationalism was left; but it is brilliant, and it does yield a genuine comment on life in its own strange way.

Thomas Middleton (ca. 1570–1627) is in some respects more in the tradition of Dekker and Heywood. Like them, he dealt in his comedies with London life, though he neither glorified nor romanticized it; instead, he drew on it for characters, sometimes almost Jonsonian in their humors, whose follies and trickeries are presented with high-spirited enjoyment. Tricksters and dupes recur in his comedies, and often they change places in the end, the trickster himself being caught out. There is something of the Latin comedy of intrigue here, too, but the plays have a boisterous realism of their own. The very titles suggest the atmosphere—*A Trick to Catch the Old One, A Mad World, my Masters, A Chaste Maid in Cheapside*. The last of these, not published until 1630 though first acted some twenty years earlier, is a rollicking comedy of folly and intrigue, with a romantic love plot taking its place on equal terms with a number of other plots which expose the stupidities, vanities, and humors of different characters. Villains overreach themselves, simpletons are gulled, different kinds of fatuity bring their appropiate rewards, cool self-interest generally pays off, and all this is presented by means of a breathless plot in which different characters are brought into contact with each other in rapid succession for the sole purpose of giving each the opportunity to precipitate his proper fate. This is typical of Middleton's comedy, which is witty, sometimes farcical, generally good-natured, and full of life. In his late comedy, *A Game at Chess* (1624), he treated a topical political theme allegorically and, though its anti-Spanish tone (it was produced just after the breaking off of negotiations with Spain for marrying Prince Charles to the Infanta) won it enormous popularity at the time, its allegorical ingenuity, and the extraordinary skill with which the characters are associated with the movement of the black and the white pieces in a chess game, have preserved it only as an exercising ground for scholars.

Like so many other dramatists of the period, Middleton collaborated with other playwrights, his most successful collaborations being with William Rowley. The one tragedy that he wrote by himself, *Women Beware Women* (probably 1612), is a powerful and somber work, written in an assured, flexible blank verse which can effectively mingle the cadences of conversation with the note of strong tragic feeling. The main plot concerns the degeneration of Bianca, wife of Leantio, after the Duke of Florence has seduced her in her husband's absence: but the play is far from a simple study in degeneration. Leantio is a merchant's agent who has "stolen" an aristocratic wife from Venice; from the beginning he hardly credits his own good fortune, and on presenting his wife to his mother expresses the hope that nothing will be done to make Bianca dissatisfied with her comparatively humble lot. Leantio's devotion to his wife cannot prevail over the claims of business, which call him from home, and in his absence the Duke, who sees Bianca at her window as he passes by in procession, falls in love with her. The scene where the mother plays at chess with Livia (who acts as procuress for the Duke) while in another room the Duke effects his seduction of Bianca is one of the great moments in Jacobean drama; but it is not, like many of Webster's scenes, an isolated moment where the play is halted while the dramatist displays his virtuosity. The action moves on with grim logic. Leantio returns, happily anticipating a blissful reunion with his wife, to find Bianca cool and ironical. When a messenger comes to invite Bianca to the Duke's, Bianca mocks her husband's fears and defies his advice (he is by this time in no position to command) not to go. Bianca grows in wantonness and hardness and Leantio in misery. He forces himself to hate his unfaithful wife and accepts the proffered love of Livia almost indifferently. There is a subplot, more closely connected with the main plot than in most Elizabethan and Jacobean tragedy outside Shakespeare, in which Isabella marries a loutish young man in order to cover her affair with Hippolito, her uncle. Having developed both the plots to a culmination of grim irony, Middleton seems to have been somewhat at a loss; in the end he kills everybody off in one of those general slaughters at an entertainment (in which murderous plans go awry and destroy the planners) so dear to the dramatist of the period. In spite of this perfunctory ending, *Women Beware Women* remains a remarkable and arresting tragedy.

Middleton's other great tragedy he wrote in collaboration with Rowley. This is *The Changeling* (1632), also an ironic story of degradation. Beatrice-Joanna, in order to escape marriage to a man she dislikes, hires De Flores, who loves her but whom she utterly despises, to murder him. She thinks she can use his devotion to serve her own ends, but finds that once he has committed the murder she is completely at his mercy and must become his mistress. The scene where De Flores comes to Beatrice to announce that his mission is accomplished, and she gradually and incredulously learns his true price for the deed, is done with psychological cunning and great dramatic irony. Even when she at last learns what he is proposing, she cannot see how she has sacrificed all claim to moral stature and is now completely in his power, physically and morally:

> Why, 'tis impossible thou canst be so wicked,
> Or shelter such a cunning cruelty,
> To make his death the murderer of my honour!
> Thy language is so bold and vicious,
> I cannot see which way I can forgive it
> With any modesty.

But at last she learns where she stands, and she becomes De Flores' mistress, achieving even a kind of masochistic satisfaction in her role. Meanwhile the way is open—ostensibly—for her to marry the man for whose love she had had her other suitor murdered. Her involvement with De Flores, and the fact that her husband would discover that he had not married a maid, compel her to further subterfuges and crimes, until inevitable discovery brings about her death, immediately before which she realizes to the full the true nature of the moral trap she had set for herself. She dies addressing her father in words that T. S. Eliot was to echo in "Gerontion":

> O, come not near me, sir, I shall defile you!
> I that am of your blood was taken from you
> For your better health; look no more upon't,
> But cast it to the ground regardlessly,
> Let the common sewer take it from distinction. . . .

The subplot (from which the play derives its title) deals with a man's disguising himself as a "changeling" or half-wit in order to make love to the wife of the keeper of the lunatic asylum. Its relation to the main plot is not of the closest, though there are some ironical parallels and contrasts which may be seen as heightening the total tragic effect. The asylum keeper's wife retains her moral control in the midst of insanity, in contrast to Beatrice, who surrenders to the madness of passion.

Other plays are ascribed to Middleton and Rowley, including an interesting version of romantic tragicomedy in *The Spanish Gypsy* (1621–22), but none approaches the stature of *The Changeling*. The quietly assured blank verse, with its supple rhythms and blending of the colloquial and the passionate, the searching tragic irony (for example, in the way Beatrice is first the superior, then the victim, and finally the emotional dependent of De Flores, and the relation of this progress to the moral meaning of the play) and the psychological penetration, are qualities of tragedy of a high order. These qualities are sufficiently akin to those displayed by *Women Beware Women* to justify us in believing them Middleton's rather than Rowley's (though Rowley seems to have had a similar kind of talent to Middleton's in tragedy). Finally, it is worth noting that in Middleton's plays, both comedies and tragedies, there is no moral disorder: he never exploits moral corruption for purely sensational purposes, or suggests (as Ford seems to do) that passion is its own justification. There is a firm moral order underlying his plays, and he lets us see it clearly in moments of crisis as well as in the general way in which the plot unfolds.

In the plays of Francis Beaumont (ca. 1584–1616) and John Fletcher (1579–1625) the Jacobean drama gives up any serious attempt to grapple with moral problems to indulge in the skillful professional exploitation of titivating, pathetic, or emotionally extravagant situations. The comedies which Fletcher wrote alone have none of the moral vigor and poetic strength of Ben Jonson at his best; they are smooth, even slick, productions, the verse tripping loosely along with extra syllables at the end of the blank verse line, the plots full of tricks and surprises, the settings generally some never-never land of romantic extravagance where heroic gesture replaces a moral code. This description applies in some degree to all the plays of this popular couple, who collaborated on over fifty in the second decade of the seventeenth century. In these plays they introduced a new kind of tragicomedy, where passion and honor whirl the action into every kind of confusion, before the casting off of a disguise or the revelation of some concealed relationship or some such device brings about the resolution. The tragic element looks forward to the heroic play of the Restoration, just as the preference of social poise to moral adjustment in so many of their comedies looks forward to Restoration comedy.

Philaster (ca. 1610) opens the series of Beaumont and Fletcher tragicomedies, and it is one of the best examples of this sort of play. Philaster, the popular heir to the throne of Sicily, has been ousted by a usurper, whose daughter Arethusa he loves and who loves him. He occasionally engages in threatening remarks about the usurping King, but, largely because of his love for the King's daughter, goes no further. After Philaster and Arethusa, meeting secretly, have confessed their mutual love, Philaster tells her that he will send his page

Bellario to wait on her and bear messages between them. This Bellario (whom the reader or audience guesses almost at once to be a girl in disguise, although nobody in the play realizes it until the end) is devoted to Philaster, who thus describes to Arethusa how he comes to have him as a page:

> Hunting the buck,
> I found him sitting by a fountain's side,
> Of which he borrowed some to quench his thirst,
> And paid the nymph again as much in tears.
> A garland lay him by, made by himself
> Of many several flowers bred in the vale,
> Stuck in that mystic order that the rareness
> Delighted me: but ever when he turned
> His tender eyes upon 'em, he would weep,
> As if he meant to make them grow again.
> Seeing such pretty helpless innocence
> Dwell in his face, I asked him all his story:
> He told me that his parents gentle died,
> Leaving him to the mercy of the fields,
> Which gave him roots; and of the crystal springs,
> Which did not stop their courses; and the sun,
> Which still, he thanked him, yielded him his light.
> Then he took up his garland and did show
> What every flower, as country-people hold,
> Did signify, and how all, ordered thus,
> Expressed his grief, and, to my thoughts, did read
> The prettiest lecture of his country-art
> That could be wished: so that methought I could
> Have studied it. I gladly entertained
> Him, who was glad to follow; and have got
> The trustiest, loving'st, and the gentlest boy
> That ever master kept.

Meanwhile Arethusa is being courted, with her father's approval, by the empty, boastful Spanish prince Pharamond, who, when Arethusa refuses to allow him to anticipate his marriage rights, comforts himself with a loose lady of the Court. They are discovered together at night, but the lady, by accusing Arethusa of keeping Bellario for her private lust, successfully blackmails the King, and Pharamond is restored to his favor. Arethusa, accused by her father of improper behavior with Bellario and charged with the same offense by Philaster himself, is rendered desperate; and after a fine tangle of events, in the course of which Philaster, Arethusa, and Bellario find themselves together in a wood under circumstances that throw further suspicion on the latter two, producing rage, passion of various kinds, explanations, and mutual but frustrated suicide attempts by Philaster and Arethusa, the truth is at last revealed, Arethusa vindicated, Bellario shown to be a girl who had forsaken her home for love of Philaster, Pharamond exposed and expelled, and Philaster restored to his kingdom. The play contains several set speeches of the kind already quoted (for example, the speech in which Bellario explains his conduct in the last act), and the tone throughout is reminiscent of Sidney's *Arcadia* except that the high Sidneian code has been reduced to something much less coherent and magnanimous. There is, of course, a superficial similarity between this sort of thing and Shakespeare's last plays; but the similarity is one of machinery rather than of tone or poetic richness.

Philaster is a "pretty" play, and it contains much pretty poetry. The same can be said of *A King and No King* (1611) which plays with a pretty prurience on the theme of incest, only to reveal at the end that the supposedly incestuous pair are not really brother and sister at all, so all is well. Beaumont and Fletcher's tragedies are similar in tone to their tragicomedies, distinguished only by a different manipulation of the conclusion. *The Maid's Tragedy*, for example (ca. 1611), perhaps the best of them, deals with a husband who discovers on his wedding night that his wife, Evadne, is the King's mistress and the marriage is to be one in name only, a cover for Evadne's affair with the King. His first reaction, apart from his frustration, is to express regret that the villain responsible for this mockery of a marriage is the King:

In that sacred word
"The King," there lies a terror: what frail man
Dares lift his hand against it? Let the gods
Speak to him when they please: till when, let us
Suffer and wait.

His second is to torture himself with thoughts of his reputation: if only his shame is not found out:

Methinks I am not wronged;
Nor is it aught, if from the censuring world
I can but hide it. Reputation,
Thou art a word, no more!—But thou has shown
An impudence so high, that to the world
I fear thou wilt betray or shame thyself.

There is a grimly comic scene when the bride and groom are welcomed the next morning with good-natured jests about loss of virginity and the wars of love, to which each responds in the way that will avert suspicion of the truth. Evadne in due course has her conscience awakened by her brother, who persuades her to murder the King when he lies in bed ready to receive her. Her husband, however, does not receive her back with open arms when he learns this, and in despair she stabs herself. The husband meanwhile has had his own troubles. Aspatia, who had been betrothed to him before he married Evadne and still loves him, seeks him out disguised as a man and provokes him to a fight in which she is slain. Evadne's brother explains everything to Lysippus, the murdered king's brother, who concludes the play by explaining that

> on lustful kings
> Unlooked-for sudden deaths from Heaven are sent;
> But cursed is he that is their instrument.

The play has some powerful and gripping moments (e.g. when, in Act IV, scene 1, Evadne finally expresses her remorse and repentance to her much-wronged and bewildered husband) and many of the passionate speeches show considerable poetic cunning. Yet, like so much of Beaumont and Fletcher, it has a certain hollowness at the core. The poetry is not integrated into the play, giving depth and richness to the dramatic situation by the subtle deployment of imagery, but is used more exhibitionistically for purposes of mere display or to give a general sense of moral confusion. These dramatists, Fletcher in particular, have been praised for the beauty of their verse, and it is true that in a play such as Fletcher's *The Faithful Shepherdess* (1608–09) there is a stylized pastoral charm which has considerable appeal; but neither of them was able to use dramatic verse consistently in that exploratory manner which is the mark of the greatest poetic dramatists. They were highly skilled professional playwrights who knew what was wanted in both the public and the private theater of their day and knew also how to tickle the somewhat jaded palates of King James I's morally shabby Court.

Beaumont's *The Knight of the Burning Pestle* (1608) must be exempted from all the generalizations above. It is a brilliant satirical comedy, mocking the popularity of Spanish romances and similar chivalric works among London prentices and their masters as well as burlesquing such urban heroics as are found in Thomas Heywood's *The Four Prentices of London.* The device of a play within a play is used with particularly happy effect, and the comments of the watching citizen and his wife on the action in which their apprentice Ralph is taking part are not only highly amusing in themselves but also achieve a cumulative effect which amounts almost to the presentation of a counterplay side by side with the main action. The aristocratic Beaumont is of course quite unsympathetic to the claims of the citizens, but this lack of sympathy, far from harming the play, purges his work for once of its besetting sentimentality and allows his wit full play.

Fletcher collaborated with other playwrights besides Beaumont, notably with Philip Massinger (1583–1640), whose early years as a dramatist were spent as Fletcher's assistant. Massinger also collaborated with other playwrights. Of the plays that he wrote alone, of which ten survive (though some nineteen surviving plays have been attributed to him), the two comedies *A New Way to Pay Old Debts* (printed 1633) and *The City Madam* (1632) are the liveliest and most successful. The former, whose plot owes something to Middleton's *A Trick to Catch the Old One* (ca. 1605), is the comedy of the overreaching of an overreacher. Sir Giles Overreach, the heartless extortioner whose financial and legal cunning has succeeded in ruining many members of the landed gentry to his own benefit, is himself caught in a trap baited with his own ambition; the preparing and the springing of the trap is presented with considerable life and color, though sometimes by means of devices which could be more fruitfully used in a Dickens novel than in a dramatic work. The characters —Wellborn, the reformed prodigal; Allworth, the good young gentleman; Greedy, the gluttonous and unscrupulous justice of the peace; Order, Amble, Furnace, and Watchall, servants to the good lady Allworth; Marall, Overreach's man who betrays his master in order to curry favor with Wellborn when he thinks Wellborn's fortunes are in the ascendant again, but does not reap the expected reward; Tapwell and Froth, the contemptible alehouse keeper and his wife—these are in the tradition of the Jonsonian comedy of humors, with hints from Fletcher. But if Massinger's comedy is Jonsonian, the differences between his comedies and Jonson's are significant. *Volpone,* the play of Jonson's which we are reminded of most in reading *A New Way,* has more than the simple moral feeling (selfishness and cruelty bring their inevitable punishment) or the crude class feeling (impoverished noblemen are still noblemen, naturally superior to rich merchants, and the attempt by upstarts to enter the ranks of the gentry is to be ridiculed and condemned) that we find in Massinger. The moral passion in Jonson is both deeper and subtler than Massinger's, and it is conveyed by the movement and imagery of the actual verse spoken by his villains, so that the moral order which is implicitly set against Volpone's code is suggested to the reader by the very language Volpone uses in professing his villainies. When Massinger tries to achieve this sort of effect, he produces simply the villain who declares his own villainy in naïve melodramatic terms; he seems to have had no notion of the possibility of building up an implicit moral order through imagery. Further, the undoing of villains in Massinger is achieved by mechanical contrivance; we do not feel that the splendid villainy of Sir Giles Overreach—and it is a splendid villainy as Massinger portrays it—is effectively challenged and destroyed by what happens to him, as we do with Volpone; he is undone because his opponents, who happen to be on the side of virtue, are even more ingenious than he is. One gets, of course, a certain warm satisfaction out of this kind of play, but it is a satisfaction of a fairly simple kind. Massinger's blank verse, though it lacks the Jonsonian overtones, has an adroit flexibility, a craftsmanlike welding of conversational rhythms with more formal elements, that pleases the ear.

Massinger's class feeling comes out strongly in *The City Madam* (1632), where the monstrous social pretensions of Lady Frugal (wife of Sir John Frugal, a London merchant) are mocked and suitably punished. Here again the moral pattern is simple, and villainy (which includes social pretension) is exposed and reformed by mere ingenious contrivance. The chief villain, Luke Frugal, brother of Sir John and left by him in charge of his family and fortune while Sir John is supposed to be away, has not quite the consistency or the dramatic probability of Sir Giles Overreach, though there is a similar power shown in his portrayal. If the moral feeling in Massinger is coarser than in Jonson, it is at least real in its simple way, as it is not in many of his contemporaries or in his successors in Restoration drama; and if Massinger's social attitude reflects that of the audiences of the private theaters, a crude hostility to bourgeois pretension on the part of the nobility, it still has some trace of the Elizabethan conception of hierarchy and order, however vulgarized, which is not to be found in Restoration comedy, where aristocracy is a matter of sophistication of speech and manners only.

Massinger's tragedies have been much admired, but T. S. Eliot's description of them as "dreary" is true of most of them. He could construct a good plot, he could manipulate blank verse with dexterity, he could rise to occasional heights of real eloquence. *The Roman Actor* (1626), which has some suggestions of Jonson's *Sejanus*, contains some scenes of power and originality; *The Duke of Milan* (printed 1623) has an ingeniously wrought action; *The Maid of Honour* (ca. 1621) is a romantic study of female virtue in a context of conflicting honor and passion which suggests Fletcher; and some of the tragedies of which he is joint author—*The Fatal Dowry* (printed 1632) with Nathan Field, *The Virgin Martyr* (1620) with Dekker—show both power and ingenuity. But the tragic vision in

Massinger, as in so many Jacobean playwrights, is eclectic and even dissipated; his world of comedy is both more credible and more coherent.

John Ford (1586–ca. 1639), after learning his trade as a dramatist in collaboration with Thomas Dekker and William Rowley, developed an interest in the psychology of frustrated and of illicit love, which produced a number of plays written between 1627 and 1633, of which the most interesting are *The Broken Heart* (ca. 1629) and *'Tis Pity She's a Whore* (ca. 1624). His almost clinical curiosity about the aberrations of the love passion is combined with that taste for the melodramatic incident and the extravagantly contrived tableau which is characteristic of so much Jacobean drama. His blank verse has a strong, somber quality, and is at its best when used to project a mood of distraught melancholy. *The Broken Heart* combines, in a crowded plot, a strange variety of themes involving love, revenge, despair, and regret. It is perhaps a sign of decadence in drama that the dramatist is unable to construct an impressive tragedy out of such essentially simple situations as those which lie at the heart of *Othello* and *Macbeth;* neither Ford nor any of his contemporary Jacobean dramatists were able to reach the profounder areas of tragic meaning through the symbolic overtones of their poetic language and the brilliant balance and manipulation of incident and character. The distractions of frustrated or immoral passion, with the extravagant speech and action to which they lead, provide both the line of the plot and the scope of the tragedy: language merely presents the action in appropriately doomed accents. In *The Broken Heart* the center of interest, and of the reader's or spectator's sympathy, keeps shifting disturbingly. Orgilus is in love with Penthea, whose brother Ithocles has forcibly married her to Bassanes, a jealous nobleman. Thus at the beginning of the play Orgilus is the wronged hero, Penthea the unfortunate heroine condemned to a loveless marriage, and Bassanes an incongruously comic figure who tortures himself and his wife with groundless jealousy. Orgilus, supposed to be out of the country, finds a way of visiting Penthea in disguise and pleads that their earlier betrothal constitutes a true marriage which would justify their secret love-making. Penthea, though returning Orgilus' love, and torn between love and wifely duty, repudiates his reasoning, but at the eventual cost of her own reason: she ends by starving herself to death. Meanwhile Ithocles has fallen in love with the Princess Calantha, the King's daughter (the scene is set in Sparta), and, tutored by his own passion, repents his earlier treatment of his sister. The spotlight shifts to him, and he becomes for the time being a sympathetic figure. Calantha looks with favor on him, and it looks for a while as though she and Ithocles at least face a happy ending. But Orgilus is still out for revenge against Ithocles, and murders him in the same scene which shows the death of Penthea. Soon afterward, the King dies. The Princess Calantha is dancing at the wedding celebrations of Euphranea (Orgilus' sister) and Prophilus when one by one messengers arrive to whisper to her the news of, first, the death of her father, secondly, the death of Penthea, and finally, the murder of Ithocles. She continues dancing with apparent gaiety—a scene which drew extravagant admiration from Charles Lamb but which is too artificially contrived to be wholly convincing dramatically—and then, her father's death having made her Queen, solemnly meets out justice. In the final scene she dies of a broken heart while kissing the cold lips of Ithocles, and the dirge which she has previously prepared for the occasion is sung as she expires. Thus the play, which starts out by concentrating on Orgilus and Penthea, shifts its main interest in turn to Ithocles and to Calantha. While there are some impressive pictures of a divided mind—notably in the speech of Penthea repudiating Orgilus' suggestion—and the whole play goes to a strangely effective melancholy music, the isolation and extravagance of the set pieces ("Sirs, the song!" cries the Prince of Argos, a rejected lover of the Princess, when she announces that she is dying) make the whole play a curiously artificial production.

'Tis Pity She's a Whore is more straightforward in its main action, though it is cumbered with some dubious comic scenes and an unnecessary number of minor machinations leading to death by violence. Its chief concern is with the incestuous love of a brother and sister. The physical passion of Giovanni for his sister Annabella is presented with an almost gloating precision. The play opens abruptly with Giovanni's unavailing attempt to persuade a friar of the lawfulness of such love, and moves on to a remarkable scene in which, after some preliminary fencing, brother and sister declare their mutual passion and surrender to it with triumphant abandon. Annabella's subsequent pregnancy makes it necessary for her to marry one of her many suitors, a nobleman called Soranzo, whose servant Vasques, acting with an inadequately motivated zeal, ferrets out the truth about the incest and plans on his master's behalf an appropriate revenge on both brother and sister. The revenge, as so often in this kind of drama, takes place at a party. Annabella, repentant, receives her brother in her room before the festivities begin and puts aside his renewed declarations of physical passion with talk of repentance and grace. He stabs her, to prevent her further defilement by her hus-

band and in the end is killed himself by Vasques' hired assassins. The atmosphere of Italian violence in which the play moves is only loosely related to the main action in which the fact of incest is presented with that curious mixture of romantic fatalism and clinical exploration which is characteristic of Ford. The moral pattern of the play is obscure. Annabella dies repentant, but from the beginning she has been the weaker character; Giovanni dies exulting in his passion, proud of having put his sister out of Soranzo's reach, and confident of seeing her again in another world. Critics have debated whether Ford is a deliberate immoralist or merely the disinterested psychological inquirer. Perhaps the simplest explanation of the theme and atmosphere of the play is that, at this late stage in the movement of Elizabethan and Jacobean drama, the theme of normal love between the sexes had been so thoroughly explored that the only way to contrive a tragedy with a new interest was to concentrate on incest. Drama, it might be said, becomes decadent when it is content to exploit the moment without any probing of cause or consequence, or when it seeks eccentric causes for common emotions, or when it uses human emotion for the simple purpose of making our flesh creep. These three categories are all found in Jacobean drama; Ford's best plays seem to come in some degree into the second.

James Shirley (1596–1666) was in full career as a dramatist when the closing of the theaters by the Puritans in 1642 put an end for the time being to the publicly acted drama in England. He was a competent professional, and wrote tragedies of Italianate intrigue and villainy or of dark passion, tragicomedies in the Fletcher tradition, and comedies of manners which in some degree point forward to the comedy of the Restoration. His best tragedy is probably *The Cardinal* (1641), a lively mixture of ambition, passion, love, and murder, reminiscent sometimes of *The Duchess of Malfi,* but never quite attaining Webster's brilliant fixing of the tragic moment. Fluent, versatile, always competent but rarely brilliant, Shirley suggests the relaxed professional rather than the original genius. His tragic world is made up of the orts and fragments of Elizabethan and Jacobean tragedy; his world of comedy (as his most popular comedy, *The Lady of Pleasure,* reveals) is moving rapidly away from the Jonsonian order toward the witty surface and unanchored sophistication of the Restoration, though it never quite gets there.

Richard Brome (d.ca. 1652) is another dramatist who manipulated Jonsonian themes. The minor dramatists of the reign of Charles I played further variations on what were by now familiar subjects.

Such new notes as were now sounded emphasized the retreat of the drama from contemporary popular life, the victory of the private over the public theater, which the closing of the theaters throughout the Commonwealth period further emphasized. The cavalier lyrist Sir John Suckling (1609–42), the clever and short-lived Thomas Randolph (1605–35), and William Cartwright (b. 1611) are among those whose plays reflect new courtly influences from France and Spain. Sir William Davenant (1606–68) experimented pallidly with new techniques for the stylization of passion and was among those who reflected a new court interest in the theories of Platonic love. This Caroline version of Platonism combined with the Fletcherian interest in honor produced the recipe which was to be important in the heroic play of the Restoration. French romances—those of d'Urfé and Mademoiselle de Scudéry—also played their part here. The modulation of the heroic world of Sir Philip Sidney into the world of Caroline gallantry shows a moral decay suggestive of the decline of a whole phase of civilization. The themes and attitudes that were to emerge in the Restoration theater were being prepared behind the scenes under the Commonwealth.

Whether a literary form, such as the poetic drama or the prose novel, has an inevitable cycle comparable to that of a human being is arguable: a great deal depends on the whole texture of the civilization within which the form flourishes. It is tempting to suppose that English poetic drama passed through a natural process of development, maturity, and decline, between, say, Marlowe and Shirley. That it passed through such a process can hardly be denied (though we must remember that in talking in such terms about literature we are talking metaphorically, not literally), but it can be doubted whether the process can usefully be considered "natural." The relation between the public and the private theater, the conditions of employment for actors and playwrights, the relation between art and entertainment, the varying atmosphere of the Court, shifts in the state of the national consciousness, the special qualities of individual genius—these and other factors in the contemporary situation had their different kinds of influence on the course of English drama during the Elizabethan, Jacobean, and Caroline periods. One fact is as clear as it is in the last analysis incapable of full explanation: English poetic drama during these years reached heights it never attained before or since. The literary historian, having discussed the drama of this age, will never again have to devote so much attention to drama (either in prose or poetry). In the Restoration drama the heroic world of the Elizabethans appears quite separated from its deep moral base, and the result is a literature that is witty or rhetorical but never truly great. And in that final fling of the Cavaliers, the last, distorted echoes of an aristocratic sensibility are heard. After that, it is to the middle classes, and their characteristic literary creation the prose novel, that the literary historian turns if he wants to follow the record of the English moral imagination as it worked through narrative art.

CHAPTER ELEVEN

Poetry after Spenser: the Jonsonian and the Metaphysical Traditions

In Spenser, as we have seen, the patriotic impulse which affected the Elizabethan imagination in so many different ways was only one of many strands which he wove together in his great poetic synthesis. Other Elizabethan poets exhibit this impulse, and the interest in English history which so often accompanied it, singly and more naïvely. William Warner (ca. 1558–1609) produced in his *Albion's England* a versified history of England in monotonous "fourteeners," a work which enjoyed great popularity in its day, and which was enlarged in subsequent editions from the four books of the original edition of 1586 to six books in 1589, nine in 1592, and sixteen in 1606, when the story was carried down to the reign of James I. It is a sobering thought that the Elizabethans, in the richest period of their great poetic flowering, were still enthusiastic over verse like this:

Which her foredooms seemed to effect in her that her succeeded,
In Queen Anne Bullen, who, for she in Lutherism proceeded,
Was hated of the Papists and envied because preferred,
And through the King's too light belief (for kings have sometimes erred)
She lost her head, and might have said, some thought, ere she did die,
That for the pleasure of a prince go many things awry.
So died the gracious mother of our now most glorious Queen,
Whose zeal in reverent Foxe his works authentical is seen.
The King's four other queens (for why he died a sexamus)
Shall pass, though Jane did bear a son to him, a king to us,
Edward the sixth, and of the same we shall deliver thus.

This is in the didactic tradition of Lydgate's *Fall of Princes* and of the *Mirror for Magistrates,* as well as of Elizabethan patriotic historical verse; the combination was rarely fortunate. Samuel Daniel (1562–1619), whom we have already noticed as a sonneteer and who was also a versatile lyrist who could produce both artfully phrased and happily cadenced short poems and longer poems of compliment and reflection in a style which Coleridge called "the natural ground of prose and verse," was seduced by the historical-didactic muse with not altogether happy results. His *The Complaint of Rosamond* (1592), a poem of almost a thousand lines in rhyme royal, is one of those gloomy pseudo-autobiographical pieces whose popularity in the sixteenth century remains a mystery: its opening lines set the tone:

> Out from the horror of infernal deeps
> My poor afflicted ghost comes here to plain it, . . .

His *Civil Wars,* of which the first four books appeared in 1595 and which was enlarged in subsequent editions but never completed, makes some attempt to present epically the same phase of English history on which Shakespeare concentrated in his history plays, and from a similar point of view. The eight-line stanzas (*ottava rima*) in which the story is carried forward move with a certain sturdiness and occasionally with eloquence; Daniel does achieve intermittently a sense of scope and design, as well as a style capable of rising to an occasion without obvious strain; but the attempt to create an epic out of relatively recent history is probably misguided: he finds it impossible to subdue his material to an epic shape.

Michael Drayton (1563–1631), a versatile poet whose sonnets we have noted and who in the course of his long poetic career tried his hand at most of the Elizabethan modes (including drama, but nearly all his plays are lost), succumbed to the didactic-historical temptation with his *Mortimeriados* of 1596, which became after much alteration the *Barons' Wars* of 1603. This account in *ottava rima* of "the lamentable civil wars of Edward the Second and the Barons" is dull and episodic, in spite of its occasional moments of passionate dialogue. Of Drayton's other historical poetry, the most interesting is that contained in *England's Heroical Epistles* (1597), modeled on the *Heroides* of Ovid: these are written in flexible heroic couplets, in a style which blends a variety of Elizabethan poetic idioms with something learned from Ovid himself, and the result often has both grace and power. But Drayton's concern with his native country found its most elaborate expression in his vast and elaborate geographical poem, *Polyolbion* (1612, 1622), "a Chorographical Description of Tracts, Rivers, Mountains, Forests, and other Parts of this Renowned Isle of Great Britain, with Intermixture of the most Remarkable Stories, Antiquities, Wonders, Rarities, Pleasures, and Commodities of the same." Descriptive, topographical, anecdotal, celebratory, this panoramic work in twelve-syllable couplets is a storehouse of lovingly recorded information about the regions of England and their legends. If it cannot be read through with pleasure today it can at least be profitably looked into as a remarkable manifestation of that special kind of interest in England bred by Elizabethan patriotic feeling (and Drayton remained Elizabethan in feeling and attitude even when writing under the Stuarts). Spenser had a similar interest, and subsumed it in the larger synthesis of the *Faerie Queene;* Drayton, like so many of Spenser's contemporaries and successors, found no adequate poetic form through which to express at length his patriotic topographical excitement. In the early seventeenth century the threads which Spenser had woven together —pastoral, patriotic, didactic, allegorical—come apart, and are found separately in those poets who came under his influence.

Of Drayton's other work, mention might be made of his early pastorals, contained in *Idea: The Shepherd's Garland,* 1593, whose eighth eclogue is an interesting pseudo-Chaucerian pastoral ballad; his two vigorous patriotic odes, "To the Virginian voyage" and "To the Cambro-Britons and their harp, his Ballad of Agincourt"; the rather coyly self-conscious fairy piece *Nymphidia; The Shepherd's Sirena,* a deftly modulated pastoral narrative in alternately rhyming iambic lines of seven syllables with an inset shepherds' song that has a delicately chiming stanza and chorus, in the purest Elizabethan tradition (though it appeared first in 1627); and *The Muses' Elizium,* his last work, published in 1630, in which, belatedly, the Elizabethan pastoral imagination finds one of its purest and happiest expressions.

The didactic muse of the Elizabethans was not, of course, always associated with patriotic or historical themes. The age produced a considerable variety of educational and philosophical verse, some of which, like Daniel's *Musophilus* (1599), a dialogue between a lover of the Muses and his worldly opponent, Philocosmus, has the grave eloquence appropriate to the poetry of intellectual discussion, while much is crudely versified instruction of no poetic value. The same year in which Daniel brought out his *Musophilus* saw the publication of another unusually interesting didactic poem, the *Nosce Teipsum* of Sir John Davies (1569–1626). This long poem in quatrains discusses the vanity of human knowledge and the importance of cultivating the individual soul: the verse moves with considerable ease, and gives both dignity and elegance to the theme, but it remains verse rather than poetry. Davies' earlier poem, *Orchestra* (1596), "a poem of dancing" in rhyme royal, presents the dance as the principle of order and pattern in the universe. A certain mild dramatic force is given to the poem by making it an argument between Antinous, chief of Penelope's suitors in Ulysses' absence, and Penelope: Antinous tries to persuade her to dance on the grounds that dancing is the basis of the cosmic order. The poem is interesting for its picture of the Elizabethan view of universal order (which can be related on the one hand to the concept of subordination and "degree" summarized in Ulysses' famous speech on that subject in Shakespeare's *Troilus and Cressida* and on the other to Milton's view of the divine harmony and the music of the spheres, as well as to other neo-Platonic notions of life as dance, that of W. B. Yeats, for example); the stanzas are modulated with considerable skill, and the poem moves with grace and liveliness. It is one of the most successful philosophical poems in English. Davies belongs, with Fulke Greville and George Chapman, to that small group of interesting Elizabethan minds who found original and often effective ways of giving poetic expression to their philosophical reflections.

The Elizabethan didactic impulse also found expression in satire. Horace and Juvenal were the chief models, the former suggesting a line of wit that was to run on to Dryden and Pope, the latter suggesting a more violent satire of direct abuse. The notion prevailed among the majority of Elizabethan satirists that satire should be rough, obscure, and violent: they wrongly derived the term from "satyr." Thomas Lodge's *A Fig for Momus* (1595) contains relatively mild satires, more Horatian than Juvenalian in tone, expressed with considerable neatness. John Donne's satires, written in the 1590's, are violent and vivid, often deliberately rough in their handling of iambic couplets and indiscriminating in their attribution of vices to the victims. Joseph Hall's *Virgidemiarum* (1597) moves between Donne's violence and the milder Horatian manner of Lodge; his themes are for the most part not the major vices but literary fashions of the day and petty meannesses and stupidities, although he professes to be anxious to "check the misordered world and lawless times." He, too, uses the rhymed iambic couplet, which now comes to be regarded as the appropriate verse form for satire. John Marston's *Scourge of Villainy*, also published in 1597, is satire of the rough kind; its almost melodramatic violence, exhibitionist striking of attitudes, and mock-heroic exaggeration gives Marston's satiric verse a flavor all its own, but it is too fitful to arouse sustained interest. Sir John Harington's *Metamorphosis of Ajax*, published in 1596, stands somewhat apart from these other Elizabethan satires. The tone of his work is clever undergraduate mock-heroic rather than satirical. Harington was also an accomplished writer of epigram, a form much cultivated by the Elizabethans. It was under the influence of the Latin epigrammatist Martial that English epigram in the Elizabethan age really grew up: Harington and Sir John Davies were two of its most successful practitioners, and the publication of their epigrams was followed by a spate of collections of epigrams in the first two decades of the seventeenth century. The Elizabethan epigram was generally a miniature satire, and provided exercise in pithy and concise expression of which English verse still stood in need. The most accomplished follower of Martial in English at this period, consummate master of epigram both satirical and commemorative, was Ben Jonson. His satirical epigrams are not obviously above those of Davies and Harington, but his epitaphs and verses of compliment and commemoration are superior to anything else done in the epigrammatic style at that time. His epitaph on the child actor Salomon Pavey is justly famous, as is the poem "On My First Son":

> Farewell, thou child of my right hand, and joy;
> My sin was too much hope of thee, lov'd boy.
> Seven years tho'wert lent to me, and I thee pay,
> Exacted by thy fate, on the just day.
> O, could I lose all father now. For why
> Will man lament the state he should envý,
> To have so soon scap'd world's and flesh's rage,
> And, if no other misery, yet age?
> Rest in soft peace, and, ask'd, say here doth lie
> Ben Jonson his best piece of poetry.
> For whose sake henceforth all his vows be such
> As what he loves may never like too much.

The Elizabethan age is popularly regarded as the great age of the singing lyric, the mellifluous poem which enchants the ear even before it appeals to the mind or the emotions. We have seen how in the earlier part of Queen Elizabeth's reign experiment with lyric measures often yielded mechanical doggerel, and we have noted, too, that many of the most successful Tudor lyrics inherit their cadences and stanza forms from the medieval lyric. But by the last years of the sixteenth century the exercising of the English language in a variety of lyric measures produced a spate of finely controlled, musically sounding lyrics, more than enough to justify the view that the Elizabethan age is the age par excellence of that kind of poetry. These lyrics are found in songbooks, in plays, and in collections of various kinds. One can only pick out a few examples. Thomas

Lodge's "Love in my bosom like a bee," from his prose romance *Rosalind,* 1590; George Peele's "His golden locks time hath to silver turned," from his *Polyhymnia,* 1590; Nicholas Breton's "Pastoral" ("Flora hath been all about") from *The Passionate Shepherd,* 1604; Thomas Nashe's "Adieu, farewell earth's bliss," with its famous third stanza:

> Beauty is but a flower
> Which wrinkles will devour:
> Brightness falls from the air,
> Queens have died young and fair,
> Dust hath closed Helen's eye.
> I am sick, I must die.
> Lord, have mercy on us!

from his comedy, *Summer's Last Will and Testament;* Thomas Dekker's "Art thou poor, yet hast thou golden slumbers, /O sweet content?" from his *Pleasant Comedy of Patient Grissill* (printed 1603), and the well-known "Golden slumbers kiss your eyes" from the same play; "Weep you no more, sad fountains," from John Dowland's *Third and Last book of Songs or Airs,* 1603—these are random selections from a rich mass of material which includes songs with music as well as spoken lyrics and which continues without a break into the middle of the seventeenth century. Nor must we forget the lyrics in the plays of Shakespeare and Ben Jonson and the incidental songs in Sidney's *Arcadia.* Shakespeare was a master of the mature Elizabethan mellifluous style, among many others, and in his narrative poems, as well as in his strange and powerful symbolic poem *The Phoenix and the Turtle,* used it with extraordinary richness. *The Phoenix and the Turtle,* with its short-lined quatrains and its combination of finely tempered verse with mystical overtones, shows Elizabethan "golden" poetry hammered out to a new fineness: this poem in many ways represents the high point of the Elizabethan lyric style. But the control, the serenity, the mastery of tempo and of modulation of tone, remained an achievement of the Elizabethan Age, a power over language which the Elizabethans achieved, which is illustrated in a great variety of ways, from narrative poems to madrigals, in the late sixteenth and early seventeenth centuries.

A lyric poet of the period who deserves more particular mention is Thomas Campion (1567–1619), composer as well as lyrist, whose experiments in combining the arts of poetry and music produced some happy subtleties in the handling of English verse rhythms. Using both classical and popular material, Campion produced a large variety of lyrical verse which, although written to be sung to specific airs, many of which Campion composed himself, conveys in its own movement and cadence sufficient verbal melody to please the ear when read apart from the music. In the address to the reader which prefaces the first *Book of Airs* (published in 1601 and edited by Philip Rosseter, who composed the music and perhaps the words for Part II of the volume), Campion wrote: "What Epigrams are in Poetry, the same are Airs in music, then in their chief perfection when they are short and well seasoned." The music gave Campion a greater freedom, or a greater subtlety, in the handling of meters, and his fine ear enabled him to use this opportunity to the full, as we find in the flexibility of such a stanza as

> Follow thy fair sun, unhappy shadow,
> Though thou be black as night,
> And she made all of light,
> Yet follow thy fair sun, unhappy shadow.

Or this:

> Will you now so timely depart,
>   And not return again?
> Your sight lends such life to my heart
>   That to depart is pain.
> Fear yields no delay,
>   Secureness helpeth pleasure:
> Then, till the time gives safer stay,
>   O farewell, my life's treasure.

Many of his best lyrics are, however, more simply regular, as "When to her lute Corina sings," "Follow your saint, follow with accents sweet" (where there is an occasional interesting variation of the basic metrical scheme), and "When thou must home to shades of underground."

Campion produced several other books of airs, as well as some masques, some technical discussions of music, and a critical tract, *Observations in the Art of English Poesie* (1602) where he attacked rhyme (in spite of the fact that he practiced it so skillfully himself) and argued for a flexible, rhymeless, quantitative English verse. His arguments were answered the following year by Samuel Daniel in *A Defence of Rhyme,* which defends rhyme on the grounds of its universality and antiquity. This ends the Renaissance controversy about rhyme and quantitative meters in England. Campion's arguments are ingenious and strongly urged, and they seem to arise in some measure from his thinking of musical rhythms in connection with verse (as later Gerard Manley Hopkins' arguments for "sprung rhythm" were to suggest a view of verse rhythms more like musical bars than the conventional metrical feet). Only once, however, is he wholly successful in practicing the rhymeless art of English poesy which he recommends in his *Observations:* this is in a poem which he gives in his discussion as one example of a classical verse form in English. The handling of vowel music and the cunning modulation of the flow of the verse in this poem more than make up for the lack of rhyme:

> Rose-cheeked Laura, come.
> Sing thou smoothly with thy beauty's
> Silent music, either other
> Sweetly gracing.
>
> Lovely forms do flow
> From concent divinely framéd;
> Heav'n is music, and thy beauty's
> Birth is heavenly.
>
> These dull notes we sing
> Discords need for helps to grace them;
> Only beauty purely loving
> Knows no discord,
>
> But still moves delight,
> Like clear spring renewed by flowing,
> Ever perfect, ever in them-
> Selves eternal.

The Elizabethan age in poetry flowed naturally into the Jacobean, and 1603, the year in which King James VI of Scotland became also King James I of England, is not a significant date in literary history. Yet there were important changes which followed James's accession. Some historians have contrasted the disillusioned years of his reign with the spacious days of great Elizabeth; the contrast could equally be made between the atmosphere of the latter years of Elizabeth's reign and that of its heyday. But changes in the atmosphere of the Court and in Court patronage were significant in an age when the arts still looked to the Court and where poets hoped for appointments that depended on the royal favor. Even so, to the literary historian the death of Spenser in 1599 is a more important date than the death of Elizabeth in 1603. Spenser, the greatest nondramatic poet of his age, drew together most of the important trends in Elizabethan thought to achieve in the *Faerie Queene,* incomplete and perhaps incapable of ever having been completed as it is, one of the most remarkable poetic syntheses in English. The poetic map of England immediately after Spenser is most clearly described in terms of the ways in which the Spenserian tradition was continued and ways of revolting against it. No single poet had the stature to continue the

Spenserian tradition as Spenser had developed it; the various elements, pastoral, allegorical, patriotic, topographical, "faerie," were handled separately, as we have seen. Aspects of the Spenserian tradition are carried on by Drayton; by George Wither (1588–1667), whose pastoral poetry has a certain grace and charm, though his satiric and didactic verse has less interest; by Wither's friend William Browne (ca. 1591–ca. 1643) whose *Britannia's Pastorals* (1613, Book II 1616) show a mixture of romantic idealization of the rustic life and realistic description, a limited and tenuous continuation of one side of Spenser; and by even more minor pastoral poets whose work is found in songbooks and other collections of the early seventeenth century.

The most interesting inheritors of the moral and allegorical side of Spenser are the brothers Giles (1585–1623) and Phineas (1582–1650) Fletcher. Giles Fletcher's *Christ's Victory and Triumph*, published in 1610 (Part I: *Christ's Victory in Heaven;* Part II: *Christ's Victory on Earth;* Part III: *Christ's Triumph Over Death;* Part IV: *Christ's Triumph After Death*), has a baroque vigor that is sometimes startling. The eight-line stanza concludes with an alexandrine which often has a Spenserian ring; there are Spenserian words such as "elamping," "ydraded," "embranded"; and the allegory is often Spenserian, as in the description of Mercy and Repentance in Part I. The verse is well managed and vigorous:

> There is a place beyond that flaming hill,
> From whence the stars their thin appearance shed;
> A place beyond all place, where never ill
> Nor impure thought was ever harbouréd;
> But saintly heroes are for ever said
>   To keep an everlasting sabbath's rest,
>   Still wishing that, of what they're still possessed,
> Enjoying but one joy, —but one of all joys blest.

The pictorial quality is rather different from Spenser's ("A star comes dancing up the orient," "And little angels, holding hands, danced all around"), and there is a fondness for punning which is sometimes more metaphysical than Spenserian ("Or maker of the man, or manner of his making," "Depraved of son should he deprived be"). Sometimes, however, the verse is almost pure Spenser:

> He was the son of blackest Acheron,
> Where many frozen souls do chattering lie,
> And rules the burning waves of Phlegethon,
> Where many more in flaming sulphur fry,
> At once compelled to live and forced to die; . . .

Or this:

> Like as a ship, in which no balance lies,
> Without a pilot, on the sleeping waves,
> Fairly along with wind and water flies,
> And painted masts with silken sails embraves,
> That Neptune's self the bagging vessel saves,
>   To laugh awhile at her so proud array;
>   Her waving streamers loosely she lets play,
> And flagging colours shine as bright as smiling day.

Some of the set descriptive pieces (that of Despair in Part II, for example) show considerable virtuosity, and the sensual and erotic picture of the temptation of Christ shows how the Spenserian school always tended to think of temptation in terms of sex. The description of Vain-glory's garden in Part II is reminiscent of Spenser's Bower of Bliss; but in Fletcher the erotic strain is often inadequately assimilated into the texture of the poetry. The straining for effect often results in a sort of incongruity which is common in this kind of poetry:

> Where all are rich, and yet no gold they owe [owe: own]
> They all are kings, and yet no subject know,
> All full, and yet no time on food they do bestow.
> (Part IV)

There are some striking and memorable phases, e.g.,

> Swelter in quiet waves of immortality

which stayed in the memory of Milton, a great admirer of the Fletchers, whose influence is seen in his early work. We cannot help thinking of Milton's "Nativity Ode" when reading this, from Part IV:

> . . . for heaven's smiling brow
> Half insolent for joy began to show:
> The early sun came lively dancing out,
> And the brag lambs ran wantonly about,
> That heaven and earth might seem in triumph both to shout.

Phineas Fletcher is less interesting, and certainly less accomplished as a poet. *The Purple Island* (1633), though it has a conventional pastoral opening, is a tedious allegory of the human body, the island corresponding in all its geographical features to the parts of the body, described in the greatest anatomical detail. The body as a castle fortified against the besieging enemy was a common medieval allegorical theme: here, with its profusion of pseudoscientific detail, it becomes insufferably tedious, allegory petering out in mere classification. *The Piscatorie Eclogues,* which appeared in the same volume, show smoothness of versification and a rather tired conventionality. *The Locusts, or Apollyonists,* published in 1627, is an expanded English version of the original Latin version, *Locustae vel Pietas Jesuitica;* it is a violent anti-Catholic poem, attacking the Jesuits, the Pope, Rome, the Greek Orthodox Church of Russia, and the doctrine of purgatory and other Catholic beliefs and practices. Book V describes the Gunpowder Plot (seen as planned in Rome, with Devils and Cardinals plotting together), and the poem concludes with praise to God for His delivery of England from Catholics and Devils. The poem contains some allegorizing in the Sackville tradition and some of its descriptions may have given hints to Milton; but for the most part its spluttering violence is unimpressive. *Sicelides, a Piscatory,* "as it hath been acted in King's College, in Cambridge," is worth mentioning chiefly as an oddity. A play written mostly in couplets, with a Sicilian setting, including among its characters Cyclops as well as two humorous "foolish" fishers to provide supposedly comic relief, with a plot in which love, female guile, supposed death, and disguise all play their parts, *Sicelides* serves to show that in a "piscatory" anything can happen.

A didactic poet of a rather different kind is John Davies of Hereford (ca. 1565–1618), whose dull verse disquisitions, *Mirum in Modum* (1602), *Microcosmos* (1603), and others show that verse was still considered the appropriate form for moral, religious, and psychological discussion. Davies (who is to be distinguished from the other John Davies discussed on page 348 was a determined writer of every kind of nondramatic poetry known to his age. Some of his epigrams have a certain coarse vigor.

Before we leave this group of didactic and religious poets, something must be said about Joseph Sylvester's (1563–1618) translation of *La Semaine, ou Création du Monde* by the French Protestant poet Guillaume de Salluste du Bartas (1544–90). This translation, entitled *Divine Weeks and Works,* appeared in 1605, and introduced an almost metaphysical violence of imagery, a deliberately incongruous use of simile and metaphor (the line "and periwig with wool the bald-pate woods" is still quoted), which helps to explain the quality of much of the imagery used in religious poetry immediately afterward. Its religious content appealed to a large section of the public of the time, who were interested more in its edifying subject matter than in its unwieldy form or baroque style, but the style inevitably had its influence. "Sylvester's Du Bartas" became the Protestant poem par excellence of its time. The young Milton read it with eagerness, and it left its traces throughout his work.

The religious poetry of Francis Quarles (1592–1644) was equally popular in the next generation. His *Emblems* (1635) popularized in England a species of writing which already had a long history in Europe. The emblem is a symbolic picture with a text and a verse exposition. It naturally tends toward an epigrammatic style: Quarles's favorite form was to cite the scriptural text, elaborate it in a fairly discursive moral or descriptive poem, add a couple of texts from one of the Church Fathers, and conclude with a four-line moral epigram. The result is poetry which is ingenious rather than inspired. Quarles has been called "something of an inferior Herbert," and it is true that he has Herbert's simple moral earnestness and a similar kind of ingenuity while lacking both Herbert's deeper devotional feeling and his ability to sublimate ingenuity to a level of poetic expression which combines passion with calmness.

The interesting if unequal work of the Catholic poet Robert Southwell (1561–95) stands rather apart from the other English religious poetry of the period. Some of his lyrics use the old "fourteeners," either broken up or in a single line, and the lilt can be very monotonous; at the same time he can combine a deliberate preciosity of language (partly Italian in inspiration) with an intense religious passion in a way that occasionally suggests Crashaw. His best known lyric, the Christmas poem "The Burning Babe," was admired by Ben Jonson and has been much praised since, and though its lilt is cumbersome and its language not always happy, it does achieve a certain visionary power.

All these poets, except perhaps Southwell, can be associated in some way with the Spenserian tradition, or at least they show what happened to the chief Spenserian themes and forms immediately after Spenser. There were also other—and stronger—elements at work in English poetry of the early seventeenth century. Ben Jonson and John Donne, each in his own way, represented in some degree a revolt against or at least a turning away from the Spenserian tradition, and the result was decisive for the future of English poetry. Jonson, with his sense of decorum, clarity, proportion, and classical form, brought to lyric poetry both a craftsmanship and a tone which owed much to the classical poets of Rome—Catullus, Martial, Horace—and at the same time never seemed far removed from colloquial English and from the tough realism of the common-sense approach. We have already noted the virtues of his lapidary verses and said something of the precise beauty of his best love lyrics. He wrote, in a great variety of measures, poems of compliment to friends and patrons, autobiographical poems about his own circumstances, different kinds of odes which included the first examples of the true

Pindaric form in English, devotional poems, epistles, elegies, "occasional" poems of many kinds, as well as songs and epigrams. Echoes of Greek and Roman poets sound throughout his work with many different notes. Who would guess at first reading that the formal elegance and limpid clarity of the well-known "Drink to me only with thine eyes" results from a cunning concatenation of passages taken from the *Epistolae Eroticae* of the late Greek prose writer Philostratus? In spite of all he learned from the classics, however, there is something highly personal, even idiosyncratic, in the tone of much of his poetry, which indicates how perfectly he was able to subsume his classical inspiration in his own temperament. If the Roman satirists suggested the terms of his outbursts of moral indignation, his moral tone is nevertheless his own, and we cannot mistake the Jonsonian air of

> Not to know vice at all, and keep true state,
> Is virtue, and not Fate.
> Next to that virtue, is to know vice well,
> And her black spite expel.
> Which to effect (since no breast is so sure
> Or safe, but she'll procure
> Some way of entrance) we must plant a guard
> Of thoughts to watch and ward . . .

or of

> It is not growing like a tree
> In bulk, doth make man better be;
> Or standing long an oak, three hundred year,
> To fall a log at last, dry, bald, and sere.
> A lily of a day
> Is fairer far in May,
> Although it fall and die that night;
> It was the plant and flower of light.
> In small proportions we just beauties see,
> And in short measures life may perfect be.

Or of this, from the "Ode to himself":

> And since our dainty age
> Cannot endure reproof,
> Make not thyself a page
> To that strumpet the stage,
> But sing high and aloof,
> Safe from the wolf's black jaw and the dull ass's hoof.

There is a relaxed, personal note in Jonson's longer verse epistles which, however, never threatens his sense of form. And always there is a sense of the essential strength and vigor of the English language; there is a virility about all Jonson's verse, but again it is a virility which often coexists with the utmost delicacy and grace.

This is to use the English poetic language differently from the way Spenser employed it. The high ornamental strain of what might be called the Petrarchan tradition in English poetry came to a climax in *The Faerie Queene,* where it was combined with other strains. But Jonson's view of the diction of *The Faerie Queene* was that "Spenser writ no language," and he deliberately moved away from the Spenserian mode toward one that was both more classical and more personal. That Jonson is the father of the "Cavalier" strain in English poetry which ran through the seventeenth century, and Donne the father of the "metaphysical" strain which ran parallel with it, and that both were different ways of reacting against the Spenserian tradition which could go no further after *The Faerie Queene,* used to be the standard interpretation of the seventeenth-century poetic scene. Like all such generalizations, it has a considerable element of truth without being wholly true. Modern scholarship has established that the Donne tradition has its roots in a tradition of rhetoric and symbolism which goes far back in European literature and is not as distinct from the Petrarchan conventions as used to be thought. Further, while the differences between Jonson and Donne are clear, their respective followers often combined the influence of the two poets, which came together more often and more easily than could be expected of essentially opposed poetic styles. Some of Jonson's more discursive, personal pieces, with their highly individual tone and their strong colloquial movement counterpointing the formal run of the verse, can be—and have been—mistaken for poems of Donne. This is not to say that Jonson and Donne wrote the same kind of poetry, or even that the "Sons of Ben" (as Jonson's followers called themselves) were also squarely in the Donne tradition; but it does mean that the fact that there were common elements in the styles of the two poets (for all their many and obvious differences) made it easier for their followers to combine elements from the style of each. Against the highly stylized artfulness of Spenser, Jonson set classical cogency and symmetry and Donne set a poetry which combined violence of personal passion with intellectual ingenuity and an imagery both starkly realistic and startlingly cunning. Both objected to the mere sweetness of the latter phases of the Petrarchan tradition as well as to the "no language" of Spenser, and for both the personality of the poet rather than the demands of a "poetic" subject and attitude determined, in the last analysis, the choice of tone and image.

In so far as the metaphysical school of poetry (the term was first used for Donne and his followers by Dr. Johnson in his discussion of Cowley in *Lives of the English Poets:* "The metaphysical poets were men of learning, and to show learning was their whole endeavour") has as its aim the introduction of a more strenuous intellectual strain into poetry, one may agree with those scholars who see George Chapman (ca. 1559–1634) as its first member. Chapman's poetry brings to the treatment of love and other themes a stern philosophical note, both Stoic and Christian, and his verse can be intellectually strenuous and sometimes obscure. *Ovid's Banquet of Sense* (1595) includes that most un-Petrarchan sonnet sequence, "A Coronet for his Mistress Philosophy," and *The Shadow of Night,* published the previous year, contains some deliberately murky writing. But the distinguishing quality of metaphysical poetry as practiced by Donne and his successors is not simply philosophical subtlety or intellectual rigor (qualities often found in the moral and didactic poetry discussed earlier in this chapter) but a peculiar blend of thought and passion, of the colloquial with the ingenious, of realistic violence and meditative refinement. If philosophy is found in Chapman and others, ingenuity is found in abundance in the Petrarchan "conceits" of conventional Elizabethan love poetry, and those who consider ingenuity of metaphor peculiar to metaphysical poetry do not seem to realize that they will find precisely this quality in almost any Elizabethan sonnet-sequence. Further, one must make distinctions among the metaphysical poets themselves, who are less like each other than has often been supposed. Donne stands apart, both chronologically and temperamentally, from the other poets to whom the term "metaphysical" is generally applied.

John Donne (1572–1631) was born and brought up a Roman Catholic, and though he later argued himself into the Anglican position and ended his life as Dean of St. Paul's, his training as a Catholic in an age of religious polemic, together with the scholastic element that was still part of the university education of his day, helped to determine the set of his mind. In his youth he combined the gaiety and sophistication of a city spark with omnivorous reading, which helps to account for the tone of curious wit in much of his early poetry. This poetry, which was not published during his lifetime but was known to a select circle through circulation in manuscript, consists of five satires, twenty "elegies" (if they are all Donne's), and the *Songs and Sonets.* The satires, written in deliberately rough couplets, have a colloquial vigor combined with a strain of ingenious ratiocination:

Judges are Gods; he who made and said them so
Meant not that men should be forc'd to them to go
By means of Angels; when supplications
We send to God, to Dominations,
Powers, Cherubims, and all heaven's Courts, if we
Should pay fees as here, daily bread would be
Scarce to kings; so 'tis. Would it not anger
A Stoic, a coward, yea a Martyr
To see a Pursuivant come in, and call
All his clothes, copes; books, primers; and all
His plats, challices; and mistake them away,
And ask a fee for coming?

They give us some vivid glimpses of the London of the period, as well as of Donne's self-arguments about religion:

On a huge hill
Cragged and steep, Truth stands, and he that will
Reach her, about must and about must go,
And what the hill's suddenness resists, win so;
Yet strive so, that before age, death's twilight,
Thy Soul rest, for none can work in that night.

The elegies are poems about love, written also in iambic pentameter couplets, dealing with the theme in a great variety of ways. Some are cynical, dealing with the paradoxes and fatuities of lust at work. Some celebrate a clandestine love with an uncomfortable realism. One, "The Autumnal," is a poem of grave compliment to an older woman apparently of high rank, opening with the well-known lines

No Spring nor Summer beauty hath such grace
As I have seen in one Autumnal face.

Some are simply exercises in wit. One, the seventeenth, celebrates variety in love. The nineteenth is a clever and lively piece of provocative bawdry, a description of his going to bed with his mistress. But the twelfth and sixteenth are strangely powerful love poems, addressed presumably to his wife (whom he secretly and imprudently married in 1601, at great cost to his career) when he had to leave her to go on a mission abroad. The passionate movement of the sixteenth, the variations in tempo corresponding to the rise and fall of the emotion, show clearly that Donne is here transmuting the naked experience directly into poetry in a way quite foreign to the Petrarchan tradition:

By our first strange and fatal interview,
By all desires which thereof did ensue,
By our long starving hopes, by that remorse

Which my words' masculine persuasive force
Begot in thee, and by the memory
Of hurts, which spies and rivals threaten'd me,
I calmly beg: but by thy father's wrath,
By all pains which want and divorcement hath,
I conjure thee, and all the oaths which I
And thou have sworn to seal joint constancy
Here I unswear, and overswear them thus,
Thou shalt not love by ways so dangerous.
Temper, O fair Love, love's impetuous rage:
Be my true mistress still, not my feign'd page. . . .

He is dissuading his wife from her rash plan to follow him abroad disguised as his page. After this initial passionate appeal, he lists the dangers with damning urgency:

Men of France, changeable camelions,
Spittles of diseases, shops of fashions,
Love's fuellers, and the rightest company
Of players, which upon the world's stage be,
Will quickly know thee, and no less, alas!
Th' indifferent Italian, as we pass
His warm land, well content to think thee page,
Will hunt thee with such lust and hideous rage
As Lot's fair guests were vexed.

The conclusion is equally powerful, but in a different way:

When I am gone, dream me some happiness,
Nor let thy looks our long-hid love confess,
Nor praise nor dispraise me, nor bless nor curse
Openly love's force, nor in bed fright thy nurse
With midnight's startings, crying out, "Oh, oh,
Nurse, O my love is slain, I saw him go
O'er the white Alps alone; I saw him I,
Assail'd, fight, taken, stabb'd, bleed, fall, and die."
Augur me better chance, except dread Jove
Think it enough for me to'have had thy love.

The *Songs and Sonets* are, however, by far the most interesting poems. They are love poems, written at different times in different moods, and addressed to different persons. Some show the same cynical strain that is found in many of the Elegies, expressed often with ingenious violence and metrical cunning:

Go and catch a falling star,
  Get with child a mandrake root,
Tell me where all past years are,

Or who cleft the Devil's foot;
Teach me to hear Mermaids singing,
Or to keep off envy's stinging,
And find
What wind
Serves to advance an honest mind.

If thou beest born to strange sights,
Things invisible to see,
Ride ten thousand days and nights
Till age snow white hairs on thee;
Thou, when thou return'st, wilt tell me
All strange wonders that befell thee,
And swear
Nowhere
Lives a woman true, and fair.

The conclusion has a characteristic turn:

Tho' she were true when you met her,
And last till you write your letter,
Yet she
Will be
False, ere I come, to two, or three.

The opening of these poems shock the reader into attention, sometimes by a question:

Now thou hast lov'd me one whole day,
Tomorrow, when thou leav'st, what wilt thou say?
Wilt thou then antedate some new made vow?
Or say that now
We are not just those persons which we were?

First the shock, then the ingenious development of the thought: this is Donne's characteristic method.

This method Donne employs equally in those poems among the *Songs and Sonets* which seems to be addressed not to casual mistresses but to someone truly and passionately loved, some perhaps to Anne More, who became his wife. Here indeed is that union of passion and ratiocination which critics have seen as Donne's chief quality. Again there is often the opening question, and then the development of the original thought in terms of ideas derived from scholastic philosophy or from new scientific notions:

I wonder by my troth what thou and I
Did, till we lov'd? Were we not weaned till then,
But suck'd on country pleasures childishly?

Or snorted we in the seven sleepers' den?
'Twas so; but this, all pleasures fancies be.
If ever any beauty I did see
Which I desir'd and got, 'twas but a dream of thee.

And now good morrow to our waking souls,
Which watch not one another out of fear;
For love all love of other sights controls
And makes one little room an everywhere.
Let sea-discoverers to new worlds have gone,
Let maps to other, worlds on worlds have shown:
Let us possess one world—each hath one, and is one. . . .

The opening, both conversational and startling, projects the reader into the poem in a way that is quite new in English poetry; once in the poem, the reader is held by the complex development of the thought which, twisted this way and that, serves to embody rather than to cool the passion. It is true that often these love poems do not quite maintain the magnificence of their opening: we have the feeling that the emotion itself has carved out the stanza form at the beginning and subsequent stanzas have to be shaped with more deliberation to the form so carved out. But on the whole it is surprising how often the ingenuity echoes in its own way the tremulousness of passion. These poems abound in memorable openings:

For Godsake hold your tongue and let me love, . . .

If yet I have not all thy love,
Dear, I shall never have it all.

Twice or thrice had I loved thee
Before I knew thy face or name, . . .

Busy old fool, unruly sun,
Why dost thou thus
Through windows and through curtains call on us—

which last is a thoroughly new rendering of the old *aubade* which goes back to early Provençal poetry.

There are other kinds of love poems in *Songs and Sonets* besides the cynical and the genuinely passionate. Some, like "A Valediction, of weeping" and "Sweetest love I do not go" sound a gentler note of protective tenderness, but again combined with intellectual cunning. Some, such as "Twickenham Garden," show a more conventional strain of exaggerated compliment, picturing the author as the afflicted lover who is hurt almost to death by the cruelty of his beloved; these, Grierson suggested, might have been written as poems of compliment to ladies of high rank. "A Nocturnal upon Saint Lucy's

Day" builds up by every kind of philosophic ingenuity a picture of the poet as reduced to a state of absolute nothingness by the death of the lady who is the subject of the poem:

> Study me then, you who shall lovers be
> At the next world, that is, at the next Spring;
> For I am every dead thing
> In whom love wrought new alchemy.
> For his art did express
> A quintessence even from nothingness,
> From dull privations and lean emptiness.
> He ruin'd me, and I am re-begot
> Of absence, darkness, death; things which are not.

Others again are merely ingenious, sometimes in satiric vein. In all, the *Songs and Sonets* alone are enough to substantiate Donne's claim to be considered an original poetic genius of a high order.

Something of the religious tensions within Donne is indicated by the strange poem, *The Progress of the Soul*, in fifty-two ten-line stanzas, in which his original intention appears to have been to trace the progress of the soul of the apple which Eve pulled (i.e., the soul of heresy) from its original appearance in Eden through all the great heretics of history, ending with Queen Elizabeth. He had almost certainly abandoned Roman Catholicism for the Church of England by the time he wrote this, but it shows clear Catholic sympathies. The original plan was modified, and the poem as we have it (not published in Donne's lifetime) carries the soul only as far as Adam's daughter Themech, "sister and wife to Cain, that first did plow." This leads to a reflection on the paradox that human progress often springs from the works of bad men, with the conclusion that moral values are relative.

> Who ere thou beest that read'st this sullen writ,
> Which just so much courts thee as thou dost it,
> Let me arrest thy thoughts: wonder with me
> Why plowing, building, ruling and the rest
> Or most of those arts whence our lives are blest
> By cursed Cain's race invented be,
> And blest Seth vext us with Astronomy.
> There's nothing simply good nor ill alone;
> Of every quality comparison
> The only measure is, and judge, opinion.

The poem is a "sullen writ" indeed, satirical, extravagant, pessimistic, its tone determined perhaps by the general disillusion with Queen Elizabeth which was abroad during her final years, especially after the execution of the Earl of Essex in February, 1601. The poem is dated August, 1601.

Donne's epigrams, and his letters of compliment to possible patrons (letters made necessary by the jolt to his career caused by his imprudent marriage), are less interesting, though two of his verse *Letters to Several Personages,* "The Storm" and "The Calm," are sharply etched pictures of the effect of these different conditions at sea on the spirits of the men aboard. The two *Anniversaries,* written as funeral elegies on the fifteen-year-old daughter of Sir Robert Drury (a girl whom he had never met) are elaborately worked out poetic arguments about the decline of the world since the death of the girl, and the discomforts of earthly life. The first, entitled "An Anatomy of the World," written and published in 1611, broods with many ingenious illustrations over the world's decay and disorder; the second, entitled "Of the Progress of the Soul" and not to be confused with the earlier poem of the same title, appeared the following year and deals in a similar way with "the incommodities of the soul in this life and her exaltation in the next." It is the latter poem which contains the often quoted metaphysical description of a blush:

> her pure and eloquent blood
> Spoke in her cheeks, and so distinctly wrought
> That one might almost say, her body thought.

The *First Anniversary* has the even better-known lines about the conflict between new thought and old values:

> And new philosophy calls all in doubt,
> The element of fire is quite put out;
> The sun is lost, and th'earth, and no man's wit
> Can well direct him where to look for it.
> And freely men confess that this world's spent,
> When in the planets and the firmament
> They seek so many new; they see that this
> Is crumbled out again to his atomies.
> 'Tis all in pieces, all coherence gone; . . .

Donne's *Divine Poems,* most though not all of which were written in the last phase of his life, when the witty and worldly "Jack Donne" of Lincoln's Inn had given way to the grave divine, explore traditional devotional attitudes with a new subtlety as well as a startling directness. In the best of these poems the paradoxes of art reflect with anguished intensity the paradoxes involved in man's relation with God. They were written after his wife's death, when Donne had put the worldly and the sensuous life completely behind him and was probing with fierce anxiety for the right relationship with eternity. Nothing could be further from the community hymn, written to reflect these aspects of religion which are common to a whole society and which therefore can be enunciated in general terms by a congregation in unison, than these strenuous religious poems:

> Batter my heart, three person'd God; for you
> As yet but knock, breathe, shine, and seek to mend. . . .

Even the puns convey the urgency:

> I have a sin of fear that when I have spun
> My last thread, I shall perish on the shore:
> Swear by Thyself that at my death Thy Son
> Shall shine as he shines now, and heretofore;
> And, having done that, Thou hast done:
> I fear no more.

There is still the question as to which is the true Church:

> Show me, dear Christ, thy spouse so bright and clear.

Sometimes, as in the longer poem in couplets, "Good Friday: Riding Westward" (a relatively early religious poem, dated 1613, four years before the death of his wife), the ingenuity of the thought is more striking than the passionate complex of thought and feeling: in this poem the main point is that he is going west, but his thoughts turn east, where Christ was crucified, and he explores the possibilities of this paradox. But even here the conclusion is grave and passionate:

> O think me worth thine anger, punish me,
> Burn off my rusts and my deformity,
> Restore thine image so much by thy grace
> That thou mayst know me, and I'll turn my face.

The nineteen *Holy Sonnets*[1] contain the core of Donne's religious poetry, and most of its finest examples. Here are not only "Batter my heart" but "Death be not proud," "At the round earth's imagin'd corners blow," and "What if this present were the world's last night?" Exactly the same combination of passion and argument as is found in the *Songs and Sonets* can be found in these poems (though perhaps the most obviously metaphysical of all Donne's religious poems is not any of the "Holy Sonnets" but the "Hymn to God my God in my sickness"). The passion here is, however, more complex; it is

[1] Donne's spelling, "sonets" in the title *Songs and Sonets* and "sonnets" in *Holy Sonnets*, has been followed because the "sonets" are not sonnets in the modern sense, whereas the "sonnets" are. The different spellings used by Donne are, however, probably accidental.

that mixture of hope and anguish that characterizes the religious man searching for the right relationship with God, aware both of his own unworthiness and of God's infinite greatness. There are, too, many traditional devices of Christian devotional literature exploited in these poems, though in Donne's own way. Donne's religious style is perhaps less absolutely novel than his secular style: the metaphysical mode thrives on paradox, and there have always been paradoxes at the heart of religious experience.

Donne's influence was felt both by secular and by religious poets. The finest of the religious "metaphysicals" was George Herbert (1593–1633), an Anglican poet who postponed taking up his religious vocation for many years, during which he faced the worldly temptations of both academic and public life, resisting them in the end (after, it must be admitted, his hopes of advancement had been frustrated) to become, during the last three years of his short life, the sweetly pious rector of Bemerton celebrated in Isaac Walton's biography. His collection of religious poems, *The Temple: Sacred Poems and Private Ejaculations*, published in 1633, show him both expressing his own sense of the conflict between the claims of worldly wit and sophistication and those of true Christian devotion, and also exploring, with a combination of colloquial ease and emblematic cunning, the significance of the main symbols and beliefs of Protestant Christianity. (Historically, Herbert's religious appeal has been both to High Anglicans and dissenters; his theology was in fact more Calvinist than was for long realized, but Calvinism had its place in the Church of England before the Civil War exacerbated theological as well as political feeling on both sides, and Herbert was firmly committed to the forms of worship of the established Church of his country.) Whether Herbert's poetry is "metaphysical" in the sense that Donne's is can be debated: recent critical opinion has tended to minimize the common elements in the poetry of those who have traditionally been regarded as the "metaphysical poets" of the seventeenth century. Affinities can be shown between Herbert's style and that of Sidney on the one hand and Wyatt on the other (but it must be remembered that the colloquial passion of Wyatt is often echoed by Donne), and it has also been argued that Herbert's manner of exploring analogies between emblematic objects (such as the human body or parts of the church building and its furniture) and religious truths is less like the individual argument of Donne's poetry than it is related to the use of the "hieroglyph" in Christian art throughout the Renaissance or, indeed, to a much older Christian tradition of exegesis through emblematic and metaphorical interpretation. But we have only to put Herbert's poetry beside

Quarles' to see the difference between a simple emblematic poetry and a poetry which uses the highest resources of art to shock the reader into new kinds of knowledge and of self-realization. There can be little doubt that Herbert learned from Donne (who was a great friend of his mother and whose poems he saw in manuscript) and that his combination of a simple and direct tone with ingenuity of argument and compelling intensity of feeling is "metaphysical" in the Donne sense. On the other hand, Herbert's poetry could never be mistaken for Donne's; its accent is wholly its own; the sensibility at work is quite un-Donnelike; and the combination of religious autobiography with presentation in due order of the great Christian themes, each associated with its proper season of the Christian year, is clearly the work of one who set his pastoral duties to his flock above the exploration of his own relationship with God—and this cannot be said of Donne's religious poetry. Herbert is artful enough in his own way—sometimes more artful than Donne in his—and he frequently uses musical devices and analogies to a greater extent than any other of the metaphysical poets.

In an early sonnet Herbert had asked

> Doth Poetry
> Wear Venus' livery? only serve her turn?
> Why are not sonnets made of thee, and lays
> Upon thy altar burnt? Cannot thy love
> Heighten a spirit to sound out thy praise
> As well as any she?

—where "thee" is of course God. He wished to bring all the resources of poetry into God's service. Yet, as a pastor, his duty was to teach Christian truths simply rather than explore his own religious emotions subtly:

> Who says that fictions only and false hair
> Become a verse? Is there in truth no beauty?
> Is all good structure in a winding stair? . . .
>
> I envy no man's nightingale or spring;
> Nor let them punish me with loss of rhyme
> Who plainly say, *My God, My King*.

If, in spite of this affirmation, Herbert's poetry is not plain in the sense that a community hymn is plain, that is largely because he draws not only on experiences which he considers common to all Christians but also on knowledge (of the Bible, of Anglican worship, of Christian doctrine, of ways of thought and feeling common to his age), and, weaving together the facts of religious experience with emblematically presented items from this knowledge, he produces poetry which arrests attention by its opening statement of its theme and maintains interest and excitement by the unexpected way it uses traditional Christian material in working the theme out. The combination of shock and repose in Herbert's poetry is something difficult to parallel in English literature. There is conflict in the poetry, yet there is calm trust; disturbed speculation yet simple faith; ingenious language—"Love enchanting language, sugar-cane, /Honey of roses . . ."—and the gentle simplicity of a wise and compassionate preacher. How these elements come together could only be demonstrated by careful analysis of individual poems; it must suffice here to refer to some of the poems which best illustrate the combination: "Redemption," "Church-Monuments" (where the sense of dissolution into dust is emblematically marked in the structure of the poem by the dissolving flow of the stanzas, which fall into each other as sand falls down an hourglass), "The Church-Floor," "Virtue," "The Bunch of Grapes," "Love Unknown," and "The Collar."

Herbert explores many ways of rendering in the shape and texture of a poem the theme which is its subject. Not only does he occasionally use "pattern poetry," as in "Easter Wings" where the two stanzas are in the shape of wings, the sense expanding and contracting as the line lengthens and shortens; but he loses no opportunity of reflecting the nature of the subject and the ebb and flow of the emotion in the run of the rhymes, the varying line-lengths, and the shifts in the tempo of the verse. He used a remarkable variety of stanza forms, constantly creating new ones to meet the needs of a new subject. He can work the simplest and commonest objects into his expression of total meaning, for he was filled with the sense of multiple analogies existing (as a result of God's design) between man, nature, and art. In "Denial" the second and fifth lines of each stanza remain unrhymed while the poet is describing his separation from God, but in anticipating his reconciliation the rhyme is "mended":

> . . . Therefore my soul lay out of sight,
> Untun'd, unstrung:
> My feeble spirit, unable to look right,
> Like a nipt blossom, hung
> Discontented.
>
> O cheer and tune my heartless breast,
> Defer no time;
> That so thy favours granting my request,
> They and my mind may chime,
> And mend my rhyme.

In "The Collar" he begins with a characteristic colloquial violence,

> I struck the board, and cried, "No more.
> I will abroad. . . ."

The rebellion against God's beneficent discipline waxes ever more violent, reflected with great precision in the movement of the verse, until the sudden change at the close:

> But as I raved and grew more fierce and wild
> At every word,
> Methought I heard one calling, *Child:*
> And I replied, *My Lord.*

There is no search, as sometimes in Donne, for the true religion; Herbert knows very well which form of Christianity is the right one; the struggle in his poetry is between the world and complete surrender to God, and even then it is often an exemplary struggle rather than a simple autobiographical confession—i.e., it is expressed so as to serve as a guide for all Christians. Perhaps no religious poet in English has so effectively combined the strongly individual with the general and exemplary. The "metaphysical" mode, as well as traditions of Christian devotional literature, helped him to do this, but the art and the sensibility are his own. The gentle charm of his prose work, *A Priest to the Temple: or the Country Parson, his Character and Rule of Holy Life,* reflects only one side of his character—the side which Walton and posterity have preferred to dwell on. His poetry shows a craftsmanship geared so perfectly both to the sensibility at work and to the theme being presented that one is tempted to see in it the perfect blending of art and religion.

Richard Crashaw (1612/13–1649), a Catholic convert who spent the latter part of his life as an exile on the continent, is generally considered with Herbert among the religious metaphysicals, though his poetry displays a sensibility and a technique equally different from Donne and from Herbert. The title of his *Steps to the Temple,* published in 1646, is a clear reference to Herbert's *Temple,* which he admired, but he had none of Herbert's quietly controlled cunning in developing a Christian theme at the same time personally and publicly; his pressing of all the senses into the service of the expression of religious passion, his use of erotic and other images of physical appetite in a deliberately paradoxical religious sense, his relish of extravagant paradox involving the secular and the divine, tears and ecstasy, the sensuous and the spiritual, show not so much the union of passion and thought which is characteristic of Donne as the deliberate search for startling and paradoxical expression which will shock and excite the reader. When Donne shocks, it is by the stark reality of the self which he reveals—his wit reflects an inner tension; and Herbert, for all his ingenuity, subdues his material beneath a quiet surface. Crashaw, with a lushness of religious experience which is typical of one aspect of the Counter Reformation throughout Europe, explores with an almost feverish enthusiasm every way of presenting the spiritual world in sensuous terms. His earliest work was a volume of Latin epigrams, *Epigrammata Sacra,* 1634, which show in pious ingenuities the kind of trick he was to exploit more elaborately in his later poems. The epigrams include the famous one on the water changed into wine, with its final line, *Nympha pudica Deum vidit, et erubuit,* which a contemporary translation (perhaps Crashaw's own) rendered: "The conscious water saw its God and blushed." This is typical of Crashaw's baroque manner, and he could be very much more elaborate than that.

Crashaw's Nativity hymn "sung as by the shepherds" concentrates with a warm passion on the babe in the cradle, and adjectives like "sweet," "balmy," "rosy," "curled," "new-bloomed" are characteristic, as, in another way, are the lines

> The babe whose birth embraves this morn,
> Made his own bed e're he was born.

"Saint Mary Magdalene, or The Weeper" is accompanied in the original volume by an emblem of a bleeding heart with the face of a weeping woman, and the following couplet:

> Lo, where a wounded heart with bleeding eyes conspire,
> Is she a flaming fountain, or a weeping fire?

In the poem he plays about with the idea of Mary Magdalene's tears, which are pearls, dew, medicine, wine, spring showers, among many other things. The imagery is pursued with an almost intoxicated ingenuity:

> O cheeks! beds of chaste loves
> By your own showers seasonably dashed;
> Eyes! nests of milky doves
> In your own wells decently washed;
> O wit of love! that thus could place
> Fountain and garden in one place.

It is this poem too, that has the well-known extravagant lines (describing the Magdalene's eyes):

Two walking baths, two weeping motions,
Portable and compendious oceans.

The "Hymn to the Name and Honour of the Admirable Saint Teresa" shows Crashaw at his most concentrated and intense. The subject obviously kindled a real passion in him, and the strength and power of the octosyllabic couplets in which he presents his contemplation of the child going to voluntary martyrdom are beyond anything else in his poetry. True, the tremulous simplicity of

Farewell house, and farewell home!
She's for the Moors and martyrdom

may sound ludicrous in some ears, though to others it has a moving gravity. It is a matter both of religious doctrine and of sensibility if not simply of "taste." But often the power is recognizable in spite of everything:

Scarce has she blood enough to make
A guilty sword blush for her sake;
Yet has she a heart dares hope to prove
How much less strong is Death than Love.

Crashaw's heavily "conceited" style and his deliberate mingling of sensuous and spiritual imagery reflects a movement that was European in scope and more influential in Italy and Spain than in England. The movement is known as "secentismo" with reference to seventeenth-century Italian literature, and secentismo in Italy is related to Gongorism (from the poet L. de Góngora y Argote) in Spain. The style was popularized in Italy by G. B. Marino's long poem, *L'Adone*, and the imagery of Crashaw's "Weeper" in particular derives from Marino and his followers (hence the term "Marinism" applied to Crashaw). Whether one considers the whole movement a disease or a laudable extension of the scope of figurative language depends perhaps on individual taste and sensibility. Like baroque in art, the style can sometimes "surprise by a fine excess" but it also drops easily into overluxuriance and vulgarity.

Henry Vaughan (1622–95) regarded himself as a disciple of George Herbert. The preface to his collection of religious poems, *Silex Scintillans*, published in 1655, condemns the "willingly-studied and wilfully-published vanities" of "those ingenious persons which in the late notion are termed wits," repudiates his own earlier secular love poetry as of this kind, and attributes the "diversion of this foul overflowing stream" to "the blessed man, Mr. George Herbert, whose holy life gained many pious converts (of whom I am the least)."

Personal misfortune, the civil troubles of the time, and the influence of his mystical brother Thomas, all helped to turn Vaughan to a poetry of religious contemplation which contains many verbal echoes of Herbert; yet, though Vaughan clearly owes so much to Herbert and to the Donne tradition, his most characteristic poems have an individuality of tone that distinguishes them sharply from any other metaphysical poetry. Vaughan is conscious of a veil which separates time from eternity, man from God, and is constantly seeking for ways to penetrate it. The world of Nature and of things is not for him, as for Herbert, a collection of hieroglyphs of the Christian story but rather a world of creatures and objects whose existence, being on a more primitive level than man's, brings them into closer touch with spiritual reality.

> I would I were a stone, or tree,
> Or flower by pedigree,
> Or some poor high-way herb, or spring
> To flow, or bird to sing!
> Then should I (tied to one sure state)
> All day expect my date;
> But I am sadly loose, and stray
> A giddy blast each way;
> O let me not thus range!
> Thou canst not change.

Childhood, too, is closer to God than the adult state, and in such a poem as "The Retreat" Vaughan tries to recapture the innocence of infancy:

> Happy, those early days, when I
> Shin'd in my angel infancy,
> Before I understood this place
> Appointed for my second race,
> Or taught my soul to fancy ought
> But a white, celestial thought, . . .
> When on some gilded cloud or flower
> My gazing soul would dwell an hour,
> And in those weaker glories spy
> Some shadows of eternity. . . .
> O how I long to travel back
> And tread again that ancient track! . . .

The mundane world was relieved by occasional private glimpses of eternity, but it was a sad fate on the whole to be cut off behind the temporal curtain. Vaughan would think of those who had penetrated it—

They are all gone into the world of light,
And I alone sit lingering here;
Their very memory is fair and bright,
And my sad thoughts doth clear—

and wish that he too, while still in this world, could see beyond the veil or else be translated at once into eternity:

Either disperse these mists, which blot and fill
My perspective still as they pass, [perspective:
Or else remove me hence unto that hill telescope.]
Where I shall need no glass.

His attitude to childhood in "The Retreat" has been compared to Wordsworth's in the "Immortality Ode," and his poem "The Waterfall"—which moves from an affectionate address to the loved water to a meditation on its mystical significance—has been considered Wordsworthian in its attitude to Nature; but the similarity is superficial in either case, especially the second. If Wordsworth might have written

Dear stream! dear bank, where often I
Have sat and pleased my pensive eye

so might James Thomson, and neither Thomson nor Wordsworth would have continued thus:

O useful element and clear!
My sacred wash and cleanser here,
My first consigner unto those
Fountains of life, where the Lamb goes!
What sublime truths, and wholesome themes,
Lodge in thy mystical, deep streams! . . .

There was a genuine mystical strain in Vaughan's thought, and sometimes as in "The World," with its arresting opening—

I saw Eternity the other night
Like a great Ring of pure and endless light,
All calm as it was bright—

it is the mystic's matter-of-factness in talking of his strange otherworldly insights that gives his poetry its most impressive quality. Much of Vaughan's poetry is conventionally ingenious in its expression of religious feeling; the minority of striking poems, which include "The Waterfall," "And do they so?," "Man," "The Night," "The Retreat," "The World," and "They are all gone into a world of light," do not always succeed in sustaining throughout the whole composition the note of mystic passion which is sometimes struck so magnificently. Vaughan's technique, one might almost say, was not quite up to his insights. His verse rang out with most power and beauty when his own quietist and mystical vision was at its most intense; when the moment of vision faded and he was left to develop his theme with mere verbal ingenuity, the quality of the poetry at once dropped.

The poetry of Thomas Traherne (ca. 1634–74) and the most interesting of his prose remained unknown until it was discovered in manuscripts at the end of the last century. His prose *Centuries of Meditations* gives the clearest and most impressive view of his quest for innocence and joy, for the incorruptible world with all its glories which can be had for the seeking. Even more than Vaughan, Traherne is dependent on his vision; for him expression is forced by the vision, and he never attains Vaughan's occasional control and calm beauty, still less the formal perfection of Herbert. Traherne's characteristic mood was a joyful primitivism; the child's unschooled appreciation of all about him was the type of the proper attitude, and his best known poem, "Wonder," expresses this:

> How like an angel came I down!
> How bright are all things here!
> When first among his works I did appear,
> Oh, how their glory did me crown!

The idealization of childhood, when, as he put it in his poem "Eden," "A learned and happy ignorance /Divided me /From all the vanity, From all the sloth, care, sorrow, that advance /The madness and the misery /Of men," suggests sometimes Vaughan, sometimes Blake, sometimes Wordsworth; and perhaps all three poets, for all their important differences, were in touch with a common mystical strain in English thought. It is at least significant that James Joyce, in the third episode of *Ulysses,* when Stephen Dedalus is meditating on the mystery of birth, the links between the generations, and the descent of all mankind from the symbolic and mystical first human pair, Adam and Eve, should quote from a description in the third of Traherne's *Centuries of Meditations:*

> The corn was orient and immortal wheat, which never should be reaped, nor was ever sown. I thought it had stood from everlasting to everlasting. The dust and stones of the street were as precious as gold: the gates were at first the end of the world. . . . Boys and girls tumbling in the street, and playing, were moving jewels. I knew not that they were born or should die; but all things abided eternally as they were in their proper places.

These, then, are the principal seventeenth-century religious poets who, in varying degrees, show, or have been thought to show, the influence of Donne. In addition to these "religious metaphysicals" there are also secular poets in the metaphysical tradition. But before we discuss these, let us turn back and consider the parallel tradition, that of the "Sons of Ben." Few if any of those poets who thought of Ben Jonson as their master were not also influenced to some extent by Donne, but in most of them the lyric strain is recognizably Jonsonian.

Robert Herrick (1591–1674) had a sensibility much less masculine than Jonson's, but, like Jonson, he turned to the classical lyric for inspiration and was concerned to achieve elegance and precision of form. His combination of classical paganism with English folk themes gave a special note to his celebrations of country festivities and seasonal customs; by temperament a hedonist, by profession (for much of his life) a country parson, by literary taste both an epigrammatist and a writer of formal lyrics of description, compliment, elegy, and love, Herrick produced his own synthesis of classical, Christian, and English which is like nothing else in seventeenth-century English literature. His *Hesperides,* published in 1648 together with his religious poems, *Noble Numbers,* opens with "The Argument of his Book" which lists the themes with which he is going to treat:

> I sing of brooks, of blossoms, birds, and bowers,
> Of April, May, of June, and July flowers;
> I sing of may-poles, hock-carts, wassails, wakes,
> Of bridegrooms, brides, and of their bridal cakes;
> I write of youth, of love, and have access
> By these to sing of cleanly wantonness; . . .
> I write of groves, of twilight, and I sing
> The court of Mab, and of the Fairy King;
> I write of Hell; I sing, and ever shall,
> Of Heaven, and hope to have it after all.

The Christian theme is something of an afterthought; he hopes to have heaven "after all" and meanwhile cheerfully offers his readers a volume containing over a thousand secular poems mostly hedonist in attitude and pagan in tone, together with a much smaller group of religious poems which show a simple confidence in his own ultimate salvation.

Though on first going to his country vicarage in 1629 (he was ejected by the Puritans in 1647 but returned after the Restoration) he appeared to languish for the city, where he had enjoyed the company of Jonson and other wits in such gatherings as he celebrated in his ode for Ben Jonson—

> Where we such clusters had
> As made us nobly wild, not mad;
> And yet each verse of thine
> Outdid the meat, outdid the frolic wine—

he turned readily to the celebration of rustic content in Horatian mood:

> Here, here I live with what my board
> Can with the smallest cost afford.
> Though ne'er so mean the viands be,
> They well content my Prue and me.
> Or pea, or bean, or wort, or beet,
> Whatever comes, content makes sweet.

The Horatian theme is enriched by strains from Catullus, Tibullus, Ausonius, Anacreon, and other Latin and Greek (but mostly Latin) lyrists. He plays all sorts of variations on the "*carpe diem*" theme:

> Gather ye rosebuds while ye may,
> Old time is still a-flying,
> And this same flower that smiles today,
> Tomorrow will be dying.

He celebrates love, as a delight rather than as a passion, and has numerous short poems of compliment to Julia or some other classically-named mistress in which a degree of metaphysical ingenuity sometimes mingles with the classical grace and formality:

> Whenas in silks my Julia goes,
> Then, then, methinks, how sweetly flows
> The liquefaction of her clothes.

The noun "liquefaction" has both a suggestiveness and precision here, which is almost metaphysical, as has the term "Protestant" in his well known "To Anthea, who may command him anything":

> Bid me to live, and I will live
> Thy Protestant to be, ...

Poems of seasonal celebration sometimes contain also an amatory or complimentary theme, as in "Corinna's Going a-Maying," and sometimes he celebrates the countryside and what it affords in the strains of Marlowe's "Come live with me and be my love":

> Live, live with me, and thou shalt see
> The pleasures I'll prepare for thee:

What sweets the country can afford
Shall bless thy bed and bless thy board.

Most of all he is aware of the rituals that mark the different points in the rustic year:

At shearing-times, and yearly wakes,
When Themilis his pastime makes,
There thou shalt be, and be the wit,
Nay more, the feast, and grace of it.
On holy days when virgins meet
To dance the hays with nimble feet,
Thou shalt come forth, and then appear
The queen of roses for that year.

"The Hock-Cart, or Harvest Home" celebrates the harvest festival in sturdy octosyllabic couplets replete with images drawn from farming activity and country cheer. Some of his poems celebrating or inviting to social feasting are reminiscent, both in movement and imagery, of Jonson's poems in similar vein; often, however, similarities between Jonson and Herrick are noted only to reveal significant differences—as in Jonson's "Still to be neat, still to be dressed," and Herrick's "Delight in Disorder," where there is a cunningly implied sense of wantonness in the details of Herrick's poem which is lacking in the graver statement of Jonson's.

Herrick's success in Romanizing his celebration of English country rituals is a belated Renaissance manifestation in English literature. While sometimes, as in "Oberon's Feast," he deals playfully with pure English folklore, on numerous other occasions he combines the Roman with the English. "A Hymn to the Lares" refers to the wassail bowl and "North-down ale," and conversely his numerous short poems describing the "ceremonies" for various Christian festivals ("Ceremonies for Christmas," "Ceremonies for Candlemas Eve," etc.) often have the air of describing a Roman ritual.

In dealing with such obvious country subjects as flowers Herrick often uses conceits which are not Petrarchan but which are hardly metaphysical. "How roses came red" or "How violets came blue" give a playfully ingenious mythological interpretation of the phenomenon he is describing, but the effect is one of ingenuousness rather than ingenuity. More interesting are those flower poems where he associates the short life of the flower with the transience of human affairs: this theme gives him some of his most attractive lyrics:

Fair daffodils, we weep to see
You haste away so soon;
As yet the early-rising sun

Has not attained his noon.
Stay, stay
Until the hasting day
Has run
But to the even-song;
And, having prayed together, we
Will go with you along.

We have short time to stay as you;
We have as short a Spring,
As quick a growth to meet decay
As you, or anything.
We die
As your hours do, and dry
Away
Like to the summer's rain,
Or as the pearls of morning's dew
Ne'er to be found again.

Some critics have professed to see a metaphysical strain in Herrick's *Noble Numbers.* It is true that occasionally there is a note somewhat reminiscent of Herbert though without Herbert's metrical variety:

Can I not sin, but thou wilt be
My private protonotary?
Can I not woo thee to pass by
A short and sweet iniquity?
I'll cast a mist and cloud upon
My delicate transgression, . . .

But the conventional view that Herrick's religious poetry expresses an almost childish faith, a naïve trustfulness that in the end God will see him through, is nearer the truth. These are mostly short poems, giving thanks for a life of modest content ("A Thanksgiving to God for his House") or expressing in deliberately childlike terms his confidence in the Christian creed ("His Creed"), or asking in advance for divine help when it will be most needed ("His Litany to the Holy Spirit"), or playing with little conceits about God and immortality. Herrick's religious poems have grace and clarity of expression; but for the most part they are curiously complacent in attitude and show none of the conflicts or deeper perceptions that we find in the "religious metaphysicals."

Thomas Carew (1594/5–1640) both praised Ben Jonson for his successful spoliation of the ancient classics—

Nor think it theft, if the rich spoils so torn
From conquered authors, be as trophies worn—

and paid tribute to Donne as the poet who "ruled as he thought fit /The universal monarchy of wit":

The Muses' garden with pedantic weeds
O'er spread, was purg'd by thee, the lazy seeds
Of servile imitation thrown away,
And fresh invention planted.

In combining the classical influence of Jonson with the metaphysical influence of Donne, Carew produced a mixture especially suited to the atmosphere of the Court of Charles I. As Sir Herbert Grierson expressed it, "in Carew's poems and Vandyke's pictures the artistic taste of Charles's Court is vividly reflected, a dignified voluptuousness, an exquisite elegance, if in some of the higher qualities of man and artist Carew is as inferior to Wyatt or Spenser as Vandyke is to Holbein." This is true Cavalier poetry, polished, gay, and witty. Without the formal precision of Jonson, the adroit Roman paganizing of Herrick, or the gentlemanly ease of his younger contemporary, Sir John Suckling, Carew has his own kind of urbanity. The gallantry of his love poems does not always conceal a cynicism at the core, but the control, the restrained touch of stylization in all his best work, shows a sense of style in living that truly reflects the Cavalier spirit of the time and is not unattractive. Occasionally, as in the well-known song, "Ask me no more where Jove bestows," he combines Jonson's lapidary elegance with a stately singing note as well as a touch of metaphysical ingenuity, and the combination is perfectly achieved. Sometimes he echoes Donne in the frank psychological curiosity with which he explores an emotional or a sensual situation (as in "To a Lady that desired I would love her" and, in a different way, "A Rapture"), but he has a tendency to laugh off the implications of his conceits with an elegant shrug, lacking Donne's ability to carry through to the end the fusion of passion and wit. It is "wit" in Carew, too—almost in the modern sense—rather than thought. There are many echoes of Donne in his poems, but the exhibitionist quality in his conceits often derives as much from Marino as from Donne. Carew's songs were meant to be sung, and lose something when merely read. His longer poems often run into mere showiness. But he had an artistic conscience; even his showiness is carefully modulated, and he always knew what he was doing.

Another heir to both Jonson and Donne is Sir John Suckling (1609–42), though both streams are shallower now. Lively, gay, very much the worldly courtier, Suckling looks to the cynical strain in Donne's early love poems and to the lighter of Jonson's lyrics. His poem, "Oh, for some honest lover's ghost" is an altogether more superficial performance than Donne's "I long to talk with some old lover's ghost." His "Hast thou seen the down i' the air" is a flippant parody (turned to satire) of Jonson's exquisite song of compliment, "Have you seen but the white lily grow." He is at his best where he combines a colloquial ease with a neatly patterned song-stanza, as in the well-known "Why so pale and wan, fond lover?" or "I prithee send me back my heart" or "Out upon it I have loved /Three whole days together." "A Session of the Poets" is a lively trotting poem in thirty four-line stanzas with a deliberately crude accentual meter, describing himself and his fellow poets competing for the laurel, only to see it given in the end by Apollo to an alderman on the grounds that "it was the best sign /Of good store of wit to have good store of coin." The poem is interesting in giving Suckling's views of his contemporaries. Carew's "muse was hard-bound, and th' issue of 's brain." Suckling describes himself as an amateur who "loved not the muses so well as his sport." The description is accurate enough: Suckling's poetry shows the Cavalier at play.

The true Cavalier poet is, however, Richard Lovelace (1618–58), whose gallantry has in it a truer strain of chivalry than Suckling's, a strain that links him with Sidney and Sir Walter Ralegh and the older tradition of Renaissance courtesy. The royalist ideal was indeed grounded in that older tradition, as we can see in Lovelace and, most clearly, in the few but noble lyrical utterances of the Scottish royalist, James Graham, Marquis of Montrose. Lovelace's "To Althea from Prison" uses imagery that is as much Petrarchan as metaphysical, but the poem brings a new kind of idealism into the English lyric of the period. The same can be said of "To Lucasta, Going to the Wars," which has the lapidary quality of Jonson at his best as well as a simple gravity of tone that we cannot find in Suckling. More metaphysical in imagery, if classical in inspiration, is the interesting poem, "The Grasshopper," where a description of the heedless grasshopper is adroitly turned into a celebration of friendship. There is something of the strength of Wyatt in Lovelace at his best, as well as echoes of the Sidneian and Spenserian association of ideal love and beauty with honor and the good life. The seventeenth-century royalist ideal was perhaps anachronistic, and a somewhat faded neo-Platonism often lay behind it; but Lovelace at least gave it effective expression.

Of the minor Cavalier poets, mention may be made of Sidney

Godolphin (1610–43), the majority of whose poems remained in manuscript until the twentieth century. He, too, has the graver note which we sometimes find in Lovelace (in Suckling's "Session of the Poets" Apollo advises Godolphin "not to write so strong"), together with a restrained metaphysical touch which adds just the right note of subtlety to the quiet clarity of his style. The influence of Donne and Jonson combine here most happily.

Richard Corbet, bishop of Oxford and Norwich (1582–1635), is a minor lyrist of the period whose character and poems reflect a robust joy of life which was to become one element in Cavalier opposition to the Puritans. His one famous poem, "A Proper new ballad, intituled The Faries' Farewell, or God a mercy Will," gives lively expression to the sense that the Puritan spirit had killed the happy superstitions of Old England:

> Farewell, rewards and fairies,
> Good housewives now may say,
> For now foul sluts in dairies
> Do fare as well as they.
> And though they sweep their hearths no less
> Than maids were wont to do,
> Yet who of late for cleanliness
> Finds sixpence in her shoe?
>
> Lament, lament, old abbeys,
> The fairies lost command;
> They did but change priests' babies,
> But some have changed your land,
> And all your children sprung from thence
> Are now grown Puritans;
> Who live as changelings ever since,
> For love of your demains.

"There never was a merry world since the fairies left dancing and the parson left conjuring," said John Selden in the middle of the century, and this remark, together with Corbet's poem, shows that there was much more than political or theological opinions involved in the Civil War and also helps to explain why the large majority of those interested in the arts and letters (Milton was the great exception) were on the royalist side.

Sir William Davenant's dramatic work and his "heroic poem" *Gondibert* are discussed in Volume II, Chapter 1, but it can be noted here that his lyric poetry is in the Cavalier tradition, combining in its way Jonsonian and metaphysical influences. The song, "The lark now leaves his wat'ry nest," is built on a conceit that is almost metaphysical in its ingenuity, but it lacks that exploratory power of the true metaphysical style. This is typical of the way the Cavalier poets modified the metaphysical conceit so as to bring it closer to the Petrarchan manner against which it had originally revolted. But Jonson and the Roman lyrical poets gave them a classical sense of form and the spirit of the age provided a gayer tone, so that the result is very different from the typical Petrarchan love poem of the Elizabethan age.

We have discussed the religious poets who in differing degrees were influenced by Donne, and the secular poets who considered themselves "Sons of Ben" even if they also show something of Donne's influence. There were also secular metaphysical poets, who continued the Donne tradition not in religious poetry but in poetry of love, compliment, elegy, or meditation. Lord Herbert of Cherbury (1583–1648), better known for his philosophical and historical writings in Latin and English and his spirited autobiography, learned from Donne to employ a precise intellectual imagery in his poetry, but he lacks Donne's immediacy and variety; the thought dominates the passion. The poetry of Henry King (1592–1669) shows Donne's influence clearly (as well as, occasionally, Jonson's grace and neatness) and in one poem, "The Exequy," an elegy on the death of his young wife, he produced a minor masterpiece which fuses passion and argument in the finest metaphysical style. John Cleveland (1613–58) was one of those in whose hands the metaphysical style turned to mere ingenuity of metaphor and simile, but a poem like "Mark Anthony" shows a mixture of metaphysical ingenuity and lusty vulgarity that was to affect poets of the Restoration, and his satirical poetry, with its strong royalist viewpoint and lively verbal tricks, was to provide suggestions for Samuel Butler's *Hudibras*.

Cleveland was extremely popular in his own day, but no less so than Abraham Cowley (1618–67), with whose poetry the metaphysical style finally works itself out. Cowley was a copious and versatile poet. Speaking of his collection of poems, *The Mistress*, published in 1647, Dr. Johnson remarked that it had "no power of seduction. Her beauty and absence, her kindness and cruelty, her disdain and inconstancy, produce no correspondence of emotion. His poetical account of the virtues of plants, and colours of flowers, is not perused with more sluggish frigidity. The compositions are such as might have been written for penance by a hermit, or for hire by a philosophical rhymer who had only heard of another sex." The modern critic is not disposed to quarrel violently with Johnson's judgment, even though he does not share Johnson's view of the metaphysical style in general. But Cowley does strike fire sometimes, and in his more Horatian moods he can be happily cogent. A thoughtful poet, he reflects in his work some of the major philosophical currents of his time, and it is not his fault if the newer streams of thought were sometimes shallow. He was a good classicist, and his imitations of Pindar set the style for the eighteenth-century Pindaric ode. His unfinished religious epic *Davideis* (in heroic couplets) is one of the several English abortions of this kind: a biblical epic professedly imitative of Virgil in style, attempting to combine neoclassic notions of the epic with Christian repudiation of pagan machinery, trying to follow classical precedent in the presentation of the material yet showing the influence of Crashaw's translation of the first book of Marino's *Sospetto d'Herode* and of Sylvester's Du Bartas—the poem was a mixture of heterogeneous motives from the start. It emphasizes, however, the transitional nature of Cowley's poetry: he looked forward to eighteenth-century neoclassical as well as backward to the metaphysicals. His prose essays are models of quiet clarity bringing the familiar autobiographical note confidently and easily into English prose. His poetry, however, is important chiefly for illustrating the progressive restriction of the poet's intellectual and emotional world as the seventeenth century moved toward its final quarter. The "dissociation of sensibility" which T. S. Eliot saw as a phenomenon of the English poetic mind throughout the eighteenth and nineteenth centuries is already present in Cowley. The metaphysical style is not really suited to his temperament or his vision of the world, and it is significant and appropriate that Johnson began his *Lives of the Poets* with a discussion of Cowley and of metaphysical poetry as a preparation for dealing with the poetry of his own century. In giving Cowley the headmaster's nod of dismissal before summoning the younger boys who are to be promoted on their merits to the leading positions in the school, Johnson was making a historical judgment with which the modern reader, whatever his opinion of the new regime, will not wish substantially to disagree.

Andrew Marvell (1621–78), however, gives us pause. His best poetry combines true metaphysical wit with perfect classical grace and poise to a greater degree than any other poet of the century. But this was not the road that English poetry was to take. Marvell—whose best poems were written in the early 1650's and were not published in his lifetime—stood alone, like Milton, creating his own synthesis out of the clashing elements swirling about him. The posthumous volume of his poems which appeared in 1681 appealed to a taste that was already out of fashion, and Marvell's own later work shows him developing a satirical strain (already evident, but far from dominant, in his early poetry) which exhibited a much more restricted kind of wit than that displayed in his finest poems; Marvell's political satires look back to Cleveland's and forward to

Dryden's. His best and most characteristic poems are those in which an adventurous wit is perfectly subdued to the quiet texture of his verse to produce a poetry at once contemplative and exciting, gravely formal and mysteriously suggestive. A precise and loving observation of nature, an ethical gravity, and an ability to put intellectual play to serious use are qualities found together in, for example, "On a Drop of Dew," which begins with the most accurate description of a dewdrop on a rose and maneuvers the picture into a symbol of the soul's relation to earth and Heaven. The wit is integral to the poem, and bound up both with its accuracy of observation and its moral feeling. "The Nymph Complaining for the Death of her Faun" is on the surface a simple poem in gently moving octosyllabic couplets, but, in the words of Eliot, "Marvell takes a slight affair, the feeling of a girl for her pet, and gives it a connexion with that inexhaustible and terrible nebula of emotion which surrounds all our exact and practical passions and mingles with them." The poem, like all of Marvell's best, is so carefully wrought that quotation cannot suggest its true quality, but an extract may give some idea of its movement:

> Thenceforth I set myself to play
> My solitary time away
> With this; and very well content,
> Could so mine idle life have spent.
> For it was full of sport; and light
> Of foot and heart; and did invite
> Me to its game: it seemed to bless
> Its self in me. How could I less
> Than love it? O I cannot be
> Unkind t' a beast that loveth me.

"To his Coy Mistress," with its wonderful manipulation of images of exaggeration—

> Had we but world enough, and time,
> This coyness, Lady, were no crime.
> We would sit down, and think which way
> To walk, and pass our long love's day.
> Thou by the Indian Ganges' side
> Should'st rubies find; I by the tide
> Of Humber would complain. I would
> Love you ten years before the Flood,
> And you should if you please refuse
> Till the conversion of the Jews—

shows not only a truly serious use of sprightly wit but also, in its threefold movement, a sense of form which provides a wholly new dimension. The second section of the poem suddenly deepens and extends the significance of the earlier wit:

> But at my back I always hear
> Time's wingéd chariot hurrying near,
> And yonder all before us lie
> Deserts of vast Eternity.
> Thy beauty shall no more be found,
> Nor, in thy marble vault, shall sound
> My echoing song: then worms shall try
> That long preserv'd virginity,
> And your quaint honour turn to dust
> And into ashes all my lust.
> The grave's a fine and private place,
> But none I think do there embrace.

The third movement conquers time by intensity of present passion:

> . . . Let us roll all our strength, and all
> Our sweetness up into one ball,
> And tear our pleasures with rough strife
> Through the iron gates of life.
> Thus, though we cannot make our sun
> Stand still, yet we will make him run.

The "Gather ye rosebuds" theme is here given new subtlety and suggestiveness by the handling of the wit and the ordering of the images.

Equally remarkable is "The Definition of Love"—

> My love is of a birth as rare
> As 'tis for object strange and high:
> It was begotten by despair
> Upon impossibility—,

"The Picture of T.C. in a Prospect of Flowers," a poem which combines delicate charm with a slowly emergent gravity, and "The Garden," which, by a finely ordered imagery and a cunning progression of thought, distills cumulatively the essence of lonely garden felicity as symbol of the unfallen life in Eden. The "Horatian Ode upon Cromwell's Return from Ireland" is another poem in which the manipulation of variety and order in the images and the carefully controlled modulation of the thought results in a unity of remarkable richness and power. Horatian in its clarity and strength, and showing other classical influences as well, it is nevertheless wholly original in its controlled variations of tone. The picture of Cromwell coming

> . . . from his private gardens, where
> He liv'd reservéd and austere

to act as the minister of fate in casting "the kingdom old /Into another mould" gives way to one of Charles at his execution:

> He nothing common did or mean
> Upon that memorable scene,
> But with his keener eye
> The axe's edge did try.

And this in turn yields to a further picture of Cromwell the conqueror, to end with the disquieting warning that

> The same arts that did gain
> A pow'r must it maintain.

Both Cromwell and King Charles are seen in a context of divine justice and order working themselves out, and this enables Marvell to be fair to them both. A similar position is taken in his longer poem in heroic couplets, "The First Anniversary of the Government under O. C.," though here the praise of Cromwell is louder and clearer.

Marvell's poems are very unequal. His long poem in eight-line stanzas "Upon Appleton House" (Lord Fairfax's seat, where Marvell lived for some years) is too discursive to respond to the poet's attempt at ordering, and the imagery is at times merely ingenious, but there are some admirable stanzas. The "Mower" poems show his love of nature put, as so often, at the service of a moral theme. The well-known "Bermudas" is quite perfect of its kind: with its rich and various imagery, musical beauty of movement, and simple gravity of feeling, it strikes "an holy and a cheerful note" to a degree rarely equaled in English poetry. His satirical verse in heroic couplets, whether the earlier "Tom May's Death," "Flecknoe," or "The Character of Holland" or the later series written after the Restoration, of which the longest is "The Last Instructions to a Painter," cannot begin to compare with his best lyrical poetry. They show a strain of cheap and boisterous cruelty and an exhibitionist wit which are quite unlike the Marvell of the other poems. Marvell was here following the new fashions of the times. It is significant that in "The Last Instructions to a Painter" Marvell was following a popular fashion of verse comment on contemporary affairs in the form of advice to a painter on what to paint and how to paint it. Much more attractive are Marvell's prose writings in defense of religious toleration.

Marvell, like Milton, was a Christian Humanist, and though he is generally regarded as a Puritan poet, his own career illustrates perfectly the dilemma of a sensitive and serious temperament caught up in a civil conflict which he deplored. Unlike Milton, Marvell could never commit himself wholeheartedly to the Commonwealth cause; he accepted it, largely because

> 'Tis Madness to resist or blame
> The force of angry Heaven's flame,

and he was friendly with many of the Parliamentary leaders. In 1657 he was appointed assistant to Milton in the Latin Secretaryship. But looking back afterward, he said that "upon considering all, I think the cause was too good to have been fought for. Men ought to have trusted God—they ought to have trusted the King with the whole matter." In his best poetry as in his character he combined the best of Cavalier wit and courtesy with the quiet gravity of a humane Puritan. But the combination was too individual and too subtle to provide a pattern for future poets.

CHAPTER TWELVE

Milton

John Milton (1608–74) stands by himself, a lonely and dedicated figure, in seventeenth-century English literature; yet no man was more profoundly affected by the events of his time. The great debate on religion and politics which divided the English nation in the middle of the seventeenth century helped to determine the course of Milton's career and the shape of his literary ambitions. The origins of the conflict were complex; James I and his son Charles I lacked the adroitness and flexibility of Queen Elizabeth in responding to the demands of an increasingly self-conscious Parliament, nor did they see in the steady rise of the commercial classes, with their economic individualism and Puritan morality, an inevitable historical process which demanded some modification of the aristocratic and paternalist view of the monarchy held by the Stuarts; and in the end Charles' lack of tact in handling Parliament, his clumsy devices for providing himself with money in the absence of Parliamentary votes of supply, his insistence on uniformity of worship and standardization of the liturgy, and his lack of realization of the state of mind of a large number of his subjects in both England and Scotland, provoked a civil conflict which ended in Charles' trial and execution in 1649 and in England's unprecedented seventeen-year experiment in non-monarchical government. On the whole, artists and men of letters were on the royalist side during the Civil War; the Court party stood for the graces of life, and royal patronage was still an important factor in a successful artistic or literary career. But many writers were torn between personal loyalty and interest on the one hand and moral or political principle on the other, and took sides with reluctance. The core of parliamentary support came from London burghers as well as from other urban centers and from the south and east of the country generally, while the Church of England, the larger part of the nobility and gentry, and the country folk of the north, west, and Midlands, supported the King. There were, of course, exceptions and anomalies. There were high-minded Puritan aristocrats who supported Parliament, and pockets of royalism in Puritan parts of the country. The antiroyalist side was far from homogeneous; political, religious, and economic motives prevailed in different proportions with different people, and on the left wing there was a host of radical sects, utopian prophets, religious idealists, and apocalyptic enthusiasts of all kinds. On the royalist side there were many who had been critical of Charles' behavior but who shuddered at the thought of bearing arms against the King; while there were others who supported the rebellion on constitutional grounds but boggled at the King's execution. The upheaval in political thinking —and political thinking at this time involved religious thinking— produced by the Civil War was tremendous; pamphlets, tracts, sermons, and proposals came from the printing presses in huge quantities, with innumerable persons (as Milton was to put it in his *Areopagitica*) "disputing, reasoning, reading, inventing, discoursing, even to a rarity and admiration, things not before discoursed or written of." For a poet like Milton, convinced of his own genius and determined to put it at the service of his country, this atmosphere was both dangerous and fascinating. Christian and Humanist, Protestant patriot and heir of the golden ages of Greece and Rome, he faced what appeared to him to be the birth-pangs of a new and regenerate England with high excitement and idealistic optimism. It was this excitement and this optimism which led him to commit himself so completely to the parliamentary side in the Civil War; and that commitment was decisive for his middle and later poetic career.

"I was born in London of an honest family; . . . My father destined me from a child to the pursuits of literature; and my appetite for knowledge was so voracious, that, from twelve years of age, I hardly ever left my studies, or went to bed before midnight." So Milton tells us in his *Second Defence of the English People*, and his stress on his early literary interests, pursued with his father's encouragement, is significant. He was given a Christian Humanist education from the start. At St. Paul's School, which he attended from 1615 or 1620 to 1625, he found a curriculum originally framed according to the Humanist ideals of Erasmus and Colet and still maintaining many of the characteristics of Renaissance Humanist scholarship. He studied Latin, Greek, and Hebrew (in addition to being tutored in Hebrew at home by Thomas Young, a Presbyterian divine), and got a thorough grounding in classical rhetoric, which he was taught to apply to the analysis of Latin and Greek prose and verse. The view of rhetoric as a noble skill necessary for the citizen who is to take a proper part in public affairs—the view of Isocrates and Cicero, not that of Aristotle, for whom it was the art of persuasion, morally neutral in itself, not yet that of Plato, for whom it was a dangerous and superficial art liable to mislead and corrupt—was the one which Milton learned at school; and this helps to explain why later as a literary man he deemed it his duty to engage in public affairs and also why, after his disillusionment over the possibility of a regenerate England resulting from the defeat of Charles, he became more and more suspicious of rhetoric, showing its abuse, and the abuse of democratic debate, in the speeches of Satan and his followers in *Paradise Lost,* and in *Paradise Regained* giving all the rhetoric to Satan, the tempter, while putting into the mouth of Jesus language deliberately stripped of all rhetorical ornament.

When Milton came to Christ's College, Cambridge, in 1625, he was already a dedicated spirit, eager to prepare himself to become a great poet. He was shocked to find scholastic disputation on trivial subjects still being used as a means of education—St. Paul's was ahead of Cambridge in its educational theories—and voiced his disagreement in his own Latin oratorical exercises. In the first of these Latin "prolusions," delivered in College before an audience of his fellow undergraduates, he referred to the unfriendliness of the majority of the audience and the small minority of his supporters, while in the third, delivered in the Public Schools, he attacked the scholastic philosophy and the barren disputes to which it gave rise, asking rhetorically what pleasure there could be in the quarrelings of crabbed old men, and describing his difficulty in getting through the long pages of verbose quibbling which he had been forced to read. "Divine Poetry," Rhetoric, and History were set against the "useless and boring controverseries and verbal wranglings [which] have no power to stir the soul." Geography, too, is recommended as an alternative subject; how much better it would be, he told his fellow students, if instead of wasting time on useless philosophical disputation they toured the whole earth with the help of a map and saw the places made famous by history and literature. Milton in this prolusion often talks in strains strongly reminiscent of Francis Bacon, whose attack in *The Advancement of Learning* on the barrenness and mere verbalism of scholastic philosophy had obviously impressed him. The second prolusion discusses the Pythagorean and Platonic notion of the music of the spheres, a notion which haunted Milton throughout his life, appealing both to his love of music and his sense of order and hierarchy, as well as to his passionate belief in purity and chastity (by which he did not mean celibacy), for only the pure and chaste could ever hope to hear that divine harmony. The fact that Milton was known in Cambridge as "The Lady of Christ's" indicates the conspicuousness of his high idealism and his aloofness from the horseplay and the immoralities that were not uncommon among the undergraduates of the time.

The young Milton began his poetic career with verse paraphrases of Psalms and Ovidian Latin elegies—the Christian and the Humanist each producing his own kind of verse. One of the main problems of his career was to be the possibility of the fusion of these two strains and the nature of the context within which they might be fused; but it is significant that he began by keeping them separate. There seems little enough connection between his version of Psalm 136, written in 1624—

> Let us with a gladsome mind
> Praise the Lord, for he is kind,
> For his mercies aye endure,
> Ever faithful, ever sure—

and a set of elegiac verses written probably in the same year:

> . . . Ecce novo campos Zephyritis gramine vestit
> Fertilis, et vitreo rore madescit humus.

> See, the bountiful daughter of Zephyr dresses the fields in new grass, and the earth is moist with glistering dew.

The Latin verses show a luxuriance, a relish of nature and, a little later, of female beauty which find no place in his early English verse. His first formal poem of any length in English is probably the "Ode on the Death of a Fair Infant Dying of a Cough" (which Milton dates "Anno Aetatis 17," but which appears to have been written in his twentieth year, in 1628), and here he does use both classical mythology and Christian ideas. The poem is an exercise, skillful enough in some of its parts, but inadequately integrated. The first part has Ovidian reminiscences as well as some Spenserian touches:

> For since grim Aquilo his charioteer
> By boist'rous rape th' Athenian damsel got,
> He thought it touched his deity full near,
> If likewise he some fair one wedded not;
> Thereby to wipe away th' infamous blot
> Of long uncoupled bed and childless eld,
> Which 'mongst the wanton gods a foul reproach was held.

Later, a more individual note is heard, a note that was to sound more clearly in "Lycidas":

> Yet art thou not inglorious in thy fate;
> For so Apollo, with unweeting hand,

Whilom did slay his dearly-loved mate,
Young Hyacinth, born on Eurotas' strand,
Young Hyacinth, the pride of Spartan land;
But then transformed him to a purple flower:
Alack, that so to change thee Winter had no power.

The infant, he continues, cannot be dead: she must be in some happy sphere above. Perhaps she was a fallen star, now reinstated by Jove? Or was she Astraea, "that just Maid who once before /Forsook the hated earth," now revisiting us? Or Mercy, or Truth? The speculations are ingenious, but inorganic. In the end, he tells the mother (who was his own elder sister: the infant was his niece) to cease lamenting:

Think what a present thou to God hast sent,
And render him with patience what he lent;
This if thou do, he will an offspring give
That till the world's last end shall make thy name to live.

The concluding consolation is perfunctory, just as the classical mythologizing is decorative rather than functional. At the same time, the poem shows considerable technical virtuosity.

Milton's quarrel with the Cambridge curriculum apparently led to a difference with his tutor and a brief rustication from the University in his second year. During the period of rustication, at home in his father's house in London, he wrote the first of his Latin "Elegies" (not, of course, elegies in the modern sense: the title refers to the verse form, not the content) to his old school-friend, Charles Diodati. The fluency and sureness of Milton's elegiac Latin verse show a remarkable mastery of the language; it shows, too, that Milton was steeped in Ovid, whose style he could reproduce with uncanny skill. He pretends in this poem to be happier by the Thames than he could be by the sedgy Cam. He describes his present life as altogether pleasant, reading, visiting the theater, or walking in the country in the spring sunshine, enjoying the beauties of nature and of handsome girls:

Nos quoque lucus habet vicina consitus ulmo,
Atque suburbani nobilis umbra loci.
Saepius hic, blandas spirantia sidera flammas,
Virgineos videas praeteriisse choros.
Ah quoties dignae stupui miracula formae
Quae possit senium vel reparare Iovis!
Ah quoties vidi superantia lumina gemmas,
Atque faces quotquot volvit uterque polus;
Collaque bis vivi Pelopis quae brachia vincant,

Quaeque fluit puro nectare tincta via,
Et decus eximium frontis, tremulosque capillos,
Aurea quae fallax retia tendit Amor; . . .

And I also visit the grove where the elms stand close together, and the noble shade of a place just outside the city. Here you may often see maidens go dancing by, stars breathing gentle flames. Ah, how often have I been struck dumb by the miracle of a beautiful form which might even make old Jove young again! Ah, how often have I seen eyes brighter than gems and all the stars that either pole moves round, necks which excel the arms of the twice-living Pelops and the Way which flows coloured with pure nectar, a brow of superb beauty, waving tresses that are golden nets flung by deceiving Love. . . .

This section of the poem ends with an eloquent description of "Alma Venus," Venus the life-giver, deserting her traditional haunts to come to London. The poem is worth dwelling on because it reveals a side of Milton which the reader of his English poems only rarely sees; yet its existence was important for Milton's poetic career.

Milton was seventeen when he wrote the verse letter to Diodati. He was writing a lot of Latin elegiac verse at this time. It was in 1626, too, that he wrote the Latin poem "On the Death of the Beadle of Cambridge University," an ingenious and skillful exercise in mythologizing, and the more serious and formal Latin elegies on the deaths of the Bishop of Winchester (Lancelot Andrewes) and the Bishop of Ely. (No sign yet of the antiepiscopal violence which Milton was to show later.) Another Latin poem of the same year, in hexameters this time, was "In Quintum Novembris." ("On the Fifth of November"), a mock heroic poem on Guy Fawkes' Gunpowder Plot in which Milton's delight in coining epic phrases, in conjuring up an atmosphere of darkness and horror, and in rousing Satanic speeches is clearly seen. The careful investigator of *Paradise Lost* would do well to study Satan's speech and the description of the "place wrapped eternally in the darkness of night" ("locus aeterna septus caligine noctis") in this Latin poem.

Among Milton's other Latin poetry written at Cambridge is the Fourth Elegy, written in 1627, addressed to his old tutor Thomas Young, in which he appears to be showing off his skill; a poem in hexameters denying that Nature is subject to old age; and the Seventh Elegy, on spring and love, which begins with an invocation to Venus and a dialogue between the poet and Cupid, and which contains some of his most sensual poetry, ending with a conventional picture of himself as Cupid's victim. It is interesting to note that when he published these elegies in the 1645 volume of his poetry he appended to the seventh and last an apology for the wantonness and levity which had led him astray: but he did not suppress any of the poems. The finest of all Milton's Latin poems is the Fifth Elegy —written probably in 1628; Milton apparently did not number his Elegies chronologically—"In Adventum Veris" ("On the Coming of Spring"), where, in a rich Ovidian verse, he describes the revival of nature, of his own poetic inspiration, and of love and joy and passion. The poem breathes sensuous enjoyment and optimism; its mythology is consistently Greek, its feeling pagan. "In Adventum Veris" is the fullest and finest expression of a side of Milton he rarely allows us to see again.

If Milton's Latin Elegies show his ability to manipulate in verse a classical paganism, his Latin "Prolusions" give some insight into his intellectual position during his years at Cambridge. He took his stand against the notion that Nature was decaying, and he championed the idea that knowledge could and should move forward in continuous progress. He was clearly on the optimistic side in the debate on the Decline of the World which was a central theme in the seventeenth century.[1] It was also in one of the prolusions that he first committed himself to the choice of his native English as his main poetic language in the future. In July, 1628, he wrote a "Vacation Exercise" in Latin, as an end-of-term entertainment, and after the Latin fooling was over—Milton amused himself by playing with some Aristotelian and Scholastic notions—he appended a personal statement in English:

> Hail, native language, that by sinews weak
> Didst move my first endeavouring tongue to speak.

With that naïve and rather engaging egotism that remained a characteristic of his throughout his life, he proceeded to tell his fellow students that he had high ambitions as a poet in the English language:

> Yet I had rather, if I were to choose,
> Thy service in some graver subject use,
> Such as may make thee search thy coffers round,
> Before thou clothe my fancy in fit sound:
> Such where the deep transported mind may soar
> Above the wheeling poles, and at Heav'ns door
> Look in, and see each blissful deity
> How he before the thunderous throne doth lie,
> Listening to what unshorn Apollo sings. . . .
> Then sing of secret things that came to pass
> When Beldam Nature in her cradle was;
> And last of kings and queens and heroes old,

[1] See Chapter 13, p. 489-90.

> Such as the wise Demodocus once told
> In solemn songs at King Alcinous' feast,
> While sad Ulysses' soul and all the rest
> Are held with his melodious harmony
> In willing chains, and sweet captivity.

He proposed to write grave poetry about the gods, about the creation of the world, and about human heroes. As for style, he wished his native language to bring him

> Not those new-fangled toys, and trimming slight
> Which takes our late fantastics with delight;
> But cull those richest robes and gay'st attire,
> Which deepest spirits and choicest wits desire.

It is doubtful whether Milton was specifically referring here to Donne and the metaphysical style; he was probably repudiating the meretricious ingenuity of some of his fellow students.

Milton was also an accomplished writer of Italian verse, and he wrote a number of Italian sonnets, probably in 1628, which, like his Latin poems, show a side of him that he hesitated to reveal in English. These poems show him as the lover, in Petrarchan style, of a foreign lady—apparently called Emilia. The expression is highly stylized, but there is a grace and a charm about much of the expression, notably in the sonnet that begins

> Qual in colle aspro, al imbrunir di sera
> L'avvezza giovinetta pastorella
> Va bagnando l'herbetta strana e bella
> Che mal si spande a disusata spera
> Fuor di sua natia alma primavera, . . .

> As, on a rugged hill, when twilight darkens,
> The young shepherdess, familiar with the place,
> Keeps watering a strange and beautiful little plant
> Which feebly spreads its leaves in the unfamiliar clime,
> Far from its native fostering springtime. . . .

One of the Italian sonnets is addressed to Diodati, telling him "con maraviglia" of his conversion to love—love not of a conventional golden-haired, red-cheeked girl, but of a "pellegrina bellezza," a foreign beauty, with lovely black eyes, the ability to speak more than one language, and an enchanting gift of song. Another gives a portrait of himself, whom he describes as gentle, candid, and steadfast, unyielding except to the arrows of Love. One of the Italian poems is a *canzone,* in which he defends his writing in Italian on the grounds that that is the language of Love. It is interesting that he imagines men and girls teasing him for writing in foreign language by assuring him that his proper language is English, in which already "the immortal guerdon of eternal leaves is putting forth its shoots to crown your locks." He was still in training to be a major English poet.

In 1629, while still at Cambridge, Milton wrote his first wholly successful English poem. This was "On the Morning of Christ's Nativity." In his Sixth Elegy—a Latin letter addressed to Charles Diodati in December, 1629—he announced that he was "singing of the heaven-born King, harbinger of peace, and of the happy centuries promised in the holy books," and the poem appears to have been intended as the first of a series in a high religious vein, celebrating different occasions of the Christian year. It consists of an introduction and hymn, both done with a combination of deliberate quaintness in imagery and conceits and a studied simplicity of feeling which produced a remarkable effect. Tillyard has compared the poem to a fifteenth-century Italian painting of the Nativity, with its combination of brilliant coloring and naïve juxtaposition of realistic and symbolic detail. It has indeed a remarkable pictorial quality, but it also has an interesting musical quality both in the handling of the language and in the form of the whole. In structure it suggests an "introduction and trio" in seventeenth-century music, with the former (in rhyme royal) more heavily orchestrated than the latter (the hymn, in an eight-lined stanza mingling short and long lines). There is a sense of movement in the poem, too: the poem states in the fourth and last stanza of the introduction that he is bringing his ode as an offering to the infant Christ—

> O run, prevent them [i.e., come before the Wise Men]
> with thy humble ode,
> And lay it lowly at his blessed feet—

and by the end of the poem the guiding star has stopped over the birthplace, the journey of the Magi is over, and the gifts have been delivered. But the real theme of the poem is the rout of pagan gods and superstitions by the divine Babe, who figures as a classical hero rather than as the suffering servant. The note of celebration is struck in the opening line:

> This is the month, and this the happy morn,

while the first stanza of the hymn illustrates the deliberately baroque quality of the imagery:

> It was the Winter wild,
> While the Heav'n-born child,

> All meanly wrapt in the rude manger lies;
> Nature in awe to him
> Had doff't her gaudy trim,
> With her great Master so to sympathize:
> It was no season then for her
> To wanton with the sun, her lusty paramour.

Milton goes on to give a picture of peace descending on the world at the nativity: the fourth stanza of the hymn banishes images of war and the fifth brings the poem to a temporary stop with its careful building up of a sense of hush:

> But peaceful was the night
> Wherein the Prince of light
> His reign of peace upon the earth began:
> The winds, with wonder whist,
> Smoothly the waters kiss't,
> Whispering new joys to the mild Ocean,
> Who now hath quite forgot to rave,
> While Birds of Calm sit brooding on the charméd wave.

The shepherds on the lawn who "sat simply chatting in a rustic row" are gradually made aware of the arrival of the "mighty Pan." The Music of the Spheres (a favorite notion of Milton's) assails their ears, and the glittering ranks of angels, guarding the divine order of the universe of which the musical harmony is the audible symbol, appear to their sight. With the picture of the divine music ringing out, the poem rises to its highest point ("Ring out ye crystal spheres") before gradually dying away to its close. For an ecstatic moment Milton's imagination would like to believe that the age of gold has been brought back to earth, and he gives an eloquent picture of its imminent arrival:

> And speckl'd vanity
> Will sicken soon and die,
> And leprous sin will melt from earthly mould,
> And Hell itself will pass away,
> And leave her dolorous mansions to the peering day.
>
> Yea, Truth and Justice then
> Will down return to men,
> Th' enamel'd arras of the rainbow wearing,
> And Mercy set between
> Thron'd in celestial sheen,
> With radiant feet the tissued clouds down steering,
> And Heav'n as at some festival
> Will open wide the gates of her high palace hall.

Milton checks this fancy with reluctance: this is not yet to be, and he goes on to give a most cunningly developed picture of the old order being routed by the new; the oracle of Apollo is now dumb, the local classical divinities pass mourning from their haunted springs and dales, "the Lars and Lemures moan with midnight plaint," the pagan gods of ancient Palestine flee away, and

> The brutish gods of Nile as fast,
> Isis and Orus and the Dog Anubis haste.

The infant Christ, like the infant Hercules strangling snakes in his cradle, "can in his swaddling bands control the damned crew." The ode then moves to a picture of the Babe being laid to rest guarded by the hierarchic orders of angels:

> And all about the courtly stable
> Bright harness'd angels sit in order serviceable.

This image of rank, order, courtliness, and stability gives Milton's conception of a harmonious universe, and on this note the poem ends.

Milton never wrote another poem quite in this style. His ode on the Passion, written soon afterward in an endeavor to continue the religious series, was left unfinished after eight labored stanzas; "this subject the author finding to be above the years he had when he wrote it, and nothing satisfied with what was begun, left it unfinished," as Milton noted later when he included the poem in the 1645 volume. Christ's passion was not a congenial subject to Milton; he preferred the heroic to the crucified Christ, his own temperament combining with the Protestant tradition to reject any mystical agonizing over the cross in favor of celebrating the divine hero who combats error and evil and by strength of will is able to resist all tempation. As we shall see, Paradise for Milton was regained not by Christ crucified but by Christ, "a second Adam in the wilderness," reenacting Adam's temptation and this time resisting instead of falling as Adam did. The Passion was not therefore a subject to which Milton's genius rose, and he rightly stopped the poem midway after experimenting unsuccessfully with a number of over-elaborate devices for expressing grief.

In his Latin elegiacs addressed to Diodati in December, 1629, Milton had mentioned that he was composing, as well as his "Nativity Ode," something simpler to be played on his native reed, and this may refer to the cheerful fragment "On May Morning":

> Now the bright morning star, day's harbinger,
> Comes dancing from the East, and leads with her
> The flowery May, who from her green lap throws
> The yellow cowslip and the pale primrose.

Or perhaps the reference is to "L'Allegro" and "Il Penseroso," which are now thought to have been written at Cambridge, probably late in his residence there. These two companion poems are skillful exercises in creating a mood by appropriate imagery and tone. "L'Allegro" opens with a mock-violent dismissal of "loathéd Melancholy" in a crashing of chords, after which the smoothly tripping solo instrument takes up the main theme. The happily modulated lines in which Milton describes a day in the life of the cheerful man show appropriate mythological and pastoral imagery developed in order to build up a mood of contented living. It is a carefully stylized picture, with the description of Euphrosyne, mirthful daughter of the west wind and the dawn, of a vine-covered rustic cottage, of milkmaids singing, mowers whetting their scythes, and shepherds making love under the hawthorn. The poem is full of light and movement. Its structure is chronological, beginning with "the dappled dawn" rising to the accompaniment of the lark's song, and going through a day of cheerful pastoral activities until sunset turns l'Allegro's thought to tournaments, pageants, poetry, and music. Milton exploits classical mythology, English folklore, and medieval romance in the course of this variegated poem. A sense of the dignity and orderliness of agricultural labor, which was to emerge again and again in Milton's poetry, gives a certain weight of significance to the pastoral imagery, which remains nevertheless lighthearted in tone:

> While the plowman near at hand
> Whistles o'er the furrowed land,
> And the milkmaid singeth blithe,
> And the mower whets his scythe,
> And every shepherd tells his tale
> Under the hawthorn in the dale.

There is a happy stylization here, a stylization even more deliberately cultivated in such an image as

> Hard by a cottage chimney smokes
> From betwixt two aged oaks,

with its careful symmetry. This is a very formal art; every activity has its proper symbols, which link the poem up at all points with a complex tradition in both art and life. In "Il Penseroso" the images are organized to present a mood of contemplation and grave intellectual activity. The coloring of this poem is darker than that of "L'Allegro": moonlight, dark woods, the song of the nightingale are appropriate symbols here. The sound of the far-off curfew, the glowing embers of a dying fire half-lighting a gloomy room, the midnight lamp of the lonely student in the tower—these images are as stylized as their counterparts in "L'Allegro," and distill a mood in the same way. Though the verse form of the two poems is the same, the pace of "Il Penseroso" is slower. Music is a pleasure to both l'Allegro and il Penseroso, but in the latter it is associated with religion and study.

> But let my due feet never fail
> To walk the studious cloisters pale,
> And love the high embowéd roof,
> With antique pillars massy proof,
> And storied windows richly dight
> Casting a dim religious light.
> There let the pealing organ blow
> To the full-voic'd choir below
> In service high and anthems clear. . . .

There is an Anglican (if not a Catholic) feeling here: Milton had not yet become suspicious of cloisters and stained glass windows and the Anglican service.

Milton took his B.A. at Cambridge in 1629 and his M.A. in 1632, then retired to his father's house in Horton, Buckinghamshire, to continue the task of preparing himself to be a great poet. Before he left Cambridge he had written, in addition to the poems already discussed, two "conceited" epitaphs (very much in style at the time) on the university carrier, an epitaph on the Marchioness of Winchester in the simpler style of Ben Jonson at his most lapidary, a sonnet on the nightingale showing a skillful blend of Italian, classical, and other influences, the more "metaphysical" sonnet in praise of Shakespeare which appears in the Second Folio of 1632, and, soon after his twenty-third birthday—in December, 1631—the sonnet "How soon hath Time, the subtle thief of youth," in which he reflects on his slowly developing maturity. Milton refused to allow himself to be hurried in his task of self-preparation. In a letter to a friend, of which two drafts are extant and with which he sent this sonnet, he replies to his friend's admonishments about his not entering on a profession. The friend appears to have suggested "that too much love of learning is in fault, and that I have given up my self to dream away my years in the arms of studious retirement like Endymion with the Moon." Milton replies that it is not "a poor regardless and unprofitable sin of curiosity" that holds him back (for how could that prevail against "a desire of honour and repute and immortal fame"?), nor "the endless delight of speculation, but this very consideration of that great commandment" (about using one's talent) that leads to his not pressing forward; such a consideration "keeps off, with a sacred reverence and religious advisement how best to undergo—not taking thought of being late, so it give advantage to be more fit."

At Horton, where his father had retired, Milton—to quote his own account in the Latin *Second Defence*—"enjoyed an interval of uninterrupted leisure, which I entirely devoted to the perusal of the Greek and Latin classics; though I occasionally visited the metropolis, either for the sake of purchasing books, or of learning something new in mathematics or in music, in which I, at that time, found a source of pleasure or amusement." He was also reading the Christian Fathers and a great deal of history, and probably much else besides. His poetic achievement was to be based on a solid foundation of knowledge. His actual poetic output during his nearly six years at Horton was small: "On Time" (if this was not written towards the end of his period in Cambridge), "Upon the Circumcision," "At a Solemn Music," *Arcades* (possibly earlier), *Comus*, and "Lycidas," together with a translation of Psalm 114 into Greek hexameters, and a verse letter in Latin hexameters to his father. "On Time" shows Milton experimenting most successfully with the verse paragraph, probably with the Italian *canzone* in mind. The manipulation of the varying line lengths, expanding or contracting to respond to the shifts of emphasis and interest until the final soaring upward in triumph of Eternity over Time—

> Triumphing over Death and Chance and thee O Time—

is handled with great skill. "Upon the Circumcision" tries to apply a similar technique to an uncongenial theme, and the result is unhappy: once again, Milton was uncomfortable in handling the theme of Christ's suffering. "At a Solemn Music" repeats the success of "On Time" in a poem of very similar structure. As Time and Eternity are set against each other in the latter poem, with Eternity soaring out in the climax, so in the latter earthly music and the divine Music of the Spheres answer each other, with the heavenly music sounding out in the end in triumphant chorus. These two short poems, in which the form is molded by the thought and emotion, show Milton already developing an architectonic power and a sure control over verse movement. They show him leaving behind the influence of Giles Fletcher's *Christ's Victory and Triumph* and Sylvester's translation of Du Bartas' *Divine Weeks,* which had been so strong in his early religious poetry, to forge a style of his own.

Arcades shows Milton in a new role, as is made clear by the subtitle, "Part of an Entertainment presented to the Countess Dowager of Derby at Harefield by some noble persons of her family, who appear on the scene in pastoral habit. . . ." Milton was probably invited to contribute to this noble entertainment by the musician Henry Lawes, who wrote the music for *Arcades,* as for *Comus.* Milton's model was the Jonsonian masque, but there is an Elizabethan freshness about the songs, and a controlled grace about the aristocratic compliment which is the purpose of the whole entertainment, that are not quite Jonsonian. It is a simple enough affair. The "noble persons of her family" in pastoral habit move across the lawn toward the Countess' country house singing the first song:

> Look nymphs, and shepherds look,
> What sudden blaze of majesty
> Is that which we from hence descry,
> Too divine to be mistook:
> This, this is she
> To whom our vows and wishes bend;
> Here our solemn search hath end.

After three more such stanzas, the Genius of the Wood (a part played by Lawes) approaches and addresses the members of the Countess' family in courtly tones:

> Stay gentle swains, for though in this disguise
> I see bright honour sparkle through your eyes. . . .

With considerable delicacy Milton moves this speech from compliment to the Countess to a discussion of his favorite Music of the Spheres and back to the Countess again. The Genius of the Wood describes his beneficent work on the Countess' estate, and then goes on to talk of his other activities:

> But else in deep of night, when drowsiness
> Hath lock'd up mortal sense, then listen I
> To the celestial Sirens' harmony,
> That sit upon the nine enfolded spheres
> And sing to those that hold the vital shears
> And turn the adamantine spindle round
> On which the fate of gods and men is wound.
> Such sweet compulsion doth in music lie,
> To lull the daughters of Necessity
> And keep unsteady Nature to her law

And the low world in measur'd motion draw
After the heavenly tune, which none can hear
Of human mold with gross unpurged ear;
And yet such music worthiest were to blaze
The peerless height of her immortal praise,
Whose lustre leads us. . . .

A second song follows, the delicate, lightly dancing

O'er the smooth enamell'd green
Where no print of step hath been,
  Follow me as I sing,
  And touch the warbled string. . . .

—which has overtones both of Puck and of Ariel. The final song, with its strangely moving opening

Nymphs and shepherds dance no more

brings the entertainment to a close, concluding with a final compliment to the Countess:

Such a rural Queen
All Arcadia hath not seen.

This is an aristocratic art, Elizabethan in feeling, courtly in tone, yet always essentially simple in manner. These songs give us some basis for speculating about what Milton might have developed into had he been a contemporary of Sidney and Spenser in fact as he was in many ways in spirit. One does not readily think of Milton as a courtly poet, or as writing from halfway up Fortune's Hill with his eye on the summit; but *Arcades* does show him for once in this role.

Milton's next aristocratic entertainment, "A Mask presented at Ludlow Castle" (generally called *Comus*, but that was not Milton's title), is a more elaborate affair. That Milton should have been commissioned to write this masque indicates that he had come to be regarded with favor by the kind of aristocratic artistic circles in which Henry Lawes was so well established. The Dowager Countess of Derby, for whom he wrote *Arcades*, lived at Harefield, only a few miles from where Milton was living at Horton, and the Earl of Bridgewater, for whose inauguration as Lord President of Wales *Comus* was written, was the Countess' stepson. So we can see how the young poet came to be invited to collaborate with Lawes in producing a masque for the Ludlow Castle entertainment. But history and his own temperament were against Milton's exploiting further his aristocratic connections and their accompanying possibilities of patronage. The issues that were to produce the Civil War were already dividing the nation: Charles I was in the midst of his sustained and ultimately unsuccessful attempt to govern without Parliament and impose his view of Church and State on the country. At the same time, something in Milton's own character led him to base his courtly entertainment on his passionately held doctrine of the mystical virtues of chastity, an odd theme for a celebratory masque at an earl's castle, and one which must have caused some eyebrow-raising at the first performance, in spite of the masque's undoubted popularity.

Comus was first published anonymously in 1637: nothing else by Milton (except the Shakespeare sonnet) had yet been published. It appeared with a dedication to the son of the Earl of Bridgewater by Henry Lawes, which includes an interesting indication of the masque's popularity: "Although not openly acknowledged by the author, yet it is a legitimate offspring, so lovely and so much desired that the copying of it has tired my pen to give my several friends satisfaction, and brought me to a necessity of producing it to the public view." The reason why Milton did not "openly acknowledge" the work is suggested by the quotation from Virgil's *Eclogues* which he chose as epigraph:

> Eheu quid volui mihi! floribus austrum
> Perditus. . . .
>
> Alas, what wretchedness have I brought upon myself!
> I have let loose the south wind upon my flowers . . .

He had written the masque because he had been requested to do so, but he did not feel himself to be really ready. So in "Lycidas," wrung from him in 1637 by "bitter constraint and sad occasion dear," he began by explaining that for a second time he had been compelled by events to pluck the as yet unripe fruit of his art:

> Yet once more, O ye laurels, and once more
> Ye myrtles brown, with ivy never sere,
> I come to pluck your berries harsh and crude,
> And with forc'd fingers rude
> Shatter your leaves before the mellowing year.

In September, 1637—two months before completing "Lycidas" and a month and a half after the drowning of Edward King, which was the occasion of the poem—he wrote in a Latin letter to Charles Diodati: "Do you ask me what I am thinking of? With God's help, of immortal fame! And what am I doing? Growing my wings and preparing for flight; but as yet my Pegasus rises on very tender pinions."

This picture of careful self-preparation to write great poetry is unmatched in the history of English literature. It shows, among other things, that Milton had the high ideal of poetry first formulated in the Renaissance: his Humanism and his Christianity combined to produce and define his poetic ambition.

Comus is in the Elizabethan masque tradition, one of the last English works of its kind. Book X of the *Odyssey*, Platonic and neo-Platonic philosophy, Spenser's description of the Bower of Bliss in Book II of the *Faerie Queene*, William Browne's *Inner Temple Masque* (treating of Circe and Ulysses), Jonson's *Pleasure Reconciled to Virtue* (a masque where Comus figures as a glutton), Peele's *Old Wives Tale*, Fletcher's *The Faithful Shepherdess*, each suggested something to Milton, and it is worth listing these varied influences if only to illustrate Milton's remarkable ability to synthesize effortlessly the results of wide reading. *Comus* opens with the attendant spirit (played by Lawes) speaking, in the calm recitative of formal blank verse, the introductory expository speech:

> Before the starry threshold of Jove's court
> My mansion is, where those immortal shapes
> Of bright aerial spirits live insphered
> In regions mild of calm and serene air,
> Above the smoke and stir of this dim spot
> Which men call Earth, . . .

He speaks of the tutelary deities of the region (managing to pay a compliment to the Earl of Bridgewater while doing so), tells of the peer's daughter and two sons coming "through the perplex'd paths of this drear wood" to greet their father, and warns of Comus the enchanter, son of Bacchus and Circe, who lies in wait to trap the unwary into his "sensual sty." He departs, and Comus enters with his rout of monsters (men and women transformed into beasts). Comus' speech, sharply distinct from the earlier formal blank verse, moves trippingly, almost tipsily, in its tones of revelry:

> The star that bids the shepherd fold,
> Now the top of heav'n doth hold;
> And the gilded car of day
> His glowing axle doth allay
> In the steep Atlantic stream, . . .
> Meanwhile, welcome joy and feast,
> Midnight shout and revelery,
> Tipsy dance and jollity. . . .
> Now to the moon in wavering morrice move,
> And on the tawny sands and shelves
> Trip the pert fairies and the dapper elves.

By dimpled brook and fountain brim
The wood-nymphs, deck'd with daisies trim,
Their merry wakes and pastimes keep:
What hath night to do with sleep?

The lilt to this sounds innocent enough (though the ear accustomed to Milton's cadences will note the occasional drunken lurch); but one of the themes of the masque is the distinction between guilty and innocent mirth, and after some thirty-five lines the tone changes, to make clear that we are here dealing with the former variety:

Come, let us our rites begin,
'Tis only daylight that makes sin,
Which these dun shades will ne'er report.
Hail, goddess of nocturnal sport,
Dark-veil'd Cotytto, t' whom the secret flame
Of midnight torches burns; . . .

A dance by Comus and his company follows, broken off by the entry of the Lady, who has become separated from her brothers and is lost in the wood. Comus falls into a more formal speech—

Break off, break off, I feel the different pace
Of some chaste footing near about this ground—

and lays his plans. The Lady enters, and in flexible verse with conversational overtones explains her plight:

. . . I should be loth
To meet the rudeness and swill'd insolence
Of such late wassailers; yet O where else
Shall I inform my unacquainted feet
In the blind mazes of this tangl'd wood?

As she dwells on her situation, the verse becomes slower and more stately:

They left me then, when the gray-hooded Ev'n
Like a sad votarist in palmer's weed
Rose from the hindmost wheels of Phoebus' wain.

But she senses the presence of Comus, and the movement of the verse changes again:

What might this be? A thousand fantasies
Begin to throng into my memory
Of calling shapes, and beck'ning shadows dire,
And airy tongues, that syllable men's names
On sands and shores and desert wildernesses.

She recalls her virtue and her chastity, and announces in somewhat stilted verse her confidence in them, then sings a song, in the hope of attracting her brothers' attention. The song is about Echo and Narcissus, a perfect piece of mythological delicacy, with the final two lines swelling out to a profounder meaning:

> Sweet Echo, sweetest nymph that liv'st unseen
> Within thy airy shell
> By slow Meander's margent green,
> And in the violet embroider'd vale
> Where the love-lorn nightingale
> Nightly to thee her sad song mourneth well:
> Canst thou not tell me of a gentle pair
> That likest thy Narcissus are?
> O if thou have
> Hid them in some flow'ry cave,
> Tell me but where
> Sweet Queen of Parley, Daughter of the Sphere.
> So mayst thou be translated to the skies,
> And give resounding grace to all Heav'n's harmonies.

Comus is ravished by the song, which moves him to an eloquent expression of admiration:

> But such a sacred and home-felt delight,
> Such sober certainty of waking bliss,
> I never heard till now.

He hails the Lady in tones reminiscent of Caliban's attitude to Miranda, and the ensuing dialogue shows him playing skillfully the role of guide and comforter to the Lady. He knows the wood, and will help her find her brothers, whom he saw recently:

> Two such I saw, what time the labour'd ox
> In his loose traces from the furrow came,
> And the swink't hedger at his supper sat.

If he is adroit enough to convince the Lady, it is no wonder that he also convinces the reader, who finds in this part of the masque some of the most charming verse, expressive of quiet joy in the English countryside and satisfaction in agricultural labor well done (which we know to have been Milton's own attitude), put into Comus' mouth. We have echoes of Puck:

> I know each lane and every alley green,
> Dingle or bushy dell of this wild wood

and of the Spenserian pastoralists. The Lady, not surprisingly, agrees to follow Comus, and as they depart the two brothers enter, searching for their sister. "Unmuffle, ye faint stars," the elder brother cries, in tones that might have been used by Romeo or some other of Shakespeare's early heroes, but as the dialogue between the brothers develops, and the elder preaches to the younger Milton's grand doctrine of the mystical virtue of chastity that always preserves from harm, something of the dramatic life goes out of the verse. The statement of the doctrine is eloquent enough, but didactically rather than dramatically.

The attendant spirit, disguised as the shepherd Thyrsis, then enters and tells of Comus, his nature and his threat, in a fine set piece of descriptive verse. The younger brother is appalled at the threat to his sister, but the elder reaffirms the young Milton's view that virtue always guarantees the safety of its possessor:

> Virtue may be assail'd, but never hurt,
> Surpris'd by unjust force, but not enthrall'd

—a view which his later contemplation of the nature of temptation led him to modify. Thyrsis explains about the magic herb which will undo Comus' enchantments, and they depart, the scene changing to Comus' palace, where the Lady is now confronted with Comus in his true colors. This is the most dramatic scene in the masque, and the give and take between Comus and the Lady is done with great spirit. The claims of sensual pleasure are pressed by Comus with a persuasive charm—this is the misuse of rhetoric which Milton was to show more profoundly in the speeches of Satan and his followers in *Paradise Lost*. Again we have the slightly tipsy lilt to the speech (faintly reminiscent of Eve's "distempered" speech on returning to Adam after eating the fatal apple):

> Why are you vext, Lady? Why do you frown?
> Here dwell no frowns nor anger; from these gates
> Sorrow flies far. . . .

To the Lady's lively reply Comus returns an even more skillful speech, denouncing "lean and sallow abstinence" and painting a seductive picture of Nature's bounty, meant to be used. He goes on:

> If all the world
> Should in a pet of temperance feed on pulse,
> Drink the clear stream and nothing wear but frieze,
> Th' all-giver would be unthank'd, would be unprais'd, . . .
> And we should serve him as a grudging master,
> As a penurious niggard of his wealth,

> And live like Nature's bastards, not her sons,
> Who would be quite surcharg'd with her own weight,
> And strangl'd with her waste fertility; . . .

The picture of Nature choked by her own unused abundance that Comus goes on to paint is brilliantly done, and shows Milton's gift for dramatic verse. For a man of his temperament, and his strongly held personal views, it is remarkable how he is able to get inside Comus' character (as later he is to get inside Satan's) and put some of his most persuasive verse into Comus' mouth. This is—perhaps it need hardly be said—a deliberately dramatic device, with Comus as with Satan, and to argue that because it is successful Satan is the "real" hero of *Paradise Lost* is as absurd as to argue that Comus is the real hero of Milton's masque—both views show a basic misunderstanding of the nature of Milton's art.

We need not follow the plot through. The Lady is rescued, Sabrina is hailed, in another charming song, to come and release her from the chair to which she is magically bound, and *Comus* ends with a cluster of songs and dances in true masque style. It is characteristic of Milton that after the dance—*innocent* mirth this time, but perhaps the distinction is not as clear as Milton intended—the attendant spirit, in his song, proclaims that "enough is as good as a feast"—

> Back shepherds, back, enough your play,
> Till next sunshine holiday; . . .

The epilogue, spoken by the spirit, suggests Ariel again:

> To the ocean now I fly,
> And those happy climes that lie
> Where day never shuts his eye,

but it ends with a Miltonic moral:

> Love virtue, she alone is free,
> She can teach ye how to climb
> Higher than the sphery chime;
> Or, if virtue feeble were,
> Heav'n itself would stoop to her.

Comus is a remarkable performance. Its freshness, variety, sureness of touch, and mastery of different tones show how far Milton had gone in developing high technical skill. Its variety is perhaps excessive; the different styles—including a not very successful imitation of the Greek *stichomythia* in some of the dialogue—are not always adequately subdued to the total design. But we must remember that this is a masque, meant to be sung and acted, and without the music and the somewhat stylized dramatic action it loses a great deal.

"Lycidas" first appeared (signed simply J. M.) in 1638, in a collection of elegies (mostly Latin) on Edward King, a fellow student of Milton's at Cambridge, who had been drowned in the Irish Sea. The sudden cutting off of a man of great promise, destined for the Church, forced Milton to face the general question of premature death in talented and dedicated young men. It is not that, as has been claimed, "Lycidas" is about John Milton rather than Edward King. But the elegy is about Lycidas and not King—by expanding the individual King into a symbolic pastoral character, standing for the young man of promise in any context, Milton makes his death more significant and the problems faced by it more disturbing. How can one face the fact that, in a world where the wicked prosper and the most incompetent people survive to get high posts of leadership, the young man who dedicates himself to a life of ideal service to his country may be cut off before he has had an opportunity of completing his training and rendering his service? As a dedicated man himself, Milton saw the implications of King's death. By adopting the traditional form of the pastoral elegy Milton was able to bring together his concepts of priesthood and of bardship in the single symbolic figure of the good shepherd who pipes and tends his flock. Further, for Milton pastoral and agricultural activity always symbolized the most elemental aspects of human endeavor; there was for him something profoundly satisfying in contemplating the annual round of the seasons, each with its appropriate rural tasks (and this makes it difficult for him in *Paradise Lost* to accept agricultural labor as a curse imposed as a result of the Fall), so that the pastoral convention is not for him an otiose tradition, but a living art form with a genuine contemporary significance.

Classical, Christian, and personal elements are fused in "Lycidas" to make an elegy both highly formal and highly individual. The famous outburst against the Anglican clergy (Milton had begun by now to take sides in the religious quarrels of his time) is not simply a personal aside; if the theme of the poem is the premature death of the dedicated poet-priest, then surely it is relevant to consider the unhappy fact that unworthy poet-priests survive to mislead the people while worthy ones die young; yet the tone is highly personal. One can find a precedent in classical or Renaissance usage for everything Milton does in "Lycidas"; yet it remains a unique poem, with a quality and a flavor all its own. The poem moves from a slow and eloquent statement of the occasion of the poem to a reminiscence of his student days with King expressed in moving and elemental pastoral terms, thence to sad reflection on the inability of guardian angels to protect their own:

> What could the Muse herself that Orpheus bore,
> The Muse herself, for her enchanting son,
> Whom universal nature did lament
> When by the rout that made the hideous roar
> His gory visage down the stream was sent
> Down the swift Hebrus to the Lesbian shore?

Even Calliope, the muse of epic poetry, could not protect her son Orpheus against the fury of the Thracian bacchanals—a thought to which Milton returns again and again in his poetry. He then goes on to wonder whether after all it might not have been better to enjoy himself while he could instead of living an austere, dedicated life, in the hope of one day becoming a great poet:

> Alas! What boots it with uncessant care
> To tend the homely, slighted shepherd's trade,
> And strictly meditate the thankless muse?
> Were it not better done, as others use,
> To sport with Amaryllis in the shade,
> Or with the tangles of Neaera's hair?

The grave eloquence of the question marks its seriousness. The answer, given by Phoebus, that fame is the spur, and fame is not to be gained in earth but in heaven, is not a true resolution of the question, and the poem moves to a new start with the interrogation of those who might have been expected to protect Lycidas. The note of elegy sounds with ever more plangency as the sense of the inevitability of the fatal accident rises; Cambridge deplores her lost son, and St. Peter laments that such a one as Lycidas should have been taken when so many bad shepherds flourish. Disgust and anger, entering the very fabric of the verse, replace elegy here, but disgust and anger will not bring back Lycidas, and the poet returns to contemplate the dead shepherd, desperately covering his body with flowers to smother his grief and frustration, and then—in a magnificent and characteristically Miltonic surge of the verse—calling on the guardian angel of England to look homeward and see her plight. Geographical imagery here, giving the whole sense of the Celtic southwest corner of England and its place in British history and mythology, is handled with great skill, and artfully put at the service of the emotion, which is both elegiac and patriotic. The ending is a double one: first, the Christian consolation of Lycidas' place in Heaven, then the return to the poet piping his sad song but determined now that it is over to face the morrow with determination. The solution to the problem posed by the poem is to turn to the task that lies to hand so long as one can:

> Thus sang the uncouth swain to th' oaks and rills,
> While the still morn went out with sandals gray.
> He touch'd the tender stops of various quills,
> With eager thought warbling his Doric lay:
> And now the sun had stretch'd out all the hills,
> And now was dropt into the Western bay.
> At last he rose, and twitch'd his mantle blue:
> Tomorrow to fresh woods and pastures new.

It is a conclusion both classical, Christian, and Miltonic. In the sober morning light the poet turns to fresh woods and pastures new. One meets grief by the assertion of purpose—a very different conclusion from Keats' answer to a very similar question, "when I have fears that I may cease to be, before my pen has gleaned my teeming brain." Keats' solution was not to "work for the night is coming," but to

> . . . stand alone, and think
> Till love and fame to nothingness do sink.

Of course the greatness of "Lycidas" does not lie simply in the movement of the thought and the emotion. The handling of the verse paragraphs, the placing of the rhymes, the varying of the line lengths, and all the devices Milton employs in order to combine the ceremonial with the personal without rending the fabric of the poem, show a mature poet at work. He may have thought his art unripe; but in fact this kind of poetic art could mature no further. He could only go further as a poet by turning to a different kind of poetry. And by the time he did that, he, and his world, had changed significantly.

Milton's period of leisured self-preparation for poetry at Horton came to an end in 1638, when he embarked on a fifteen-month period of European travel, most of it spent in Italy. Professor Hanford has called Milton's Italian journey "one of the great *Wanderjahre* of literary history, a moment of contact between cultures comparable with the Italian journeys of Erasmus and of Goethe," and the description is apt enough, for Milton went abroad in a spirit of high purpose, to visit distinguished men of letters, absorb the atmosphere of Mediterranean culture, and establish, as it were, the European context of his ambitions as native English poet. He spent two months in Florence, where he demonstrated his skill as a Latin poet before one of the important literary societies there—one of the "private academies," as Milton called them, in which Italy at that time abounded, where literary men met for readings and conversation. "No time," wrote Milton of his Florentine stay in the *Second Defence,* "will ever abolish the agreeable recollections which I cherish of Jacob Gaddi, Carolo Dati, Frescobaldo, Coltellino, Bonomatthei, Clementillo, Francini, and many others. From Florence I went to Sienna, thence to Rome, where, after I had spent about two months in viewing the antiquities of that famous city . . . I continued my route to Naples. There I was introduced . . . to John Baptista Manso, Marquis of Villa, a nobleman of distinguished rank and authority, to whom Torquato Tasso, the illustrious poet, inscribed his book on friendship." Milton had a wonderful time in Italy, taking an active part in the cultural life of the cities he visited and making many friends. His friendship with Manso produced a set of complimentary verses in Latin hexameters entitled "Mansus," where he paid tribute to Tasso's patron and ended, characteristically, by talking about himself, expressing the wish that it would be his lot to find such a friend if he embarked on epic accounts of "our native kings," and of the wars of Arthur against the Saxons. Manso was also one of those Italians who addressed Latin complimentary verses to Milton, included in the prefatory matter to the 1645 edition of Milton's poems. The Italian visit produced a revival of Milton's Latin versifying; these included a poem to the Roman poet Giovanni Salzilli and several short tributes in hexameters to the Neapolitan singer, Leonora Baroni.

Although Milton spoke out freely on religious matters in Italy—he tells us in the *Second Defence* that on his departure Manso "gravely apologized for not having shown me more civility, which he said he had been restrained from doing, because I had spoken with so little reserve on matters of religion"—this did not prevent him from enjoying himself and making friends and admirers.

"When I was preparing to pass over into Sicily and Greece,"—to quote again from Milton's account in the *Second Defence*—"the melancholy intelligence I received of the civil commotions in England made me alter my purpose; for I thought it base to be travelling for amusement abroad, while my fellow-citizens were fighting for liberty at home." But he took his time about returning. He visited Rome again (where he estabished contact with the important musical circles there), and Florence, thence to Bologna, Ferrara, Venice (where he spent a month and shipped home the books he had collected in Italy), Verona, Milan, and along Lake Leman to Geneva, where he met the distinguished Protestant scholar and theologian Giovanni Diodati, uncle of his friend Charles Diodati. He finally reached England at the beginning of August, 1639, in that uneasy period between the settlement of the so-called First Bishops' War and the outbreak of the Second in 1640. Milton settled down in London, undertaking the education of his two orphaned nephews, Edward and John Philips, and later taking in also some other pupils. He pondered on education, and at the same time (not immediately seeing it as his duty to offer his services to the antiroyalist cause) meditated on topics for an epic and on plans for a drama on the subject of the Fall. His self-preparation as a poet was still continuing.

King Charles had summoned the Short Parliament in 1640 in the hope of getting a money vote, but Parliament insisted on redress of grievances first, and Charles dissolved Parliament in disgust after three weeks. The Second Bishops' War ended in October after the defeat of Charles' army by a Scottish force, and Charles had to summon Parliament again. This, the Long Parliament, turned at once to the punishment of those who had advised the King in his absolute course—notably the Earl of Strafford and Archbishop Laud—and then proceeded to legislate for the regularizing of parliamentary procedure and the curbing of the royal authority. The Long Parliament had a narrow Puritan majority, who introduced a bill for the abolition of episcopacy and the reorganizing of the Church. This "root and branch bill" aroused the strong opposition of the substantial minority who wished to see a moderate episcopacy and a certain amount of toleration in church matters (in other words, to revert to the position of the Church of England before Laud had imposed his uniform ceremonial and method of worship). The two sides engaged in a fierce pamphlet war, and it was into this war that Milton entered with an anonymous pamphlet supporting his old tutor Thomas Young. Bishop Hall had published, in December, 1640, a moderate enough defense of a limited episcopacy, under the title, *A Humble Remonstrance to the High Court of Parliament*. Young and a group of his fellow ministers wrote a reply (the authors' combined initials formed the word "Smectymnuus," under which name the pamphlet appeared), and this reply was in turn answered both by Hall and by James Ussher, Archbishop of Armagh. Milton joined in on Hall's side, his first pamphlet *Of Reformation in England and the Causes that have hitherto hindered it,* appearing just before the replies to Smectymnuus by Hall and Ussher and not directly referring to the controversy; but Milton's subsequent antiepiscopal pamphlets enter more directly into the controversy, and are concerned to refute Hall and Ussher. Milton produced five pamphlets in all on this subject, between April, 1641, and March, 1642, and their titles indicate the continuous dingdong nature of the argument. The second was *Of*

Prelatical Episcopacy, and whether it may be deduced from the Apostolical Times, by virtue of those Testimonies which are alleged to that purpose in some late treatises; one whereof goes under the name of James, Archbishop of Armagh. Then *Animadversions upon the Remonstrant's Defence against Smectymnuus* in July, 1641, and *The Reason of Church Government Urged against Prelaty* in February, 1642. In the same month as the latter appeared a pamphlet on the other side, whose title is also instructive: *A Modest Confutation of a Slanderous and Scurrilous Libel entitled Animadversions upon the Remonstrant's Defence against Smectymnuus.* And in March came Milton's *An Apology against a Pamphlet called a Modest Confutation of the Animadversions upon the Remonstrant against Smectymnuus.*

The main thought in Milton's antiprelatical pamphlets was that the English Reformation had not been completed in Tudor times, and now was the time to complete it. He has the true Protestant view of the Reformation, rejoicing to recall "how the bright and blissful Reformation (by divine power) struck through the black and settled night of ignorance and antichristian tyranny." He asks himself, in his first pamphlet, "how it should come to pass that England (having had this grace and honour from God, to be the first that should set up a standard for the recovery of lost truth, and blow the first evangelic trumpet to the nations, holding up, as from a hill, the new lamp of saving light to all Christians) should now be last and most unsettled in the enjoyment of that peace, whereof she taught the way to others." He replies by interpreting the ecclesiastical history of England from the time of Henry VIII, and distinguishing three "hinderers of reformation"—antiquarians (whom he distinguishes from "useful and laudable" antiquaries), libertines, and politicians. *Of Reformation in England* is a vigorously argued pamphlet, marshaling evidence from history and literature (he cites Dante, Petrarch, Chaucer, and Ariosto, as well as ecclesiastical writers) and pressing its points forcefully and with a certain dignity in a prose whose long sentences are managed with considerable rhetorical skill. *Of Prelatical Episcopacy* turns to the arguments of the other side, and refutes them point by point in what to the modern reader is tedious detail, though here, as in the former pamphlet, there comes through clearly Milton's view of the lamentable gap between the simple Gospel injunctions and the elaborate paraphernalia of ecclesiastical systems. Milton is particularly anxious to deny (as his opponents were anxious to maintain) that modern episcopacy could be deduced from the practice of apostolic times. "The pure and living precept of God's word only" is the proper guide for Christians. "But if any shall strive to set up his ephod and teraphim of antiquity against the brightness and perfection of the gospel; let him fear lest he and his Baal be turned into Bosheth." *Animadversions* deals in a more satirical way with Hall, whose arguments he sets out and replies to in question-and-answer form, often turning the argument *ad hominem* in what Milton considered a sportive manner. *The Reason of Church Government* (the first to appear with the author's name) is an elaborately reasoned defense of the presbyterian form of church government against the episcopal; there is no sportiveness here, only an earnest and scholarly argument. *An Apology* shows how the debate had deteriorated into personalities. Milton had himself been personally attacked by this time, and he replied in kind, showing his characteristic ability to identify himself with a cause and to regard autobiography as defense of the cause. This pamphlet is full of picturesque abuse, and parts are in a style of colloquial flippancy which, while popular in controversial literature of the time, does not wear well. This manner, with the progress of the debate forced upon Milton, led to a pettiness and lack of generosity that are found all too often in Milton's controversial prose.

There is something else, however, which is found in these antiprelatical pamphlets which is purely Miltonic and which throws much light on Milton's state of mind at this time. He was still the dedicated poet, though the necessities of the time might take him temporarily into other kinds of writing. On his return from Italy he had been full of poetic plans, and was desolated to find that his friend Charles Diodati, to whom he had looked forward to talking of his Italian triumphs and his literary intentions, had died the previous year. In the Latin elegy on Diodati—an eloquent and skillful pastoral elegy—he cannot resist saying something of the plans for an epic he had hoped to discuss with his friend. After repeating the refrain

Ite domum impasti, domino iam non vacat, agni,
Go home unfed, my lamb, your master now has no time for you,

he proceeds:

Ipse ego Dardanias Rutupina per aequora puppes
Dicam, et Pandrasidos regnum vetus Inogeniae,
Brennumque Arviragumque duces, priscumque Belinum,
Et tandem Armoricos Britonum sub lege colonos;
Tum gravidam Arturo fatali fraude Iogernen,
Mendaces vultus, assumptaque Gorlois arma,
Merlini dolus. O, mihi tum si vita supersit,
Tu procul annosa pendebis, fistula, pinu
Multum oblita mihi, aut patriis mutata camenis

> Brittonicum strides! Quid enim? omnia non licet uni
> Non sperasse uni licet omnia. . . .

For my part, I shall tell of the Dardanian ships in the Rutupian sea, and of the ancient kingdom of Inogen, daughter of Pandrasus, and of the chiefs, Brennus and Arviragus, and old Belinus, and of the Armorican settlers who at last came under British law; then of Igraine pregnant with Arthur by a fatal trick, the features of Gorlois and his arms falsely assumed by Merlin's trickery. O then, my pipe, if further life remains to me, you shall hang far away on some old pine tree, wholly forgotten by me, or else sound forth in harsher tones a British theme to your native muses. What then? One man cannot do everything, nor can one man hope for everything.

These were themes from early British history, and he intended to choose among them for his epic. With the kindling of his imagination at the prospect of a new and regenerate England arising out of the completion of the Reformation for which he was pleading in his antiprelatical pamphlets, he thought of himself more and more as the poet of that brave new world, waiting for the completion of God's deliverance to utter forth his mighty harmonies. He thinks now more of divine than of secular subjects. But he does still think of poetry, and his poetic ambitions are higher than ever. Who else but Milton could end a pamphlet on church government as Milton ended *Of Reformation in England,* with a passionate outburst expressing his faith in a reformed and greater England of which he will be the poet?

O how much more glorious will those former deliverances appear, when we shall know them not only to have saved us from greatest miseries past, but to have reserved us for greatest happiness to come! Hitherto thou hast but freed us, and that not fully, from the unjust and tyrannous claim of thy foes; now unite us entirely, and appropriate us to thyself, tie us everlastingly in willing homage to the prerogative of thy eternal throne. . . .

Then, amidst the hymns and hallelujahs of saints, some one may perhaps be heard offering at high strains in new and lofty measures to sing and celebrate thy divine mercies and marvellous judgments in this land throughout all ages; whereby this great and warlike nation, instructed and inured to the fervent and continual practice of truth and righteousness, and casting far from her the rags of her old vices, may press on hard to that high and happy emulation to be found the soberest, wisest, and most Christian people at that day, when thou, the eternal and shortly expected King, shalt open the clouds to judge the several kingdoms of the world, and distribute national honours and rewards to religious and just commonwealths, shalt put an end to all earthly tyrannies, proclaiming thy universal and mild monarchy through heaven and earth; where they undoubtedly, that by their labours, counsels, and prayers, have been earnest for the common good of religion and their country, shall receive above the inferior orders of the blessed, the regal addition of principalities, legions, and thrones into their glorious titles, and in supereminence of beatific vision, progressing the dateless and irrevoluble circle of eternity, shall clasp inseparable hands with joy and bliss in overmeasure for ever.

This is a remarkable outburst to find in a pamphlet on episcopacy. It is the true voice of the young Milton, but it is also the voice of his times, combining with the immense ambition of the poet the utopian optimism of the Puritan reformer. We must remember this tone of boundless optimism when we come to assess the nature of Milton's disillusion at the failure of the Commonwealth and the restoration of Charles II.

The personal note emerges in the most unexpected places in his prose pamphlets. In the *Animadversions* he turns suddenly from a contemptuous dismissal of one of the Remonstrant's arguments to contemplate with almost mystical fervor the coming heaven on earth. The prose is tremulous with excitement as he addresses God:

O perfect and accomplish thy glorious acts! for men may leave their works unfinished, but thou are a God, thy nature is perfection: shouldst thou bring us thus far onward from Egypt to destroy us in this wilderness, though we deserve, yet thy great name would suffer in the rejoicing of thine enemies, and the deluded hope of all thy servants. When thou hast settled peace in the church and righteous judgment in the kingdom, then shall all thy saints address their voices of joy and triumph to thee, standing on the shore of that Red Sea into which our enemies had almost driven us. And he that now for haste snatches up a plain ungarnished present as a thank-offering to thee, which could not be deferred in regard of thy so many late deliverances wrought for us one upon another, may then perhaps take up a harp, and sing thee an elaborate song to generations. . . . Come forth out of thy royal chambers, O Prince of all the kings of the earth! put on the invisible robes of thy imperial majesty, take up that unlimited sceptre which thy Almighty Father hath bequeathed thee; for now the voice of thy bride calls thee, and all creatures sigh to be renewed.

After this it is not surprising that in the *Apology for Smectymnuus*, after rebutting charges of unchastity made against him by his opponents, he goes on to elaborate his theory of chastity, explaining how he came to hold it, and the Platonic and Christian authorities for it, concluding significantly: "Nor did I slumber over that place [in the Bible] expressing such high rewards of ever accompanying the Lamb with those celestial songs to others inapprehensible, but not to those who were not defiled with women, which doubtless means fornication; for marriage must not be called a defilement."

Even in the serious and scholarly argument of *The Reason of Church Government* Milton manages to become autobiographical, beginning the second book by expressing regret that the advancement of knowledge should require controversy, which was not really his task. "But when God commands to take the trumpet and blow a dolorous or a jarring blast, it lies not in man's will what he shall say or what he shall conceal." He explains that his "sharp but saving words" are, unfortunately, necessary. "I should not," he goes on, "choose this manner of writing, wherein knowing myself inferior to myself, led by the genial power of nature to another task, I have the use, as I may account it, but of my left hand." At this point, while admitting that "I shall be foolish in saying more to this purpose," he cannot resist the urge to go on and talk about his career and ambitions, mentioning the praise his poems had received in Italy, his determination "to fix all the industry and art I could unite to the adorning of my native tongue," and the kinds of poetry he contemplated writing:

> Time serves not now, and perhaps I might seem too profuse to give any certain account of what the mind at home in the spacious circuits of her musing hath liberty to propose to herself, though of highest hopes and hardest attempting; whether that epic form whereof the two poems of Homer and those other two of Virgil and Tasso are a diffuse, and the book of Job a brief, model: or whether the rules of Aristotle herein are strictly to be kept, or nature to be followed, which in them that know art and use judgement, is no transgression but an enriching of art: and lastly, what king or knight before the conquest might be chosen in whom to lay the pattern of a Christian hero. . . .

After epic, he goes on to consider tragedy, wondering "whether those dramatic constitutions, wherein Sophocles and Euripides reign, shall be found more doctrinal and exemplary to a nation." There are dramatic models in Scripture, too, "a divine pastoral drama in the Song of Solomon" and "the majestic image of a high and stately tragedy" in the Apocalypse of St. John. Finally, he considers the possibilities of the lyric, either in the Greek style of Pindar or Callimachus or in the style of the Hebrew poetry of the Old Testament. Milton concludes this autobiographical digression by explaining that he was originally intended for the Church, "till coming to some maturity of years and perceiving what tyranny had invaded the church, that he who would take orders must subscribe slave and take an oath withal, which, unless he took with a conscience that would retch, he must either straight perjure or split his faith; I thought it better to prefer a blameless silence before the sacred office of speaking, bought and begun with servitude and forswearing. Howsoever, thus church-outed by the prelates, hence may appear the right I have to meddle in these matters, as before the necessity and constraint appeared." It is clear already that Milton was not going to find it easy to go along with any major Christian sect. Though he had thrown in his lot with the Presbyterians, a few years later he was to complain in a sonnet of "the new forcers of conscience under the Long Parliament," and he moved ever closer to the Independents and to Cromwell, who supported them, finding himself eventually among the small Cromwellian group committed to the execution of the King.

It was Milton's precipitate marriage, probably in the spring of 1642, that helped to move him toward a more independent and liberal position in ecclesiastical as in other matters. After years of dedicated chastity, he suddenly turned all his passionate idealistic thought about a perfect mate onto a flighty young girl of royalist family, imagining that her dumbness in his presence was a sign of modest thoughtfulness and looking forward to an intellectual as well as a physical companionship which he felt he had fully earned. Both were rapidly disillusioned; and Mary Powell soon returned to her parents' home on a visit from which she did not return until a reconciliation was patched up in the summer of 1645. The emotional shock to Milton was enormous and, with his usual gift for deriving general conclusions from a personal situation, he immediately set himself to discover and to proclaim publicly the legal and other problems involved, and their solution. Marriage was meant to be a perfect companionship, spiritual, intellectual, and physical, and if through well-meaning misjudgment it turned out to be something very different, release should be made possible. This was the position he argued in *The Doctrine and Discipline of Divorce,* published in August, 1643. It was because his ideal of marriage was so high, not because he took a low view of it, that he pleaded for easiness of divorce. The personal note rings out with sad naïveté in Chapter III.

> The soberest and best governed men are least practised in these affairs; and who knows not that the bashful muteness of a virgin may ofttimes hide all the unliveliness and natural sloth which is really unfit for conversation? Nor is there that freedom of access granted or presumed as may suffice to a perfect discerning till too late; and where any indisposition is suspected, what more usual than the persuasion of friends that acquaintance, as it increases, will amend all? And lastly, it is not strange though many who have spent their youth chastely, are in some things not so quick-sighted, while they haste too eagerly to light the nuptial torch, nor is it, therefore, that for a modest error a man should forfeit so great a happiness, and no charitable means to release him, since they who have lived most loosely, by reason of their bold accustoming prove most successful in their matches, because their wild affections, unsettling at will, have been as so many divorces to teach them experience. Whereas the sober man honouring the appearance of modesty, and hoping well of every social virtue under that veil, may easily chance to meet, if not with a body impenetrable, yet often with a mind to all other due conversation inaccessible, and to all the more estimable and superior purposes of matrimony useless and almost lifeless;

and what a solace, what a fit help such a consort would be through the whole life of a man, is less pain to conjecture than to have experience.

It is the virtuous man, with no experience of women, who is most likely to make a fatal error of judgment in marriage, while the rakes, having sown their wild oats, have learned from experience and choose more wisely when they come to marry. Alas, what boots it with uncessant care. . . .

Milton's defense of divorce naturally provoked much opposition, which led him to write, in 1644 and 1645, three further pamphlets in more controversial vein, one citing the opinions of an earlier divine who had favored divorce, another reinforcing his arguments with a great play of scriptural texts, and a third replying, with a wealth of sportive abuse, to an opponent who had attacked his first divorce pamphlet. Meanwhile Parliament, now dominated by the Presbyterian party, who were anxious to silence opposition views, had passed an act requiring all books to be licensed by an official censor. Milton and his printer ignored this, and an inquiry was ordered. Though nothing further developed, Milton's blood was up; once again, personal situation and general principle combined to produce a passionately held conviction. The result was *Areopagitica* in 1644, a classic defense of liberty of the press, where Milton's highly individualistic temper led him to put forward arguments which, while familiar to nineteenth-century liberal thought, were new and strange indeed in the seventeenth century. Truth will prevail over error only in open conflict; and in any case (an unexpected argument from a passionate Puritan Christian) truth is not in its single wholeness capable of being grasped by men, each of whom may only discover a single, and different, fragment:

Truth indeed came once into the world with her divine Master, and was a perfect shape most glorious to look on; but when he ascended, and his apostles after him were laid asleep, then straight rose a wicked race of deceivers, who . . . took the virgin Truth, hewed her lovely form into a thousand pieces, and scattered them to the four winds. From that time ever since, the sad friends of Truth, such as durst appear, imitating the careful search that Isis made for the mangled body of Osiris, went up and down gathering limb by limb still as they could find them. We have not yet found them all, Lords and Commons, nor ever shall do, till her Master's second coming.

Truth is strong, but not single:

For who knows not that Truth is strong, next to the Almighty. She needs no policies, nor stratagems, nor licensings to make her victorious—those are the shifts and defences that error uses against her power. Give her but room, and do not bind her when she sleeps, for then she speaks not true, ...

Yet it is not impossible that she may have more shapes than one. What else is all that rank of things indifferent, wherein Truth may be on this side, or on the other, without being unlike herself?

There is the indignity, too, of being subject to the ferula like a schoolboy. "When a man writes to the world, he summons up all his reason and deliberation to assist him; he searches, meditates, is industrious, and likely consults and confers with his judicious friends, after all which he has done he takes himself to be informed in what he writes, as well as any writ before him." Who is any parliamentary censor to challenge John Milton? In any case, controversy strengthens truth, and to believe things merely on authority is no real belief. Good can only be known by evil, truth by falsehood, virtue by trial against the temptations of the world. "To sequester out of the world into Atlantic and Utopian polities, which never can be drawn into use, will not mend our condition; but to ordain wisely as in this world of evil, in the midst whereof God hath placed us unavoidably." Or again: "I cannot praise a fugitive and cloistered virtue unexercised and unbreathed, that never sallies out and sees her adversary, but slinks out of the race, where that immortal garland is to be run for, not without dust and heat." There is a note of patriotism, too, in the pamphlet, and of expectation of great things to happen shortly in England. "Lords and Commons of England," he exclaims, "consider what nation it is whereof ye are . . ." The roar of debate going on in the country is a sign of health and vigor: some wonderful dispensation will soon be vouchsafed.

Now once again by all concurrence of signs, and by the general instinct of holy and devout men, as they daily and solemnly express their thoughts, God is decreeing to begin some new and great period in his Church, even to the reforming of reformation itself. What does he then but reveal himself to his servants, and, as his manner is, first to his Englishmen.

Areopagitica is a noble and eloquent plea, overwhelmingly optimistic in tone even though one of the premises of the argument is the inaccessibility of total truth to men as a result of the Fall. Much of it would seem to come more appropriately from the pen of a John Stuart Mill than that of a seventeenth-century Puritan. That Milton could write this classic piece of liberal pamphleteering is one of many indications of the complex nature of his Christian Humanist mentality.

In 1644, between his first and second divorce pamphlets, Milton published his little treatise *Of Education,* in the form of a letter to Samuel Hartlib, whose known interest in educational reform and in the ideas of John Comenius made him an obvious recipient of such a communication. Milton is here concerned with the training of an elite in regional academies containing about a hundred and thirty pupils and a staff of about twenty. His educational ideal is a Christian Humanist one; he defined the end of learning as "to repair the ruins of our first parents by regaining to know God aright, and out of that knowledge to love him, to imitate him, to be like him," and shortly afterwards declares, in the true spirit of Renaissance Humanism, "I call . . . a complete and generous education that which fits a man to perform justly, skilfully, and magnanimously all the offices, both private and public, of peace and war." He opposes early emphasis on such "abstract" studies as rhetoric and logic, insisting on a great variety of substantial reading in Latin and Greek, from the point of view of the usefulness of their content (including agriculture, geometry, astronomy, geography, medicine, and natural history) and not merely of their stylistic elegance. Thence the students proceed to classical writers on ethics and economics, "and either now or before this, they may have easily learned at any odd hour the Italian tongue." Politics comes next, and then (Hebrew together with "the Chaldee and the Syrian dialect" now having been learned) biblical studies and church history, and only after that come "choice histories, heroic poems, and Attic tragedies," and rhetoric and logic follow at a still later stage. Regular exercise, walks in the country, fencing, and recreation "with the solemn and divine harmonies of music" are also prescribed. The curriculum is of course impossibly large by modern standards, but it must be remembered that Milton is concerned (though he never explicitly says so) with training a ruling class of specially gifted people. It is interesting that Milton should see his pupils as gaining scientific and practical knowledge through reading appropriate Latin and Greek works; unlike some nineteenth-century English defenders of the classics, he saw classical culture not only as a source of "sweetness and light" but also as a means of instruction in the material things of civilization. The specifically Christian side of his program takes up less space; but that was because there was such universal agreement on its importance that he did not have to dilate on it.

Looking back afterward on his earlier writings, Milton wrote in the *Second Defence* that he came to write on marriage, education, and freedom of the press by a simple logical process:

When the bishops could no longer resist the multitude of their assailants, I had leisure to turn my thoughts to . . . the promotion of real and substantial liberty, which is rather to be sought from within than from without, and whose existence depends not so much on the terror of the sword as on sobriety of conduct and the integrity of life. When, therefore, I perceived that there were three species of liberty which are essential to the happiness of social life—religious, domestic, and civil; and as I had already written concerning the first, and the magistrates were strenuously active in obtaining the third, I determined to turn my attention to the second, or the domestic species. As this seemed to involve three material questions, the conditions of the conjugal tie, the education of the children, and the free publication of the thoughts, I made them objects of distinct consideration.

One cannot help thinking, however, that this is rationalization after the event and that it was Milton's personal circumstances and interests that impelled him to write on these subjects at this time.

Meanwhile, Milton was moving steadily away from the Presbyterians, whom he came to regard as narrow and intolerant, toward the Independents, who eventually gained control of Parliament and began to think more and more in terms of a republic. Between 1646 and 1648 Charles was defeated and imprisoned, escaped to renew the Civil War, and was finally defeated again. Milton was writing no pamphlets at this time; he wrote a few sonnets reflecting his views of various contemporary events, continued teaching his nephews and others, published a volume of his minor poems, worked on a history of Britain, continued to meditate on his future epic, and watched with interest the tide of affairs. Charles was brought to trial on January 20, 1649, and executed ten days later. The execution was the work of a determined minority who were resolved to end the *mystique* of kingship once and for all. It is probable that Milton by this time had moved very close to the position of this minority. At any rate, barely a fortnight after the execution there appeared the first of his third series of pamphlets, concerned with constitutional questions and the rights of the people against tyrants: this was *The Tenure of Kings and Magistrates*, designed to prove—in the words of its subtitle—"that it is lawful, and hath been held so through all ages, for any who have the power, to call to account a tyrant, or wicked king, and after due conviction, to depose, and put him to death, if the ordinary magistrates have neglected or denied to do it. And that they who of late so much blame deposing, are the men that did it themselves." It is a carefully reasoned argument, based on both historical precedents and general moral principles, in favor of the revocability of the supreme civil power. "Since the king or magistrate holds his authority of the people, both originally and naturally for their good in the first place, and not his own, then may the people, as oft as they shall judge it for the best, either choose him or reject him, retain him or depose him, though no tyrant, merely by the liberty and right of freeborn men to be governed as seems to them best." Milton was going behind Stuart theories of divine right and Tudor theories of absolutism to a liberal political tradition common to medieval and Renaissance thought, and at the same time looking forward in some degree to John Locke's *Second Treatise on Civil Government.* From now on Milton's identification with the group that brought about Charles' execution and the setting up of the Commonwealth was complete. The result was that he became the official apologist of the regicides before Europe as well as an important servant of the new government. In March, 1649, he was appointed Latin Secretary to the Council of State (the post was also called Secretary for Foreign Tongues). He had postponed writing his greatest poetry until he was sure that his period of self-preparation was complete, and now history had caught him up and he had to postpone it further.

In addition to conducting the Government's foreign correspondence in Latin, Milton was now required to defend its policy publicly. The execution of Charles had shocked Europe, and in England there was still a great deal of personal feeling for the dead King, a feeling exploited by the publication in February, 1649, of *Eikon Basilike,* "the true portraiture of his Sacred Majesty in his solitudes and sufferings" in the form of a record of his supposed self-communings during his last years (though actually invented by Bishop Gauden). Milton undertook to destroy the effect of this dangerously popular work, with its sentimental, idealizing picture of the King, and in *Eikonoklastes* ("the Image-breaker"), published in October, 1649, he produced a stinging attack on the royal character as revealed in *Eikon Basilike.* Though he begins with some generosity—"To descant on the misfortunes of a person fallen from so high a dignity, who hath also paid his final debt both to nature and his faults, is neither of itself a thing commendable, nor the intention of this discourse"—the work soon becomes insistently carping in tone, ingeniously pressing every point that can be made against the King's character and behavior, tracing his actions in political and ecclesiastical matters in considerable detail. His purpose is to destroy the image of the saint and martyr built up by Bishop Gauden and replace it by that of a vain and hypocritical tyrant. In the very first chapter he seizes with glee on the fact that Charles had "so little care of truth in his last words, or honour to himself, or to his friends, or sense of his afflictions, or of that sad hour that was upon him, as immediately before his death to pop into the hand of that grave bishop who attended him, for a special relique of his saintly exercises, a prayer stolen word for word from the mouth of a heathen fiction praying to a heathen god; and that in no serious book, but the vain amatorious poem of Sir Philip Sidney's Arcadia; a book in that kind full of worth and wit, but among religious thoughts and duties not to be named; nor to be read at any time without good caution, much less in time of trouble and affliction to be a Christian's prayer-book." That Milton was the first to recognize this plagiarism testifies to his own intimate knowledge of *Arcadia,* a work which in other circumstances he would have been glad to praise.

The next stage of Milton's official pamphleteering for the Commonwealth involved a European rather than a purely English audience. The French scholar Claude Saumaise, generally known as Salmasius and now living in Holland, had been commissioned by the exiled Charles II to write a public attack in Latin on those who were responsible for the execution of Charles I, and the result was his *Defensio Regia pro Carolo I.* This appeal to Europe by a distinguished scholar was dangerous for the Commonwealth Government, and Milton replied with a long Latin reply, *Ioannis Miltoni Angli pro Populo Anglicano Defensio contra Claudii anonymi, alias Salmasii, Defensionem Regiam.* This *Defence of the English People* is a detailed and scornful reply to Salmasius, mingling legal, historical, and moral arguments with fierce personal attacks on the character, scholarship, and grammar of Salmasius. The defense seems to have been effective; Salmasius, now living at the court of Queen Christina of Sweden, left in disgrace and died soon afterward. But other champions took up the fight against the regicides. A powerful anonymous work appeared in 1652, with the rhetorical title, *Regii Sanguinis Clamor ad Coelum, adversus Parricidas Anglicanos,* "The Cry of the King's Blood to Heaven against the English Parricides." To this Milton replied with *Joannis Miltoni Angli pro Populo Anglicano Defensio,* the *Second Defence of the English People,* which appeared in May, 1654. This, too, contains much personal abuse, directed against Alexander More, whom Milton wrongly took to be author of the *Regii Sanguinis Clamor;* Milton had received personal abuse in the *Clamor* and gave at least as good as he got. But there is also a note of high patriotic eloquence in the work, and, in addition, those revealing autobiographical passages in which he countered abuse by talking of his own education and ambitions. He talks of his youth, his friendships, his studies, his Italian visit, his feelings when the Civil War broke out, in a long passage which is of the first importance for the student of Milton's mind. He explains and defends his entry into controversial pamphleteering.

> I saw a way was opening for the establishment of real liberty; that the foundation was laying for the deliverance of man from the yoke of slavery and superstition; that the principles of religion, which were the first objects of our care, would exert a salutary influence on the manners and constitution of

the republic; and as I had from my youth studied the distinctions between religious and civil rights, I perceived that if ever I wished to be of use, I ought at least not to be wanting to my country, to the church, and to so many of my fellow-Christians, in a crisis of so much danger; I therefore determined to relinquish the other pursuits in which I was engaged, and to transfer the whole force of my talents and my industry to this one important object.

Milton's identification of himself with the cause he championed was never more clear.

The personalities into which the controversial habits of the age pushed Milton led him at last to a work devoted wholly to a defense of himself. More, not unnaturally resenting Milton's violent attack on himself for a work which he had not written, replied with a fierce attack on Milton, in which he particularly sneered at his crude vanity in taking it upon himself to lay down the law to Cromwell (who became Lord Protector in 1653). Milton's reply, *Joannis Miltoni pro se Defensio contra Alexandrum Morum,* "John Milton's Defence of Himself against Alexander More," appeared in 1655: it is personal and abusive and of little interest to the modern reader. It is interesting, however, that Milton shows himself sensitive to More's charge that he employed "language of unwashed foulness, words naked and indelicate," and he replied not only by returning the charge ("No shade could veil your filthiness, not even that notable fig-tree") but also by citing illustrious precedents for the use of plain, naked words —Sallust, Herodotus, Seneca, Plutarch, "the gravest of authors." Further, if it is to be considered indecent to speak frankly about "subjects abundantly gross," "how often will you have to charge with indecency and obscenity Erasmus, . . . Thomas More, . . . the ancient fathers of the church, Clemens Alexandrinus, Arnobius, Lactantius, Eusebius, when they uncover and cast derision upon the obscene mysteries of the old religions!"

After this there was a pause in Milton's pamphleteering until after Cromwell's death in 1658, when he addressed himself to the question of the relation between the civil and the ecclesiastical power in a pamphlet entitled *A Treatise of Civil Power in Ecclesiastical Causes.* Milton had never been satisfied with any sort of church establishment, his highly individualistic temperament reinforcing the Protestant conception of every man with his Bible constructing his own path to God (though C. S. Lewis has shown that the insistence on spiritual leaders and followers was also a Protestant characteristic in the sixteenth and seventeenth centuries). "Seeing, therefore, that no man, no synod, no session of men, though called the church, can judge definitely the sense of scripture to another man's conscience, which is well known to be a general maxim of the Protestant religion; it follows plainly, that he who holds in religion that belief, or those opinions, which to his conscience and utmost understanding appear with most evidence or probability in the scripture, though to others he seem erroneous, can no more be justly censured for a heretic than his censurers." It is the same argument that he had urged in *Areopagitica;* man can only embrace the truth as he sees it. (He does not, however, push his principles so far as to wish toleration for those whose view of the truth forbids them to accept scripture as a divinely authoritative work at all; he was Milton after all, not John Stuart Mill.) The *Treatise* was addressed to Parliament in the vain hope of producing a practical effect. A second pamphlet on the same subject, *Considerations touching the likeliest means to remove Hirelings out of the Church,* appeared in 1659, after Cromwell's son, Richard Cromwell, had given up the attempt to carry on his father's position and the Rump Parliament (what remained of the Long Parliament after the dismissal of the Presbyterians in "Pride's Purge" in 1648) was recalled by the army to consider the position. Hopeful as ever, Milton saw in this turn of events a chance of moving nearer his ideal commonwealth, and sketched out a plan for an almost unsalaried clergy drawn only from those truly eager for spiritual service, instead of a class of ecclesiastics representing "a distinct order in the commonwealth, bred up for divines in babbling schools, and fed at the public cost, good for nothing else but what was good for nothing."

With the political situation fluid again, and the question of what form of government England should have again under discussion, Milton with an almost pathetic hopefulness published his *Ready and Easy Way to Establish a Free Commonwealth.* And yet the optimism is somewhat forced, as the note of premonition in the introduction shows: ". . . If their absolute determination be to enthrall us, before so long a Lent of servitude, they may permit us a little shroving time first, wherein to speak freely, and take our leaves of liberty." But the optimism rises as he continues: "Now is the opportunity, now the very season, wherein we may obtain a free commonwealth, and establish it for ever in the land, without difficulty or much delay." And later: ". . . few words will save us, well considered; few and easy things, now seasonably done." There is a new tone of almost desperate pleading in parts of this brief tract, in which he recommends to favor his favorite scheme of a single Parliament "in perpetuity of membership for life," a stable oligarchy of the best men chosen by a properly qualified electorate. The pamphlet aroused interest and produced replies, and a second, enlarged edition appeared on the very eve of the Restoration, by which time any possibility of a new republican form of government had vanished. The conclusion of the second edition has a nostalgic eloquence, as though Milton really knew that history had overtaken him:

> What I have spoken, is the language of that which is not called amiss "The good old Cause;" if it seem strange to any, it will not seem more strange, I hope, than convincing to backsliders. Thus much I should perhaps have said, though I was sure I should have spoken to trees and stones; and had none to cry to, but with the prophet, "O earth, earth, earth!" to tell the very soil itself, what her perverse inhabitants are deaf to. Nay, though what I have spoke should happen (which thou suffer not, who didst create mankind free! nor thou next, who didst redeem us from being servants of men!) to be the last words of our expiring liberty. . . .

The Restoration of Charles II brought all Milton's political hopes to an end, destroying at the same time his vision of a reformed and regenerate England which had sustained him for so long. Further political pamphleteering was now useless. Only in 1673, two years before his death, he turned again to pamphleteering to argue in *Of True Religion, Heresy, Toleration, and the growth of Popery*, in favor of toleration of all creeds based on honest interpretation of God's word, however mutually different, and against that one species of Christianity that imposes a man-made tradition on all.

Meanwhile, he had gone blind, the left eye beginning to go in 1644 and total blindness developing by 1652. His enemies saw God's judgment in this, but Milton accepted his affliction with dignity and fortitude, comparing himself, in the *Second Defence*, to "those wise and ancient bards whose misfortunes the gods are said to have compensated by superior endowments." The record of Milton's adjustment to the fact of his blindness is plain in his writings. First, the famous sonnet on his blindness, "When I consider how my light is spent," showing momentary rebellion turning to trust in God's purpose for him —"They also serve who only stand and wait." (So, in *Paradise Regained*, Jesus meditates on his Father's purpose for him, and concludes that he must trustfully await its manifestation.) Then the dignified passage in the *Second Defence*, comparing himself to blind heroes and sages of old. Then the lines at the beginning of Book III of *Paradise Lost:*

> . . . nor sometimes forget
> Those other two equall'd with me in fate,
> So were I equall'd with them in renown,
> Blind Thamyris and blind Maeonides,
> And Tiresias and Phineus, prophets old.
> Then feed on thoughts, that voluntary move

> Harmonious numbers; as the wakeful bird
> Sings darkling, and in shadiest covert hid
> Tunes her nocturnal note. Thus with the year
> Seasons return, but not to me returns
> Day, or the sweet approach of ev'n or morn,
> Or sight of vernal bloom, or summer's rose,
> Or flocks or herds or human face divine;
> But cloud instead, and ever-during dark
> Surrounds me, from the cheerful ways of men
> Cut off, and for the book of knowledge fair
> Presented with a universal blank
> Of Nature's works, to me expunged and ras'd,
> And wisdom at one entrance quite shut out.
> So much the rather thou, celestial light,
> Shine inward, and the mind through all her powers
> Irradiate; there plant eyes; all mist from hence
> Purge and disperse, that I may see and tell
> Of things invisible to mortal sight.

And then in the beginning of Book VII:

> Standing on earth, not rapt above the pole,
> More safe I sing with mortal voice, unchang'd
> To hoarse or mute, though fall'n on evil days,
> On evil days though fall'n, and evil tongues;
> In darkness, and with dangers compast round,
> And solitude; yet not alone, while thou
> Visit'st my slumbers nightly, or when morn
> Purples the East: still govern thou my song,
> Urania, and fit audience find, though few.

And in the end he makes a tragic hero of the blind Samson.

Milton wrote sonnets intermittently throughout his life, some of them mere exercises, but most reflecting his attitude to contemporary events and often showing him in undress, as it were. He used the sonnet form with an originality and a variety which mark him out as one of the great sonneteers of England; but he did not go back to the Elizabethan sonneteering tradition, which was dead by Milton's time. He went to Italy independently, adopting the Petrarchan (not the "Shakespearean") form and in doing so giving a new vitality to the English sonnet. He seems to have been influenced by the Italian sonneteer Giovanni della Casa in his shaping of the sonnet as a continuous verse paragraph, with the thought cutting across the rhyme divisions and the division into *octave* and *sestet*. His early sonnet "O Nightingale" is an accomplished exercise; his reflections on his late maturing in "How soon hath Time, the subtle thief of youth," shows him using the sonnet form to produce a personal utterance that combines dignity of tone, flexibility of movement, and mastery of structure. During the Civil War he wrote sonnets of an "occasional" nature, such as "When the assault was intended to the city," with its quiet formality, or the sonnets of compliment to friends, "Lady that in the prime of earliest youth," or those to the Lady Margaret Ley and to Mr. Henry Lawes (whose friend he remained although Lawes was a devoted Royalist). "I did but prompt the age to quit their clogs" gives his vigorous reaction to the reception of his divorce pamphlets, while "On the New Forcers of Conscience under the Long Parliament" (a *sonetto caudato,* or "tailed" sonnet with a coda or tail of six extra satiric lines) shows Milton's kind of ironic humor:

Men whose life, learning, faith and pure intent
  Would have been held in high esteem with Paul
  Must now be nam'd and printed heretics
  By shallow Edwards and Scotch what d'ye call:
    But we do hope to find out all your tricks,
    Your plots and packing worse than those of Trent,
        That so the Parliament
    May with their wholesome and preventive shears
    Clip your phylacteries, though baulk your ears,
        And succour our just fears,
    When they shall read this clearly in your charge:
    New Presbyter is but Old Priest writ large.

A similar rough sportiveness is found in his sonnet "On the Detraction which followed on my writing certain Treatises," with its deliberately humorous rhymes. The sonnets of compliment to Fairfax and Cromwell reflect his admiration of these antiroyalist heroes; that to Cromwell is an appeal to him not to accept the proposed limitation of freedom to preach. "Peace hath her victories /No less renown'd than war," he eloquently reminds him:

Help us to save free conscience from the paw
Of hireling wolves whose gospel is their maw.

The indignant eloquence of "On the Late Massacre in Piemont" has a fine Miltonic ring and shows how flexibly Milton could use the sonnet form, while the charming "Lawrence, of virtuous father virtuous son" gives a glimpse of a Milton who rarely appears in the poems: it is an invitation to dinner ("of Attic taste, with wine, whence we may rise /To hear the lute well touch'd, or artful voice /Warble immortal notes and Tuscan air") to a young friend. Of the two sonnets to his friend Cyriack Skinner, one is a pleasantly modulated appeal to relax:

> For other things mild Heav'n a time ordains,
> And disapproves that care, though wise in show,
> That with superfluous burden loads the day,
> And when God sends a cheerful hour, refrains.

The same year (1655) he wrote to Skinner of his blindness in the sonnet, "Cyriack, this three year's day these eyes." The conclusion is in the vein of the *Second Defence:*

> What supports me, dost thou ask?
> The conscience, friend, to have lost them overplied
> In liberty's defence, my noble task,
> Of which all Europe talks from side to side.
> This thought might lead me through the world's vain masque
> Content though blind, had I no better guide.

Finally, there is "Methought I saw my late espoused saint," a simply eloquent and moving sonnet about his dead second wife, who died in February, 1658.

The Italian sonnet had not originally been used only to write of love, though English sonneteers before Milton, developing only one aspect of the Petrarchan tradition, had assumed so. Milton knew Tasso's "heroical sonnets" of compliment and praise, and took the hint in his sonnets to Fairfax, Cromwell, and Sir Henry Vane. For originality, variety, and craftsmanship Milton's sonnets are unique in the language.

Two other works of Milton must be mentioned before we go on to discuss his last and greatest poetry. These are his *History of Britain,* begun in the 1640's and published in 1670, and the Latin work *De Doctrina Christiana* ("Of Christian Doctrine"), worked on at different periods of his life. The latter work, not published until 1825, is an elaborate presentation of Milton's own interpretation of Christianity, of great interest as providing the logical and theological basis on which *Paradise Lost* was to be reared (though the principles of the *De Doctrina* are never as clear in *Paradise Lost* as one might expect them to be after reading the former work). The *History,* which never gets further than the Roman conquest, shows Milton's interest in the early history of his country, which he at one time explored thoroughly for possible epic themes. He used his sources with critical care, and went to the original authorities whenever he could. He cannot help moralizing the story as he goes, for to his mind his nation's story was full of warnings and useful lessons; but the work remains in its way an impressive original rendering of the history of a difficult period. The long paragraphs and rather hurried style make it difficult for modern readers to read comfortably, with the result that it is less well known than other early histories which have some claim on our attention.

Milton meditated many subjects, from both British and biblical history, before he finally decided on the Fall as the theme for his great epic. There exists a manuscript of his in which he jotted down a great variety of subjects both for epic and for plays. A list of twenty-eight incidents from Roman, British, and early English history begins with "Venutius, husband of Cartismandua" and ends with "Edward Confessors divorsing and imprisoning his noble wife Editha, Godwins daughter"; the list includes the suggestion that "A Heroicall Poem may be founded somewhere in Alfreds reigne, especially at his issuing out of Edelsingsey on the Danes; whose actions are wel like those of Ulysses." The biblical themes include "Abram from Morea, or Isack redeemd," "Baptistes" ("beginning from the morning of Herods birth day"), "Sodom" ("the scene before Lots gate"), "Herod massacring, or Rachel weeping," "Christ Bound," "Christ Crucified," "Christ Risen," and "Lazarus." The biblical subjects are presented mostly as subjects for tragedies. There are two lists of biblical *dramatis personae*, one including Michael, Heavenly Love, Lucifer, Adam, Eve, Conscience, Death, Faith, Hope, and Charity, with a Chorus of Angels, and Labour, Sickness, Discontent, Ignorance and others as "mutes." The other includes Moses, Justice, Mercy, Wisdom, Lucifer, Adam, Eve, and others. There is a summary of the action of *Paradise Lost* in five acts, with Moses speaking a prologue, and brief notes on over fifty other biblical subjects. There is an elaborate summary of the action of a play called *Adam Unparadiz'd*. But, though he may well have begun *Paradise Lost* as a drama, Milton cannot have worked long at it before deciding that the epic was the appropriate form for a great poetic work on a theme of such universal implications. How much of *Paradise Lost* he had written before the collapse of all his political hopes with the Restoration, we cannot say. Some parts would appear to have been written between the writing of the *Second Defence* and his last pamphlets just before the Restoration, while much of the latter part of the poem must have been written after the period of confusion and danger which Milton went through in 1660. Professor Hanford suggests that the second half of *Paradise Lost* was written between Milton's third marriage in February, 1663, and his giving his young friend and pupil Thomas Ellwood the completed manuscript to read in September, 1665. It was published in 1667.

At long last, Milton had written that poem "doctrinal to a nation" that he had been determined to write from his earliest years. It was inevitably a very different poem from the one whose Platonic idea haunted him in his Cambridge and Horton days, and different, too, from the poem he would have written had he not lived to see the wreck of all his hopes for a regenerate England. In the invocation at the beginning of Book VII he notes the change in his circumstances while denying that there has been any change in his voice:

> More safe I sing with mortal voice, unchang'd
> To hoarse or mute, though fall'n on evil days;

Unchanged to hoarse or mute, certainly, but changed in subtler ways. *Paradise Lost* was a richer, profounder, and maturer epic because of what Milton had gone through before he completed it. A decorative poetic treatment of the Christian story of the Fall was no novelty in European literature. A younger Milton might have added another, and probably the most workmanlike as well as the most deeply felt, to the number of naïve poems of this kind, modeling himself on Sylvester's translation of Du Bartas whose superficial influence is so clearly seen in *Paradise Lost* as we have it but whose tone and texture is so utterly different from Milton's poem. Milton's *Paradise Lost* is a poetic rendering of the story of the Fall in such a way as to illuminate some of the central paradoxes of the human situation and illustrate the tragic ambiguity of man as a moral being.

Paradise Lost was a heroic poem, but its theme was to be far above the themes of conventional heroic poems. To narrate the story of the Fall of Man was

> sad task, yet argument
> Not less but more heroic than the wrath
> Of stern Achilles on his foe pursued
> Thrice fugitive about Troy wall, or rage
> Of Turnus for Lavinia disespous'd,
> Or Neptune's ire, or Juno's, . . . ;
> If answerable style I can obtain
> Of my celestial patroness, who deigns
> Her nightly visitation unimplor'd,
> And dictates to me slumb'ring, or inspires
> Easy my unpremeditated verse:
> Since first this subject for heroic song
> Pleas'd me, long choosing and beginning late,
> Not sedulous by nature to indite
> Wars, hitherto the only argument
> Heroic deem'd, . . .

The "answerable style" demanded a verse which allowed of both a dignity and a flexibility, an ability to rise to the most sublime heights and at the same time to indicate through changes in movement shifts in moral attitude, differences in cosmic status, and the relationship between the four great theaters of action—Heaven, Eden, Hell, and (by suggestion and implication only, yet most strongly and significantly), the ordinary, familiar postlapsarian world. The popular view that Milton in *Paradise Lost* had but one voice, and that an organ one, is wholly unjustified. No epic poet was a master of such a variety of styles as Milton, and the variety with which he could use "English heroic verse without rime" (as he calls it in his preliminary note on the "measure," in which he somewhat unnecessarily attacks rhyme and sees himself as recovering ancient liberty to English heroic poetry) can be seen at once if we put, say, Satan's first speech in Book I, rallying his fallen host, beside the trancelike, nightmare tone of Eve's description of her dream to Adam in Book V, and then turn to God's gentle teasing of Adam about his desire for a mate in Book VIII or the tipsy lilt of Eve's speech when, returning to Adam from the fatal tree, she makes her apology for being late in a rush of words "with countenance blithe." Or we might consider the description of ideal nature in the first account of Eden in Book IV, the primal courtesy of Adam and Eve's mutual talk before the Fall, the simplicity and freshness of Eve's speech in Book IV beginning "Sweet is the breath of morn," in some respects quite different from yet in others similar to the gentle penitential tone of her speech in Book X, "Forsake me not thus, Adam," in which the moral recovery of the pair begins. As for Milton's epic similes, often considered as merely elaborate poetic exercises, these have an important function in the poem as providing the only link between cosmic scenery of the epic and the world of ordinary men in their day-to-day activities throughout all of history and geography.

Milton's statement of his theme at the beginning of Book I not only follows epic precedent in making such an opening statement; it also, in a remarkably sustained verse paragraph, indicates the ambitious and comprehensive nature of his task and establishes his status as an epic poet on a higher moral plane than the Latin and Greek classics.

> Of Man's first disobedience, and the fruit
> Of that forbidden tree, whose mortal taste
> Brought death unto the world, and all our woe,
> With loss of Eden, till one greater Man
> Restore us and regain that blissful seat,
> Sing Heav'nly Muse, that on the secret top
> Of Oreb or of Sinai didst inspire
> That shepherd, who first taught the chosen seed
> In the beginning how the Heav'ns and Earth

Rose out of chaos: or if Sion Hill
Delight thee more, and Siloa's brook that flow'd
Fast by the oracle of God, I thence
Invoke thy aid to my advent'rous song,
That with no middle flight intends to soar
Above th' Aonian Mount, while it pursues
Things unattempted yet in prose or rhyme.
And chiefly thou, O Spirit, that dost prefer
Before all temples th' upright heart and pure,
Instruct me, for thou know'st; thou from the first
Wast present and with mighty wings outspread
Dove-like satst brooding on the vast abyss
And mad'st it pregnant. What in me is dark
Illumine, which is low raise and support;
That to the height of this great argument
I may assert eternal providence
And justify the ways of God to men.

The placing of the pauses, the rise and fall of the emotion, the high emotional charge in which the poet's sense of dedication and of communion with the great biblical figures of the Old Testament is communicated, the supplicatory cadence of the appeal to have his darkness illumined and his mind elevated, and the powerful simplicity of the concluding statement of his purpose—all this represents poetic art of a high order. Milton had experimented much with the verse paragraph in his earlier poems, and in *Paradise Lost* he was able to handle it with a variety and a structural cunning that go beyond anything else of the kind in English poetry. Classical echoes mingle with stark English simplicities and with overtones of meaning deriving from Milton's awareness of the precise meaning of relevant words in the Hebrew Bible. ("Dove-like satst brooding o'er the vast abyss," for example, is Milton's rendering of the precise meaning of the word in Genesis 1:2 translated by the Authorized Version as "moved"—"And the Spirit of God moved upon the face of the water"—but explained by both Jewish and Christian commentators as implying brooding and hatching. "This is that gentle heat that brooded on the waters, and in six days hatched the world," wrote Sir Thomas Browne in *Religio Medici.*) It is worth noting that Milton wrote of "the ways of God to men," not something like "designs of Deity to all mankind"; nothing could be more simply and effectively put than the statement of his purpose.

Paradise Lost shows Milton as Christian Humanist using all the resources of the European literary tradition that had come down to him —biblical, classical, medieval, Renaissance. Imagery from classical fable and medieval romance, allusion to myths, legends, and stories of all kinds, geographical imagery deriving from Milton's own fascination with books of travel and echoes of the Elizabethan excitement at the new discoveries, biblical history and doctrine, Jewish and Christian learning—all these and more are found in this great synthesis of all that the Western mind was stored with by the middle of the seventeenth century. Like *The Faerie Queene,* Milton's epic is a great synthesizing poem, but Milton's synthesis is more successful than Spenser's because he places his different kinds of knowledge—biblical, classical, medieval, modern—in a logical hierarchy, and never mingles, as Spenser often does, classical myth and biblical story on equal terms. If all the resources of classical mythology are employed in order to build up an overwhelming picture of the beauty of Eden before the Fall, that is because Milton is saying that here, and here only, were all the yearnings of men for ideal gardens fully realized—

> Hesperian fables true,
> If true, here only, . . .

The description of Eden in Book IV is indeed one of the finest examples of Milton's use of pagan classical imagery for a clearly defined Christian purpose.

> The birds their choir apply; airs, vernal airs,
> Breathing the smell of field and grove, attune
> The trembling leaves, while universal Pan
> Knit with the Graces and the Hours in dance
> Led on th' eternal Spring. Not that fair field
> Of Enna, where Proserpin gath'ring flow'rs,
> Herself a fairer flow'r, by gloomy Dis
> Was gather'd, which cost Ceres all that pain
> To seek her through the world; nor that sweet grove
> Of Daphne by Orontes, and th' inspir'd
> Castalian spring, might with this paradise
> Of Eden strive; . . .

There is a tremulous glory in this description of ideal nature fully realized, and repetitions such as "airs, vernal airs," and "gath'ring flow'rs, herself a fairer flow'r" help to give the proper emotional quality to the verse. The classical imagery is neither purely decorative nor as solidly grounded in reality as the biblical groundwork of the story: Milton uses myth for what it is, the imaginative projection of all man's deepest hopes and fears. Matthew Arnold cited the lines about Proserpin and Ceres as a touchstone of great poetry, but did not pause to inquire why. It is in the combined suggestion of infinite beauty and of foreboding and loss that Milton manages to capture precisely the sad sense of transience which accompanies all postlapsarian response to beauty, and thus even while describing a prelapsarian scene he introduces overtones of the Fall. And more than that—these overtones emphasize a paradox that lies at the very heart of *Paradise Lost*, namely, that only after one has lost something ideally lovely can its true worth be known; the Fall is necessary so that we may pursue the ideal, in the teeth of all the obstacles that now confront us, with a deeper sense of its desirability.

Critics have objected to Milton's use of the apostrophe in such words as "gath'ring flow'rs" as though this were something monstrously artificial, instead of his indication that he meant the words to be spoken as they are pronounced in ordinary speech, not with the artificial "poetic" articulation of syllables not normally sounded. He writes "gather'd" and not "gathered," because some poets wrote the latter form intending the word to be pronounced "gatheréd."

Book I shows us the fallen angels in Hell beginning to recover from their defeat and prostration. The high-sounding rhetorical verse in which Milton describes and which he puts into the mouths of these great and perverted creatures indicated both that Milton had grown suspicious of rhetoric (perhaps because of his disillusion with the Long Parliament debates) and that he was aware that evil had its own attractiveness, which he was careful not to minimize. The speeches of Satan and his followers in Books I and II are magnificent in their way, "Miltonic" in the popular sense of the word; they represent the attractiveness of plausible evil. If evil was never attractive there would be no problem for man. It is because high-sounding rhetoric can so easily "make the worse appear the better reason" and that man so easily thrills to grandiose rantings about honor and revenge uttered with all the mock passion and the theatrical trimmings of a Nuremberg rally, that Satan is so great a danger. To see Satan as a hero because Milton goes out of his way to show the superficial seductiveness of this kind of evil is to show an extraordinary naïveté. The descriptions of Satan's regal state at the beginning of Book II is a magnificent evocation of all the barbaric splendor which the Greeks (and Milton with them) so shuddered at in the Persians. As for the supposed nobility of Satan, it does not take a very close reading of his speeches to see that a self-frustrating spite is his dominant emotion and that it is just when he uses the most impressive heroic terms that his language most lacks meaning. Of course, there are traces of true heroism in him. Milton was making the point that *corruptio optimi pessima*, the corruption of the best becomes the worst, as well as the subtler point that every great human virtue has its moral dangers and can appeal for the wrong reasons.

The scenes in Heaven, in Book III and elsewhere, are by common consent the least effective parts of the poem. Milton was here too detailed in his anthropomorphism. The nonsensical charge that he lacked a specific visual imagery (as though specific visual imagery was always essential to great poetry) is quite beside the point here, for the trouble is that there is too much of it. If he had been content, as he was in the magnificent description of Eden, to use large general terms highly charged with the appropriate emotion as a result of their cadence and tone and of the whole poetic movement of the context, he would have done better. Abstract images of light and joy could have rendered God more effectively than literal descriptions and earnest defensive arguments put into His mouth. Another reason for the relative ineffectiveness of these parts of the poem is that God continually gives the *logical* (not the poetic) answer to all the doubts we feel about the fairness of allowing an innocent couple to be so cunningly tempted and then drastically punishing them and their descendants. We cannot help taking God's arguments as arguments, and arguing back as we read. And as the arguments are far from invulnerable, the poem suffers. The purely logical case for God —that He made man with free will and therefore, even though God knew before the creation of man that man would fall, man's Fall was man's own fault and properly punished; and that the Christian scheme of redemption (even though, on Milton's own showing, it would save only a tiny minority of men in human history) was the product of pure mercy and love, an undeserved blessing which showed God repaying good for evil—is full of fallacies as Milton and Milton's God argue it. Indeed, so inadequate is this presentation of the purely formal case for God that Milton's picture in Book III of God insisting that after the Fall *someone* must be punished, Adam or anybody else who might be found, if justice is to be satisfied, strikes one as unchristian and positively evil:

> He with his whole posterity must die,
> Die he or Justice must; unless for him
> Some other able, and as willing, pay
> The rigid satisfaction, death for death.

This picture of a judge telling the court after a murderer has been found guilty that in order that justice must be done somebody, the guilty man or some member of the jury or the public, must be hanged—it doesn't matter who so long as there is a hanging—is very far from the Christian doctrine of atonement. Clearly, Milton's heart was not fully in this sort of justification of the ways of God to men, whatever he might have consciously thought. His poetic instinct was better than his logical powers, and the true justification of the ways of God to men lies in the way in which it emerges as the poem develops that virtue can only be achieved by struggle, that the Fall was inevitable because a passive and ignorant virtue, without the challenge of an imperfect world, cannot release the true potentialities of human greatness. Of course, the cost of making such a release possible was enormous; but that was part of the nature of things as well as part of *la condition humaine*.

The poem recovers magnificently with Satan's arrival in Eden in Book IV, and it is a fine symbolism which makes us see Eden, in all its unfallen glory, first through Satan's eyes. Milton takes his time in bringing his camera to focus on Adam and Eve. He moves round the garden first, showing the varied glories in imagery at once general ("ambrosial fruit of vegetable gold") and highly evocative before showing us—again with Satan acting as the camera eye—to the noble, naked dignity of our first parents. Nothing could be more simply passionate than the summing up of this great description:

> So hand in hand they pass'd, the loveliest pair
> That ever since in love's embraces met, . . .

Adam's reception of Raphael in Book V gives Milton the opportunity to emphasize the beauty of prelapsarian simplicity:

> Meanwhile our primitive great sire to meet
> His god-like guest walks forth, without more train
> Accompani'd than with his own complete
> Perfections; in himself was all his state,
> More solemn than the tedious pomp that waits
> On princes, when their rich retinue long
> Of horses led, and grooms besmear'd with gold
> Dazzles the crowd and sets them all agape.

Here the familiar postlapsarian world is brought in by a simple contrast, but Milton has many subtler ways of doing it. Milton seems to be fascinated by innocent nakedness; he emphasizes the pair's nakedness, especially Eve's, again and again:

> . . . Meanwhile at table Eve
> Minister'd naked, and their flowing cups
> With pleasant liquors crown'd. . . .

He had already, at their very first appearance, given his picture of innocent sexuality and emphasized that here, and neither in perpetual celibacy nor in the barren artificialities of the courtly love tradition, lay the true use of sex. There is indeed an oblique war carried out by Milton throughout *Paradise Lost* against conventional notions of heroism (which turn out to be diabolical) and against conventional attitudes to sex, both courtly and Puritan. Again and again there is an implicit contrast made between the Garden of the Rose tradition and the Garden of Eden and between the heroic gestures of romance and the true heroism of the virtuous man.

Of course, as innumerable editors have pointed out, Milton uses all the epic devices he could find in classical epic. But the significance of his use of these devices is not that, knowing he was writing an epic, he used appropriate epic devices. It is that he found a way of making most of these devices work poetically in expanding the meaning of the paraphrasable content of the poem. Further, these epic devices represent but a small proportion of the different means he uses—in imagery, vocabulary, cadence, paragraphing, shifts of tone, etc.—to give poetic effectiveness to his story. Far too much critical attention has been spent on pointing out parallels between *Paradise Lost* and earlier epics, instead of emphasizing the highly individual way in which Milton uses his epic machinery.

Raphael's account of the war in Heaven, which occupies part of Book V and all of Book VI, is poetically the least original part of *Paradise Lost*. There is an inherent difficulty in a situation where one of the protagonists is Almighty God, all knowing and all powerful, who can bring anything to pass merely by willing it. Military conflict seems otiose, and God's deliberations on what to do ("Nearly it now concerns us to be sure /Of our omnipotence") appear absurd. In the same way the posting of angelic guards round Eden to prevent Satan's entry, when God has already told the angels that Satan will enter and successfully tempt Adam and Eve, is mere gesturing. Even the building up of Abdiel into a hero as the only one of the angels in Satan's group to defy him to his face seems pointless: what was Abdiel doing among Satan's host anyway? The nearer Milton approaches the defiances and conflicts of classical epic the less convincing *Paradise Lost* is. Angelologists like C. S. Lewis can argue that the wounds suffered by the angels in the conflict are perfectly consistent with Milton's conception of their natures, but that is beside the point. The whole physical conflict, which falls between allegory and history, is misconceived. There are memorable descriptive passages in this part of the poem, but they do not possess the rich suggestive power of other parts. Raphael's account of the creation in Book VII is more poetically effective, with Milton drawing ingeniously on imagery from Genesis, the Psalms, Proverbs, Job, and Plato. But here too the poem is marking time; its true progress is halted. We return to the true Miltonic poetic texture in the scene in

Book VIII where Adam tells Raphael of his own experiences after his creation.

Book IX is one of the great books. From the self-tormenting spitefulness of Satan we move to the sweetly courteous difference of opinion between Adam and Eve about the propriety of Eve's gardening alone in another part of Eden that morning, for a change. We are left to assume, though this is never stated, that this suggestion was put into Eve's mind by Satan when he lay by her ear in the form of a toad as she slept the previous night. But neither she nor Adam is yet fallen, and the quiet grace of their discourse illustrates at its best a quality which Milton always tried to bring into his verse when describing the behavior and conversation of the pair before the Fall. (The faults of his style in such passages are more a Wordsworthian oversimplicity than a "Miltonic" heaviness, as in "No fear lest dinner cool.") When Adam consents to let Eve go, knowing that "thy stay, not free, absents thee more," we feel that Eve, having, woman-fashion, won her point, does not really want to act on it and only goes because she feels her previous insistence makes it necessary that she should. They part reluctantly, and as Eve slowly slides her hand out of her husband's Milton uses the richest resources of classical mythology to dwell for the last time on her innocence and beauty. It is a slow and moving passage, as though Milton is reluctant to have them part. Eve promises to be back "by noon amid the bow'r, /And all things in best order to invite /Noontide repast." She will be back to make lunch, in fact. But that lunch was never made or eaten. At noon Eve was standing beneath the forbidden tree, the arguments of the cunning serpent reinforced by her own appetite; and the noontide repast that both she and her husband eventually ate was the fatal apple. Milton's lingering on this final moment when prelapsarian man and woman stood hand in hand for the last time produces its own haunting emotion. We are made to realize fully that Eve, for all her promises, will never return again—not *this* Eve, not the unfallen bride with her innocent display of her naked beauty; the woman who tripped back to Adam with a branch of the forbidden tree to give to him was a very different person.

The temptation scene itself shows the skilled orator taking advantage of simplicity. Eve is "our credulous mother," and she is fooled by the cunning serpent, whose final effort is significantly compared by Milton to the speech of "some orator renown'd /In Athens or free Rome." If she had known more she would have been more suspicious of this plausible eloquence; but she could not know more without eating of the forbidden Tree of Knowledge; and so the paradox is emphasized. Her sin was disobedience, it is true; but what caused her to commit this sin was credulity. She was taken in by cunning lies, never having met with lies or cunning before. Is credulity sinful and suspicion a virtue? It is the problem of Othello's trusting Iago. There is no solution; only a moral paradox at the heart of the matter.

Eve falls through credulity; Adam falls because he does not realize that the duty of an unfallen man who wants to help a fallen beloved is not to share her sin, and so render them both helpless, but to intercede for her while he is yet sinless. In a cunning parody of the courtly love tradition, Milton has Adam eat the apple as (in Eve's delighted words) a "glorious trial of exceeding love." And so they both become irresponsible and fatuous. Eve had changed as soon as she had eaten the apple, bowing to the tree in drunken worship, and spilling out her story to Adam in the most brilliant of all "Sorry I'm late, but—" speeches in English poetry. Now sex becomes guilty, shame follows self-consciousness, the pair bicker with sullen regret (how different the tone of their speech here from its earlier tone!), and Book IX ends in disillusion and bitterness. Book X charts the change that begins to take place on earth and in Hell as a result of the Fall, but its most interesting passages are those showing us the gradual process of recovery on the part of Adam and Eve. Adam's bitter repudiation of Eve—"Out of my sight, thou serpent!" —is followed by Eve's beautifully modulated penitential speech which we have already noted. And so at last they come to prayer and repentance.

The final part of *Paradise Lost* (which was, incidentally, first published in ten books and then rearranged in twelve) shows Michael displaying or narrating the future history of the world to Adam. It is a miserable story, from Cain's committing the first murder to the final picture of the world going on "to good malignant, to bad men benign, /Under her own weight groaning, till the day /Appear of respiration to the just /And vengeance to the wicked." The story of Christ's passion and triumph, which breaks the dismal chronicle with a momentary gleam of light and elicits in Adam his great hail to the "fortunate fall"—

> O goodness infinite, goodness immense,
> That all this good of evil shall produce,
> And evil turn to good—

is not, as Michael reveals the story, the culmination but only an incident in the long story, and is in some respects a less cheering incident than the quiet beauty of the picture of the earth returning to normal after the flood, never again to be so overwhelmed:

> . . . but when he brings
> His triple-coloured bow, whereon to look
> And call to mind his cov'nant: day and night,
> Seed-time and harvest, heat and hoary frost
> Shall hold their course, till fire purge all things new,
> Both Heav'n and Earth, wherein the just shall dwell.

This, with its sense of satisfaction in the procession of the seasons and man doing his daily agricultural labor, everything in its due time, gets us close to the heart of the poem.

In the end Milton and Adam turn from grandiose public hopes to the "paradise within," content with the prospect of "with good /Still overcoming evil, and by small /Accomplishing great things." Adam and Eve leave their former Paradise with quiet confidence, to face a world of work and endeavor and mutual help. Milton could not praise a fugitive and cloistered virtue, could not conceive of a life of pure meditation, could not imagine life in Eden lasting. At the same time he had lost his earlier confidence that Heaven on Earth could be restored by a regenerate, fully reformed England. Public virtue became for him almost a contradiction in terms, and only private virtue was real. The arts of public virtue, notably rhetoric, were suspect. In *Paradise Regained* he was to make this point even clearer, for Satan tempts Christ there to the public life, which he rejects, with all its accompanying splendors. This was not a wholly new view of Milton's, for, together with the public ambitions of his early years, he had felt also the necessity of submitting himself quietly and patiently to God's purpose for him—as Christ does in *Paradise Regained.* The sonnets on his twenty-third birthday and on his blindness should not be forgotten when we come to consider how far the turn to the "paradise within" represented a radical change in Milton as a result of the failure of his political hopes for England. On the other hand, the change, though it should not be exaggerated, cannot be denied. We have only to put the line

> Peace to corrupt no less than war to waste

from Book XI of *Paradise Lost* beside the line from his sonnet to Cromwell

> Peace hath her victories
> No less renow'd than war . . . .

to see a startling result of that change. Another result was the relegation of the "Miltonic" style to the Devil's side. The high rhetorical manner, invocations such as

> Power and Dominions, Deities of Heav'n

and exhortations such as

> Awake, arise, or be for ever fall'n

belonged to Satan's speech, to the public manner, to evil; God, angels, and men when they were not imitating Satan, spoke in a quieter and more carefully modulated tone. Those who think that *Paradise Lost* is a silly poem redeemed only by its organ tones—a poem to be read for its sound and not its sense—are taking Satan's view as Milton saw it.

All great works of literature contain more than their ostensible subject: starting from a particular set of beliefs, a story such as the biblical story of the Fall or a journey through the underworld, the true poet, in presenting his material, keeps reaching out at every point to touch aspects of the human situation which are real and recognizable whatever our beliefs may be. But through turns of phrase, handling of imagery, simultaneous exploitation of the musical and the semantic aspects of words and of all the evocations and suggestions that can be obtained from allusions to the great mythological imaginings of mankind, the poet turns his story and his creed into a unique means of shedding light on man. The combined knowledge of man's nobility and his weakness, the sense of man's looking back or forward to a golden age coupled with the knowledge that, partly because of the very characteristics of man as man, such a golden age can be envisioned but never realized, the sense that man's life is governed by chance and linked always with the movements of the day to night and back to day, with the passing of the seasons, with resolutions that fluctuate and moods that alter, but a sense, too, that only a determination to do what can be done at the moment of decision can ever achieve anything—all this and a thousand more such archetypal ideas are carried alive and passionately into the mind of the reader by *Paradise Lost*. The poem has its barren patches, and the arguments about free will in Heaven may leave us unconvinced. But as a poem the subject of *Paradise Lost* is less the logical justification of the ways of God to men than the essential and tragic ambiguity of the human animal. Expanding his meaning by every kind of poetic device to include almost all that Western man had thought and felt, pivoting the action on a scene which, as Milton describes it, illuminates immediately the paradox of man's ambition (at once good because noble and bad because arrogant) and human love (both bad because selfish and because passion clouds the judgment and good because unselfish and self-sacrificing), linking the grandiose action at every point to suggestions of man in his daily elemental activities in fields, cities, and on the ocean, developing all the implications of man's perennial desire for a better world with the continuous awareness of man's tendency to trip himself up and turn his very virtues into snares—achieving all this in spite of the plot, or at least by expanding the plot into something infinitely more than its summarizable meaning, by placing an image where it will speak most richly and by linking up units to each other so that the chorus of implication grows ever richer, reverberates ever more widely, Milton, operating as a poet rather than as a theologian or moralist, in spite of himself probes more deeply into man's fate than his formal scheme would seem to allow. Work was a punishment for the Fall, but images of daily work well done are used throughout the poem to establish a note of satisfaction and recovery. Perpetual spring gave way after the Fall to the procession of the seasons, yet it is the procession of the seasons itself that gives meaning and dignity to human life as Milton reveals it by the pattern of image and suggestion in his poem. And in the end, Paradise, the ideal world of innocent idleness, has become uninhabitable. As they look back on it for the last time, the angels guarding it seem dreadful figures from another world. It is a great and memorable ending:

> . . . for now too nigh
> Th' archangel stood, and from the other hill
> To their fix'd stations all in bright array
> The cherubim descended, on the ground
> Gliding meteorous, as ev'ning mist
> Ris'n from a river o'er the marish glides
> And gathers ground fast at the labourer's heel
> Homeward returning. High in front advanc'd,
> The brandish'd sword of God before them blaz'd
> Fierce as a comet, which with torrid heat
> And vapour as the Libyan air adust
> Began to parch that temperate clime; whereat
> In either hand the hast'ning angel caught
> Our ling'ring parents, and to th' eastern gate
> Led them direct, and down the cliff as fast
> To the subjected plain,—then disappear'd.
> They looking back, all th' eastern side beheld
> Of Paradise, so late their happy seat,
> Wav'd over by that flaming brand, the gate
> With dreadful faces throng'd and fiery arms.
> Some natural tears they dropp'd, but wip'd them soon;
> The world was all before them, where to choose
> Their place of rest, and Providence their guide.

> They hand in hand with wand'ring steps and slow
> Through Eden took their solitary way.

The image of the laborer returning homeward in the evening sets the emotional tone of this concluding passage: always for Milton, daily agricultural labor duly accomplished was a highly charged symbol of satisfaction in human achievement. Eden becomes hot and frightening. Below, the "subjected plain" awaits them—subjected in the literal Latin sense of lying below them and in the other sense of awaiting their conquest of it. The simple phrase, "so late their happy seat," renews the elegiac tone with memories of lost felicity. But natural tears give way to the pioneering spirit of hope. "The world was all before them." And so they go forth, hand in hand yet in a sense solitary; they know now that, while mutual love and help sweeten all human toil, complete communion between individuals is impossible, for love and comradeship are bound up with self-interest. All is here said that can be said about man's capacity to hope in spite of despair, about loneliness and companionship, about the healing effects of time and the possibility of combining bewilderment with a sense of purpose, man as both elegist and pioneer. The style, with its quiet gravity, is more characteristically Miltonic than the Milton-Satan style which most people think is the invariable style of *Paradise Lost*. The manipulation of the pauses alone shows the highest art.

Paradise Regained and *Samson Agonistes* were published together in 1671, the former apparently written after the publication of *Paradise Lost*. There is no clear evidence as to when *Samson* was written, but theme and versification together with the date of publication suggest that it was one of his latest works if not his final achievement, though some scholars have suggested an earlier date. Both works had clearly been long maturing in Milton's mind. *Paradise Regained* is a much more limited poem than *Paradise Lost*, dealing only with one specific aspect of Christian story in four books. Milton is here treating of the temptation of Christ in the wilderness as what might be called a ritual re-enaction of the original Fall, only this time with temptation withstood instead of succumbed to. Taking the order of the temptations from the account in Luke, not in Matthew (where the order is different) Milton, following a well-established Christian tradition, sees in it an undoing of the Fall. Christ faces the wiles of Satan *quasi homo*, as Man not as God (and Milton always preferred to see Christ as heroic man rather than as God incarnate), and his triumph is therefore redemptive for mankind. As God tells His angels:

> He [Satan] now shall know I can produce a man
> Of female seed far abler to resist
> All his solicitations, . . .
> That all the angels and ethereal powers,
> They now, and men hereafter, may discern
> From what consummate virtue I have chose
> This perfect man, by merit call'd my son,
> To earn salvation for the sons of men.

Satan's motive in tempting Christ—and again Milton is here following a well-established tradition—is both to find out if he is really the prophesied Messiah and to tempt him to destroy his perfection and messianic claims by committing specific sins. Satan is here a rather seedy character compared with the fallen angel of *Paradise Lost;* his address to his fellows in Book I, announcing his determination to find out who this man is, is a sullen and shabby affair, the rhetoric sounding hollow, as though Satan did not believe himself in the possibility of his own success. The interest soon shifts to the mind of Christ, whom we see communing with himself after his forty days in the wilderness without food, wondering what God has in store for him, and determined to await patiently the revelation of His purpose. Satan's first appearance to him, in the likeness of "an aged man in rural weeds," produces a quiet dialogue in which the cunning persuasiveness of the supposed innocent old pauper as he suggests that by turning stones into bread Christ would both save himself from starvation "and us relieve with food," is met by a firmly quiet, slightly contemptuous reply which is characteristic of Christ's speech to Satan throughout the poem. His first remark is simply

> Who brought me hither
> Will bring me hence, no other guide I seek.

When Satan's suggestion becomes more specific, Christ calmly points out that God supported Moses on the mount and Elijah in the wilderness: "Who dost thou then suggest to me distrust?" Christ also states that he knows Satan's identity—which, we cannot help feeling, gives him a quite unfair advantage over Eve, who did not know who spoke through the serpent. Christ's calm refusal to do anything which might suggest distrust of God—and it must be emphasized that the temptation to turn stones into bread is not, as Milton presents it, a temptation to gluttony, but a temptation to distrust—produces a change in Satan's style, which becomes steadily more persuasive and rhetorical. That rhetoric, the art of persuasion, is here on the side of evil is abundantly clear. Christ's language is quiet, precise, even homely, the language of private not public discussion. Satan, having been recognized, proceeds to build himself up as at once heroic and pitiful, a character worthy of respect and at the same time deserving of compassion, and flattery is added to this cunning mixture of boasting and self-pity. It is a remarkable speech, ending with deliberate art on an elegiac note:

> This wounds me most (what can it less) that man,
> Man fall'n shall be restor'd, I never more.

Christ is not fooled:

> To whom our Saviour sternly thus replied.
> Deservedly thou griev'st, compos'd of lies
> From the beginning, . . .

He goes on to taunt Satan with having been the deceiver of man through the oracles of the pagan world; but "God hath now sent his living Oracle /Into the world." Satan counters this hopelessly with the argument that he loves virtue though he does not follow it, adding that God allows sinners to approach his altar, and therefore Christ should give access to him. Christ replies tersely:

> Thy coming hither, though I know thy scope,
> I bid not or forbid; do as thou find'st
> Permission from above; thou canst not more.

So the first temptation ends, Satan temporarily disappears, and Jesus is left alone in the wilderness:

> for now began
> Night with her sullen wing to double-shade
> The desert; fowls in their clay nests were couch'd;
> And now wild beasts came forth the woods to roam.

The quiet desolation of the scene is significant. The hero is alone in the waste land. Satan tempts him to take easy ways out, later trying to persuade him to exchange his lonely private life for the glories and satisfactions of a successful public career. But all temptations to public life are refused, and Jesus remains a private man at the end of the poem.

Book II gives us a glimpse of the disciples wondering what has happened to their master, then moves to Satan reporting to his devils his lack of success and repudiating contemptuously Belial's fatuous advice to "set women in his eye" in favor of further temptations "of worth, of honour, glory, and popular praise." We then turn to Jesus, communing with himself again, wondering what is to happen to him. Satan returns, this time in courtly garments, and brings on a magnificent banquet, a temptation to luxury and sensuality, but the Saviour's quiet contempt persists. "And with my hunger what hast thou to do? /Thy pompous delicacies I contemn." Satan turns to argue Christ's lack of power and authority. How can he save the world without these? "Money brings honour, friends, conquest, and realms"—

> They whom I favour thrive in wealth amain,
> While virtue, valour, wisdom sit in want.
> To whom thus Jesus patiently replied:
> Yet wealth without these three is impotent. . . .

Significantly, Jesus goes on to cite examples from both biblical and classical history of heroes who, their work over, returned to private life. As for power, "he who reigns within himself, and rules /Passions, desires, and fears, is more a king."

In Book III Satan, with increasing cunning and all kinds of verbal trickery, makes more explicit the contrast between private and public life:

> These God-like virtues wherefore dost thou hide?
> Affecting private life, or more obscure
> In savage wilderness, wherefore deprive
> All earth her wonder at thy acts, thyself
> The fame and glory, glory the reward
> That sole excites to high attempts the flame
> Of most erected spirits, . . . ?

This is coming more shrewdly home: Milton in "Lycidas" had recognized that "Fame is the spur . . ." But Jesus replies with cold contempt that the praise of the rabble is not worth having. (An un-Christlike argument, surely, but one that reflects Milton's own disillusion with public opinion in England.) Conventional glory is won by meaningless and destructive wars. Patience and temperance are the true virtues, and Job and Socrates are cited. This leads Satan to press the moral aspect of the conquest of the evil by the good: would not the deliverance of Israel from the Roman yoke be a good thing? (Even as Milton had thought the deliverance of England from episcopacy and Charles I would be a good thing.) The argument here is pressed closely: a righteous war against the heathen is urged. But again Jesus replies coldly: "All things are best fulfill'd in their due time." ("They also serve who only stand and wait," in fact.) He will continue "Suffering, abstaining, quietly expecting /Without distrust or doubt." Satan presses his point with a magnificent picture, both historical and geographical, of the power-pattern in the Middle East and Mediterranean, with a ringing use of place names reminiscent for the first time of *Paradise Lost,* and offers his help and advice to Jesus in regaining David's throne. But again Jesus answers coldly, repudiating with quiet contempt "much ostentation vain of fleshly arm." As for the people of Israel, they serve for their sins, and will be called back to God in His own time.

Book IV shows Satan employing all "the persuasive rhetoric /That sleek'd his tongue" to build up a magnificent picture of the civilization of Greece and Rome. Here we have the grand style of *Paradise Lost.* A brilliant evocation of the whole world of Roman civilization, with a sense of the color and movement and variety of the whole Roman world, is followed by an equally brilliant evocation of the wisdom of Greece. To the first, offered by Satan in exchange for Jesus' homage, Jesus replies (becoming ever more contemptuous of the now desperate Satan): "I never lik'd thy talk, thy offers less." To the second he replies with more careful arguments. The wisdom of the Greeks is not dismissed with contempt. There is a note of genuine compassion when he says of the Greek philosophers

> Alas! what can they teach, and not mislead,
> Ignorant of themselves, of God much more, . . .

And though Greek philosophy has its virtues, they are pale beside the Hebrew prophets. "Sion's songs" are better than Greek literature (which is not to say that Greek literature is bad). The biblical prophets "with our Law, best form a king." Satan, frustrated and furious, carries Jesus back to the wilderness and tries, ridiculously, to frighten him with a night of storm and "hellish furies." The next morning he replies quietly to Satan's attempt to frighten him: "Me worse than wet thou find'st not." Enraged and desperate, Satan brings Jesus to a pinnacle of the temple, on which he sets him, hoping that he will call on angels to support him and thus both reveal his identity and at the same time lose it by invoking divine aid for his personal safety, or else fall and be destroyed. But neither of these things happens: Jesus stands unaided; Satan is confounded. An angelic choir hails Jesus' triumph over temptation and Jesus himself

> Home to his mother's house private return'd.

The identification of the private life with virtue and the public with evil could not be more emphatic. This is how Milton's own experience had led him to interpret the story of the temptation in the wilderness.

The Book of Job as well as Spenser's *Faerie Queene* (Book II, Canto VIII) and Giles Fletcher's *Christ's Victory and Triumph* gave suggestions to Milton for *Paradise Regained,* and of course he drew on established Christian tradition. But the "brief epic" is nevertheless remarkably original in treatment, in its presentation of the conflict between public ambition and quiet trust. If the character of Jesus suffers somewhat as a consequence—he seems an oddly cold and stoical character, with none of the warmer virtues—it must be remembered that in this poem he is opposing the false charm of rhetoric and resisting the temptation to exchange the "Paradise within" for grandiose public action.

In *Samson Agonistes* Milton dramatized the bare story from Judges in the form of a classical tragedy in which Aeschylus' *Prometheus Bound* and Sophocles' *Oedipus at Colonus* served as models. His introduction explains that tragedy is "the gravest, moralest, and most profitable of all other poems." Aristotle's theory that tragedy has "the power by raising pity and fear, or terror, to purge the mind of those and such like passions" is cited, and every effort is made to prove that tragedy is of the highest seriousness. He explains that he has followed the ancient model, both in plot and in verse form, and that "according to ancient rule and best example" the action is kept "within the space of 24 hours." A Greek tragedy on a biblical theme is perhaps Milton's final way of reconciling his Christianity with his Humanism.

The tragedy is in the form of a series of dialogues between Samson and the various people who visit him, one at a time, with intervening monologues by Samson, comments by the chorus, and the final reported account of Samson's death in pulling down the heathen temple on the Philistines. In the course of the action Samson gradually (and not always in a continuous forward movement) recovers a proper state of mind, which combines penitence, recognition of the nature of his earlier fault and the justice of his present fate, and a confident submission to whatever destiny God has in store for him. The temptations which face him, a blind prisoner of the heathen Philistines, are despair on the one hand and a belief in his ability to decide his own destiny (instead of waiting on God's revelation of His purpose) on the other. In the end, God's purpose is revealed, and he goes to participate in the Philistine festival knowing that that is what God wishes him to do. His death in destroying his enemies was the destiny prepared for him.

The theme of the play is the process of Samson's recovery, and each of the characters who visit him—his father Manoa, his wife Dalila, the Philistine giant Harapha, and the Philistine officer—represent different temptations, in resisting which he proceeds further toward recovery. We see him first lamenting his present state, "Eyeless in Gaza at the mill with slaves," and contrasting it, with bitter self-reproach, with his former career as a dedicated servant of God and a hero of his people. The verse moves from a firm and flexible blank verse to a more complex lyric measure where cunningly varied line lengths and deliberately varied metrical feet respond to the movement of the emotion:

> O dark, dark, dark, amid the blaze of noon,
> Irrecoverably dark, total eclipse
> Without all hope of day!
> O first created beam, and thou great word,
> "Let there be light, and light was over all,"
> Why am I thus bereav'd thy prime decree?
> The sun to me is dark
> And silent as the moon,
> When she deserts the night,
> Hid in her vacant interlunar cave. . . .

The Chorus, in a similar varied measure, comments on Samson's state and contrasts it with his former heroic exploits for his people. Samson, in discussion with the chorus, tells some of his story and distinguishes (rightly, in Milton's view) between his own wrongdoing, for which he takes the blame, and the follies and sins of omission of Israel's governors, which are really responsible for the present state of his people. The Chorus, in a well-known interlude, debate the question of God's justice with a passionate to-and-fro movement which indicates the emotional earnestness with which Milton posed the question. Manoa, Samson's first visitor, then comes to rub salt into Samson's wounds (though not consciously) by saying "I told you so" about his marriage to a Philistine woman. Samson responds with a mixture of self-reproach and self-respect. Manoa, whose bustling confidence that he can make everything come out well in the end reminds one a little of Oceanus in *Prometheus Bound,* looks forward to a happy ending, but such talk depresses Samson and he becomes more and more hopeless, verging on the sin of despair. Manoa leaves to try and arrange Samson's ransom, leaving Samson to give passionate expression to his hopelessness and the Chorus to ponder the baffling ways of God, who raises a man up from earliest youth to a high destiny, only to dash him down again in middle life.

The entry of Dalila, announced by the Chorus in terms which make clear that she is decked out in all her finery, brings a new temptation. She explains that she betrayed Samson for love of him, not expecting the Philistines to blind and imprison him, but hoping they would simply cut his hair to remove his great strength and leave him to her uxorious care. She is not lying: she is proffering to Samson a dangerous kind of love, and wants him back.

> Mine and Love's prisoner, not the Philistines'.

This is not Milton's concept of marriage, and when Dalila actually suggests that a blind Samson is better off than a seeing one, as being more completely under her loving protection, we see clearly that Milton is attacking here a variant of the courtly love tradition (with the man as "love's prisoner") which he attacked in other ways in *Paradise Lost*. It is a real temptation, because sex is involved, and the savagery with which Samson forbids Dalila to approach him indicates his fear of succumbing if once he allows physical contact between them. His repudiation of her stings her into a spiteful declaration of her determination to seek appreciation from the Philistines, and she goes, leaving the Chorus to ponder the strange power of physical love. Harapha then comes to taunt Samson, who answers his bravado with calm and confident words:

> All these indignities, for such they are
> From thine, these evils I deserve and more,
> Acknowledge them from God inflicted on me
> Justly, yet despair not of his final pardon
> Whose ear is ever open.

He vindicates his earlier career with dignity, and in the end chases Harapha from the scene by merely making a pretended motion toward him. The Chorus hail Samson's reviving spirits, and note that patience is the true exercise of saints.

The Philistine officer now enters and summons Samson to give an exhibition for the Philistine lords at their feast of Dagon. Samson returns a contemptuous negative, but then, contemplating his growing hair and returning strength, suddenly begins to feel "some rousing motions in me," indicating a divine impulse to go with the messenger after all. He leaves in high dignity, telling the Chorus:

> Happ'n what may, of me expect to hear
> Nothing dishonourable, impure, unworthy
> Our God, our law, my nation, or myself;
> The last of me or no I cannot warrant.

Manoa returns, confident that he can secure his son's release, looking forward to a completely restored Samson, with eyesight as well as strength given back. His optimistic speculations are interrupted by a shout from the temple of Dagon, and he exchanges apprehensive speculation with the Chorus. The announcement by a messenger, in a set speech in the true Greek dramatic tradition, of Samson's end brings comment by the Chorus (who are careful to point out that Samson died "self-kill'd /Not willingly"—he was not guilty of the sin of suicide) and a final realization by Manoa that the end is heroic and fitting:

> Come, come, no time for lamentation now,
> Nor much more cause: Samson hath quit himself
> Like Samson, and heroicly hath finish'd
> A life heroic, . . .
> Nothing is here for tears, nothing to wail
> Or knock the breast, no weakness, no contempt,
> Dispraise, or blame, nothing but well and fair,
> And what may quiet us in a death so noble.

The Chorus echo this thought:

> All is best, though we oft doubt,
> What th' unsearchable dispose
> Of highest wisdom brings about,
> And ever best found in the close.
> Oft he seems to hide his face,
> But unexpectedly returns
> And to his faithful champion hath in place
> Bore witness gloriously; whence Gaza mourns
> And all that band them to resist
> His uncontrollable intent.
> His servants he, with new acquist
> Of true experience from this great event,
> With peace and consolation hath dismiss'd,
> And calm of mind, all passion spent.

Samson Agonistes is the only successful Greek tragedy in English, but its inner substance is not really Greek; the theme of a fallen hero's achievement of a new and subtler kind of heroism is not Sophoclean, but Christian in a very Miltonic way. The autobiographical overtones in the play are obvious and have often been commented on. Whether *Samson* was Milton's final work or not, it can be taken as his last word on his own situation. This passionately individual Christian Humanist poet, so powerfully enmeshed in the history of his own time, with his great sense of poetic mission, his deflection into public service, reaching the full flower of his poetic achievement in the midst of a civilization in which he had completely lost faith, presents a fascinating and moving picture. He was the greatest English nondramatic poet and the last English poet to take and use as his poetic heritage everything that Western civilization, with its twin origins in Hebrew and classical thought, had so far achieved.

CHAPTER THIRTEEN

Prose in the Sixteenth and Seventeenth Centuries

THE INTELLECTUAL CONFLICTS and shifting tides of opinion in the sixteenth and seventeenth centuries are more directly shown in the prose of the period than in its poetry. Pamphleteering of all kinds, polemical religious argument, political, educational, and literary theorizing, flourish now as never before, with the result that the literary historian has to deal with a mass of miscellaneous prose most of which can hardly be called strictly "literature," yet which, in addition to providing an occasional work of real literary merit, provides an interesting view of the state of English prose style and the various ways in which English prose was being exercised and developed. Besides this large quantity of miscellaneous prose writing, there are devotional works, sermons, translations of many different kinds, histories, biographies, accounts of contemporary events, and prose fiction (both translation of Italian *novelle* and original work). Two forces are seen at work in most of this varied prose writing: first, the breakthrough of colloquial speech, with its vigor and raciness, into the written word, and secondly, the attempt to mold a consciously artistic English prose style. The two forces are, surprisingly enough, often found in conjunction, with colloquial vigor and over-elaborate parallels or antitheses alternating in the same work. No permanent resolution was achieved in the sixteenth or early seventeenth centuries, in spite of the occasional prose triumphs of the age. Though an impersonal devotional prose developed, descending from the devotional prose of Rolle and Hilton in the fourteenth century, and a biblical prose was wrought by the English translators of the Bible from Tyndale to the translators of the Authorized Version of 1611, it remains true that nearly all prose writers of the Elizabethan and immediately subsequent period wrote a highly idiosyncratic prose: there was, except for prayer and biblical translation, no common tradition of prose style on which individual writers could play their own variations, as eighteenth-century writers had from Addison on; every prose writer had first to solve the problem of creating his own style.

We can see colloquial prose disciplining itself into effective written speech in such documents as the fifteenth-century *Paston Letters,* family letters which, while wholly informal and unliterary, nevertheless have style—the style of fluent, educated speech, only slightly less discursive than actual speech would be. It is, however, a naïve prose, unsuited for any heavier burden than that of exchange of family news. Similarly naïve is the narrative prose of the English translation of the *Gesta Romanorum,* a collection of tales compiled in Latin in the late thirteenth century and translated into English in the middle and later fifteenth century. These popular stories of adventure and magic were put into an English whose style suggests that of the oral teller of tales. The same can be said of the very popular collection of saints' lives known as the *Golden Legend,* originally compiled in Latin by Jacobus de Voragine and translated into English in the second quarter of the fifteenth century, and of the English versions of the *Travels of Sir John Mandeville.* A more artful prose was demanded by the religious controversies which began in England over a century before the Reformation. The pre-Reformation Lollard movement, coinciding as it did with an extension of the ability to read among laymen, produced theological controversy in the vernacular on both sides: hitherto those who were not themselves clerics had for the most part received, and been content to receive, their religious education through preaching and oral instruction, but now both attackers and defenders of the ecclesiastical *status quo* began to appeal to the people in vernacular literature. The most distinguished fifteenth-century prose work resulting from the religious controversies provoked by the Lollards was Reginald Pecock's *The Repressor of Over Much Blaming of the Clergy,* written in the middle of the century. This humane and reasonable defender of the Catholic position against the Lollards—his sweet reasonableness with heretics led to his own prosecution as a heretic in the end—was concerned to find a way of putting into English, theological and other abstract concepts which had not hitherto been expressed in that language. The result is a work full of strange invented words and odd inversions; but though the style is often awkward and even puzzling, it remains a remarkable single-handed attempt to enlarge the potentialities of English prose for serious discourse, and it has an impressive dignity for all its oddness.

Various experiments in the handling of a utilitarian English prose were made in the fifteenth century; among them are treatises on medicine, hunting, hawking, and political theory, mostly translated from the French or Latin. The finest literary prose of the century was that of Malory's Arthurian stories, already discussed in Chapter 5. Malory's prose, magnificent though it is for its purpose, had no significant influence on the future course of English prose narrative; it is rather the final achievement of medieval prose narrative than the first beginnings of a modern style. William Caxton, who printed Malory and gave his collection of Arthurian stories the title *Morte Darthur* by which it has been known for centuries, was himself a prolific translator as well as a pioneer printer. His translated *Recuyell of the Histories of Troye*, published at Bruges in 1475, is the first printed book in English. Caxton's importance as a printer is paramount; after his return to England in 1476 following a long stay abroad, first as merchant and then as printer, he printed much of the best of older English literature available to him, including Chaucer, Gower, and Malory, together with prose romances, translations of Latin classics (including works or parts of works by Cicero, Virgil, Ovid, and Boethius), and numerous works of piety, morality, and information. But Caxton is also important as a translator and a writer of English prose, if only for the vast quantity of translated material that he produced and made available. His translations tend to be dominated by the originals; he had not a strong enough sense of English style to be able to turn a foreign language into clear idiomatic English possessing a firm sentence structure of its own; he often paired a French and an English word together as if uncertain which was the proper one to use and hoping that at least one of them would achieve the desired effect; and he frequently got lost in long sentences. But he struggled tirelessly with the English language, trying to find an "English not over rude, ne curious, but in such terms as shall be understanden by God's grace," and he thus takes his place as one of the important exercisers of English prose in one of the most interesting transitional periods of its history.

Humanism and Protestantism, whose impact on English life and thought at the end of the fifteenth and the beginning of the sixteenth century has been briefly described in Chapter 5, made their own contributions to the development of English prose. Sir Thomas More, whose Latin *Utopia*, published in 1516, marks his chief literary contribution as a Humanist, made his contribution to English prose mainly in his religious works. His polemical writings against the reformers begin with the *Dialogue* "of images, praying to saints, other things touching the pestilent sect of Luther and Tyndale," published in 1528, and continue with a series of belligerent attacks on Tyndale against whom he defended the orthodox Roman Catholic position. The original *Dialogue* is by far the liveliest of these, for its dramatic form (it consists of a series of conversations between himself and a messenger, with brisk interruptions and interludes of cheerful anecdote) gives More the opportunity to display his humor and the verve of his colloquial style. His other controversial religious works are strange mixtures of pedantry, piety, robust humor, scurrility, and railing. Rhetorical tricks of denunciation are found side by side with passages of earnest analysis on the one hand and of rollicking vulgarity on the other. The intrusion of colloquial vitality into his most serious prose discussions is a constant feature of More's work. From the point of view of the development of English prose, the colloquial element was important as helping to keep alive in written English the invigorating element of good speech, though More never found a style which for any length of time successfully domiciled happily together the vernacular vigor and more formal qualities. His style reflected the paradox (or so it has seemed to some) of a man who was both saint and humorist.

More interesting and far more appealing than his attacks on Tyndale is his *Dialogue of Comfort against Tribulation,* written when he was in the Tower of London awaiting death. Cast in the form of a conversation between two Hungarian gentlemen anticipating possible martyrdom if the Turkish advance continues, it discusses with searching honesty the fears and hopes of a Christian in prospect of "shameful and painful death." It is the most personal of his works and reveals most clearly the nobility as well as the charm and humor of his character. Even in dealing with a subject of this immense gravity he introduces his illustrative anecdotes, his jests, and what in a later age would have been called music-hall stories, and for once the reader accepts the mingling of grave and gay as the appropriate reflection of the mind of a resolute Christian determined that even while awaiting martyrdom he will not lose sight of the humor of daily life and will take comfort from the more innocent of human follies, including his own.

William Tyndale (d. 1536), More's opponent in his religious controversies, is more distinguished as the great pioneer of English Bible translation than as a religious pamphleteer and theological writer. His prose writings on religious questions possess a speed and vigor which More's style lacks; he has a way of conveying to the reader an almost gay conviction of his own rightness, by the rapid accumulation of arresting short clauses; yet he has not More's humor, though his writings reflect an ebullience of character that we do not detect in More, for all the latter's fondness for the humorous anecdote. The theological points on which More and Tyndale differed so strongly are bound up with the whole pattern of religious controversy of the age, and that is more a subject for the historian of religious thought than for the literary historian. One point of difference is illustrated by the story told by the Protestant martyrologist John Foxe in his *Acts and Monuments:* Foxe tells how, in discussion with a "learned man" who was praising the Pope's law above God's, "Master Tyndall . . . answered him, I defy the Pope and all his laws, and said, if God spare my life ere many years I will cause a boy that driveth the plough shall know more of the Scripture than thou dost." Tyndale's attitude toward the Pope and the ecclesiastical hierarchy in general, and his view of the Bible and its authority in Christian life, were essentially that of the Lollards in an earlier generation. The Bible was the supreme authority in religious affairs and the King was equally the supreme authority in civil matters. Tyndale held, too, that it was the individual's state of mind, rather than his actions, which earned him salvation; that is, in theological terms, he set faith above good works. But no easy summary can do justice either to Tyndale's views or to More's. They were both involved in that great controversy over the nature of Christian discipline and authority, the relation between faith and works, the true vehicle of the Christian tradition, and (to use the title of one of Tyndale's works) "the obedience of a Christian man," which raged throughout the sixteenth century and later and wrought so much change in the European scene. As Professor C. S. Lewis has pointed out, both were at their best when arguing for positions which were really common ground between them.

The sermon was a literary form more apt for the development of a formal prose than the controversial religious pamphlet. The Middle Ages had developed its own traditions and styles of preaching (as the lay reader can gather from Chaucer's *Pardoner's Tale*), and the medieval homiletic tradition did not dry up suddenly at the Renaissance but continued to influence, in varying ways, the preacher's methods and devices. Nevertheless, new styles and new kinds of sophistication came into English preaching in the sixteenth and seventeenth centuries. The sermons of Dean Colet combined powerful rhetoric with high idealism in a notable manner; Bishop Fisher introduced humanistic variations into an essentially medieval homiletic style, rising on occasion to a grave and gentle eloquence; Hugh Latimer (ca. 1490–1555) was a great popular preacher who knew how to make effective use of the most casual and anecdotal material, preserving an appearance of impromptu speaking which greatly added to the immediacy of the effect. The Elizabethan settlement, completed with the establishment of the thirty-nine articles in 1571, produced the Church of England, Catholic in profession but national in character, repudiating the authority of the Pope but episcopal in organization, a national Catholic Church stripped of the abuses of Rome but resisting the demands of the Puritans for extreme simplicity and severity in worship, for the abolition of episcopacy, and for granting spiritual authority to individuals who claimed it on the grounds of grace vouchsafed to them and of preaching ability. The settlement provided a wide roof under which different shades of opinion could shelter together, as later divisions into "high" and "low" Church (both within the Church of England) were to testify; but it left out both Roman Catholics and the more extreme Puritans. The Puritans, to whom preaching the Word was a sacred obligation, would have had a greater effect on English preaching if they had not eventually been forbidden to preach by the repressive legislation introduced in support of the establishment by Archbishop Whitgift. Fortunately, the Church of England produced early in its history a succession of learned and able ecclesiastics who brought preaching in England in the late sixteenth and early seventeenth centuries to a new level of literary art. The Puritan preachers, who re-emerged under the Commonwealth and later strongly influenced the style of nonconformist preaching, are important in the history of the spoken sermon; but the great Anglican preachers are of more concern to the literary historian.

The term "Puritan" has been used with many shades of meaning. Those who accepted Calvin's theology and also demanded that his system of church government be set up in England on the grounds that it was the one proper system to be discovered from the text of the New Testament and was therefore compulsory for all true Christians, represented the hard core of the party. But there were Calvinists prominent in the Church of England well into the seventeenth century; the active controversy between Puritan and Anglican in Queen Elizabeth's reign centered on the method of church government. The Church of England was committed to episcopacy, and the Puritans were equally committed to opposing the whole notion of an episcopal hierarchy. It must be remembered that Henry VIII's reformation did not affect the theology, the hierarchy, or the ritual of the Church in England; it merely removed the Pope's authority at the top of the hierarchy and substituted that of the King. The short reign of his son, Edward VI, gave free play to more purely

Protestant forces, but with the accession of Edward's sister Mary, in 1554, England was reconciled with Rome and those vocal Protestants who did not escape to Geneva were vigorously persecuted. The exiles returned on the accession of Elizabeth in 1558, considerably embittered by the Marian persecutions, much more uncompromising in their Calvinist views, and hopeful that with a Protestant queen now on the throne they could look forward to the implementation in England of the Calvinist form of church government. But Elizabeth deliberately avoided both extremes in the religious controversies she found prevailing on her accession; she sensed the nation's combination of conservatism and nationalism in religious matters in spite of the brilliance and passion of the Puritan propagandists, and her settlement was Protestant, national, and antipapist without being anti-Catholic. She retained the bishops—whether as necessary machinery for implementing her own authority over the Church, in the spirit of her successor James' remark, "No Bishop, no King," or for more disinterested reasons, need not concern us. The result was a spate of Puritan criticism of the bishops, both as individuals and as an institution.

The bishops eventually set up machinery to silence their critics, controlling both the press and the pulpit, but no sooner was the machinery completed when the anonymous pamphleteer who called himself Martin Marprelate began to issue his series of spirited attacks on the bishops. These pamphlets, which appeared in 1588 and 1589, have tremendous vigor; popular in style, colloquial in speech, full of witty taunts, vulgar jeers, and all the humorous rhetorical tricks of an expert street-corner orator, they introduced a new manner into religious pamphleteering. Though Martin Marprelate was never discovered, his printers were caught, and that put an end to the pamphlets, but not before they had so disturbed the bishops that they hired writers to attack Martin in his own style. One of these anti-Martinist pamphlets was by Lyly, others were for long erroneously attributed to Nashe; some of them succeed in capturing Martin's exuberant vitality of style. Nashe may have written the pamphlet called *An Almond for a Parrot,* which shows his characteristic command of racy invective and picturesque exaggeration. At any rate, Nashe's undisputed prose writings, which include satirical pamphlets and a picaresque novel, show these qualities to a most remarkable degree. The Elizabethan satirical pamphlet, as practiced by Nashe, Lodge, and others, thus owes something to the style developed by Elizabethan religious controversy.

If religious and other controversies helped to stimulate the development of a polemical prose style, a more profound shaping of English prose was going on at the same time by means of the discipline of translation. The earliest and one of the most significant of the great Elizabethan translations was Thomas North's *Lives of the Noble Grecians and Romans* (1579), translated from Plutarch via the French of Amyot. North's Plutarch provided the Elizabethans in large measure with their view of the ancient world; he provided the personalities, the political and domestic details, the "properties," not only for Shakespeare in his Roman plays but also for the educated Englishmen of the time. His style is vigorous, idiomatic and flexible, and it is significant that Shakespeare sometimes follows him almost verbatim. Sir Thomas Hoby's translation, published in 1561, of the greatest of all the "courtesy books," Castiglione's *Il Cortegiano*, "The Courtier," made available to Englishmen a notable exposition of the high Renaissance ideal of the gentleman—an ideal combining the two medieval alternatives, the active and the contemplative life, the whole seasoned with a passionate neo-Platonic sense of a graduated ascent from earthly to divine beauty. Hoby's style is uneven and not really able to cope consistently with the happy eloquence of the original Italian; but Castiglione's picture of an ideal Court done with such liveliness and enthusiasm, with dramatic dialogue and incidental short stories, does communicate itself in Hoby's translations for all its occasional uncertainties. Hoby was influenced in some degree by Sir John Cheke's view that English should be used in its native purity, uncorrupted by borrowings from other languages; but Cheke went to extremes in his advocacy of "pure and unmixed" English—his spelling reform and his ardent Saxonism can be seen in his curious translation of Matthew and part of Mark—while Hoby only intermittently seeks for the Anglo-Saxon equivalent of a word of Romance or Latin origin.

The Italian *novella*—"trifling tale," as Sir Thomas Hoby translates the word, but that perhaps only indicates his own fundamental seriousness of mind—so important as providing plots for Elizabethan drama, also attracted English translators. William Painter's *Palace of Pleasure*, published in 1566 with a second volume in 1567, contains a large variety of such stories, many taken not directly from the Italian but from the rather more verbose French versions in Belleforest's *Histoires Tragiques*. The authors include Boccaccio, Bandello, Cinthio, and Margaret of Navarre, as well as Livy, Herodotus, and Plutarch. Geoffrey Fenton's *Tragical Discourses*, published in 1567, contains Italian *novelle* elaborated and moralized. George Pettie's *Petite Palace of Pettie his Pleasures*, 1576, tells a dozen stories from classical sources (mostly Ovid and Livy) in an elaborate rhetorical style in which we first see sustained that characteristic Elizabethan attempt to achieve a literary prose through a careful use of parallels, antitheses, balanced similes, and the other devices associated with euphuism. Lyly's *Euphues*, briefly discussed in Chapter 7, develops this style, which is modified somewhat in the sequel, *Euphues and his England;* in the prose dialogue of his plays Lyly advances to a true courtly prose with a charm and delicacy of its own.

The noblest achievement of sixteenth-century English prose translation was, however, done on the Bible. The Wycliffite versions had been renderings from the Latin of the Vulgate; they had, moreover, been made before printing came to England, and could not therefore have the circulation that the printed Bible could have. The sixteenth-century movement was both Protestant and Humanist in impulse—the former in that it sprang from the desire to make available to the ordinary reader the one original source of Christianity, and the latter in its determination to translate from the original Hebrew and Greek. The combination of the two impulses is symbolized by the fact that William Tyndale, pioneer translator of the Bible into English from the original languages, published in 1529 a translation of Erasmus' *Exhortation to the Diligent Study of Scripture* in which the great Humanist uttered words that were heartily echoed by the Protestant translator:

> I would that all women should read the Gospel and Paul's Epistles, and I would to God they were translated into the tongues of all men, so that they might not only be read and known of the Scots and Irishmen but also of the Turks and Saracens. . . . I would to God the plowman would sing a text of the Scripture at his plowbeam and that the weaver at his loom with this would drive away the tediousness of time. I would the wayfaring man with this pastime would expel the weariness of his journey. And to be short I would that all the communication of the Christian should be of the Scripture, for in a manner such are we ourselves as our daily tales are.

This, of course, was not orthodox Catholic doctrine. The medieval Church took the view that ordinary folk should not read the Bible themselves, but should have appropriate portions of the Vulgate interpreted to them by properly trained experts. The demand for a vernacular Bible was a feature of many medieval heresies, and was sternly resisted by the Church. As the criticism of the Church that was eventually to bring about the Reformation spread in England as elsewhere, the demand for Bible translation also grew. The Church shifted its ground somewhat in the face of this growing demand and began to object to the Wycliffite translations because they were erroneous rather than because they made the Bible readily accessible to the public. Sir Thomas More, discussing Bible translation in 1528, made it clear that in his view the Church could only have condemned the Wycliffite versions if they were textually corrupt and contained heretical notes, and he accordingly assumed that these versions did in fact have these faults. More's main objections to Tyndale's translation were its heretical glosses and its untraditional terms.

Official opinion against vernacular Bible translation was, however, slow in changing, and Tyndale did his work secretly abroad. The first edition of his New Testament was seized at the printer's in Cologne in 1525, before the printing was complete, and Tyndale moved to Worms, where he brought out two editions of the work in the same year. He then turned his attention to the Old Testament, having acquired a very respectable knowledge of Hebrew, and published his version of the Pentateuch in 1531. A version of the Book of Jonah appeared the following year, and in 1534 he brought out a revised edition of his New Testament, to which was added a translation of select passages from the Old Testament Prophets. Further revisions of the New Testament appeared in later years. Tyndale's New Testament circulated widely, though surreptitiously. The translation was officially condemned by the ecclesiastical authorities in England as well as in a royal proclamation of 1530 which, however, significantly affirmed the royal intention of providing for an authorized translation when the time was ripe. Attempts were made to trap Tyndale into coming to England. He was eventually betrayed in 1535, and burned at the stake at Vilvorde the following year.

Tyndale was a strongly Protestant translator who deliberately rendered (to Thomas More's horror) *ecclesia* as "congregation" not "church," *charis* as "favor" not "grace," and so on, because he wished to avoid the Roman Catholic implications of the established terms. And because he rendered the New Testament from the Greek (Erasmus' edition, with help from his Latin version) and the parts of the Old Testament he translated from the Hebrew, instead of following the traditional Roman Catholic view that the Vulgate was the true Christian text, he was bound to introduce certain novelties into men's conception of the Bible. Further, he shared with Luther the view that a biblical rendering should respect the language of the common man and be clear and straightforward, and this led him to an occasional phrasing which sounds too brightly popular to ears accustomed to the statelier prose of the Authorized Version. But his simplicity gives his prose, for all its occasional oddness to modern ears, a special charm, and though later translators added a more liturgical note to Tyndale's honest clarity, they retained the basic simplicity, which remains the norm of narrative prose in the Authorized Version. Tyndale had a true gift of phrase, and introduced many words, phrases, and cadences which remain unchanged in the Authorized Version. The English language was richer for his biblical endeavors, and the line of Bible translation which led unbroken to the Authorized Version had been begun. As far as the New Testament went, all subsequent English renderings to 1611 and beyond were in effect revisions of Tyndale or of his revisers, and his translation of the Pentateuch and other parts of the Old Testament gave Protestant Christianity a rich store of words and phrases (including "scapegoat," "mercy seat," "long-suffering" and many more) which became a permanent part of the English language.

In 1535—five years after Henry VIII's proclamation condemning Tyndale's translation yet affirming the royal intention of eventually providing for an authorized translation—the first complete English Bible appeared, the work of Miles Coverdale, a man inspired by the same ideals as Tyndale but milder and more compromising in character. This was not the authorized version for which the English bishops were preparing, but Coverdale assumed that his work (which was probably printed at Zurich) would be acceptable to the King, to whom it was dedicated. A later edition of Coverdale's Bible, published in 1537, bore the legend: "Set forth with the King's most gracious license." The main battle had been won, and the 1537 quarto edition of Coverdale's Bible was in a sense the first "authorized version" of the Bible in English. (Since the King was by now "supreme head" of the Church as well as of the State, his "license" implied a twofold authorization.) Coverdale had not Tyndale's scholarship in Hebrew and Greek, and his translation was admittedly derived from later Latin and German versions. He mentions "five sundry interpreters" whose work he drew on, and these were fairly certainly the Zurich Swiss-German Bible of 1524–29 (by Zwingli and Leo Juda), Luther's German Bible, Pagninus' Latin Bible of 1528, the Vulgate, and Tyndale's New Testament and Pentateuch. For the Old Testament, except the Pentateuch, the Zurich Bible is his primary source, with occasional renderings of Pagninus and Luther preferred to those of the Zurich version. The basis of his Pentateuch is Tyndale's, and Tyndale also influenced Coverdale's rendering of Jonah. Coverdale's New Testament is a revision of Tyndale largely by the Zurich text. When his other authorities left him in genuine doubt, he fell back on the Vulgate.

Lacking Tyndale's original scholarship, Coverdale was free to choose renderings and phrasings that pleased his ear rather than satisfied a demand for strict scholarly accuracy. He possessed a fluency which sometimes produced a fine flowing cadence and at other times led him into diffuse paraphrase. His fluency had a permanent effect on the style of the English Bible, for it was he more than any other single translator whose sense of rhythm produced that musical quality which is particularly evident in the Authorized Version of 1611. His influence did not work only through "Coverdale's Bible" of 1535 and its later editions, for Coverdale put his services at the disposal of later official translators and his revisions of phrasing in subsequent versions helped significantly to mold the style of the Authorized Version. In 1537 appeared a composite version, known as "Matthew's Bible," made up of Tyndale's translation of as much of the Old Testament as he had translated, Coverdale's translation of the remainder of the Old Testament, and Tyndale's New Testament (the professed translator Matthew, whether a real or a fictitious person, being introduced to cover up the Government's inconsistency in now allowing parts of a translation they had earlier vehemently condemned). This version, like the edition of Coverdale's Bible of the same year, was "set forth with the King's most gracious license," and it was strongly supported by the bishops. More important, it was the basis for the series of revisions that culminated in the King James, or Authorized Version of 1611. Its imperfections were freely admitted by the bishops, even though Archbishop Cranmer promoted it as strongly as he could, and the Great Bible, a revision of Matthew's Bible made by Coverdale at the instance of the King's minister Thomas Cromwell, was published in April, 1540. In this version (which shows, in the Old Testament, the influence of Sebastian Münster's Latin translation) Coverdale introduced many of the felicities of phrasing that have remained in the English Bible.

The Great Bible ran into many editions, but there were continuous suggestions of a further major revision. On the death of Edward VI the progress of English Bible translation was temporarily halted. The Catholic Queen Mary on her accession stopped abruptly the printing of vernacular Bibles in England. Many of the Protestants most interested in Bible translation went into exile, and it was at the colony of these exiles at Geneva that the next English translation of the Bible was made. This, known as the "Geneva Bible," published at Geneva in 1560, was a thorough revision of the text of the Great Bible after the original Hebrew of the Old Testament and in the New Testament a revision of Tyndale after the original Greek and Beza's Latin New Testament of 1556. The Geneva translators had the help of such other versions and aids to translation as had recently appeared on the Continent, and they made full use of it. Their version was the most accurate and scholarly English translation that had yet been made, and though it is not officially in the direct line of succession of the Authorized Version, it was in fact heavily drawn upon by the King James translators. On the whole, the Geneva translators sacrificed style to accuracy, and there is a pedantic flavor about the work, particularly noticeable in the spelling of Old Testament proper names, which follows the Hebrew exactly. The Geneva Bible is the first English Bible to break up the Old Testament text into numbered verses, a perhaps unfortunate practice which has persisted until the "Bible designed to be read as literature" of our own day. The Puritan habit of text-quoting must have been largely responsible for this desire to have each verse numbered for ease of reference. The profuse marginal notes were another feature of the translation displeasing to modern eyes as it was to Elizabethan Anglicans.

The accession of Queen Elizabeth in 1558 marked a reversion to a middle-of-the-road Protestant policy. The Great Bible was again regarded as the official version and ordered to be set up in churches (the Geneva Bible, being the work of more extreme Protestants who were considerably to the "left" of Elizabeth's position, was not officially recognized). In 1568 the Great Bible was superseded by a further revision made by a company of bishops and hence known as the "Bishops' Bible." This version was not, however, altogether successful. A combination of the work of different revisers working with little common policy or discipline, it is patchy and uneven, and in accuracy considerably behind the Geneva Bible, which continued to be the most popular translation in England until after 1611. Finally, when James I ascended the throne in 1603 he appointed a company of learned men consisting of the most competent Hebrew and Greek scholars available (excluding, however, those who were antagonistic to the Anglican Church) to prepare a great new revision. This work, begun in 1604 and completed in 1611, after meticulous and carefully coordinated labor, has remained *the* English Bible ever since. It was as accurate a translation of the available Hebrew and Greek texts as the combined scholarship of the age could make; but, more than that, the company of translators who worked on it were sufficiently sensitive to the demands of a biblical prose in keeping with the finest stylistic achievements of Tyndale and Coverdale that again and again they seemed to be able to strike the right note with unerring felicity. True, the style of the Authorized Version was in some degree archaic by now, and the revisers were thus deliberately perpetuating a biblical style which was something apart from contemporary English prose, a style that had been forged in almost a century's experimentation. The Authorized Version, it must be remembered, was not a new translation, but a revision, ostensibly of the Bishops' Bible but in fact making as much use of the Geneva Bible. It was the culmination of the successive versions of which Tyndale's was the first. And though archaic in its time, it had a great influence on the rhythms and the vocabulary of later English prose, especially in the seventeenth and the nineteenth centuries.

There were other biblical versions produced during this period which were not in the line of succession of the Authorized Version. There was, for example, the Bible translated by Richard Taverner, published in 1538, which was an independent revision of Matthew's Bible which received no official recognition. Sir John Cheke's rendering of Matthew and part of Mark, which remained unpublished until 1843, is interesting for its determined attempt to provide genuine English equivalents of ecclesiastical terms from the Greek and Latin; thus "parable" becomes "biword," "proselyte" becomes "freshman," "crucified" becomes "crossed." But the most important English Bible outside the main tradition of the Protestant translations of the sixteenth and early seventeenth centuries was the Roman Catholic translation from the Vulgate, of which the New Testament appeared at Rheims in 1582 and the Old Testament at Douai (Douay) in 1609–10. The moving spirit in the preparation of this version was Cardinal Allen, president of the English College at Rheims—the college had moved from Douai to Rheims in 1578 on account of the expulsion order against English residents issued by the magistrates in that year—and a distinguished Bible scholar. Writing in Latin to a friend in September, 1578, Allen explained how the Catholic preachers were at a disadvantage compared with the Protestant, who were familiar with the English Bible and did not therefore need to translate extempore from the Vulgate when preaching to a popular audience. The Catholic preacher, he said, was liable to stumble in his English renderings, which would make a bad impression on his hearers. Although it were perhaps better that no translation into *barbaras linguas* were made, yet the disadvantages the Catholic cause suffered by not having an English version while the Protestants had were sufficient to overrule the traditional objections to vernacular versions. The result was a scholarly rendering of the Latin Vulgate text. The emphasis was on accuracy rather than on stylistic grace, and though the Rheims and Douay Bible is a notable English translation it has not the independent literary merit, nor has it had the influence, of the Authorized Version.

The Book of Common Prayer of 1549, the work of Archbishop Cranmer and others, happily combines the earlier tradition of liturgical prose with the new tradition of Protestant biblical translation. Its style derives in large measure from the stately Latin liturgical prose of the medieval service book used in the diocese of Salisbury, known as the *Use of Sarum,* as well as from the devotional Books of Hours, originally in Latin but occasionally in English, in the fourteenth and fifteenth centuries and (with significant doctrinal differences) after the Reformation. The version of the Psalms and other biblical passages in *The Book of Common Prayer* was that of the Great Bible of 1540–i.e., Coverdale's revision of Matthew's Bible. The combination of Latin and English, medieval and modern, liturgical, devotional, and biblical styles was not only remarkably effective from the literary point of view; it also symbolized and exhibited that unique combination of the traditional and the reforming which was such a significant aspect of the English Reformation. *The Book of Common Prayer,* which was confirmed as the official Church of England prayer book under the Elizabethan settlement, remains eloquent testimony to the English genius for preserving continuity amid change.

Humanism and the Reformation meet in English Bible translation, the former providing the philological tools, the latter the religious impulse. Meanwhile, both humanistic and religious prose continued independently. Sir Thomas Elyot (ca. 1490–1546) produced in 1531 *The Book of the Governor,* an English contribution (though deriving from Erasmus, the Italian Patrizzi, and other European sources) to the abundant Renaissance literature of instruction for members of the ruling class, of which, as we have seen, Castiglione's *Il Cortegiano* is the most impressive. Elyot's book shows a profound belief in the importance of order or "degree," and it stresses equally practical, intellectual, and esthetic education. His prose is consciously artful, but not excessively tricked out with any of the euphuistic devices by means of which writers later in the century tried to give literary dignity to their style. He combines stateliness and clarity; he uses anecdote and allusion adroitly, but with no great liveliness; and the result is workmanlike without being exciting. Elyot's later work includes miscellaneous translations and popularizations of medical, political, and educational subjects, and the first significant Latin-English dictionary. Roger Ascham (1515–68) is an attractive Protestant Humanist whose *Toxophilus* (1545) is a patriotic treatise on archery as an English national sport done with liveliness and charm; it is cast in dialogue form, but the appeal of the work derives less from the exploitation of the dramatic possibilities of the dialogue than from the personal observation and the lovingly described detail in the pictures of English life. His educational treatise, *The Schoolmaster,* published after his death in 1570, is concerned first with the practical details of teaching, advocating gentleness and patience instead of the rod, and, secondly, with the method of teaching Latin. His attitude is narrowly Humanist; he advocates the imitation of select classical authors for the proper molding of style and shows the characteristic Humanist contempt for medieval romances. For all his charm and gentleness, especially evident in the discussion of teaching methods, he shows the narrowness of the Protestant Humanist: "In our forefathers' time, when Papistry, as a standing pool, covered and overflowed all England, few books were read in our tongue, saving certain books of Chivalry, as they said, for pastime and pleasure, which, as some say, were made in monasteries by idle monks or wanton canons, as one for example, *Morte Arthure,* the whole pleasure of which book standeth in two special points, in open manslaughter and bold bawdry." Ascham also attacks rhyme, and inveighs against the immorality of the Italianate Englishman and "the enchantments of Circe, brought out of Italy to mar men's manners in England." Ascham's prose style has a plain vigor; it is not, however, the plainness of colloquial speech that he affects, but a studied plainness deriving from his belief in the native strength of the English language (he was like Sir John Cheke, though less extreme, in his preference for words of English origin) and a deliberate balancing of sentences and alternation of long sentences with short. Cheke, whom we have already mentioned as a purist in his vocabulary and author of an odd translation from the New Testament, was a notable Greek scholar and teacher; he produced in 1549 a prose pamphlet entitled *The Hurt of Sedition* which sets forward with great force the Tudor position with regard to rebellion (and so helps to explain, for example, Shakespeare's attitude in *Henry IV Part I* and elsewhere) and does not show his Saxonism as his biblical translation does, employing a style of no great individuality or distinction. Thomas Wilson (ca. 1525–81) is another English Humanist, whose most important work is *The Art of Rhetoric,* published in 1553 and in a revised and enlarged edition in 1560. This can reasonably be called the first modern handbook of English composition, though its sources are to be found in Quintilian and Cicero. He anticipates euphuism in his advocacy of similes drawn from natural (or unnatural) history and in his advice on the pairing and balancing of clauses; yet he is no advocate of artificiality, condemning "inkhorn terms" and recommending a style without affectation and excessive Latinisms. His own style can be unduly rhetorical at times, but, like so many Elizabethan prose writers, he has the gift of enlivening discussion with anecdote.

History and biography were also fields in which Elizabethan prose exercised itself. Edward Hall (ca. 1499–1547) produced in his *Union of the two Noble and Illustre Families of Lancaster and York* an account of English history from Henry IV to Henry VIII from what might be called the official Tudor viewpoint; he showed the pattern as developing from trouble through tragedy to Tudor redemption, thus fixing what has been called the "Tudor myth," which some critics have seen as so important a clue to the understanding of Shakespeare's history plays. Hall's style was condemned by Ascham as "indenture English" (i.e., coupling together words of similar meaning in pairs, for emphasis and rhetorical effect: "all regions which by division and dissension [are] vexed, molested and troubled [are] by union and agreement relieved, pacified and enriched"), but at his best Hall can use this device to give gravity and even dramatic power to his writing. He is a rhetorical writer who balances his sentences with deliberate and sometimes excessive art. He is also a historian who sees a grand moral pattern in history and spares no effort to bring out in relief the high points of his story. Sir Thomas More had done something similar on a smaller scale in his Latin *History of Richard III* (written 1513–14 but not published until 1565) which was translated into English and appeared in the collected folio edition of More's English works in 1557.

Raphael Holinshed's *Chronicles,* of which the first edition appeared in 1577 and the enlarged second edition (the one which Shakespeare used) in 1587, is a compilation of English, Scottish, and Irish history deriving from a variety of earlier sources (including Hall, and Sir Thomas More's *Richard III*). The original plan was an ambitious "universal cosmography" projected by the London printer Reginald Wolfe, but the completed work was much less comprehensive. It did, however, include geographical as well as historical accounts of the countries dealt with. The *Description of England* included in the *Chronicle* is by William Harrison, who writes in a cheerful, rapid, anecdotal style, pleasingly garrulous, and gives much valuable information about the England of his day. The *Description of Scotland* is translated by Harrison from the Scots version (by John Bellenden, 1536) of the Latin history of Scotland by the Scottish Humanist Hector Boece, published in 1527. Holinshed had other collaborators, and the total result is a somewhat discursive work, with the history lacking the sharp outlines of Hall, but clearly told, with a feeling for the lively incident and high patriotic tone.

Tudor patriotism encouraged the chronicler and the historian, and at the same time the Renaissance view of history as a "mirror for magistrates," a source of moral lessons for the ruler of a state, helped to increase the vogue for history. Patriotism also encouraged antiquarian study, which begins to become important at this period, with Archbishop Parker, John Stow, John Speed, John Leland, and William Camden. Each of these made important contributions to the study of English antiquities. Parker, with the help of his assistant John Josselyn, pioneered in the study of Anglo-Saxon, one of his motives being to show the national nature of the English Church even in Anglo-Saxon times and so demonstrate the historical continuity of the Church of England. Leland, realizing that the dissolution of the monasteries and the dispersal of their libraries might destroy forever important literary documents, embarked on (to cite the title of one of his major works) "a laborious journey and search for England's antiquities" and also produced a Latin list of British authors and their works which represents the true beginning of English literary scholarship. Leland's cataloguing work of British authors was continued by the violently Protestant John Bale and the violently Catholic John Pits. Stow, with Parker's help, edited a number of medieval English chronicles; he also edited Chaucer, and produced a *Summary of English Chronicles* in 1565, *The Chronicles of England* in 1580 (entitled *Annals* in later editions) and, his most important work, *A Survey of London* in 1598. Speed (like Stow, originally a tailor by trade) was antiquary, historian, and cartographer, but it is as a cartographer that he is most important. Camden's *Britannia*, easily the greatest antiquarian work of the period, was published originally in Latin in 1586 and appeared in English in 1610.

At the other extreme from the local topographical work of antiquaries is the grandiosely conceived world history, of which the most impressive example in English is Ralegh's *The History of the World*, published unfinished in 1614. Ralegh's work is a remarkable mingling of the medieval and the Renaissance—and perhaps can be used as evidence by those who maintain that the Renaissance marked no real change in human thought. Based (as far as historical information goes) entirely on secondary sources, it is an attempt to see a providential pattern working through world history—history which begins with the Creation, accepts the biblical record of events implicitly, yet shows a shrewd critical mind at work in dealing with postbiblical events and in commenting on men and affairs. There is a certain majesty in the grand moral pattern which Ralegh sees unfolding in the events he describes, and the moral eloquence of the style provides the proper tone for this sort of history, with its somber sense of the brevity of individual life and the vanity of human plans. The medieval *ubi sunt* theme is here, and Ralegh has the medieval sense of human affairs as a pageant directed and watched by God; but he has a sense of the heroic too, an admiration for skill and magnanimity wherever found, and a feeling for parallels and contrasts between past and present. He did not get beyond 168 B.C.

The sixteenth century saw the rise of a new interest in biography as well as in history. Sometimes, as in More's work on Richard III, the impulse is historical and the biography becomes a species of history, but another motive sometimes manifested itself. This was the desire to commemorate and celebrate a distinguished figure, not as in a medieval saint's life, where the narrative tended to be typical and exemplary, but out of personal admiration, affection, or curiosity. The Humanists, both in England and abroad, developed a tradition of writing eulogistic biographies of their fellows (deceased or still living). These are often in Latin, such as the group of biographies of Humanists (including Colet, Linacre, Fisher, More, and Latimer) brought out by George Lily in 1548. The most distinguished representative in English of this *genre* in the sixteenth century is William Roper's life of his father-in-law, Sir Thomas More. This is written with an affectionate gravity, in a prose style which, in spite of its long and somewhat cumbersome sentences, succeeds in conveying the writer's personal attitude and interest; the dialogue, where the sentences are shorter and the voices strangely authentic, is particularly successful.

John Foxe's *Acts and Monuments,* published in English in 1563 after the publication of an original Latin version at Basel in 1559, is biography of a different sort. Foxe's aim was to write the story of Christian martyrs of all times, and he added in successive editions detailed accounts, from the Protestant point of view, of the persecution of Protestants under Mary. Foxe's work is not all original, for he includes narratives of others in various degrees of abridgement. The effect of the work is cumulative; in spite of a cumbersome English style, the succession of detailed incidents in the portion dealing with the Marian persecutions does succeed in creating a lively impression of the dedicated heroism of the martyrs and the senseless malice of their persecutors. The book (known, since an edition of 1776, as *The Book of Martyrs*) was an immensely influential piece of Protestant hagiography. Foxe's anti-Catholic bias is, of course, strong; but he never consciously distorts his material, much of which was drawn from the accounts of eyewitnesses which he obtained after his return from exile on the accession of Queen Elizabeth. Further, he was a genuinely humane man who disapproved of cruelty whichever side practiced it; it is this humanity which provides the note of passion in his account of individual sufferings, rather than exultation at the thought of proving the wickedness of his religious opponents.

Among the Protestant writers in the brief reign of the Catholic Mary may be mentioned John Ponet or Poynet, whose *Short Treatise of Politique Power,* written in exile and published anonymously abroad in 1556, the year of his death, attacked with eloquence and spirit the whole conception of Tudor monarchy. There were not many writers of the time who questioned the view that the ruler, as God's vicegerent, cannot be lawfully attacked by his subjects; Ponet attacked it with vigor, undercutting the whole position of those who saw disobedience to the ruler as disobedience to God and who held that only God and never his subjects could punish an erring ruler, by an appeal to natural law as understood in medieval political thought. And that reminds us that the Tudor despotism was a Renaissance invention; the position maintained, for example, by Sir John Cheke in *The Hurt of Sedition* was strictly modern; Ponet, though antipapal, was more medieval in his political thought than some Protestant Humanists, which illustrates some of the difficulties of writing intellectual history.

Among the miscellaneous themes to which Elizabethan pamphleteers devoted their attention, the denunciation of real or fancied evils was a favorite. Stephen Gosson's *School of Abuse,* published in 1579, is chiefly remembered for having provoked Sidney's *Defence of Poesie* in reply. Gosson's work is not in its own right an important piece of criticism; it is a routine denunciation of contemporary literature and the theater; but it is of some interest as an exercise in rhetorical invective. The subtitle—"containing a pleasant invective against Poets, Pipers, Players, Jesters and such like Caterpillars of a Commonwealth"—shows something of his exhibitionist style. His balanced sentences, alliteration, and other stylistic devices show the artful rhetorician as much as the indignant moralist:

> Oh what a wonderful change is this! Our wrestling at arms is turned to wallowing in ladies' laps, our courage to cowardice, our running to riot, our bows into bowls, and our darts to dishes. We have robbed Greece of gluttony, Italy of wantonness, Spain of pride, France of deceit, and Dutchland of quaffing. Compare London to Rome, and England to Italy, you shall find the theatres of the one, the abuses of the other, to be rife among us. . . . In our assemblies at plays in London, you shall see such heaving and shoving, such itching and shouldering, to sit by women; such care for their garments, that they be not trod on; such eyes to their laps, that no chips light in them; such pillows to their backs, that they take no hurt; such masking in their ears, I know not what; . . . such ticking, such toying, such smiling, such winking, and such manning them home, when the sports are ended, that it is a right comedy to mark their behaviour, to watch their conceits, as the cat's for the mouse, . . .

Other pamphleteers also attacked the abuses of the time, more often from a general conservative viewpoint than from an extreme Puritan position; bewailing the lost virtues of Old England, denouncing new fashions and follies, as Philip Stubbes, in his *Anatomy of Abuses* (1583), attacked the wearing of starched ruffs by women. ("The women there use great ruffs and neckerchers of holland, lawn, cambric, and such cloth, as the greatest thread shall not be so big as the least hair that is; and lest they should fall down, they are smeared and starched in the devil's liquor, I mean starch . . .") George Whetstone's *Touchstone for the Time* (1584) similarly denounces the "many perilous mischiefs bred in the bowels of the city of London." And there were many other similar pamphlets.

Gosson was answered (as well as by Sidney) by Thomas Lodge in his privately printed and suppressed pamphlet, *Honest Excuses.* Lodge was better at attack than defense, however, and his *Alarm against Usurers* (1584) and *Wit's Mercury* (1596) contain—especially the latter—some lively pictures of contemporary abuses in a style where a rhetorical euphuism struggles with a robust realistic humor, the realistic humor winning in the end. The best of all the Elizabethans in this vein, however, is Thomas Nashe, whose *Anatomy of Absurdity* ("containing a brief confutation of the slender imputed praises to feminine perfection, with a short description of the several practices of youth and sundry follies of our licentious times; no less pleasant to be read, than profitable to be remembered, especially of those who live more licentiously, or addicted to a more nice stoical austerity"), published in 1589, shows him employing every kind of verbal and rhythmic device to arrest the attention of the reader. Nashe's characteristic mixture of roaring colloquialism and fancy rhetoric is more successful than might be imagined, especially in his later work, such as *Pierce Penniless, his Supplication to the Devil,* an extraordinary combination of character portraits of types, anecdote, abuse, preaching, fiction, and sheer high spirits. Nashe became involved in a fierce pamphlet war with Gabriel Harvey, whom he abuses fiercely in *Pierce Penniless* and elsewhere. His *Lenten Stuff* shows Nashe's roistering exhibitionist style to best advantage; it is a mock-heroic celebration of the red herring, in which the most fantastic Latinisms take their place in a style which is nevertheless colloquial and popular in tone. He finds the origin of the herring in the metamorphosis of Hero, after she and Leander had come to their tragic end:

> To recount *ab ovo,* or from the church-book of his birth, how the herring first came to be a fish, and then how he came to be king of fishes, and graduationately how from white to red be changed, would require so massy a tome as Holinshed; but in half a pennyworth of paper I will epitomize them. Let me see, hath anybody in Yarmouth heard of Leander and Hero, of whom divine Musaeus sung, and a diviner Mûse than him, Kit Marlowe?

Two faithful lovers they were, as every apprentice in Paul's churchyard will tell you for your love, and sell you for your money; the one dwelt at Abydos in Asia, which was Leander; the other, which was Hero, his Mistress or Delia, at Sestos in Europe, and she was a pretty pinckany and Venus priest; and but an arm of the sea divided them; it divided them and it divided them not, for over that arm of the sea could be made a long arm. In their parents the most division rested, and their towns that like Yarmouth and Leystoffe [Lowestoft] were still at wrig wrag and sucked from their mothers' teats serpentine hatred against each other. Which drove Leander when he durst not deal above board, or be seen aboard any ship, to sail to his lady dear, to play the didopper and ducking water spaniel to swim to her, nor that in the day, but by owl-light.

Leander, after he is drowned, is changed into a ling (the fish), and Hero to a herring. The detailed invention with which the story is told shows a most fertile vein of fantasy, as well as a Rabelaisian wit. Here, for example, is the account of what happens to Hero's nurse after her metamorphosis:

The nurse or mother Mampudding, that was a cowering on the back side while these things were a tragedizing, led by the scritch or outcry to the prospect of this sorrowful heigho, as soon as, through the revalled button-holes of her blear eyes, she had sucked in and received such a revelation of Doomsday, and that she saw her mistress mounted a cockhorse and hoisted away to hell or heaven on the backs of those rough headed ruffians, down she sunk to the earth, as dead as a door nail, and never mumped crust after. Whereof their supernalities (having a drop or two of pity left after the huge hogshead of tears they spent for Hero and Leander) seemed to be something sorry, though they could not weep for it, and because they would be sure to have medicine that should make them weep at all times, to that kind of grain they turned her which we call mustard-seed, as well as she was a shrewish snappish bawd, that would bite off a man's nose with an answer and had rheumatic sore eyes that ran always, as that she might accompany Hero and Leander after death as in her lifetime; and hence it is that mustard bites a man so by the nose, and makes him weep and water his plants when he tasteth it; and that Hero and Leander, the red herring and ling, never come to the board without mustard, their waiting maid; and if you mark it, mustard looks of the tanned winscot hue of such a withered wrinkle-faced beldam as she was that was altered thereto. . . .

Whippet, turn to a new lesson, and strike we up "John for the King," or tell how the herring scrambled up to be King of all fishes. So it fell upon a time and tide, though not upon a holiday, a falconer bringing forth certain hawks out of Ireland—

and off Nashe goes to another piece of absurd invention, told in the same extraordinary style. There is nothing like this in English again until we come to some parts of Joyce's *Ulysses,* though Sir Thomas Urquart's translation of Rabelais, done in the middle of the seventeenth century, has something of Nashe's linguistic gusto and inventiveness. Nashe is one of the great individual prose stylists in English.

Nashe's rambling narrative, *The Unfortunate Traveller, or The Life of Jack Wilton* (1594), is a picaresque tale of adventure, perhaps suggested by the Spanish *Lazarillo de Tormes*. The picaresque or "rogue" novel was a suitable form for prose narrative in the infancy of the novel, for it did not demand any real integration of plot, but, by taking its hero on a series of adventures in different places, enabled the author to engage in a great variety of miscellaneous descriptive writing. *The Unfortunate Traveller* has been called the first English historical novel (the hero, who tells his story in the first person, was supposed to have lived much earlier in the century, and Nashe introduced some pseudohistorical episodes), but it is not really important as a contribution to the development of English prose fiction. Its basis is episodic narrative linked by memory and coincidence; and though Nashe had an eye for detail and the writing has a vivid pictorial quality as though everything is seen in brilliant sunlight, its discursiveness and complete formal irresponsibility make it very much less than a novel. It contains some remarkable individual stories, and is written in a style considerably simpler, with shorter sentences, than that of *Lenten Stuff*. It has its place in the history of English fiction, but as an interesting individual experiment rather than an "influence."

Robert Greene, like Nashe, was dramatist, pamphleteer, and writer of prose fiction. His *Groatsworth of Wit bought with a Million of Repentance* (1592, best known for its early reference to Shakespeare) is an autobiographical pamphlet written with verve but with no great distinction of style. Greene wrote a number of pamphlets, moving from a moderately euphuistic style to a more racy and colloquial one. His "conny catching" pamphlets, which have the ostensible object of putting the reader on his guard against the rogues and tricksters of London, reveal his extensive knowledge of London's underworld, and he tells his stories of swindles and immoralities with all the zest of a good crime reporter. Indeed, there is something of the journalist in the Greene of these later pamphlets, though his earlier work shows the more pretentious man of letters. His earlier writing includes romantic prose tales deriving in both style and kind of subject from Lyly's *Euphues*, which had many imitators in the 1580's. But in his romances, too, there is a progressive shedding of excessive rhetoric; the later ones, *Pandosto* (1588) and *Menaphon* (1589), being clearer in narrative outline and less prone to rhetorical digressions and elaborate soliloquies than the earlier. Thomas Lodge was another who combined pamphleteering with the writing of prose tales deriving from Greek romance. His *Rosalind* (1590), like Greene's *Pandosto*, was used by Shakespeare. The style of Lodge's prose romances is formal and rhetorical, influenced by Lyly (whose *Euphues* is discussed in Chapter 7), but at his best Lodge's narrative prose has a flow and a control that makes it much more satisfactory to the ear than many examples of the euphuistic style; the artificiality is there, but it is subdued to the narrative, which moves with conspicuous ease.

Perhaps the Elizabethan writer of prose fiction who is of most historical interest is Thomas Deloney, whose three tales (or groups of tales), *Jack of Newbury, The Gentle Craft*, and *Thomas of Reading*, all written in the 1590's, show him as the storyteller of the bourgeois craftsman. *Jack of Newbury*, for example, deals with the weavers: the hero is a heroic weaver who rises to become a famous and wealthy clothier employing large numbers of people. *The Gentle Craft* deals with the shoemakers, and contains the tale which Dekker used as the plot of his *Shoemakers' Holiday*. Deloney portrays and appeals to the new middle classes of the time, revealing the bourgeois society which arose after the medieval craft guilds had been replaced by the domestic system of manufacture. His style is somewhat pedestrian, but straightforward and competent, and the dialogue is particularly good. The details of the lives and activities of hardworking craftsmen, kind employers, and disguised noblemen posing as apprentices not only throw interesting light on the Elizabethan social scene: they also show the first faint outline of the mature English novel, which was to develop as the special contribution to literature of the middle classes, for long concerned with the relationship between social classes, the possibilities of advancement from one class to another, and in general with the relation between gentility and morality.

It is sometimes difficult to distinguish Elizabethan fiction from Elizabethan reporting. Dekker's graphic picture of London smitten by plague, *The Wonderful Year* (1603), is a piece of reporting, but it shows the macabre imagination of some of the late Elizabethan and Jacobean playwrights. This, for example, is hardly straight journalism:

> What an unmatchable torment were it for a man to be barred up every night in a vast silent charnel-house, hung to make it more hideous with lamps dimly and slowly burning, in hollow and glimmering corners; where all the pavement should instead of green rushes be strewed with blasted rosemary, withered hyacinths, fatal cypresses and yew, thickly mingled with heaps of

dead men's bones; the bare ribs of a father that begat him lying there, here the chapless hollow scull of a mother that bore him, round about him a thousand corpses, some standing bolt upright in their knotted winding sheets, others half mouldered in rotton coffins, that should suddenly yawn wide open, filling his nostrils with noisome stench and his eyes with the sight of nothing but crawling worms. And to keep such a poor wretch waking, he should hear no noise but toads creaking, screech-owls howling, mandrakes shrieking . . .

Dekker also followed Greene and Nashe in producing accounts of the London underworld, as in *The Seven Deadly Sins of London, News from Hell brought by the Devil's Carrier, The Belman of London,* and *Lanthorne and Candlelight,* all published between 1606 and 1608. *The Gull's Hornbook* (1609) gives a lively picture of varieties of fools and rogues in London with an irony that is humorous rather than biting.

Nothing better illustrates the range of the Elizabethan imagination, even when ostensibly merely reporting contemporary events, than to set side by side the accounts of London low life just discussed with Richard Hakluyt's final version of his great book of voyages, *The Principal Navigations, Voyages, Traffiques and Discoveries of the English Nation,* which appeared in three volumes between 1598 and 1600. Hakluyt was a compiler and editor, and he brought together accounts by many different hands of all the great English voyages of discovery and adventure that he could lay hands on. His motive was both scientific and patriotic; he wished to bring together all the available knowledge about distant lands and the sea routes to them, and to testify to the glory and enterprise of English seamen. The collection includes Sir Walter Ralegh's exciting and haunting *Discovery of Guiana* and his *Report of the Fight about the Azores* (from which Tennyson got the material for his famous ballad of the *Revenge*), both of which had been previously published independently; Edward Hare's account of Sir Humphrey Gilbert's last voyage, pedestrian in style but epic in content; accounts of voyages by Drake and Hawkins; and hundreds of others, some told in a vivid, heroic style, others more flatly. Much of what we know of the great Elizabethan voyagers and their adventures comes from Hakluyt's collection. None of the other collections of accounts of voyages has the appeal of Hakluyt's. Samuel Purchas, an ambitious geographer who took all history as well as geography for his province, produced in *Purchas his Pilgrimage* (1613) an encyclopedic survey of the world and its peoples past and present, and in 1625, in four large folio volumes, *Hakluytus Posthumus, or Purchas his Pilgrims,* which drew on his earlier work and on Hakluyt's unpublished papers in an attempt to provide a complete "history of the world in sea voyages and land travel by Englishmen and others." The work is not, however, a coherent unity, nor does it have the attractiveness of Hakluyt.

We have already mentioned the religious controversies between Puritans and Anglicans, to which the Marprelate pamphlets are one of the liveliest contributions from the Puritan, anti-episcopal side. The story of Elizabethan religious prose is not, however, confined to the record of this kind of popular controversy; the argument was also conducted on a high philosophical and theological level by scholars and thinkers who brought to bear much heavier artillery than lively abuse. The details of this more formal controversy are not strictly the concern of the literary historian. But since it lies behind, and indeed produced, Richard Hooker's great Anglican prose work, *Of the Laws of Ecclesiastical Polity*, some reference must be made to it. Hooker gave the final Anglican answer to the Puritan position which had been maintained most forcefully by Thomas Cartwright in three replies to John Whitgift's pro-episcopal answer to certain Puritan works (this gives some idea of the house-that-Jack-built chain of events, reminiscent of Milton's early career as a prose pamphleteer). Cartwright's position cannot be easily summarized, but in general it is not unfair to say that he was arguing for a theocracy: church discipline is also civil discipline, which it commands, and the Christian ruler, working through the same kind of church officers that Calvin instituted at Geneva, applies the "Word of God" as revealed in the Bible and interpreted by God's duly "called" Presbyterian ministers. The ecclesiastical discipline, which Cartwright and those who thought as he did wished to see imposed, touched every aspect of human activity and recognized no distinction between religious and civil or even between matters essential and matters indifferent: the religious authorities claimed control over everything, and the state was in fact subordinate to the church.

Richard Hooker (1554–1600) published the first four books of his *Ecclesiastical Polity* in 1594 and the fifth in 1597. The other three were published posthumously, and there was for long some doubt as to their authenticity, but this is now accepted, though it is clear they are not in their final form. The work as a whole is a masterpiece of exposition which involves legal and philosophical as well as theological argument. Hooker had none of Cartwright's tendency to see the world in two opposed colors, one divine and therefore alone proper, the other merely human and therefore evil. He sees reason, the law of nature, as coming from God, as providing a light by which men can achieve worthy things. Scriptural law does not govern the whole of life; there are numerous matters not dealt with by Scripture to be considered and weighed by reasonable Christian men and agreed upon in the light of their reason. Further, times change, and what is the most effective way of achieving the Church's purpose at one time may not be so at another. The whole question of episcopacy is discussed not only with reference to the question of the apostolic succession, but also with regard to history, tradition, and convenience. He has a feeling for tradition and at the same time realizes that different circumstances require different procedures; he has a sense of the community of all Christians, together with keen concern for the position and function of an English national Church; he sees scriptural injunction as requiring to be supplemented by reasonable inference and common counsel; he sees the civil ruler as legal head of the English Church, but he assumes that the ruler, with the advice of the properly established civil and ecclesiastical bodies (i.e., Parliament and Convocation), will proceed according to the laws of the Church, which in fact he makes into law by implementing, and would never for a moment consider him to be above those laws (he is no supporter of the new, extreme notions of Tudor despotism). Above all, Hooker has a flexibility of mind which enables him to wind into his argument with cumulative reasonableness. No summary can do justice to the majestic ordering of his case, moving from a general discussion of law in Book 1, to a consideration of the scope of scriptural or divine law in Book 2, to the place of the national Church within the State in Book 3, to the Church's control of her own position free of both Rome and Geneva in Book 4, and so on. On the whole, the first two books lay down the general principles, and the later books discuss their application. At the bottom of all Hooker's argument lies his sense of the divine, creative, ordering, and multiple nature of law, "whose seat is the bosom of God, whose voice the harmony of the world." He is basically opposed to the monolithic position of Cartwright, although, of course, it would be wildly anachronistic to seek in his work any trace of the modern liberal position with regard to universal toleration of all creeds. He is immensely erudite without being exhibitionist; never flustered, never merely doctrinaire. His argument has gaps, and few modern readers would find it wholly acceptable; but it remains a remarkable single-handed attempt to produce a complete intellectual explanation and vindication of the theory and practice of the English Church as established under Elizabeth. Hooker's prose is that of a scholar and thinker; there is no showing off, no stylistic gymnastics, but always a careful functional use of language. His sentences are often long, but rarely cumbersome, for the movement of clauses mirrors the movement of his mind. It is a ratiocinative prose, as much a lawyer's as a philosopher's perhaps, but calm, dignified, and always molded by its subject. There are occasional flashes of lively popular language, and a subdued, somewhat quizzical sense of humor, quite different from the flashier wit of the writers of the Elizabethan underworld. *Of the Laws of Ecclesiastical Polity* is one of the very few English classics of its kind.

While churchmen debated the theory and practice of church government, the secular mind of Francis Bacon (1561–1626) was meditating an ambitious scheme for laying anew the foundations of human knowledge on which could be reared an ever-increasing understanding and control of nature. To this scheme he gave the general name of the Great Instauration (or Renewal). Reacting against scholastic philosophy and against all a priori thinking and systems of thought derived deductively from premises laid down by authority, the Great Instauration, basing knowledge on observation, would restore a truer relationship between the observing mind and observed nature and so make scientific progress possible. For Bacon, "the furthest end of knowledge" was not theoretical insight but "the relief of man's estate"; it was to be for "the benefit and use of man." The sequence was to be from observation to understanding to practical application. Bacon proposed to himself six stages in the realization of his scheme, beginning with the classification of existing knowledge, with a precise mapping of all gaps and deficiencies, and proceeding through the development of a new, inductive, logical method (the New Organon) and the collection of basic data to provide lists of examples of the new method in operation, thence to a preliminary report of the achievements of the method, and finally to a full-dress presentation of the new philosophy and method and its results in explaining the natural phenomena of the universe. The sixth and final stage could not of course be reached by any single individual: it represented the eventual aim of human knowledge. Of the other five stages, the first is represented by Bacon's *Advancement of Learning* (1605, with an enlarged Latin version in 1623); the second by the unfinished Latin work, *Novum Organum*, which appeared together with a general statement of the aims and plan of the Great Instauration (*Magna Instauratio*) in 1620; and the others only by fragments.

Bacon was not the first to propose an inductive scientific theory, or to attack scholasticism; nor did his writings achieve a philosophic revolution of the kind which Descartes brought about a generation later. Further, he was not in touch with the actual achievements of contemporary science, was ignorant of and sometimes hostile to new advances in astronomy and medicine and curiously uninfluenced by the revival of Greek science and Platonic mathematics which were so important for the scientific achievements of the Renaissance.

Nevertheless he spoke with prophetic eloquence of the new conception of knowledge and its function, popularizing a point of view which was to become increasingly significant later in the century. His diagnosis of much of the accepted philosophy of his time as mere verbal jugglery had something of the same effect as the work of the more popular of the logical positivists and semanticists of the 1930's: "For the wit and mind of man, if it work upon matter, which is the contemplation of the creatures of God, worketh according to the stuff and is limited thereby; but if it work upon itself as the spider worketh his web, then it is endless, and brings forth indeed cobwebs of learning, admirable for the fineness of thread and work but of no substance or profit."

The Advancement of Learning is in two books: the first states and answers arguments that have been brought forward against learning and the second providing a detailed classification of all the kinds of knowledge, with the deficiencies noted. The argument against learning comes from theologians, from politicians, and from the habits and studies of learned men themselves. The first he answers in their own terms; the second he answers by an appeal to history and experience; and in tackling the third he admits that here are "three vanities in studies" which have been responsible for attacks on learning in general. These "vanities" or "distempers" of learning are in ascending order of gravity, fantastic and exhibitionist styles of writing, the kind of logic chopping which degenerates into mere verbalism, and "delight in deceiving and aptness to be deceived; imposture and credulity." The greatest error of all, however, is "mistaking or misplacing the last or furthest end of knowledge"—which is control over nature for the benefit of man. Book I concludes with positive arguments to prove the dignity of learning, both "divine proofs" and "human proofs." Bacon, it should be noted, conceded the study of divinity to the divines, distinguishing between God's word, as revealed by Him and studied by His ministers, and God's work, the natural world, the province of scientific inquiry; but though the separation between theology and philosophy had been made before (e.g., by William of Ockham), Bacon makes the separation to protect science from religion (to use modern terms) not, as Ockham had done, to protect faith from reason. Thomistic philosophy did not make this separation, subsuming philosophy in theology, but later scholastic thought did sometimes recognize a "twofold truth." Such a division was found useful by seventeenth-century thinkers such as Bacon and Hobbes in providing a clear field for secular thought.

Book II of *The Advancement of Learning* is a brilliant piece of classification, full of the witty definitions and apt and lively phrases so characteristic of Bacon's vigorous expository style; but in spite of this the modern reader will find this sort of detailed schematization somewhat tedious. Among the many interesting definitions, that of poetry might be singled out, for it is curiously Freudian: "it [poetry] doth raise and erect the mind, by submitting the shows of things to the desires of the mind; whereas reason doth buckle and bow the mind unto the nature of things." (The dwindling number of those who profess to believe that Bacon wrote Shakespeare's plays might reflect on this definition of poetry and consider whether it could possibly be made to apply to *Hamlet* or *Othello*.)

The *Novum Organum* contains the famous account of "the four classes of idols which beset men's minds," a fine example of the imaginative wit which Bacon so often displayed in making his points. The Idols of the Tribe (deriving from the limitations of human nature), the Idols of the Cave (deriving from personal character and idiosyncrasies), the Idols of the Marketplace (popular superstitions and confusions), and the Idols of the Theatre ("because in my judgment all the received systems are but so many stage-plays representing worlds of their own creation after an unreal and scenic fashion"), all militate against the proper use of observation and reason. Again, this reminds us of a modern semanticist analyzing the sources of verbal confusion or of a psychologist explaining the origins of irrational prejudice. Bacon was not himself a great scientist or a great philosopher; he was a master of prose exposition whose colorful and memorable phrases helped to popularize a new view of science.

The New Atlantis, published incomplete in 1627, is a slight work; it describes how a group of seafarers come upon an unknown island in the South Sea, where they are hospitably entertained and told of the high state of morality and civilization prevailing there, notably of the wonders of Salomon's House, a research institution in the description of which Bacon illustrates his own ideas of how research should be carried on. It all seems rather naïve in an age when scientific research is as highly developed and as much taken for granted as it is now; but it is interesting as providing further evidence of Bacon's desire to popularize his views of the importance of experimental science, that "commerce between the mind of man and the nature of things, which is more precious than anything on earth" as he called it in his *Magna Instauratio*.

Bacon's *Essays*—beginning with a volume of ten essays, written in a pungent aphoristic style, in 1597, with expansions and additions and a progressively more discursive style in the volumes of 1612 and 1625, the last containing fifty-eight essays—consist of reflections on human affairs by a practical psychologist who wishes to base his ethical prescriptions on a sound knowledge of human nature. The essay as a literary form had been invented by Montaigne shortly before Bacon adopted it; but Montaigne, with his rambling curiosity about himself and his genial and sceptical humanism, represented a different side of Renaissance thought. The easy flow of Montaigne's prose represented a relaxed self-consciousness far removed from the impersonal wisdom affected by Bacon, whose early essays read almost like a series of proverbs. It is the aphoristic element in his style that makes so many of his sentences—particularly his opening sentences—memorable and quotable. "What is truth? said jesting Pilate; and would not stay for an answer." "Men fear death as children fear to go in the dark; and as that natural fear in children is increased with tales, so is the other." "Revenge is a kind of wild justice . . ." "He that hath wife and children hath given hostages to fortune." "A man that hath no virtue in himself ever envieth virtue in others." The essays deal as much with public as with private life, discussing "great place," nobility, "seditions and troubles," empire, and "the true greatness of kingdoms and estates," as well as truth, death, parents and children, marriage, envy, love, and "wisdom for a man's self." He speaks as a man of the world, illustrating his generalizations by references to history (often classical history) and his own experience. Realistic in politics, shrewd but not coldly calculating in practical affairs, Christian in a general theistic way with more than a touch of Stoicism, occasionally rising to a somber eloquence in discussing time and change and death or led into the display of a personal enthusiasm as in the essay on gardens, Bacon in his essays is an impressive if hardly an endearing character. There is a moderately Machiavellian side to his thought: "The best composition and temperature is, to have openness in fame and opinion; secrecy in habit; dissimulation in seasonable use; and a power to feign, if there be no remedy." He is reconciled to human nature: "Why should I be angry with a man for loving himself better than me?" He knows how to relax with a variety of delights, but it is significant that he ends his essay on "masques and triumphs" with the sentence: "But enough of these toys." Montaigne in one way, Bacon in another, are very far from the medieval mind; and they are far, too, from some of the more passionate movements of their own time. It is hardly extravagant to suggest that Bacon lives in the same world as Benjamin Franklin, not in that of the author of *Piers Plowman,* or in that of Spenser or Milton or George Herbert.

Bacon's *History of Henry VII* (1622) is a conscientious study of that king's policy in the light of which he is able to give an integrated picture of the events of his reign. The work shows Bacon's interest in statecraft, his political and legal knowledge, his command of an effective narrative and expository style, and a historico-psychological imagination which enabled him to put imaginary speeches into the mouths of his characters in the manner of classical historians. Others of Bacon's works, more or less fragmentary contributions to the six-fold plan of the Great Instauration, were published in various collections of his literary remains after his death.

If Bacon separated God's word and God's work in order to be able to concentrate freely on the latter, Sir Thomas Browne (1605–82) divided his attention between the two, investigating the facts of nature with a Baconian empiricism (though with a religious excitement at the ingenuity of the Creator thus revealed, which Bacon wholly lacked) and at the same time glorying in his acceptance by faith of religious mysteries on which his imagination loved to dwell. Browne was both Baconian experimentalist and Christian mystic, author both of *Pseudodoxia Epidemica* (generally known as *Vulgar Errors*), an exposure of erroneous notions about nature held by the credulous, and of *Religio Medici*, a discursive statement of his religious faith with a deliberate emphasis on wonder and mystery. The impact of the "new philosophy" in the seventeenth century naturally differed according to the temperament of the individual. Browne had a "unified sensibility" in the sense that he could move freely between mystery and experiment and saw no conflict between the duty of the man of science and that of the man of religion. This is related to his genial autobiographical manner of discussion and his interest in what might be called philosophy as play; if in discussing one kind of truth you are also aware of another kind, you will not be too intense in your method of presenting either.

The relation—sometimes the conflict—between science and religion becomes henceforth an important aspect of English thought. Although seventeenth-century theological controversy for the most part ignored the new science, its effects were indirectly visible in the great debate between those who believed optimistically in inevitable progress and those who held that the world was steadily declining. The classic statement of the pessimistic position was Godfrey Goodman's massive work, *The Fall of Man, or the Corruption of Nature Proved by the Light of our Natural Reason*, published in 1616. This was answered by George Hakewill's *Apology of the Power and Providence of God in the Government of the World*, published in 1627, with enlarged editions in 1630 and 1635. The argument as to whether the world had steadily declined from an original Golden

Age or was steadily progressing and improving represents two poles of human thought which are perhaps always with us; but the seventeenth century saw the conflict brought into focus with particular clarity. It was this debate which underlay the conflict between Ancients and Moderns which developed later in the century; whether the classical literature of the Greeks and Romans represented a summit of human literary achievement which later ages could never quite reach, or whether modern refinement and ingenuity could surpass the achievements of the ancient world, was an argument which flowed from the larger debate on the decline of the world. The narrowing of the issue in this way reflects a contraction of the intellectual universe of the late seventeenth and early eighteenth centuries as compared with that of the earlier seventeenth century. The comfortable deistic solution of the science-religion conflict, making God the First Cause who retired from the universe after the creation, the divine watchmaker who made and wound up the watch before leaving it to be admired and investigated by the pious and the curious, was the eighteenth-century systematization of a position implicit in Bacon. Scientific progress then becomes increasingly successful in discovering how the watch was made and how it works, while literary progress is measured by the degree to which writers equal or perhaps even excel the great achievements of the classical world.

Sir Thomas Browne remained at the still center of the controversies of his day, cultivating an inclusive tolerance which enabled him to reconcile almost anything with almost anything else. *Religio Medici*—which circulated for some time in manuscript, and appeared in two unauthorized editions in 1642, before the appearance of the authorized edition in 1643—might almost be called an exercise in inclusiveness of thought and feeling. The very title—"the religion of a doctor"—emphasizes a reconciliation of traditional opposites, the numinous and the scientific; for, as Browne points out in the very first sentence, the world does not generally consider doctors to have any religion at all. His favorite image is the circle, his favorite concept the microcosm. The prose of *Religio Medici* is so richly harmonized that one might almost say that its meaning is conveyed vertically rather than horizontally. Browne's constant endeavor is to break down distinctions and include all things in a single context. In sentence after sentence he reaches out to embrace apparent contradictions and bring them together; each sentence—or at least each paragraph—is thus a microcosm of the book as a whole. Consider, for example, his discussion of the relation between Protestants and Catholics:

> We have reformed from them, not against them; for (omitting those Improperations and Terms of Scurrility betwixt us, which only difference our Affections, and not our Cause,) there is between us one common Name and Appellation, one Faith and necessary body of Principles common to us both; and therefore I am not scrupulous to converse and live with them, to enter their Churches in defect of ours, and either pray with them, or for them.

Here we have the whole of *Religio Medici* in little: reformation does not imply disagreement; any admission of difference is softly tucked away within brackets; and at the end there is the cunning suggestion that praying *for* somebody (which would really indicate that we are concerned for him because he is not of our faith) amounts to the same thing as praying *with* him (which indicates that we *are* of the same faith). The actual statement of the case—an appeal for toleration—is reinforced by stylistic devices and by every kind of quasi-logical suggestion that can be derived from language.

Religio Medici begins with a definition of the author's brand of Christianity, a definition which gradually expands to include, by a "general charity to Humanity," virtually all faiths professed by men. Though a member of the Church of England ("there is no Church whose every part so squares unto my Conscience; whose Articles seem so consonant unto reason, and as it were framed to my particular Devotion, as this whereof I hold my Belief, the Church of England"), Browne "could never divide myself from any man upon the difference of an opinion, or be angry with his judgment for not agreeing with me in that from which perhaps within a few days I should dissent my self." By various quasi-logical and autobiographical devices he brings all humanity into the circle of his own faith. Faith and reason are at first distinguished:

> As for those wingy Mysteries in Divinity, and airy subtleties in Religion, which have unhing'd the brains of better heads, they never stretched the *Pia Mater* of mine. Methinks there be not impossibilities enough in Religion for an active faith; the deepest Mysteries ours contains have not only been illustrated, but maintained, by Syllogism and the rule of Reason. I love to lose myself in a mystery, to pursue my Reason to an *O Altitudo!* . . . I can answer all the Objections of Satan and my rebellious reason with the odd resolution I learned of Tertullian, *Certum est, quia impossibile est.* I desire to exercise my faith in the difficultest point; for to credit ordinary and visible objects is not faith, but persuasion.

But though faith and reason are thus opposed, they are eventually reunited, if not logically at least symbolically, by being discussed in terms of each other and by the inclusion of both in a third term, such as God's Wisdom, which created the world to be "studied and contemplated by Man: 'tis the Debt of our Reason we owe unto God, and the homage we pay for not being Beasts." God's work and God's word are distinguished, but again only to be reunited: Nature is the Art of God. This being so, "there are no Grotesques in Nature." Every created thing is beautiful and wonderful in its way. Man himself is a little world. "We carry with us the wonders we seek without us: there is all Africa and her prodigies in us, we are that bold and adventurous piece of Nature, which he that studies wisely learns in a compendium what others labour at in a divided piece and endless volume." God's work is also a book, like His word. "Thus there are two Books from whence I collect my Divinity; besides that written one of God, another of His servant Nature, that universal and public Manuscript, that lies expans'd unto the Eyes of all; . . ."

Religio Medici continues with the adducing of examples showing the inclusive attitude at work. Both the miraculous and the scientific explanations of the same phenomenon are accepted; atheism is explained away as never having really existed; pagan gods are included in the Christian scheme; soul and body, life and death, are so defined as to include each other. Martyrdom is deprecated as symbolizing an exclusive rather than an inclusive attitude. And even when Browne has reluctantly to concede that salvation is granted by God only to Christians, he adds significantly: "yet those who do confine the Church of God, either to particular Nations, Churches, or Families, have made it far narrower than our Saviour ever meant it." Part II of the work is, logically enough, a discussion of charity, the state of mind which favors maximum inclusion. It is essentially an autobiographical illustration of his own charitable and tolerant disposition: "Methinks there is no man bad, and the worst, best." He can exclude nobody from his charity, and, as "every man is a Microcosm, and carries the whole World about him," his own tolerance takes on universal dimensions. The work concludes with the author's submission to the will of God.

Browne's style, with its coupling of Anglo-Saxon and Latin words and its sentences composed of an arrangement of fairly short clauses rising and falling in a carefully contrived cadence, is in many respects a reflection of his sensibility. "Do but extract from the corpulency of bodies, or resolve things beyond their first matter, and you discover the habitation of Angels, which if I call the ubiquitary and omnipresent Essence of God, I hope I shall not offend Divinity: for before the Creation of the World God was really all things." The Latinisms here are introduced with a deliberate relish; they reflect that savoring of words and attitudes which is part of Browne's literary character. But it is worth noting that this sentence works up to a crucial statement which is itself expressed (except for the one word "Creation") in words of Anglo-Saxon origin: "for before the Creation of the world God was really all things." Browne's stylistic artifice is perhaps more obvious in *Hydriotaphia* (*Urn Burial*) and *The Garden of Cyrus*, published together in 1658. In the former, the digging up of some old sepulchral urns "in a field of old Walsingham" provokes Browne to eloquent meditation on burial customs of the past and on the mysteries and solemnities of mortality. The opening sentence of the Epistle Dedicatory sets the tone of the work:

> When the Funeral pyre was out, and the last valediction over, men took a lasting adieu of their interred Friends, little expecting the curiosity of future ages should comment upon their ashes, and, having no old experiences of the duration of their Reliques, held no opinion of such after-considerations.

Historical curiosity, philosophical speculation, mystic contemplation, and the suggestiveness and sonority of a rich and carefully manipulated vocabulary, combine to make *Hydriotaphia* a remarkable piece of virtuosity. The antiquarian, the Platonic mystic, the Christian moralist, and the artist all contribute to the total effect, but the artist is generally in the ascendant. "We whose generations are ordained in this setting part of time, are providentially taken off from such imaginations; and being necessitated to eye the remaining particle of futurity, are naturally constituted unto thoughts of the next world, and cannot excusably decline the consideration of that duration, which maketh Pyramids pillars of snow, and all that's past a moment." The artifice here is patent, as it is in the well-known passage beginning "What Song the Syrens sang, . . ." which includes the remarkable sentence: "But to subsist in bones, and be but Pyramidally extant, is a fallacy in duration." *The Garden of Cyrus*, in its riot of speculation concerning the quincunx pattern in heaven and earth, combines a scientific air with a poetic tone in a strange and fascinating way. Sometimes, the vocabulary is almost a parody of the scientific: "The *Reticulum* by these crossed cells makes a further digestion in the dry and exuccous part of the Aliment received from the first Ventricle." But more characteristic is the famous paragraph which begins the concluding movement of the work:

> But the Quincunx of Heaven runs low, and 'tis time to close the five ports of knowledge; we are unwilling to spin out our awaking thoughts into the phantasms of sleep, which often continueth præcogitations; making Cables of

Cobwebs, and Wildernesses of handsome Groves. Beside Hippocrates hath spoke so little, and the Oneirocritical Masters have left such frigid Interpretations from plants, that there is little encouragement to dream of Paradise itself. Nor will the sweetest delight of Gardens afford much comfort in sleep; wherein the dullness of that sense shakes hands with delectable odours; and though in the Bed of Cleopatra, can hardly with any delight raise up the ghost of a Rose.

No more fascinating evidence exists of the coexistence in the seventeenth century of new scientific ideas and old notions of authority, and of the "hydroptic thirst" for all knowledge, ancient and modern, than the vast encyclopedic treatise by Robert Burton (1577–1640), *The Anatomy of Melancholy,* published in 1621, with several revised editions between 1624 and 1651. This work, now regarded as a rich anthology of curious notions, picturesque anecdotes, and varied quotations from both ancients and moderns, was intended as a scientific examination of the various distempers of the mind to which Burton gives the generic name "melancholy"—a medical and psychological work in which all known knowledge on the subject would be presented. If it has long been valued as a source of quaint or suggestive quotations or as a work to be dipped into and relished for its oddity, this is because the comprehensiveness of Burton's aim, the transitional nature of the age he lived in, and his own mixture of sympathy, curiosity, erudition, superstition, and common sense, gives his work a texture and a flavor that can be found neither in the medieval world nor in the modern scientific world after the foundation of the Royal Society. The organization of the book into discussions of the symptoms, causes, and cure of different kinds of melancholy is logical enough, but no central principles provide coherence to the whole. Unbounded curiosity about man and a humane and sensible concern for his welfare are perhaps Burton's chief qualities; they are sufficient to give a tone but not to provide a method or a principle of integration to his work. The elaborate and detailed synopses to each "partition" of the work testify to Burton's methodological intentions, but the digressions and the illustrative anecdotes remain the most memorable parts of his book. The long section on "heroical or love melancholy," with its powers, causes, symptoms, and cures, is the richest part of the book to modern eyes and its quizzical yet sympathetic tone, its profusion of information with a refusal to come down on any side of a controversy, is characteristic of Burton. We must not forget, however, that Burton was an Anglican priest by profession, and when he discusses religious melancholy, as he does in his final section, he mingles religious consolation with the humanist advice to avoid extremes and extravagances. "Thy soul is eclipsed for a time, I yield, as the sun is shadowed by a cloud; no doubt but those gracious beams of God's mercy will shine upon thee again, as they have formerly done: those embers of faith, hope and repentance, now burned in ashes, will flame out afresh, and be fully revived." This is a somewhat different Burton from the writer who, discoursing of the "prognostics" of love melancholy, remarks:

> Go to Bedlam for examples. It is so well known in every village, how many have either died for love, or voluntarily made away themselves, that I need not much labour to prove it; *Nec modus aut requies nisi mors reperitur amoris* [love knows no limit or escape save death]: death is the common catastrophe to such persons.
>
> *Mori mihi contingat, non enim alia*
> *Liberatio ab aerumnis fuerit ullo pacto istis.*
>
> [Would I were dead, for nought, God knows,
> But death can rid me of these woes.]

But quotation can give no conception of the variety and multiplicity of Burton's extraordinary work, in which religion and science intermingle, medicine and psychology are set against a cosmic background, and ironic observations of the human comedy are made the excuse for a display of an almost irresponsible erudition. Burton's prose style is flexible and varied; he can be colloquial, pedantic, picturesque, or epigrammatic. The perpetual interlarding of his English with Latin quotations produces a strange mosaic effect. Perhaps it can be said that Burton had no style; there is too much variety and digression. *The Anatomy of Melancholy* is, however, a remarkable work, a significant symptom of the times and a *tour de force* without parallel in English literature.

That the seventeenth century is a watershed in the history of English thought is sufficiently proved by the fact that it saw the publication of work by Bacon, Browne, Burton, and Hobbes. Thomas Hobbes (1588–1679), materialist, rationalist, and empirical psychologist, broke completely with tradition and endeavored to work out a new science of man by the application of "natural reason" to the understanding of "bodies." "The word *body*, in the most general acceptation, signifieth that which filleth, or occupieth, some certain room, or imagined place; and dependeth not on the imagination, but is a real part of what we call the *universe*. For the universe, being the aggregate of all bodies, there is no real part thereof that is not also body . . ." Causality was reducible to motion, the ultimate effective principle in a reality that was made up of "bodies." Hobbes' *Leviathan* (1651) attempts, with ruthless logic, to deduce a complete political theory from his view of man which is in turn based on a view of the human passions which in its turn is derived from his materialist view of sensation. There are empirical elements in Hobbes' psychology as well as elements deductively inferred from his general view of body and motion. On the whole, however, the *Leviathan* is a closely reasoned and brilliantly phrased argument in which Hobbes builds up from his analysis of man, a theory of the state as essentially an instrument for preventing perpetual conflict between men. Its aim is security, freedom from the perpetual risk of sudden death—at almost any price. For men, Hobbes maintains, are naturally prone to strive for ever increasing power. "I put for a general inclination of all mankind a perpetual and restless desire of power after power, that ceaseth only in death." Thus, without a civil power to control them, they would live in perpetual civil war, and human life would be "solitary, poor, nasty, brutish and short." To avoid such a state, men have made an implicit contract with each other to surrender their natural rights to do as they think fit, on condition that everyone else does the same, and to set up some individual or group as guarantor and enforcer of that contract. The individual or group—who is not a party to the contract—thus becomes the representative of all, and only by obedience to him can man have any chance of a decent life. Disorder, social and political chaos, with the attendant chance of sudden death, is for Hobbes the ultimate basis of all good political action, just as vanity, each individual's restless desire for increasing power, is the main principle of disorder and conflict. Life is sweet at any price, and while there is no supreme good for Hobbes, there *is* a supreme evil, the prospect of sudden death. The best way of organizing a commonwealth, for Hobbes, is the way which, at whatever cost, minimizes that prospect. As for religion, that was to be decided by the ruler as a purely civil matter.

Hobbes's was an individual contribution which had no great influence on English political or ethical thought. Popularly regarded as an arch-atheist and archmaterialist, as well as the defender of absolutism, he could play no part in shaping the future of English thought, which, with characteristic compromise, moved in the direction of Deism and constitutional monarchy. Locke, not Hobbes, was to be the great philosopher of the eighteenth century, as Newton (who proved the existence of a designing creator by showing how the universe was mathematically ordered) was to be its scientist. But the boldness and individuality of Hobbes's thought, and the picturesque liveliness of his language, made him a significant, though an isolated, figure in his day. He was a symptom, too: one could not imagine his work appearing in an earlier age, and it would have been surprising (though not impossible) in a later. Bacon tried to break down medieval thought; Hobbes was filling a vacuum left by its decay.

For all the signs of modernity and secularism in seventeenth-century philosophical prose, the dominant interest of the age was religion, and there were many more books devoted to religious subjects—collections of sermons, devotional and theological works, works of exposition, exhortation, and controversy—published between 1600 and 1660 than works of any other kind. Sermons, both spoken and written, enjoyed a popularity which the modern reader finds hard to understand. Puritans and Anglicans alike stressed the importance of preaching, which in the Elizabethan period was often highly controversial (Puritan preaching being often suspect as dangerous to the Elizabethan settlement) but which in the reigns of James I and Charles I was generally more hortatory or expository. Many skills were involved, including those of rhetoric, logic, and theological and linguistic scholarship, and they were employed in a great variety of ways. The range of styles and manners was enormous, from the rousing of the emotions by passionate and grotesque imagery to the most closely reasoned *explication de texte*. The Middle Ages had developed its own *artes praedicandi* and medieval techniques are often found still flourishing in the seventeenth-century sermon. A popular tradition of sturdy and colorful exhortation and an erudite tradition of subtle commentary existed side by side, with every kind of gradation in between and every kind of permutation and combination of the two. Of the scores of notable preachers of the period, we might single out for mention three great Anglicans—Lancelot Andrewes, whose fame has been revived in our own time by T. S. Eliot, John Donne, and Jeremy Taylor.

Lancelot Andrewes (1555–1626), whose sermons were published individually or in groups before the posthumous *XCVI Sermons* appeared in 1629, has a packed, intense style, in which an argument is developed with subtle insistence and sometimes an almost hypnotic iteration. The cumulative effect of his short, condensed sentences, with their probing for the precise meaning of a biblical text, can be very powerful, though his thought is not easy to follow and the rhetorical ingenuity manifested in the plays on words can be excessive. Donne's sermons (of which six were published individually during his lifetime and three collections were published posthumously, in 1640, 1649, and 1660) have a more obvious appeal, at least to the modern reader, with their mixture of the colloquial, the intellectual, and the mystical. Like those of Andrewes—and indeed like nearly all the sermons of the time—they are carefully worked out arguments, whose structure from a citation of the text to its amplification, illustration, and application, can only be appreciated by a careful reading of the whole; but his shifts in tone, his awareness of the claims and distractions of the everyday world in the midst of his religious ecstasies, his ability to break out into great passages of rhapsody or elegy or sheer power, often lead him to break the bound of the formal organization of his sermon. His own personality enters into his preaching in unexpected ways and places, and the mixture of intellectual and emotional elements can produce, as in his poetry, a strange and powerful utterance. It may be, as Eliot has said, that "about Donne there hangs the shadow of the impure motive," that he "lacked spiritual discipline" compared with Andrewes; but the result is often to make his preaching more individual and more interesting. Donne's prose style tends to fall into long sentences made up of linked short clauses, arranged in parallel rather than in series, as it were; neatness in subordination of clauses in the total pattern of the sentence was an achievement of the next age. Both Andrewes and Donne also produced devotional works, which bring the reader into more intimate contact with their religious meditations. Andrewes' devotional manual, originally written in Greek, appeared in an English translation in 1647 as *Private Devotions;* it is sometimes known by the Latin title of *Preces Privatae*. Donne's *Devotions upon Emergent Occasions* (1624), a record of his religious meditations during a long and serious illness, is simpler in style than his sermons, and has a vivid personal quality in its tone and idiom.

There were plain preachers in the first half of the seventeenth century as well as those who employed a highly colored rhetorical or metaphysical style, and it was the style of plain preaching that was to come to the fore after the Restoration. But the most impressive as well as in many ways most distinctively Anglican sermons and devotional works of the period were not of the plain school. The most conscious stylist of them all was Jeremy Taylor (1613–67), whose early *Liberty of Prophesying* (1647), a thoughtful and moving plea for toleration, is written in a simpler style, cogent in its earnest lucidity, than his later work. *Holy Living* (1650), a devotional manual concerned with the conduct of Christian life in all its phases, both personal and social, is a kind of work which had been fairly common in the Middle Ages but which had not been produced in England since the Reformation. The prose has a fuller eloquence than that of *The Liberty of Prophesying*, but it has not the richer luxuriance of *Holy Dying* (1651), a work in the medieval tradition of the *ars moriendi*, drawing on a long tradition of religious thought and feeling about death and the contempt of this world, but with its elaborate rhetorical style drawing new music out of these old themes. Combining classical and Christian sources, making use of details of contemporary life as well as of biblical and classical history and literature, employing a strong visual imagination to find concrete illustrations for general ideas, Taylor succeeds in giving new weight and harmony to some of the great traditional themes of his religion. His sentences, like those of so many prose writers of the period, consist of clauses arranged in extended sequence, with parallel clauses modifying or answering or emphasizing each other. Taylor cultivated a similar style for his sermons, of which several collections were published in his lifetime.

Of preachers and devotional writers on the Puritan side, mention might be made of Thomas Adams (whose date of birth is unknown and who died in or soon after 1653), a great preacher who knew how to use allegorical and other devices in order to stir the conscience of London audiences, and Richard Baxter (1615–91) whose numerous tracts and exhortations, as well as his long autobiographical work, *Reliquiae Baxterianae*, long remained popular. His two best known works, *The Saints' Everlasting Rest* and *Call to the Unconverted* (1657), manuals of practical religion, took an important place in the Evangelical tradition in both England and America. A very different character from these was the Anglican Thomas Fuller (1608–61), biographer, historian, antiquary, preacher, essayist, and divine, an attractive and versatile writer whose *Holy State* (1642), a book of practical conduct, is an eclectic work in which common sense, Christian feeling, belief in a social hierarchy, and a taste for the illustrative anecdote and character sketch, combine to produce a series of essays and sketches rather than a wholly unified work. Fuller was (among other things) a wit, a realist, and a *raconteur*. His *History of the Worthies of England* is a collection of English biographies arranged by counties in their alphabetical order, a remarkable storehouse of information, anecdotes, and miscellaneous facts and stories of all kinds. Information about the "natural commodities," manufactures, buildings, and proverbs of each county are given, before he proceeds to give biographical notes on the "worthies." Fuller got his information from earlier antiquaries (such as Camden, Speed, and Stow) as well as from his own researches: he traveled over the country interrogating those who had known any "worthies," consulting local records and examining places and buildings. His other works include *The Church History of Britain,* published in 1655 together with *The History of the University of Cambridge,* in both of which the antiquarian and anecdotalist combine with the recorder of his own times.

Fuller's biographies are the work of a lively and discursive antiquarian; those of Izaak Walton (1593–1683) are different both in tone and intention. His *Lives* of John Donne, Henry Wotton, Richard Hooker, George Herbert, and Bishop Robert Sanderson, first published separately between 1658 and 1678, represent a characteristically gentle combination of realistic biography and idealizing hagiography. His portrait of Donne—whom he knew only in the final phase of his career, the pious Dean of St. Paul's—concentrates on his character as a divine, seeing in his entering on holy orders a parallel with the life of St. Augustine: "Now the English Church had gained a second St. Austin; for I think none was so like him before his conversion, none so like St. Ambrose after it! and if his youth had the infirmities of the one, his age had the excellencies of the other; the learning and holiness of both." His facts are not always correct—he makes some serious errors particularly in his life of Hooker, whom he never knew—but the simple charm of his narrative, with its graceful style and gentle tone of honest admiration, makes his biographies classics of their kind. "Charm" also is the obvious term to apply to that wholly delightful book, *The Compleat Angler* (1653), one of the great pastoral works in English, in which a fishing manual is transformed by the infusion of the author's personal feeling, his love of rural peace, of song, of clean and well-cared-for country inns, and of his fellow men, into an enchanting picture of human contentment in a realistic and not a Utopian setting. The form of the work is a series of conversations between Piscator, the angler, and other characters whom he meets in the course of his five days' fishing expedition. Piscator instructs the others in fishing, and they discourse, fish, and sing together, dining in the evening at a convenient inn, where the hostess is neat and courteous, and innocent mirth, with singing over a cup of barley wine, is enjoyed by all. The subtitle of the work, "The Contemplative Man's Recreation," provides a clue to its atmosphere. Beneath the simple account of a week's fishing, talking, and making innocently merry is a sense of the ideal fisherman as the type of Christian gentleness and humility: ". . . he found that the hearts of such men, by nature, were fitted for contemplation and quietness; men of mild, and sweet, and peaceable spirits, as indeed most Anglers are: these men our blessed Saviour, who is observed to love to plant grace in good natures, though indeed nothing be too hard for him, yet these men he chose to call from their irreprovable employment of fishing, and gave them grace to be his disciples, and to follow him, and do wonders."

Finally, something remains to be said about the seventeenth-century prose form known as the "Character." This was defined by Sir Thomas Overbury, one of its practitioners, as "a picture (real or personal) quaintly drawn in various colours, all of them brightened by one shadowing." It is essentially a portrait of a type rather than an individual, often done with an almost exhibitionist wit. The form derives from the Greek natural philosopher Theophrastus, whose *Characters* begin with a brief description of a vice (such as dissimulation, flattery, loquacity, superstition, and so on) and then go on to describe the typical possessor of that vice. ("Distrustfulness is a disposition to suspect all men of dishonesty. The Distrustful Man is this sort of man. When he has sent one of his slaves to buy provisions he sends another one after the first to find out exactly what they cost. In travelling he carries his own money and sits down every few hundred yards to count it." etc.) All Theophrastus' *Characters* deal with vices: if he also wrote characters of virtues they have not survived. The first collection of characters in English was Joseph Hall's *Characters of Virtues and Vices,* published in 1608. Hall is much less succinct in expression than Theophrastus; his sketches are longer and he is less the witty observer of men than the Christian moralist seeking to improve his readers by warning or example. As he says in his Proem to Book I (which deals with virtues): "Virtue is not loved enough; because she is not seen: and Vice loseth much detestation; because her ugliness is secret. . . . What need we more, than to discover the two to the world? This work shall save the labour of exhorting and dissuasion." Hall is livelier in Book II (the vices) than with virtues, where the tones of the preacher sometimes suggest themselves. He has his own kind of wit, as the conclusion of his character of the busybody shows: "He knows not why, but his custom is to go a little about and to leave the cross still on the right hand. One event is enough to make a rule: out of these rules he concludes fashions, proper to himself; and nothing can turn him out of his course. If he have done his task, he is safe: it matters not with what affection. Finally, if God would let him be the carver of his own obedience he could not have a better subject: as he is, he cannot have a worse."

Characters or Witty Descriptions of the Properties of Sundry Persons (1614), by Sir Thomas Overbury and others, shows the Character becoming a more deliberate exercise of wit. "A good woman is a comfort, like a man. She lacks nothing but heat. Thence is her sweetness of disposition, which meets his stoutness more pleasingly; so wool meets iron easier than iron, and turns resisting into embracing." "A Puritan is a diseased piece of Apocrypha: bind him to the Bible, and he corrupts the whole text: ignorance and fat feed are his founders; his nurses, railing, rabies, and round breeches: his life is but a borrowed blast of wind; for between two religions, as between two doors, he is ever whistling." These Characters are less concerned with general moral issues than with giving pictures of types common in England at the time, and they are thus of great interest to the social historian. The picture of the Amorist throws some light on Hamlet: "Is a man blasted or planet-strooken, and is the dog that leads blind Cupid; . . . He is never without verses and musk comfits, and sighs to the hazard of his buttons; . . . He is untrussed, unbutton'd and ungartered, not out of carelessness, but care. . . ."

The fashion was now in full swing, and Overbury's collection was followed by John Earle's *Microcosmography* (1628–29), the work of a careful artist whose characters combined effective wit with genuine moral feeling. Earle is less of an exhibitionist than many of the character writers of the period; his wit is put at the service of a kindly curiosity about his fellow men, as in his well-known sketch of "A Child":

> A Child is a man in a small letter, yet the best copy of Adam before he tasted of Eve or the apple; and he is happy whose small practice in the world can only write his character. He is nature's fresh picture newly drawn in oil, which time, and much handling, dims and defaces. His soul is yet a white paper unscribbled with observations of the world, wherewith, at length, it becomes a blurred notebook. He is purely happy, because he knows no evil, nor hath made means by sin to be acquainted with misery. He arrives not at the mischief of being wise, nor endures evils to come, by foreseeing them. He kisses and loves all, and, when the smart of the rod is past, smiles on his beater. . . . We laugh at his foolish sports, but his game is our earnest; and his drums, rattles and hobby-horses, but the emblems and mocking of man's business.

Some of the titles of Earle's characters show his range: "A Young Raw Preacher," "A Mere Dull Physician," "A Mere Formal Man," "A Young Gentleman of the University," "A She Precise Hypocrite," "The Common Singing-Men in Cathedral Churches."

Later Character writers tended to move from the general picture to the individual portrait. Samuel Butler (whose Characters were written in the late 1660's but not published until 1759) was concerned with contemporary follies and eccentricities, and all his sketches are sharply satirical. But after him the character becomes more individualized, and by the time Addison and Steele make use of the form in their *Tatler* and *Spectator* essays it has become the individual character portrait, ready to join the other streams that flowed into the English novel.

CHAPTER FOURTEEN

Scottish Literature to 1700

How far Scottish literature can be properly said to be the concern of the historian of English literature is a debatable question. Before the Union of the Scottish and English Parliaments in 1707, and to an even greater extent before the Union of the Crowns in 1603, Scotland was an independent kingdom with a vigorous culture of its own and in many respects a closer cultural relationship with the European continent (particularly France) than England had. But the northern kingdom was smaller and poorer than the southern, which made frequent attempts to dominate its neighbor, sometimes successful; lowland Scotland and northern England were geographically and linguistically more closely akin than northern England and southern England; and Scotland was comparatively slow in developing as a unified nation. These three facts make it sometimes difficult to define the identity of Scottish literature even before 1603, while after 1603 the increasing number of Scottish writers who wrote in English for English readers makes the difficulty even greater—great enough, indeed, to make it very much a matter of arbitrary choice whether someone like Drummond of Hawthornden, or James Thomson (author of *The Seasons*), or Tobias Smollett is considered in an English or a Scottish context. But in the Middle Ages, when Scots was a literary language with both a national tradition and a European perspective, the fact of an identifiable Scottish literature and Scottish literary tradition is unquestionable.

Even in the medieval period, however, the situation is complicated, though in a different way. In the Anglo-Saxon or Old English period of English literature the language spoken in what is now Scotland was either one of three Celtic languages, or Norse, or the same language that was spoken and written in northern England as far south as the Humber. Much of Lowland Scotland during this period was linguistically part of Northumbria. The borders between England and Scotland were continually shifting, and the mélange of

Scots, Picts, Strathclyde Britons, Norsemen, and Anglo-Saxons which (with a sprinkling of Normans) was to make the Scottish people was still in the formative process. Gregory Smith has pointed out that the fragment of *The Dream of the Rood* carved in runes on the Ruthwell Cross in Dumfriesshire (probably about the year 800) might have been carved, so far as the language is concerned, in Edinburgh or in York. At this period, Scotland was (in the words of a modern Scottish historian) "partly a piece of England, speaking English, partly a Norwegian colony, speaking Norse, and the rest three independent kingdoms, speaking three separate Celtic languages." Gradually the kings of Scotland won the eastern Lowlands from Northumbria and the north and the west from Norway, and the languages of Scotland shook down into two—"Scots" (which the medieval Scots called "Inglis"), originally identical with the Anglian speech of northern England, and the Celtic language we know as Scottish Gaelic. The former was spoken and written in the Lowlands, the latter in central, western, and northern Scotland. Early Scots is thus a form of English written in Scotland by Scotsmen. But by the fifteenth century, when the phase of the language which we call Middle Scots develops, Scots has become a highly complex literary speech, used by all the Scottish writers in non-Gaelic Scotland in the golden century which produced, in the so-called "Scottish Chaucerians," Scotland's greatest poets. Scotland's struggle for independence against the English kings Edward I and Edward II at the end of the thirteenth and beginning of the fourteenth centuries had helped to mold a heterogeneous group of people into a nation and to give it a strong national feeling; while the genius of the early Stuart kings in the fifteenth century encouraged the production of a national culture. Between about 1430 and 1513, when the disastrous Battle of Flodden undid at a blow so much of the first four Stuarts' work, Scottish literature, using Middle Scots as its literary language, showed a poise, a maturity, and a national character to a degree never afterward equaled, even though the literary language survived for another century and even though in the eighteenth century a deliberate attempt was made by a handful of writers, notably Robert Fergusson and Robert Burns, to revive a native Scottish literature by drawing on the spoken Scots vernacular.

The Scottish literature we are concerned with here is that written in Early and Middle Scots; Scottish Gaelic literature belongs to the Celtic world and has no place in a history of this kind. (At the risk of confusing the reader, it must be repeated that Middle Scots was called "Inglis" by those who wrote in it, and "Scottis" was the name they gave to Gaelic.) Much medieval Scottish literature has not survived: many tales, romances, and popular poems exist as titles only, listed in *The Complaint of Scotland* (1549), while Dunbar's "Lament for the Makars," probably written about 1500, mentions many poets whose works have not come down to us. The earliest name in Scottish literature is Thomas the Rhymer, or Thomas of Ercildoune, who is supposed to have lived in the thirteenth century and to have written a romance, *Sir Tristrem;* the existing northern romance of that title (mentioned in Chapter 2) used to be attributed to Thomas. But he is altogether too shadowy a figure to be able to move clearly from the world of mythology into that of history. As we have noted, early Scots represents the same form of Middle English that was spoken in the northern half of England, and any romance written in the northern form of Middle English before the fifteenth century might as easily have been written in Scotland as in England. No separate discussion of Scottish metrical romances is therefore necessary, even though diligent Scottish historians have found a distinctively Scottish tone in some of them. They belong to the general medieval cycles of romance, and their language is a northern form of English. Even John Barbour (ca. 1320–95), whose historical metrical romance *Bruce* deals in a patriotic spirit with recent Scottish history, is not yet writing in a language or a tradition distinctively Scottish. But Barbour's feeling and manner are distinctively Scottish. Though his form is that of the romance, he is writing history, of the trials and achievements of a Scottish hero who won through against overwhelming odds, regaining his country's independence from England. The spirit is more heroic than romantic, suggesting more the *chansons de geste* than the later courtly French romances. Barbour writes to preserve the memory of great deeds:

I wald fain set my will
Gif my wit micht suffice theretil,
To put in writ a soothfast story
That it last aye furth in memory,
Sa that na time of length it let,
Na gar it wholly be forget. [gar: make, cause]

Barbour tells his story with vigor and precision, and his accounts of combats are done with carefully selected details. The patriotic note is sounded throughout, and the theme of freedom occasionally breaks to the surface as in the famous outburst:

A! fredome is a noble thing.
Fredome maiss man to have liking:
Fredome all solace to man givis:
He livis at ease that freely livis. . . .

The *Bruce* makes a very respectable beginning to a national literature.

Andrew Wyntoun's *Oryginale Chronykil of Scotland,* written about 1400, is versified history (in Barbour's octosyllables) of no great literary interest, but Blind Harry's *Wallace,* celebrating the earlier hero of the Scottish War of Independence, is a romance which has none of Barbour's claims to historical accuracy. Blind Harry is only a name, traditionally associated with the *Wallace.* The poem, in decasyllabic couplets, was written in the latter part of the fifteenth century; it treats Wallace as a popular hero, and the narrative is full of life and variety, though metrically somewhat plodding. This is an unsophisticated art, and its appeal lies in the very naïveté with which character is described and the story unfolded. It long retained popularity in Scotland, and an early eighteenth-century version in later Scots was avidly read, with violently patriotic enthusiasm, by the young Robert Burns.

The achievement and prestige of Chaucer naturally had its influence on the Scottish writers of the fifteenth century, but it is an influence that has often been overestimated. Of the so-called "Scottish Chaucerians"—King James I (if he really was the author of *The Kingis Quair*), Robert Henryson, William Dunbar, Gavin Douglas—only the first can be properly called Chaucerian; the others, while of course they learned from Chaucer, worked in a European context with differing degrees of individual genius. *The Kingis Quair* ("The King's Book") is the story, told in the first person, of how James I of Scotland, when a prisoner in England, saw and fell in love with Lady Jane Beaufort, who later became his wife. Born in 1394, James was captured at sea by the English in 1406 and kept as a virtual prisoner in England until 1423, when he married Jane Beaufort, niece of the powerful Duke of Exeter and of his equally powerful brother the Bishop of Winchester, and returned to Scotland as a result of a Scottish-English settlement. *The Kingis Quair* is attributed to James in the only extant manuscript of the poem, dating from the late fifteenth century and thus written some seventy years after the poem was presumably composed, but whether it is actually by him is doubtful. The mingling of Scottish and English forms in the language of *The Kingis Quair* may represent the language of a Scot who spent seventeen years of his life in England, but it may even more plausibly be taken to be language of a Scottish poet who was consciously imitating Chaucer. The poem, in rhyme royal stanzas (hence the adjective "royal"), opens with a picture of the poet sleepless in bed, taking up Boethius to read and led by his reading to reflect on the uncertainties of fortune. He thinks how, unlike Boethius (who fell from high to low estate), he himself found fortune first his foe and then his friend. (This makes clear that the poem, whether by James or not, must have been written after James had been freed from his imprisonment, for he is referring to the change from his years of imprisonment to his later state as a free man and a successful lover.) As he muses, dawn comes, and he hears the matins bell ring; the bell seems to say to him: "Tell on, man, what thee befell." So he proceeds to tell his story. First he gives an account of how he sees the beautiful Jane Beaufort from his prison window and immediately falls in love with her: there are clear reminiscences here of the imprisoned knights falling in love with Emily in Chaucer's *Knight's Tale*. Then he has a vision in which his spirit is transported above to "the glad empire of blissful Venus." He has an interview with Venus, in which he seeks her aid; she sends him to Minerva, who gives encouraging advice, and then his spirit descends again to a pleasant river bank "enbroudin all with fresche flouris gay" where he beholds a great variety of animals and eventually finds Fortune and her wheel. Fortune instructs him how to climb, and then he awakes. The poem ends with expressions of thankfulness for his present happiness.

The Kingis Quair is a conventional poem in a medieval mode which was common throughout Europe. Its style and language owe something to Chaucer and to Lydgate (though the author mentions only Chaucer and Gower as "my maisteris dere" in his concluding stanza). But in spite of the use of common conventions and the echoes of other writers, the poem has a freshness and an individuality that set it apart from the majority of medieval dream allegories in the Rose tradition. Whether or not this is an autobiographical poem written by King James, the personal touch is real and vivid, and the use of this poetic form to tell a story of individual courtship gives a new turn to the courtly love tradition. Though *The Kingis Quair* was not the first poem to link courtly love with marriage, it was the first to do so in this concrete and detailed way. The sense of agitation that overcomes him on seeing the lady from his window is conveyed in a stanza at once stylized and realistic:

> And in my hede I drewe ryght hastily.
>   And eftsones I lent it forth ageyne,
> And sawe hir walk, that verray womanly,
>   With no wight mo bot onely women tueyne.
>   Than gan I studyé in myself and seyne,
> 'A! suete, ar ye a wardly crëatúre,
> Or hevinly thing in likeness of natúre?'

The fluctuations of emotion are conveyed with a wry vigor; the usual references to classical gods and goddesses have a certain sprightliness; the descriptions of flowers and animals and fishes in the scene by the river are both formal and vivid:

> That full of lytill fischis by the brym,
> Now here, now there, with bakkis blewe as lede,
> Lap and playit, and in a rout can swim [can: did]
> So prattily, and dressit tham to sprede [dressit: addressed]
> Thair curall fynnis, as the ruby rede, [curall: coral]
> That in the sonne on thair scalis bryght
> As gesserant ay glitterit in my sight. [gesserant: shining mail]

The list of heraldic animals, with its "There saw I" formula deriving originally from Statius, has its unexpected touches, such as the line that reads:

> The lytill squerell, full of besyness.

The Kingis Quair has neither Chaucer's metrical cunning nor his complex of ironic and sympathetic attitudes; it is perhaps basically a literary exercise by an amateur; but in its handling of detail in describing both inward states and external scenes it is curiously appealing.

Robert Henryson is the first Middle Scots poet with the range and artistry to achieve major stature. Little is known of his life; he was schoolmaster at Dunfermline, and was born in the first half of the fifteenth century, and he was dead by 1508, when Dunbar's "Lament for the Makars," which refers to him as dead, was first printed. Henryson's *Fables* (most, but not all, out of Aesop) are narrative poems done with humor and verve and a flexible handling of the rhyme royal stanza. The humor is not Chaucer's; it is based more on the accurate placing of realistic detail; but Henryson does use Chaucer's trick of giving pretentious language to animals, with ironic effect, as in the tale of the town mouse and the country mouse, where the town mouse sniffs disdainfully at her sister's rustic fare:

> 'My fair sister' (quod scho), 'have me excusit.
> This rude dyat and I can not accord.
> To tender meit my stomok is ay usit,
> For quhylis I fair alsweill as ony Lord. [quhylis: at times]
> Thir wydderit peis, and nuttis, or thay be bord, [wydderit: withered]
>
> Wil brek my teith, and mak my wame fful sklender,
> Quhilk was before usit to meities tender.' [quhilk: which]

The country mouse visits the town mouse's rich home, and the two sisters enjoy a splendid feast in the pantry, though the country mouse cannot help asking suspiciously:

> 'Ye, dame' (quod scho), 'how lang will this lest?'

They eat and drink and sing "haill yule, haill!" until their festivities are interrupted by the entry into the pantry of the steward, on which

> They taryit not to wesche, as I suppose. [wesche: wash]

The country mouse has scarcely recovered from her shock and terror, when Gib the cat enters, and she escapes from him with difficulty. And so she leaves, flinging a last word to her urban sister:

> Almichtie God, keip me fra sic ane ffeist!

All this is more than "pawky" Scottish humor: there is a counterpointing of formal and colloquial elements which marks the mature artist and an ease in handling of the verse which is far removed from the mechanical doggerel so common among English poets in the century after Chaucer.

"The Cock and the Fox" tells the same story as Chaucer tells in his Nun's Priest's tale, and again the tone and style are Henryson's own, though of course he owes something to Chaucer. The fox talks to the cock of the cock's father:

> Off craftie crawing he micht beir the Croun,
> For he wad on his tais stand and craw. [tais: toes]
> This was na le; I stude beside and saw. [na le: no lie]

The force and precision of "I stude beside and saw" are typical of Henryson's narrative style. Or consider this stanza from "The Fox and the Wolf," where the Fox is making his confession to Friar Wolf:

> 'Art thow contrite, and sorie in thy Spreit
> For thy trespas?' 'Na, Schir, I can not duid: [duid: do it]
> Me think that hennis ar sa honie sweit,
> And Lambes flesche that new are lettin bluid;
> For to repent my mynd can not concluid,
> Bot off this thing, that I haif slane sa few.'
> 'Weill' (quoth the Wolff), 'in faith, thow art ane schrew.'

Some of the material in these thirteen *Fables* comes from the medieval Reynard cycle and the majority of the stories themselves come from Aesop, probably the Latin version of the Englishman Walter (Gualterus Anglicus). But the handling throughout is artful and original. Henryson appends a "Moralitas" to the end of each fable, where the simple didacticism (as well as the genuine piety) of the schoolmaster replaces the humorous vivacity of the storyteller: the fables themselves, however, are complete without these dull appendages.

Henryson's most sustained and serious work is his narrative poem, *The Testament of Cresseid,* which continues Chaucer's story to tell of Cressida's end. Here he handles rhyme royal with much greater weight than in the *Fables;* the verse moves with impressive gravity against a clearly visualized realistic background, and there rises as the story proceeds a deep note of compassion, always characteristic of Henryson, very different from Chaucer's quizzical irony. The poem opens with a description of the poet trying to keep himself warm on a winter evening: it is a powerful and precise picture, reminding us that the Scottish medieval poets were the first in Europe to move away from the idealized Mediterranean setting of so much European literature and treat realistically of nature as they knew it. Indeed, Henryson accepts his own country, its manners, climate, and social customs, as a natural background for his poetry to a degree unique among medieval poets. *The Testament of Cresseid* opens with no formal rose garden, but with a vivid winter scene:

> The Northin wind had purifyit the Air
> And sched the mistie cloudis fra the sky,
> The froist freisit, the blastis bitterly
> Fra Pole Artick come quhisling loud and schill,
> And causit me remufe aganis my will.

The poet sits at home huddled over a fire, and cheers himself up with a drink and a book:

> I mend the fyre and beikit me about, [beikit: warmed]
> Than tuik ane drink my spreitis to comfort, [spreitis: spirits]
> And armit me weill fra the cauld thairout;
> To cut the winter nicht and mak it schort,
> I tuik ane Quair, and left all uther sport,
> Writtin be worthie Chaucer glorious,
> Of fair Creisseid, and worthie Troylus.

And so he goes on to tell the sequel of the story Chaucer told. It is done with gravity and tenderness, with sharp realistic touches and a quiet eloquence. Cressida, smitten with leprosy, leaves her father to enter the leper house:

> Quhen thay togidder murnit had full lang, [murnit: mourned]
> Quod Cresseid: "Father, I wald not be kend. [kend: known]
> Thairfor in secreit wyse ye let me gang

Into yone Hospitall at the tounis end.
And thidder sum meit for Cheritie me send
To leif upon, for all mirth in this eird [leif: live]
Is fra me gane, sic is my wickit weird." [weird: destiny; sic: such]

She goes out, with her cup and clapper, and on entering the hospital she lay "in ane dark Corner of the Hous allone" and made her lament. The lament is a formal complaint, effectively using the *ubi sunt* theme. The climax of the poem is handled with a beautiful restraint. Cressida goes out to beg with the other lepers, and Troilus, at the head of a company of Trojan knights, rides by.

Than upon him scho kest up baith hir Ene,
And with ane blenk it come into his thocht [blenk: look]
That he sumtime hir face befoir had sene.
But scho was in sic plye he knew hir nocht, [plye: plight]
Yit than hir luik into his mynd it brocht
The sweit visage and amorous blenking
Of fair Cresseid sumtyme his awin darling.

He gives alms to the lepers and Cressida, when she discovers who he is, falls into a swoon. On recovering, she prepares for death, bequeathing her body to worms, her cup and clapper and money to her fellow lepers, and the ring she had got from Troilus back to him again. When, on her death, Troilus receives his legacy, his heart nearly bursts for sorrow, and he says:

"I can no moir; [moir: more]
Scho was untrew, and wo is me thairfore." [scho: she]

Sum said he maid ane Tomb of Merbell gray,
And wrait her name and superscriptioun, [wrait: wrote]
And laid it on hir grave quhair that scho lay,
In goldin Letteris, conteining this ressoun:
"Lo, fair Ladyis, Crisseid, of Troyis toun,
Sumtyme countit the flour of Womanheid,
Under this stane, lait Lipper, lyis deid."

The superb restraint of this ending marks perhaps Henryson's finest achievement as an artist.

Something of the same quiet gravity is seen in Henryson's *Orpheus and Eurydice*, especially in the complaint of Orpheus, with its musical refrain

Quhair art thou gone, my love Euridices.

Robene and Makyne is a lively pastoral ballad of great charm, suggesting the old French *pastourelle*. Among his other poems, *The*

Bludy Serk (Shirt), a religious allegory done with vividness and power, is the most impressive. Henryson has not Chaucer's range or complexity, but within his own fairly wide limits he is a literary artist of great skill and integrity.

William Dunbar (ca. 1460–ca. 1520) is a very different poetic character. A brilliant and versatile craftsman, in whose hands Middle Scots became a virtuoso instrument, he was also a man of powerful original personality who imposed his own character, with a vigor that is sometimes startling, on everything he wrote. He of course knew the work of Chaucer and Gower and Lydgate, paying tribute to the first as "rose of rethoris [eloquent writers] all" and referring to the "sugurit lippis and tongis aureate" of the other two; but he is no disciple of any of them. The vitality and originality of his work is in startling contrast to the plodding dullness of so much fifteenth-century English poetry. In his verse we see with an almost Hogarthian vividness the life of late fifteenth-century Edinburgh—the court of James IV and his Queen at Holyrood, the jostling for benefices among the clergy, the activities of merchants and lawyers, all the teeming activities of nobility, churchmen, and citizenry. Dunbar's portraits of Edinburgh life are unique in medieval literature, not only for their variety and brilliance of detail, or for the verbal craftsmanship and manipulation of innumerable stanza forms which they display, but also for their complex counterpointing of secular and religious, of the relish of surface color combined with the somber underlying sense of the transience of all earthly things and the ultimate relation of everything to the Passion of Christ. A Court poet and a rollicking abuser of the Court, a highly personal poet who draws on his own shifting moods and experiences to find themes for his verses and at the same time a poet with a profound sense of the conventions of medieval literature, a poet very much of his own time and country who nevertheless draws heavily on Latin and French elements to construct a poetic language which is almost an international medium and yet powerfully Scottish, a Goliardic poet full of rollicking wit and sometimes of outrageous obscenity and a devotional poet whose richly echoing religious poems chime hauntingly across the centuries—these are some of the paradoxes of Dunbar's character. If he lacks Henryson's gentleness and quietly ironic sympathy, he has a range and a virtuosity beyond Henryson's.

In his most formal poetry Dunbar employed an "aureate" Scots drawing directly on Latin for the weightier part of its vocabulary (Latin was of course the scholarly language of Europe and one of the literary languages of Scotland at this time). In set pieces like "The Thrissil and the Rois" (written to celebrate the marriage of James IV of Scotland to Margaret Tudor of England in 1503) he employs the medieval Rose tradition—the May morning, the dream, and the rest of it—with an accent of his own. "The Goldyn Targe," in some respects his most ambitious poem, is a dream allegory in which the aureation of the language achieves a very special effect:

> Ryght as the stern of day begouth to schyne [stern: star]
> Quhen gone to bed war Vesper and Lucyne, [begouth: began]
> I rais and by a rosere did me rest; [rosere: rose garden]
> Up sprang the goldyn candill matutyne,
> With clere depurit bemes cristallyne, [depurit: purified]
> Glading the mery foulis in thair nest;
> Or Phebus was in purpur cape revest [or: before]
> Up raise the lark, in hevyns menstrale fyne
> In May, in till a morrow myrthfullest.

The Latin words here slow down the pace of the verse and provide an apt gravity for this serious didactic poem. But the effect is quite different from that obtained by aureation in his religious lyrics, as in "Ane Ballat of our Lady":

> Hale, sterne superne! Hale, in eterne,
> In Godis sicht to schyne!
> Lucerne in derne for to discerne [lucerne in derne: lamp
> Be glory and grace devyne; in darkness; be: by]
> Hodiern, modern, sempitern,
> Angelicall regyne! [queen of angels]
> Our tern infern for to dispern
> Helpe, rialest rosyne.
> *Ave Maria, gracia plena!*
> Haile, fresche floure femynyne!
> Yerne us, guberne, virgin matern [yerne: move; guberne: govern]
> Of reuth baith rute and ryne. [both root and stream of pity]

It is a remarkable achievement to have constructed a Scots language in which a Latin line can take its place naturally. But this is more than a cleverly chiming use of words. The note of ritual celebration and the note of appeal, of beseeching, are sounded simultaneously. The macaronic tradition in medieval religious poetry is here given a new meaning and purpose.

The same poet can write begging letters to the king (with a variety of refrains—"my painful purse so prickles me," "your Grace beseech I of remeid," "excess of thought does me mischief," and many others); or purely "occasional" poems like that on his headache or the "Meditatioun in Wynter" with its fine evocation of a medieval northern winter:

In to thir dirk and drublie dayis, [drublie: wet]
Qhhone sabill all the hevin arrayis [when sable covers all
With mystic vapouris, cluddis, and skyis, the heavens]
Nature all curage me denyis
Off sangis, ballattis, and of playis. . . .

He can reflect wryly on the difficulty of knowing how to conduct himself in a censorious world:

How sould I rewill me or in quhat wys, [rewill: rule]
I wad sum wyse man wald devys;
Sen I can leif in no degre, [leif: live]
Bot sum my maneris will dispys.
Lord God, how sould I governe me?

The poem continues for ten stanzas, each with the same refrain ("Lord God, how sould I governe me?"), the poet mocking (or half-mocking) himself as well as the society he lives in. Dunbar is a great master of the refrain, using it for every purpose from low humor to sublimity, and often combining self-mockery with serious irony.

His poems addressed to the King show an attitude both familiar and respectful: many of them are petitions (for most of his life Dunbar sought in vain for ecclesiastical preferment) in which general moral advice is combined with personal reproof or specific requests, with every variety of humor, irony, or mock humility. Many of these petitionary poems have titles suggesting that they are concerned with general moral problems—"Of Discretion in Asking," "Of Discretion in Geving," "None May Assure in this Warld"—and it is fascinating to watch how Dunbar counterpoints the general and the particular. He can write a humorous "Welcome to the Lord Treasurer," a self-deprecating "Petition of the Gray Horse, Auld Dunbar," a general "Complaint to the King," a charmingly complimentary poem of new year greeting to the King, a brilliantly rollicking account "Of a Dance in the Quenis Chalmir," a complaint addressed to the Queen against James Dog, the keeper of her wardrobe, with the refrain "Madame, ye haff a dangerous Dog!" followed by another poem about the same James Dog when he had got from him what he wanted, with the refrain this time "He is na Dog; he is a Lam." He satirizes every kind of abuse at Court, at the law-courts, and among the shopkeepers in poems packed with life and color. His "Dance of the Sevin Deidly Synnis," in a fast moving twelve-line stanza, is both brilliantly pictorial and full of movement, one of the most impressive and original renderings of this common medieval theme. His vivid account of the war between the soutars (shoemakers) and the tailors, in a similar stanza, has the same speed and vivid handling of detail;

it is followed by an "amends" to the tailors and soutars for the satire on them in a much simpler stanza beginning

> Betuix twell houris and ellevin,
> I dremed ane angell came fra Hevin
> With plesand stevin sayand on hie, [stevin: voice;
> Teylouris and Sowtaris, blist be ye. sayand: saying]

The refrain, "Taylors and Soutars blest be ye" runs with grave irony throughout the ten stanzas of the poem. Dunbar could use the medieval dream convention for every purpose from stately compliment to private feuding. His roistering "flyting" (poetic warfare—a tradition in Scots poetry) with Kennedy, with its rich and varied vocabulary of abuse and its rapid movement geared cunningly to an elaborate eight-line stanza, is a masterpiece of its kind.

At first sight, one is inclined to divide Dunbar's poems into the ceremonious and the familiar, but, though it is easy to distinguish the two extremes, many of his most characteristic poems combine both notes with remarkable skill, and in that combination lies much of their appeal. He can play his own variations on every kind of traditional form—e.g., in his long narrative poem, *The Tua Mariit Wemen and the Wedo* ("The Two Married Women and the Widow") he adopts the structure of the French *chanson d'aventure* and the tone (in some degree) of the *chanson de mal mariée* to give a lusty, realistic picture of female immorality—a kind of comic parody of courtly love poetry where the love involved is mere animal lust. In this poem Dunbar uses the old alliterative verse form:

> Apon the Midsummer evin, mirriest of nichtis,
> I muvit furth allane, neir as midnicht was past,
> Besyd ane gudlie grein garth, full of gay flouris,
> Hegeit, of ane huge hicht, with hawthorne treis; . . .

In over five hundred lines of robust dialogue between the three characters Dunbar paints a picture of female animality and unscrupulousness which might have been suggested in some degree by Chaucer's Wife of Bath, but which is quite different in tone. It is typical of Dunbar that he should open the poem with a ceremonious description of the traditional midsummer evening: it is only when he proceeds to give an account of the overheard conversation of the three women that we begin to realize how far the poet is taking us from the medieval rose garden.

Dunbar's best known poem is his "Lament for the Makars" (Poets) with its haunting Latin refrain, *Timor mortis conturbat me*. But he has many poems which show the same kind of musical gravity. Of these perhaps the most powerful is his poem on the Resurrection of Christ, with its refrain *Surrexit Dominus de sepulchro:*

> Done is a battell on the dragon blak,
> Our campioun Chryst confountet hes his force;
> The yettis of hell ar brokin with a crak, [yettis: gates]
> The signe triumphall rasit is of the croce,
> The divillis trymmillis with hiddous voce, [divillis trymmillis: the devils
> The saulis are borrowit and to the blis can go, tremble; borrowit: relased]
> Chryst with his blud our ransonis dois indoce:
> *Surrexit Dominus de sepulchro.*

Here the imagery of chivalry is put to religious purposes ("the dragon black" is of course Satan) and the note of chivalric adventure combines with that of Christian awe and liturgical sonority to produce poetry of remarkably rich texture.

Dunbar was a great metrist, and used an extraordinary variety of stanza forms, some of which seem to be original with him. Latin hymns, Goliardic verse, the Church service (which he sometimes parodies), the various stanza forms of Provençal poetry, are only some of the many influences—Latin, English, continental—which helped to shape his richly various poetry. The influences are all assimilated into his own highly idiosyncratic personality. The lack of tenderness in his verse has put off those who expect all Scottish poetry to be like Burns at his most sentimental or at least like the gentle Henryson. But Dunbar has a good claim to be considered the finest artist among them all. It is significant that modern Scottish poets, wishing to free themselves from the sentimentalities of a debased Burns tradition, should have raised the cry: "Back to Dunbar."

Gavin Douglas (ca. 1475–1522) lived to see the confidence and vivacity of the reign of James IV give way to the depression and confusion that followed the disastrous battle of Flodden in 1513 when the King himself together with the flower of Scottish chivalry was slain fighting against the English. His poetic career belongs to the pre-Flodden period, and shows him combining medieval convention, new modes from the Italian Renaissance, metrical and verbal virtuosity, and (at times) a sharply original sensibility. *The Palice of Honour* is an elaborate dream allegory written in a tricky nine-line stanza with an exuberance of poetic properties and an exhibitionist verbal dexterity which mark the poem as a show piece. He employs aureation as Dunbar did, and his coined words help him in the difficult task of finding rhymes (which are restricted to two in each nine-line stanza). The variety of effects obtainable from a poetic diction which ranged from elaborate Latinate terms to vigorous colloquial Scots enabled Douglas to change his tone more frequently than we find in most medieval dream allegories, and contrasts between the stately and the vigorous, the richly enameled and the grotesque, musical chiming and a deliberately harsh emphatic speech, are to be found frequently. The work concludes with a "ballad of honour" in three stanzas in which the first has two internal rhymes to the line, the second three, and the third four:

> Haill, rois maist chois til clois thy fois greit micht!
> Haill, stone quhilk schone upon the throne of licht!
> Vertew, quhais trew sweit dew ouirthrew al vice, . . .[1]

King Hart is a much less elaborate allegory in a simpler eight-line stanza, dealing with the heart's (or soul's) adventures with Dame Pleasance and others: in the end, Age knocks at the gate, Youthheid and others flee, and King Hart prepares for death. It is a vigorous handling of a common medieval theme.

Douglas' most remarkable achievement was his translation of Virgil's *Aeneid* into Middle Scots rhyming couplets. This is not only a pioneer work—the earliest rendering of Virgil into any branch of the English language—but also a remarkable production in its own right. Though the impulse to render Virgil into his native literary language represents a kind of interest which it is legitimate enough to consider as part of the complex of movements we call the Renaissance (in fact, Douglas tells us that he was moved to try his hand at a genuine translation because of his annoyance with Caxton's fake version), it is because he renders Virgil so vividly in terms of the life and color of the medieval world he knew that Douglas succeeds so well. There is a precision and a vitality about Douglas's version which, if it does not give us the Tennysonian Virgil with its heavy emphasis on the "*lacrimae rerum*" side which has become the fashion since the nineteenth century, does give us a genuine epic Virgil full of strength and movement and emotional conviction. It is the epic rather than the elegiac Virgil that he gives us. Neither Scots nor English is as compact a language as Latin; expansion is inevitable, particularly in a verse rendering; and, on the whole, Douglas expands with tact and skill. The freshness and ease of movement of Douglas' rendering cannot be readily illustrated by a short extract, but here (in a slightly simplified spelling) is a passage from Book I describing Aeneas before Dido:

[1] The reader will read Middle Scots more easily if he remembers that "i" is used to lengthen the preceding vowel, as in *rois,* and "qu" or "quh" is the English "wh."

Up stude Enee, in clear licht shining fair,
Like til ane god in body and in face,
For his mother grantit her son sic grace;
His crisp hairis were plesand on to see
His favour gudly, full of fresh beautie,
Like till ane younker with twa laughand ene;
Als gracious for to behold, I wene,
As ivoire bone by craft of hand weill dicht,
Or as we see the burnist silver bricht,
Or yet the white polist marble stane shine,
When they bene circulit about with gold sa fine.
Or ever they wist, before them all in hy,
Unto the queen thus said he reverently: . . .

Equally if not more remarkable are Douglas' Prologues to the individual books, especially those to Books VII, XII, and XIII, which give pictures respectively of winter, spring, and summer of a kind that are not easily—if at all—paralleled in medieval literature. The loving particularization of detail, the sense of atmosphere and landscape, with which he describes the Scottish scene at different times of the year show both a quality of observation and a kind of *Einfühlung* that are not generally considered medieval qualities and which are not indeed found elsewhere in European literature for two and a half centuries. The Middle Ages did well enough with spring—and Douglas' picture of May at the beginning of Book XII is for this reason his least original—but for a picture of a northern winter landscape rendered with a combination of faithful observation and moral feeling we can only turn to Douglas:

Sour bitter bubbis, and the showris snell [bubbis: blasts]
Seemit on the sward ane similitude of hell, [snell: keen]
Reducing to our mind, in every steid,
Ghostly shadowis of eild and grisly deid,
Thick drumly skuggis derknit so the heaven; [drumly: turbid; skuggis:
Dim skyis oft furth warpit fearful levin, shadows; levin: lightning]
Flaggis of fire, and mony felloun flaw, [flaw: blast]
Sharp soppis of sleet, and of the snipand snaw. [snipand: biting]
The dowie ditches were all donk and wait,
The low valley flodderit all with spate,
The plain streetis and every hie way
Full of flushis, dubbis, mire and clay. [flushis, dubbis: puddles]

The effect of the description is largely cumulative, and it needs to be quoted at length. He describes the bare moors and hillsides with "herbis, flouris, and grasses wallowit away," the naked woods, the plight of the birds, the "puir laboureris and busy husbandmen" who "went wet and weary draglit in the fen," the sheep huddling under banks, and the domestic animals kept "by manis governance, on harvest and on simmeris purveyance." The picture concludes with an account of the East wind:

> Wide where with force so Eolus shoutis schill [schill: shrill]
> In this congealit season sharp and chill,
> The caller air penetrative and pure [caller: fresh]
> Dasing the blood in every creäture,
> Made seek warm stovis and bien firis hot,
> In double garment clad and wylie-coat [wylie-coat: waistcoat]
> With michty drink, and meatis comfortive,
> Agane the stormy winter for to strive.

This is from the Prologue to Book VII; the description of a June day in the Prologue to Book XIII is equally fine. It is in descriptions like these that the full force of the native element in the Scots vocabulary can be brought out. Incidentally, Douglas was the first to call his language "Scottis" rather than "Inglis." In describing the problems of translation in his Prologue to Book I he explains:

> And yet forsooth I set my busy pain,
> As that I couth, to make it braid and plain,
> Kepand na Sudroun bot our own langáge,
> And speakis as I lernit when I was page.
> Nor yet sa clean all Sudroun I refuse
> Bot some word I pronounce as nychbour dois.
> Like as in Latin bene Greek termis some,
> So me behuvit whilom, or than be dumb,
> Some bastard Latin, French, or Inglis use,
> Where scant were Scottis; I had na other choiss.

Douglas was an assured poet, confident of his craft, blending personal experience and literary convention with conscious artistry. His allegorical work tends to be either overloaded with tricks of the trade or, conversely, pedestrian in movement if not in diction; but his *Aeneid,* with the Prologues, represents a degree of poetic art of which no poet south of the Border was capable in the century and a quarter after Chaucer.

Sir David Lindsay (ca. 1486–1555) was for more than two centuries after his death the most popular Scottish poet in Scotland, but the reason was theological rather than literary: as Allan Ramsay was to put it:

> Sir David's satires helped our nation
> To carry on the Reformation,

And gave the scarlet dame a box
Mair snell than all the pelts of Knox. [snell: sharp]

The traditional view of him as an early Protestant helping by his satirical verses to expose the abuses of the Catholic Church has obscured his real interest as a Court poet deeply concerned with the state of the kingdom and projecting that concern in a great variety of ways in his poetry. Scotland after the disastrous battle of Flodden was in a state calculated to arouse concern; during the minority of the infant King James V the country was rent with divisions between pro-French and pro-English parties, and the glories of James IV's reign seemed very far away indeed. Lindsay's first poem, *The Dreme,* is a dream allegory in which the plight of John the Common Weill (John Commonwealth) is exposed in that character's vivid complaint of the state of the realm:

Allace, quod he, thow seis how it dois stand
With me, and quhow I am disherisit
Of all my grace, and mon pass of Scotland, [mon pass of:
And go, afore qhuare I was cherisit. must leave]
Remane I heir, I am bot perysit. [perysit: laid waste]
For there is few to me that takis tent [takis tent: pay heed]
That garris me go so raggit, rewin and rent. [garris: makes]

He casts his eye over all the regions of Scotland and finds injustice and violence, "unthrift, sweirnes [sloth], falset, povertie, and stryfe," everywhere. The picture of a corrupted Scotland is set in a larger vision of the earth, the planets, heaven and hell, but it is the vivid detail of the descriptions of contemporary Scotland that remains in the mind, and such passages as the introductory account of the poet's January walk by the sea preceding his falling asleep and dreaming. The Complaint of John the Common Weill comes at the end of the poem, as the climax of the dream, after which the poet, awakened by the salute of guns from a newly arrived ship, takes up his pen to write of his vision and advise the young king "to rewle thy realme in unitie and peace."

Lindsay had been the King's companion and attendant when James was a small child, and as a result the relation between the two was intimate, which gives a curiously personal tone to those poems in which the poet addresses his royal master. In *The Complaynt of Schir David Lyndsay,* a spirited and attractive address to the King in easily moving octosyllabic couplets, he reminds him of their former relationship:

I tak the Queenis Grace, thy mother,
My lord Chanclare, and mony other, . . .
I tak thame all to beir witnys . . .

How as ane Chapman beris his pak,
I bure thy grace upon my bak,
And, sumtymes, strydlingis on my nek,
Dansand with mony bend and bek.
The first sillabis that thow did mute
Was *pa, Da Lyn:* upon the lute
Than playt I twenty spryngis, perqueir, [perqueir: by heart]
Qhhilk was gret piete for to heir.

The poem goes on to attack the King's bad advisers, but Lindsay's real purpose is to ask for money: this is a begging letter, like so many of Dunbar's poems, but its tone is more intimate than Dunbar's, full of an affectionate humor which is very different from Dunbar's wilder variety. Another poem in a similar vein is a complaint put into the mouth of Bagsche, "the Kingis auld hound"; and he has other minor satirical poems and "flytings."

The Testament of the Papyngo is a more elaborate "complaint," in the form of the last words of the King's parrot. It is a highly colored poem in rhyme royal, attacking the laziness, greed, and hypocrisy of the clergy (who are birds, as are all the characters of the poem) and showing that panoramic vision of Scottish history and circumstances so characteristic of Lindsay. The moral indignation is not consistently integrated into the fabric of the poem, but there are moments of fine satiric invention and a memorable incidental elegy on James IV. An even more comprehensive didactic work is *Ane Dialog Betwuix Experience and ane Courteour,* in jogging octosyllabic couplets (with some incidental stanzaic variations), which relates the present woes of Scotland to the whole past, present, and future of the country with surprisingly little poetic life. Or at least what poetic life there is in the poem is smothered by its tedious length.

Lindsay's masterpieces are his enormously long moral-allegorical play, *Ane Satire of the Thrie Estaitis* and that lively, realistic, humorous, deftly manipulated verse tale, *The Historie of ane nobil and wailyeand squyer William Meldrum* (generally known as *Squire Meldrum*). The former is an astonishingly successful handling of an unpromising form, and herald of a Scottish drama which history was to frustrate. It was first performed in 1540 (but not with any of the texts that have survived), and was revived, in an abbreviated version, with immense success at the Edinburgh Festival in 1948. It is more than an attack on the abuses of the Church for which it was so long remembered: it is a picture of man in his moral and psychological condition and in his social and economic environment presented through allegorical figures who are at the same time lively characters behaving with a forceful individuality of a kind that illuminates rather than obscures their allegorical function. Very roughly, the plot is about Rex Humanitas (King Humanity) who, going back on his promise to amend his ways and rule well and justly, is seduced by Lady Sensuality; Flattery, Falsehood, and Deceit join the King's company, each taking new hypocritical names (Flattery, for example, calls himself Devotion). Verity reproves the King and others; Chastity laments that she is cast out; Diligence and Solace consider what can be done. The entry of Divine Correction results in the departure of Sensuality and the King's receiving Good Counsel, Verity, and Chastity. Good Counsel advises the King on his duty as a ruler, and Diligence summons the Three Estates. There follows an "interlude" concerning a Poor Man and a Pardoner, the latter a richly comic figure and at the same time an embodiment of the evils associated with his kind. Then comes the second part of the main play. But a continuation of the summary would be pointless: it sounds like a typical medieval morality, except for its length and the number of characters. The interest of *Ane Satire* lies not in its plot but in the magnificently realized detail of speech and action with which it is carried forward. Neither summary nor quotation can do justice to the verve, the color, the combination of genuine *saeva indignatio* at human vice with a relish for the follies and foibles of mankind, which characterize this work. In the second part, John the Common Weal is a central figure, and Lindsay uses him to present with pity and dignity the claims of the "common man." The play is as full of compassion as it is of humor, as full of detailed social and psychological observation as of moral generalizations. The rhyming couplets (varying from octosyllables to decasyllables) give way on occasion to other verse forms; but everything *moves,* and though the plot is too diffuse for the play to hang together as a tightly knit unity, and the verse too simple to achieve anything like the overtones of poetic statement that Elizabethan poetic drama is capable of, the projection of a vision of man, in terms which allow both the liveliest humor and the deepest moral feeling, is achieved.

For *Squire Meldrum* one can make no such claim; it is an altogether less ambitious work—based on the lives of an almost contemporary couple—done with complete success. It represents the medieval romance brought down to earth, as it were, with traditional chivalric and modern realistic elements neatly counterpointed. The modern reader may peruse its sprightly octosyllables with Butler's *Hudibras* in his mind—somehow, it is difficult to resist thinking of

Hudibras when reading *Squire Meldrum*—but in fact its tone is wholly different, not mocking or satirical, but humorous in an interested and friendly way. Altogether, it is a rather unexpected poem to find at the end of Scottish medieval literature.

Of anonymous medieval Scottish poetry outside the ballads, the most characteristic are poems which show the conventional situations of the European lyrical forms sharpened and localized by a colorful realism, such as "The Wowing of Jok and Jynny" and two accounts of popular festivities, "Christis Kirk on the Grene" and "Peblis to the Play." These last two poems have been attributed both to James I and James V, more plausibly to the latter, and they represent a tradition which has never really died out in Scottish literature, though it has suffered some strange mutations.

The Reformation came to Scotland more violently than it came to England and it disrupted the national culture to a far greater degree. A sign of the times was that remarkable collection of poems known as the *Gude and Godlie Ballatis,* of which the earliest surviving edition belongs to 1567, but which had very probably appeared in earlier editions in the 1540's. This is a Protestant work, Lutheran in tone, divided into four sections, of which the first is a Catechism, both in prose and in verse, the second a group of sixteen "spiritual sangis," the third "certaine ballatis of the Scripture," and the fourth "The Psalmes of David with uthir new Pleasand Ballatis." Some of the poems in the collection are translations of Lutheran hymns, and there are traces of Danish and Swedish as well as French influence. The tone of some of the verses in the first part is reminiscent of modern Negro spirituals:

> Moyses upon the mount Sinay,
> With the great God spak face for face,
> Fastand and prayand but delay, [but: without]
> The tyme of fourtie dayis space.
> O God be mercyfull to us.

The "spiritual sangis" contain poems based on medieval hymns and carols (e.g., "To us is borne a bairne of bliss" and "In dulci jubilo") as well as hymns of Lutheran origin ("Faithful in Christ, use your riches richt") and others which sound a more individual note, for example:

> Richt soirly musing in my mynde,
> For pitie soir my hart is pynde, [pynde: pained]
> Quhen I remember on Christ sa kynde,
> that savit me:
> Nane culd saif from Thyle till Ynde,
> bot only He.

But by far the most interesting section is that containing the "new Plesand Ballatis," which have been, significantly, "changit out of prophanc ballatis in godlie sangis for avoydance of sin and harlatrie." Here popular songs have been made over into religious poems, sometimes successfully, sometimes with ludicrous results. It is not difficult to see what has happened in this song:

Johne, cum kis me now,
Johne, cum kis me now;
Johne, cum kis me by and by
And mak no moir adow.

The Lord thy God I am,
That Johne dois thee call;
Johne representit man,
By grace celestiall.

Sometimes the transformation of a secular song into a religious poem is remarkably successful:

All my Lufe, leif me not,
  Leif me not, leif me not;
All my Lufe, leif me not,
  Thus myne alone:
With ane burding on my bak, [burding: burden]
I may not beir it I am sa waik;
Lufe, this burding from me tak,
  Or ellis I am gone.

The antipapal note is sometimes sounded, and when this is combined with the rollicking chorus of thc original popular song, the result is curious:

The Paip, that pagane full of pryde, [Paip: Pope]
  He hes us blindit lang;
For quhair the blind the blind dois gyde,
  Na wonder baith ga wrang:
Lyke prince and king he led the ring
  Of all iniquitie:
Hay trix, tryme go trix,
  Under the grene wod-tree.

The best are often the simplest, such as

Go, hart, unto the Lamp of licht,
  Go, hart, do service and honoúr;
Go, hart, and serve him day and nicht,
  Go, hart unto thy Savïoúr.

And the simple substitution of God or Christ for the name of the lover can change a love lyric into a religious poem of considerable appeal:

> All my hart, ay this is my sang,
> With doubill mirth and joy amang;
> Sa blyith as byrd my God to sang:
> Christ hes my hart ay.

It is clear that the Reformers, for all their zeal against the drama and against popular entertainments and their suspicion of most secular imaginative literature, had ears and voices of their own.

The question of religion in Scotland was not to be settled until the end of the seventeenth century, and between 1560 and 1689 the country was frequently torn apart by civil and religious conflict. The death of James V in 1542, after a second disastrous defeat of a Scottish army by the English, left Scotland with an infant Queen and quarreling religious and political parties. A Parliament summoned without the proper royal authority in 1560 implemented John Knox's views and established the reformed faith in Scotland. The following year young Mary Queen of Scots, who had been brought up in France, arrived in Scotland to begin her troubled and tragic reign. Her arrival was celebrated by Alexander Scott in a poem entitled "Ane New Yeir Gift to the Quene Mary, Quhen scho come first hame." After welcoming the Queen, Scott proceeds to give her lengthy advice about reverencing the "true kirk" (Scott was a reformer, though a moderate one), founding her reign on the four cardinal virtues of wisdom, justice, fortitude, and temperance, punishing wicked and unchaste pastors, righting the wrong of the poor, and making all the estates of the realm attend to their proper business, to end with an elaborately chiming alliterative stanza of compliment and greeting:

> Fresch, fulgent, flurist, fragrant flour formois, [Flurist: flourishing;
> Lantern to lufe, of ladeis lamp and lot, formois: beautiful]
> Cherie maist chaist, cheif charbucle and chois;
> Smaill sweit smaragde, smelling but smit of smot: [smaragde:
> emerald: but smit of smot: without trace of stain]
> Noblest natour, nurice to nurtour; note
> This dull indyte, dulce dowble dasy deir,
> Send be thy sempill servand Sanderris Scott: [send be: sent by]
> Greting grit god to grant thy grace gude yeir.

This aureate and artful language is in the tradition of the fifteenth-century Scottish poets, though its virtuosity is more deliberately precious than that of Henryson or even Dunbar. We know little about Alexander Scott's life: most of his poetry is found in the Bannatyne Manuscript (the collection made by George Bannatyne in 1568, which preserves so much medieval Scottish poetry), and so must have been written before 1568. He is a musical and craftsmanlike lyrist who wrote songs for Court airs and verses in accepted lyric stanzas, a poet who obviously leans rather heavily on the tradition in which he is writing, taking from it rather more than he gives to it; but he *is* in a tradition, and this gives his art both grace and confidence. He can sing to May in the medieval mode:

> O lusty May, with flora quene,
> The balmy dropis frome Phebus schene, [schene: beautiful]

or musically lament his parting from his love:

> Departe, departe, departe,
> Allace! I most departe,
> From hir that hes my hart,
> With hairt full soir,
> Againis my will indeid,
> And can find no remeid,
> I wait the panis of deid
> Can do no moir.

Many of his love poems are delicately wrought, revealing not only a cunning ear but also a personal feeling both deep and gentle. He can also be vigorously satirical (as in "Ane ballat maid to the derisioun and scorne of wantoun wemen") and amusingly mock-heroic, as in the lively "Iusting and debait up at the Drum, Betuix W[a] Adamsone and Johnie Sym."

Scott was a Court poet, and it must be remembered that Scotland continued to have a Court until Mary's son, James VI, went south in 1603 to become James I of England. Some of the other Court poets of the first half of the sixteenth century may be represented among the anonymous lyrics of the Bannatyne manuscript. James VI took a scholar's interest in poetry: one of his tutors was George Buchanan, known throughout Europe as a poet and dramatist in Latin. James wrote an essay on the technique of writing Scottish poetry, he translated some French and other poetry, and he produced passable verses himself. The chief poet of his Court was his friend William Montgomerie (ca. 1545–ca. 1611), whose remarkable long poem *The Cherry and the Slae* is one of the latest and most original handlings of the medieval Rose tradition. The complex musical stanza in which this poem is written was to be revived in the eighteenth century with interesting results. Here is the first of the poem's 114 stanzas:

> About ane bank, quhair birdis on bewis [bewis: boughs]
> Ten thousand tymis thair notis renewis

Ilke houre into the day: [ilke: every]
The Merle and Mavis micht be sene, [Merle, Mavis:
The Progne and the Phelomene, blackbird, thrush]
Quhilk caussit me to stay:
I lay and leynit me to ane bus, [bus: bush]
To heir the birdis beir, [beir: song]
Thair mirth was sa melodius,
Throw nature of the yeir:
Sum singing, sum springing,
With wingis into the sky:
So trimlie, and nimlie,
Thir birdis they flew me by.

The poem, in its elaborate and leisurely way, seems to have as its central theme an argument as to whether the poet should pursue the perfect and perhaps unattainable cherry or be content with the more ordinary sloe, but the arguments, moralizings, and "pithy" apothegms of abstract characters such as Hope, Experience, Courage, and Reason take the poem far from this simple debate between two possible objects of love, though where precisely they take it is not easy to discover. The fascinating stanza in which the poem is written is first found in a poem entitled "The Bankis of Helicon," which may also be by Montgomerie, who may have invented the stanza on this occasion (it goes to a tune of the same name). King James, in his *Reulis and Cautelis to be observit and eschewit in Scottis Poesie*, discussed "all kyndis of cuttit and brokin verse, whairof new formes are daylie inventit according to the Poetes pleasure," and Montgomerie was apparently one of those who "inventit" them according to his pleasure.

Another elaborate and musical stanza is that employed by Montgomerie in his poem "The Solsequium" (marigold):

Like as the dumb solsequium, with care ourcome
Dois sorrow, when the sun goes out of sicht,
Hings doun his head, and droops as dead, nor will not spread,
Bot locks his leaves through languor all the nicht,
Till foolish Phaeton rise
With whip in hand,
To purge the crystal skyis
And licht the land.
Birds in their bour waitis for that hour
And to their prince ane glaid good-morrow givis;
Fra then, that flour list not till lour,
Bot laughis on Phoebus loosing out his leavis.
So stands with me, except I be where I may see
My lamp of licht, my lady and my luve; . . .

The stanza conveys a musical gravity which fits perfectly with the poem's mood. Montgomerie also wrote sonnets, metrical versions of psalms, and love lyrics in a variety of stanza forms. He engaged in a "flyting," too, the "Flyting of Montgomerie and Polwart," which has the comic exuberance of its kind. Such graceful love songs as "Sweet hairt, rejoice in mind" are rather like Alexander Scott's in the same vein. Montgomerie was a Court poet and song writer, and much of his best work consists of song lyrics written in a European courtly tradition. Scots poetry was still very much in the orbit of European culture.

Of the other Scottish poets of the period, John Stewart of Baldynnis (ca. 1550–ca. 1605) is an interesting craftsman who produced an abridged version of *Orlando Furioso* in decasyllabic quatrains and a considerable amount of technically interesting verse, including the charming "Of Ane Symmer House"; William Fowler (1562–1612), a versatile poet whose best work is contained in his sequence of sonnets called *The Tarantula of Love*—some of these have a quiet gravity and control that is impressive; and Mark Alexander Boyd (1563–1601), a shadowy figure who wrote in Latin, Greek, and French and produced one remarkable sonnet in Scots, "Fra bank to bank, fra wood to wood I rin." These were all writers of Court verse, untouched by the fiercer moods of the Presbyterians. But there were Presbyterian poets who did more than produce metrical versions of the Psalms. Alexander Hume (ca. 1560–1609), Presbyterian minister, deliberately set out to write a more serious kind of poetry than the Court poets were capable of. "In princes' Courts," he wrote in the preface to his *Hymns or Sacred Songs* (1599), "in the houses of greate men, and at the assemblies of yong gentilmen and yong damosels, the chief pastime is to sing prophane sonnets, and vaine ballads of love, or to rehearse some fabulous faits of Palmerine, Amadis, or such like raveries." The serious and devotional lyrics he wrote in his somewhat Anglicized Scots are of no great interest today; but once he succeeded in writing a well-nigh perfect poem, a limpid, beautifully modulated picture, in a simple four-line stanza, of a summer's day from dawn to dusk, entitled "Of the Day Estivall."

The Union of the Crowns in 1603 brought a change in the Scottish literary landscape. The migration of James to England, as well, of course, as the prestige and achievement of Elizabethan English poetry, encouraged the Scottish poet to try the English literary language, and the group of Scots poets at the English Court in the early part of the seventeenth century—Sir Robert Aytoun, Sir David Murray, Sir Robert Ker, Sir William Alexander—wrote exercises, sometimes skillful, sometimes stiff, in which, the whole man not being able to operate, mere convention tended to take control. William Drummond of Hawthornden (1585–1649) stayed at home, a quiet scholarly man who admired Sidney and knew, as well as the English poets, Ronsard and Tasso and Marino, not to mention Virgil and Petrarch. His love poetry is elegantly conventional in an English and not a Scottish way; sometimes, in personal elegiac or religious verse, he strikes out something more individual and complex, but in general one is inclined to agree with Ben Jonson's charge that he "smelled too much of the schools." James Graham, Marquis of Montrose (1612–50), in character and reputation something of a Scottish Philip Sidney, gave his literary and political loyalties to the English Cavalier tradition which at this time had no true equivalent in Scotland. The Court poet in Scotland had now no native center to turn to, with the result that Scottish Court poetry and music came to be transcribed and collected by individual gentlemen for their own nostalgic pleasure instead of being actively created and published. So a man like Montrose, loyal to his King and his Court, naturally turned to the Cavalier tradition in England. He wrote only a handful of poems, some of which seem to have been achieved by sheer strength of character; it is significant that, in his very last poem, written on the eve of his execution, the force of the expression demands one Scots word, "airth" (direction), on which the whole poem pivots.

Lacking the Court as a cultural center, turning more and more to England for literary inspiration, it would seem that the Scottish writer had now no choice but to accept English as his literary language, even if that involved splitting his personality in some degree (for Scots was still the *spoken* language of non-Gaelic Scotland). But the situation does not develop as simply as that. Some time in the middle of the turbulent seventeenth century there appeared a new kind of Scots poem, "The Life and Death of the Piper of Kilbarchan, or the Epitaph of Habbie Simson," by Robert Sempill of Beltrees (ca. 1595–ca. 1668). This vulgar, vigorous, rollicking poem, written for amusement by a member of the landed gentry, is not written in a literary language but in a Scots vernacular. For Scots has now become a vernacular, drawing on popular speech rather than on an artistic tradition. Sempill writes jocularly, amusingly, almost patronizingly. Here is his opening stanza:

Kilbarchan now may say alas!
For she hath lost both game and grace,
Both *Trixie* and *The Maiden Trace*; [names of tunes]
But what remead? [remead: remedy]

For no man can supply his place:
Hab Simson's dead.

If we put this beside a stanza by Alexander Scott or Montgomerie (not to say of Dunbar or Henryson) we see at once a difference of weight: though Scott and Sempill both use images drawn from popular speech, Scott's language is more highly charged, it has more gravity and greater reverberation. "Habbie Simson" is sprightly popular verse written for amusement by an amateur, and written in a language which by this time few educated people felt to be suitable for the highest kind of art. True, it draws on a tradition of poetry of popular revelry which earlier had produced such poems as "Christis Kirk on the Grene" and "Peblis to the Play," but it is frivolous rather than truly humorous because it does not grow out of that tradition but uses it with what almost might be called condescension. This is not to say that "Habbie Simson" is not an important poem; it is indeed important historically, both for drawing attention to the possibilities of folk humor as a way of bringing the vernacular back into current poetry and for suggesting the mock elegy as a poetic form, and for reviving an old stanza form which was to play such an important part in eighteenth-century Scottish poetry; but it lacks a dimension. The Scottish vernacular came more and more to be associated with rusticity, and Scots dialect verse, written more or less phonetically in a mood of patriotic primitivism or of music-hall humor, replaced poetry written in a full Scottish literary language in which the whole man could speak. Between Sempill of Beltrees and Burns, Scottish vernacular poetry had to learn how to be the product of the whole man, how to achieve scope and density—in short, how to recover the lost dimension.

The difference between a vernacular and a literary language is that in the latter case there is a literary tradition, arising out of the different forms of the spoken language and transcending them, which reflects back on the spoken language and gives it a steady relationship to the national culture. Once the literary tradition is broken, once there is no literary language growing out of the spoken language (however different from it it may be, and however many artificial elements may have been added), the spoken language is bound to disintegrate into a series of regional dialects. So, after the Norman Conquest of England, the central literary position of West Saxon was lost, since French replaced Anglo-Saxon as the literary language, and Middle English fell into a series of regional dialects. Only after the re-establishment of English as the literary language of England did a linguistic norm emerge and, while differences between spoken dialects persisted, the language was pulled together by the integrating force of a literary tradition. Similarly in Scotland, Middle Scots, in virtue of its literary tradition, had been a language and not a vernacular; Scots became a mere vernacular only after the literary language of most of its serious writers had ceased to be Scots. How to use the *vernacular* as a *language* in serious literature was the problem faced by the eighteenth-century Scottish poets. The problem was never permanently solved, for English remained the main language of serious expression; it was solved occasionally and temporarily, partly by happy accident, partly by the intervention of genius.

Of the ballads, one of the acknowledged glories of Scottish literature, we have spoken in an earlier chapter. Something must be said, however, of Scottish literary prose. There is not a great deal, for it developed late (as it does in any culture) and succumbed to English relatively early. Latin was the language of Scottish historians and moralists well into the fifteenth century and later. A treatise on *The Craft of Deyng* (dying), attributed to the mid-fifteenth century, is the first known piece of Scots prose that has any claim to be considered literary; it has an attractive simplicity and directness. Other Scots prose of this century seems to consist entirely of translations, such as Gilbert Hay's competent rendering of three French works on knighthood, warfare, and government and John Gau's *Richt Vay to the Kingdom of Heuine* (1533), a Protestant work from the German (via the Dutch) published in Sweden. Murdoch Nisbet based his Scots version of the New Testament on Wyclif, probably about 1530; it is of more philological than literary interest. John Bellenden (b. 1495) translated Livy and Hector Boece's Latin *History of Scotland* in the 1530's; his prose is workmanlike and unadorned. But by far the most interesting Scots prose work of the sixteenth century is *The Complaynt of Scotland,* of doubtful authorship, published apparently in Paris in 1549. It is based on a French work, *Le Quadrilogue invectif* by Alain Chartier, and the author applies to Scotland, Chartier's description of the unhappy state of his country. *The Complaynt* is dedicated to the Queen Mother, Marie of Guise, in a heavily loaded "aureate" style, which has, however, a certain stateliness and dignity. This is the most artful Scots literary prose yet to have appeared. In a prologue addressed to the reader, which follows the dedication, the author explains that he is going to proceed in a simpler language, "domestic Scottis langage, maist intelligibil for the vulgare pepil," though he explains that "it is necessair at sum tyme til myxt oure langage with part of termis drewyn fra Lateen, be rason that oure Scottis tong is nocht sa copeus as is the Lateen tong." The main part of the complaint—long and detailed—does use a simpler Scots than the aureate dedication. But the complaint is interrupted by a "Monolog Recreatif." This is a curious and most interesting section. It opens with an account of the author setting out for a walk on a summer evening; the sunset is described in meticulous detail, then night comes, and passes, and the sun rises. There follows an extraordinary description—highly mannered, yet with a certain vivid realism—of the various beasts and birds and the different noises they make on waking. Other scenes follow, and eventually we follow the author away from the seashore (where he has spent some time) inland to a company of shepherds, with whom he gets into conversation. This is a pastoral set piece. One of the shepherds discourses at length on the advantages of the rustic life, citing innumerable authorities, but at last he is interrupted in the full tide of an account of the horrible corruption of cities by his wife, who says: "My weil belovit husband, I pray thee to decist fra that tideus melancolic orison . . ." She proposes that they tell stories instead, and the proposal meets with general approval. So they tell tales and dance and sing, and the names of their tales, songs and dances are listed in a long catalogue which is one of our main sources of knowledge of the lost literature of Scotland. The author then enters a meadow, falls asleep, and continues the main burden of his complaint by means of a vision.

Lindsay of Pitscottie's *Historie and Cronicles of Scotland* (1575) is a continuation of Boece's Latin history in Scots, done with considerable liveliness and full of memorable anecdotes. By this time the Reformation had turned more and more Scotsmen's eyes away from their old ally France and toward Protestant England. The Geneva Bible was in use among many Scottish Protestants, and partly under its influence and partly as a result of a deliberate attempt to address a wider audience, Scottish prose came to adopt more and more English forms. John Knox's vigorous polemical prose shows this movement. His *History of the Reformation,* written in the 1560's but not published until 1644, uses a deliberately Anglicized Scots. The result of this was for a while that Catholic writers clung to Scots and Protestant writers used a more Anglicized written language. Ninian Winzet challenged Knox vigorously in an extremely forceful colloquial Scots prose. The ultimate victory of the Reformation in Scotland, however, together with many other factors, social, educational, and economic, altered this picture. Though the Church of Scotland (like the lawyers of Scotland) asserted its independence of England by using a forthright spoken Scots, written prose came more and more to be English, and by the middle of the seventeenth century a Scottish literary prose hardly existed. It was to be revived again only in the dialogue of certain Scottish novels; but the Scottish novel was born too late for it to provide a means for the continuation of a full Scots literary prose.